LATIN AMERICA
Social Structure and Political Institutions

LATIN AMERICA

Social Structure and
Political Institutions

JACQUES LAMBERT
Translated by HELEN KATEL

UNIVERSITY OF CALIFORNIA PRESS
Berkeley, Los Angeles, London

University of California Press
Berkeley and Los Angeles, California

University of California Press, Ltd.
London, England

First published as *Amérique Latine:
Structures sociales et institutions politiques,*
© 1963 by Presses Universitaires de France

ISBN: 0-520-00689-5 *(Cloth)*
0-520-00690-9 *(Paper)*

Library of Congress Catalog Card Number: 67-29784
Printed in the United States of America

Acknowledgments

Our thanks to Professor Antonio Lago Carballo of the University of Madrid, who was kind enough to supplement the bibliography in Spanish, and to Professor G. Margadant of the Independent University of Mexico City, who read this manuscript and made helpful suggestions.

Contents

Tables

Introduction

"Latin America Appears on the Scene" was the title of Tibor Mende's outstanding series of articles, published in 1952. Actually "Return Performance" might have been more appropriate, for Latin America had previously played a major international role. In 1545, when precious metals from Huancavelica and Potosí began flowing into Spain they gave Spain her financial supremacy and, by spreading throughout Europe, hastened the advent of capitalism.

Early Latin American Colonial Development

Iberian and especially Spanish settlements in America had developed both early and swiftly. At the beginning of the eighteenth century, the English had not yet left the Atlantic shore to venture inland and an almost empty continent lay in front of them. By then the Spaniards had been for almost a century the masters of organized empires with millions of subjects in Central America and the Andean plateaus. The natives had been cultivating the land before the conquerors landed and continued to do it for them. The Spaniards and Portuguese had also established settlements and had set up an efficient administration along the coastline of huge territories stretching from California to the Rio de la Plata. Humboldt, who traveled over Latin Amerca from 1799 to 1804, estimated its population at about 17 million, at a time when the United

States did not have over 5 million inhabitants. Mexico alone
had a larger population than the United States.

It is true that the economic and social structure that was
later to impede Latin America's evolution was already being
shaped. But under the colonial system, when the colonizers'
success was measured by the amount of precious metals and
tropical produce supplied to the home country, the stern tutelage of the Spanish and Portuguese administrations over
American trade, the concentration of the land in the hands of
a few, and the enslavement of native labor had fostered rather
than hindered the prosperity of colonial empires. Until the
eighteenth century America loomed in the eyes of the world as
an Iberian-dominated continent.

Latin America's Delayed National Development

After her early start, Latin America—as thoroughly exploited as she was poorly developed—fell into a deep slumber
induced by the colonial system. The intellectual awakening of
the late eighteenth century and the independence won in the
first quarter of the nineteenth were felt in Latin America only
as ceaseless, nightmarish political upheavals. The revolutions
that brought independence separately to the various parts of
Latin America were local in character so that the continent
was eventually parceled into twenty sovereign states, some of
them too small and too sparsely populated even today. Being
neither social nor economic in character, the revolutions in
independent nineteenth century Latin America left intact or
sometimes even strengthened the existing obsolete social structure in the various countries. This structure had formerly
helped the home country to exploit its colonial empire, but its
persistence was to become a serious hindrance to national
economic and social development.

Thus, most of the Latin American states retained long after
independence a colonial social structure that was hardly compatible with diversified economic growth or an egalitarian
ideology and democratic institutions. Power struggles among
individuals or groups were the consequence. The unshakable
obsolete social fabric dissociated the economic and social evolution of Latin America from that of the United States and

western Europe. For a large part of Latin America, the nineteenth century was a wasted century; even for the most favored countries, such as Argentina, Brazil, Chile, Mexico, Uruguay, the first half of that century was wasted. By the end of the nineteenth century, the United States had a larger population than the whole of Latin America, and, while the 80 million North Americans were rich and literate, most of the 60 million Latin Americans remained illiterate and in a state of wretchedness. Compared to fast-growing Western Europe and Anglo-America, Latin America had turned into an underdeveloped continent.

Eclipse in the Nineteenth Century

In the nineteenth century, America meant the United States, and Latin Americans had to accept the fact that the people who in their opinion should have been called "North Americans" or "United Statesmen" were called "Americans." Europe and English-speaking America received a distorted image of Latin America in which there was no place for the bulk of her population.

In Europe, especially in France, Latin Americans were regarded as likable aristocrats—tin, silver, coffee, or cattle barons who shuttled between the Sorbonne and Monte Carlo— expatriates in seach of a life of culture and luxury. This misleading image concealed the extreme poverty and ignorance of the masses, and gave credibility to the myth of a fabulously wealthy continent.

On the other hand, to the United States, which saw in the Caribbean a caricature of Latin America's backwardness, the image was one of utter squalor and violence. Here were selfish feudal landlords, bloodthirsty generals, crooked politicians (all lumped together under the derogatory term of *caudillos*), who were always at one another's throat but always managed to stay in power just long enough to get rich. Surely it was the duty of good neighbors who believed themselves wiser to help these people, who apparently were incapable of governing themselves; obviously, they had to be subjected to the discipline of U. S. Navy expeditionary forces.

It took a long time for these clichés to die. They masked for too long the awakening of Latin America which began in the second half of the nineteenth century at the southern tip of the continent, far from the United States. From there, the movement spread after World War I, and even more so after World War II.

The ignorance on both sides was as dangerous for the United States as for Latin America because it bred a mutual lack of understanding stemming respectively from contempt and resentment. This ignorance and contempt led the United States to maintain her policy of military interventions in the Caribbean too long and to delay giving any economic aid. Ignorance and resentment in Latin America produced in turn a pathological sensitivity toward the United States that is the most widespread common trait of all those countries, and that today thwarts the efforts of the United States to hasten economic and social progress.

Rediscovery of Latin America After World War II

After World War II Latin America again attracted widespread attention. Just before the war, which the United States saw coming and was anxious to stay out of, she had to work out a Good Neighbor Policy in order to create a continental front of American neutrality, and this left no room for contempt or ignorance. When the war ended and the Cold War began, the structure of international organizations gave Latin America a diplomatic weight that none of the Great Powers could afford to ignore. Within the United Nations, fragmentation into small countries was an asset to Spanish-speaking Latin America. Portuguese Latin America, on the other hand, despite her almost equal size, had only one seat because she had escaped fragmentation. At the time when the newly formed United Nations was composed of only its fifty-one founding members, twenty were Latin American—eighteen of them Spanish-speaking. The United Nations General Assembly was Spanish-American before becoming Afro-Asian.

This privileged position did not endure: the birth of so many new independent nations in Africa and Asia has greatly lessened the weight of the Latin-American bloc within the international organizations, which now have over a hundred members. But, while Spanish rang out so forcefully at the meetings,

Latin America became better known, and the old image of republics of operetta or tragedy was forgotten. Of course, there are still some backward countries in Latin America with purely personal dictatorships and frequent military coups, but in the largest ones—Brazil, Argentina, Mexico, Colombia, Venezuela—and the two small peaceful nations of Uruguay and Costa Rica, the era of the caudillos is over, just as is that of the enlightened despotism of cultured aristocracies.

The Awakening of the Middle Classes

In all the most advanced countries and to some degree in the others, aggressive middle classes have taken over. They are composed almost exclusively of city dwellers but constitute a large segment of the population, since the cities themselves have expanded so swiftly. Everywhere the embryonic proletariat, consisting of workers and more recently, in some cases, of peasants, is trying to wrest power from the middle classes. The nineteenth century caudillos and aristocrats had shaken off colonial domination in the name of political freedom, but had retained the colonial economic and social structure; the new classes now in power in the various countries are trying to complete the process of decolonization by building more egalitarian and economically independent societies. The working class, fighting for power, thinks that the process is not fast or thorough enough; in the past few years, peasants have also been demanding integration into a society that has been treating them as subjects instead of as citizens.

The political life of this new Latin America is as troubled as before; revolutions, dictatorships, military coups are almost as frequent in the more developed countries as in the others, but these political troubles are of a different nature. Rigid stereotypes must be put out of mind if the meaning of this political ferment is to be understood. No longer does it stem simply from personal or clan rivalries; neither is it the doing of ambitious military men, nor the product of the supposedly volatile Latin American temperament. It is the almost inevitable result of cumulative economic and social backwardness that is now intolerable to nations determined to move forward at an accelerated pace.

Today, except for the Argentine Republic and Uruguay, Latin American countries remain underdeveloped, although in most of them rapid economic and social advances are taking place. No one can dismiss these efforts: if they bear fruit, Latin America's demographic potential, her natural resources, and the quality of her elites will create new nations that could alter the world balance of power.

Demographic Potential

Since the beginning of the twentieth century, the population has been increasing faster in Latin America—even without a large influx of immigrants—than anywhere else in the world. The birth rate among the overwhelming mass of the population—as poor as it is illiterate—is still 40 or 50 per thousand, just as before the dissemination of birth control methods; at the same time, under the influence of civic-minded elites who are part of European cultural life, the use of simple low-cost public health techniques has brought the death rate down to an average of 10 to 15 per thousand, and it will in all likelihood continue to decrease rapidly in the near future.

In forty years, from 1920 to 1960, the population of Europe grew by 23 percent, as compared to 126 percent in Latin America. Around 1900, Latin America with her 63 million inhabitants was far less populated than the United States; by 1960 she was far ahead, with 202 million people. If the present rate of increase of 2.9 percent a year persists until the end of the century, which is most likely, the population of Latin America, which was 240 million in 1965, will reach almost 700 million in 2000, that is, twice the number of English-speaking people on the North American continent. By the end of this century Brazil, which in 1960 had the largest population in Latin America with her 70 million inhabitants, might be one of the great powers in terms of population (over 180 million), while Mexico, which had only 34 million inhabitants, should by then have over 100 million.

However, such rapid population growth is not in itself a harbinger of power or prosperity. On the contrary, the present population growth in some underdeveloped countries of the Middle East and Southeast Asia, although slower than in Latin America, is nevertheless seriously hindering their economic and social progress. When population increases, there is a possibility that any economic achievements may merely keep a greater number of people in the same state of wretchedness. Crowding also makes it harder to raise the level of productivity. Nevertheless, most Latin American countries are in a better position than other underdeveloped countries to afford a rapid population growth because, except for some points in the West Indies, Central America, and perhaps Mexico, Latin America is sparsely populated, and suffers from too low a population density.

Economic Potential

The low population density in Latin America—11 inhabitants per square kilometer—is not misleading, as it is in some areas that include huge, totally uninhabited deserts. There are few truly unproductive regions in Latin America; these are in northern Mexico, northern Chile, and on the Pacific coast in Peru, as well as on the high stretches of the Andes. Deserts occupy no more than 6 percent of the land; if one includes areas at high altitude or those with an erratic water supply, such as the region subject to recurrent droughts in northeastern Brazil, the total area unfavorable to settlement does not exceed 25 percent of the continent.

It is always arbitrary to speak of a territory as being habitable by a given number of people, since this depends as much on the type of people as on the nature of the land; very rough estimates are valid only for a given level of technology. With this reservation in mind, Latin America as a whole is highly habitable. A 1958 estimate by Harrison Brown, a specialist in geological chemistry at the California Institute of Technology, is for two billion inhabitants, almost twice what he suggests for the English-speaking countries of North America. He probably had in mind primarily the potential food resources, but the natural resources needed for industrialization are equally abundant. Lack of coal in Latin America, which would have been an insuperable obstacle to industrial growth in the nineteenth century, can now be compensated for by an abundance of oil, hydroelectric potential, and also, it seems, by the availability of fissionable materials.

Bearing in mind that these figures are only estimates and

not precise calculations, one can say nonetheless that if by the end of this century the Latin America peoples can use efficient development methods, their continent could easily accommodate 700 million inhabitants, and still leaving ample room for growth. The density of 63 to 70 inhabitants per square mile that will probably prevail in Latin America at the turn of the century might even afford a better economic and social use of the land than today's density, which is only a third of this.

As elsewhere, the rapid rate of population increase is placing too heavy a burden on the Latin American peoples, and a lower fertility would ease their lot. Poverty that feeds on too rapid population growth can only increase the probability of new revolutions. If the sacrifices imposed on the present generation were not so heavy as to paralyze economic and social development, they might help future generations because a larger number of people would better match the vast expanse of the land and the wealth of natural resources.

The land and natural wealth are there; the too small population is increasing too fast. But since World War I the governments have been acting with determination to hasten economic and social development. Great advances have already been made in Brazil, Mexico, Chile, and Argentina. Some countries have reached the point of economic takeoff. But, before the advent of general prosperity, much is still lacking; what is needed is capital, the elimination of an obsolete social structure, greater literacy among the masses, slower population growth, and political stability. Nevertheless, Latin America is one of the areas where financial and technological assistance, if given and accepted without ulterior motives, may be the most efficient way of fighting underdevelopment, and where far-reaching results may be achieved within a short time.

Latin America's Dual Background

Although helping Latin America entails some sacrifices, the results may be highly rewarding: a wealthy and powerful Latin America would, in all likelihood, be able to contribute a great deal to solving or alleviating the most serious of world conflicts. Beyond ideological conflicts and power rivalries that range the Communist and capitalist countries in opposing camps lies the division of countries into developed and under-developed. That division is further embittered as racial animosities and resentments left over from the colonial past are compounded with differences in culture and living standards.

Latin America does not fully belong to either camp in any of these respects. Latin American countries as a whole are equally tied to both groups by some of their features, namely their stage of development, their ethnic makeup, and the role of colonization in their history. Without being fully aware of it, Latin America is ambivalent in the conflict between rich and poor nations, between the European white man and the colored peoples, the former colonizers and the former colonial peoples. She may in the end give her allegiance to either camp according to the generosity or greed, the skill or clumsiness, of the great powers. But if any of the Latin American countries become great powers, their dual background could help them to work out a constructive neutralism, to mediate between the two camps, and possibly to prepare a reconciliation.

Ethnically, Latin America as a whole does not fully belong either to the white or to the colored group. European influence is very strong because the Iberian colonization was followed after independence by an influx of Europeans from many areas who made up a large segment of the population; furthermore, in every Latin American country, European culture predominated for centuries as the undisputed national culture. Nevertheless, except for Argentina and Uruguay, a large segment of the population is today of Indian and, in places, African stock.

The most characteristic ethnic feature of the people of Latin America is that, while there are Europeans, Indians, and Africans, there is an even larger number of Latin Americans who are a blend of the three. Little does it matter whether the conquerors from Spain or Portugal lived with Indian and Negro women because (unlike the English) they had no race prejudice or because their possible prejudices were discarded since they came without families, as conquerors and not as immigrants. The fact is that Latin America has become the land of racial mixture.

Race mixture has always been so widespread that any accurate ethnological breakdown has become very difficult. How could it be otherwise when, through the blending of Europeans, Indians, Africans, and even some Asians which has gone on since the start of colonization, there are not only whites, Negroes, and brown people, but countless others in between so that individuals can be differentiated not by their color but only by their particular shade?

The figures provided by W. S. and E. Woytinsky [1] may be regarded as very rough estimates; the facts to be retained are

TABLE 1

ROUGH ESTIMATE OF THE ETHNIC COMPOSITION
OF LATIN AMERICA IN 1950
(in millions)

Region	Total Population	White	Brown [a]	Negro
Central America	51	·9	31	11
South America	111	52	40	19
Total	162	61	71	30

[a] Brown means the pure Indians as well as the mestizos and the mulattoes. In Latin America "mestizo" applies only to the mixture of European and Indian.

merely that the mestizos and mulattoes are probably the largest group; that South America is far more European than Central America but that in neither region are pure Europeans in the majority, as shown in table 1.

The diversity of the mixtures and of the intermediate blends prevents any brutal racial confrontation. If racial barriers were wanted by anyone, they could be erected only between individuals. Latin Americans know that any strict segregation, besides being dangerous, is not even possible. Further mixing is constantly watering down racial differences, and who knows whether Latin America is not thus preparing the only workable solution to the racial problem by melting all the races

[1] W. S. Woytinsky and E. S. Woytinsky, *World Population and Production*, New York, 1953, p. 51.

down into this new brown or gray hue that some of her sociologists regard as the embryo of a universal race?

Political Turmoil

No one disputes the value of the Latin American approach to racial problems, although it tends to be overestimated by those who would conclude that because there is no segregation, neither is there any racial prejudice or discrimination. Where political life is concerned, on the other hand, Latin America is hardly ever held up as an example. Abroad and even at home the phrase "Latin American political regime" has come to mean an arbitrary, inept, and short-lived regime. It has become almost a tenet in political science that the only thing Latin America has to offer in that field is the examples of failures so frequent that one is tempted to attribute them to a congenial inability of Latin Americans to govern themselves.

The fact is that in no other part of the world has political life been so stormy: five assassinations of heads of states between 1955 and 1961; over thirty military coups between 1940 and 1965, and even two real social revolutions—in Bolivia in 1952 and in Cuba in 1959. Nowhere else have there been so many short-lived constitutions; nowhere else have personal dictatorships disguised themselves so well behind a façade of legality.

It may seem paradoxical to speak of value in Latin American political experience, and especially to seek models in it for other nations. In fact, however, the Latin American political experience is far from being as disheartening as alleged. Frequent criticism stems from the following three mistakes that tend to distort the usual political judgments:

(1) Erroneous generalizations that stem from the tendency to base generalizations on any subject on those instances where the factors that are being studied are present. This should not be done unless the size of the whole population is taken into account as well.

(2) The tendency to rely on legal appearances rather than on social reality. Political institutions—and the men who operate them—are judged according to the stability of the institutions and the frequency of the political and social disorders they are unable to forestall. This should not be done without

considering the fact that these institutions reflect widely differing situations in the respective countries; besides, the people of these countries may assign them different goals, some of which may be more difficult to reach than others.

(3) Judging political institutions according to their conformity to a given pattern. It remains to be seen whether some deviations have not molded the institutions to the particular needs of a country.

Hasty generalizations about Latin America based on the number of states involved in a particular type of crisis have resulted in an exaggerated estimate of political instability. As far as national constitutions are concerned, it is true that a total of over 180 Latin American constitutions in 150 years is disquieting. It should be noted, however, that these changes have centered in a group of states, large in number but with relatively small populations (Venezuela having the largest). Out of the 70 successive constitutions since 1900, 43 involved six countries: Bolivia, the Dominican Republic, Haiti, Honduras, Nicaragua, and Venezuela; Venezuela is at the head of the list with 22 successive constitutions promulgated since her independence in 1811. However, in 1960 the combined populations of all six countries did not total even 24 million.

Insofar as any generalization is in order, it is certainly wiser to base it on five other countries, Argentina, Brazil, Colombia, Mexico, and Chile, whose combined populations total about 150 million. Since 1900 they have not written more than seven constitutions. This does not mean that they have not had their share of political upheavals: in each one of them, the constitution has been suspended or misapplied because of military coups or personal dictatorships. Nevertheless, the fact that the same institutions have lasted means that despite temporary troubles they fit those countries' political needs and hence are eventually reinstated.

Superficial generalizations on the volatility of political life in Latin America and the fragility of her institutions must be tempered by the statement that this occurs in the majority of the countries, but not among the majority of the over-all population. Although political life is often stormy for this majority, the long-term trend is toward balance.

Even in the most advanced Latin American countries, political life is stormy. How could it be otherwise when most of these countries are underdeveloped, are progressing at a stepped-up pace and hence have highly unstable societies? Stability of political institutions in itself is no virtue, for it may mean that the society is at a standstill and is resigned to this. If stability were all that mattered, the model political regime would be the one imposed upon Japan by the Tokugawa rulers for two and a half centuries—a regime of perfect immobility. Conversely, the instability of political regimes does not necessarily mean that the institutions are bad or badly applied, for revolutionary reforms may be needed to cope with frequent emergencies.

It is obvious that Latin America is afflicted with such frequent political upheavals because historical processes have been enormously speeded up. Thus, a mere few years have brought her changes that were spread over five whole centuries in Europe. Capitalism was already flourishing in western Europe and the United States when Latin America had only won her independence. Iberian domination and the very nature of a society of conquerors, with slavery and forced labor, preserved an archaic social structure that had disappeared several centuries earlier in more advanced countries. Since Latin America has become independent, she has had to undergo first the revolutions that attended the uniting of sovereignties broken up by feudalism in the Middle Ages, then the bourgeois revolutions that withdrew the monopoly of public administration from the nobility in the seventeenth and eighteenth centuries, then the revolutions of the nineteenth century that brought the proletariat into political life, and finally the social reforms of the twentieth century. This telescoping of history creates a state of permanent social emergency. Time is so short that the clock strikes for a new revolution before the preceding one has been completed. Different eras coexist and the Middle Ages mingle with Modern Times.

In Argentina around 1850, Rosas was only finishing his task of unifying the territory (something the Capetians had done in France centuries earlier), while English capitalism was beginning to change the province of Buenos Aires and the Pampa. The aristocracy had held uncontested power for barely forty years when Leandro started preparing the third estate for accession to power by founding the Radical Civic Union. A period of democracy that did not extend beyond the purely political field lasted from only 1916 to 1930, with Irigoyen as president. In 1943 a form of people's fascism started under Perón. None of these revolutions was completed. In the political confusion that has prevailed in Argentina since 1955, the old feudal political forces are still confronting the bourgeoisie and the proletariat.

Latin American countries have gone through far more political turmoil than Europe, but the very archaic point of departure of their evolution in the nineteenth century should be kept in mind. Hence, it is not certain that the upheavals have actually been more numerous, at least in the countries where three-quarters of the population are concentrated, that is, Argentina, Brazil, Chile, Colombia, Mexico, and the two small favored countries of Costa Rica and Uruguay. Political turmoil only seems permanent because, having been postponed for three centuries, it has been squeezed into a span of a few years.

Value of the Latin American Political Experiment

It is true that many African and Asian countries are facing today the same problems of acceleration, and must even more rapidly correct backward conditions that are worse than those in Latin America. In spite of this, the regimes of some of these developing countries seem more stable than Latin American regimes. But the overwhelming majority of the countries whose development started after World War II demand less of their political institutions. Having realized that it is difficult to change a society quickly without restricting the freedom of its members, they have more or less completely and openly given up democratic forms of government and even legality. Personal or party dictatorship, rigged elections, and arbitrary conduct of the affairs of state enable some of the developing countries some of the time to achieve a degree of political stability, at least on the surface. Instead of bursting out in the open, political upheavals are merely disguised as palace intrigues involving only a small group of people.

Latin American is different: the people who up to now have formed the body politic of those countries have always been reluctant to forsake for long the ideal of political and especially of individual freedom. That is the price they would have had to pay for the convenience of arbitrary totalitarian forms of government that appear to speed up economic and social progress. The Latin American countries differ from other underdeveloped countries mainly in the fact that their culture has never been severed from western European culture. Like the western European countries, they were deeply influenced by the liberal thinking of the eighteenth and nineteenth centuries—thinking that was born in Latin America at the same time as in Europe and North America.

Changes that elsewhere have taken centuries can be made in a few years only by the painful sacrificing of freedoms grounded in law or custom. It is difficult to achieve them through the normal operation of democratic government. Since Latin America wishes to sacrifice neither state-planned development nor freedom, she oscillates between government by law and despotic government by decree, between dictatorship and democracy.

The attempt of developing countries to preserve freedom may be a heavy handicap, and possibly the Latin Americans are wrong not to resign themselves to authoritarian regimes. On the other hand, accepting the convenience of authoritarian arbitrary regimes may be the real threat to their future. In that case, the Latin Americans are right not to give up political freedom and the guarantees afforded by law, no matter what price they must pay. In any event, in appraising their political life it should be kept in mind that these are developing countries with many handicaps to overcome. The remarkable fact is not that dictatorships have occurred from time to time, but rather that they have been short-lived.

In no other part of the world have more persistent efforts been made to preserve freedom under such unfavorable circumstances. The Latin American experiment does not deserve to be scorned because it has been painful. To the extent that a part of Latin America may finally succeed in overhauling its obsolete economic and social structure without curtailing too much or for too long the freedoms she loves, the political regimes that enable her to do so are worthy of careful study, even if they have not followed the traditional pattern of representative democracy.

Latin American Regimes of Presidential Dominance

The usual form of Latin American constitutional regime, to which almost all the countries revert after any interruption in their normal operation, has been copied from the United States presidential regime. In constitutional terms, the typical Latin American regime is not very different from the North American one, and is also called a presidential regime. The similarity of names is unfortunate, however, because it promotes the mistaken assumption that the Latin American regimes function best whenever they more closely resemble their North American model. In fact, however, they should depart from the model in order to better fulfill the special needs of the developing countries. Latin America adopted what is called the presidential regime, but if the term is defined by the way the presidential regime operates in the United States, such a regime no longer exists in Latin America. It has given way to an original Latin American regime whose peculiarities conform to the experience of Latin American politicians rather than the wishes of the framers of the constitution.

The differences from the North American presidential regime are significant enough to justify a different terminology which would better reflect the originality of the Latin American form. In order not to depart too much from the accepted name, we shall call it the *regime of presidential dominance*.

In North America, the traditional presidential regime still rests on a balance of powers, although in practice the need for government action has weakened the rigid separation between the executive and legislative branches provided by the framers of the Constitution. Numerous lines of communication had to be set up between the president, who alone is responsible for policy, and Congress, which alone makes the laws for the president to apply. The concerted operation of both powers required this. The Constitution provided for some lines of communication: presidential veto, senatorial ratification of treaties and of presidential appointments, but they were not enough. Additional procedures which were easier to operate emerged through practice. They were: congressional leadership to be exercised by the majority leader, and the granting of patronage to senators—in other words, whatever made it easier for the president to manage Congress. The balance of power remains, since the president, who is answerable only to the electorate, is actually in charge of the executive branch; and Congress, which cannot be dissolved by the president, can influence presidential policy by passing or vetoing the legislation he needs to carry out that policy. Congress has the means to do this and uses them quite often in the United States. In the true presidential regime as it emerged and developed in the United States, none of the powers is dominant under normal conditions. This could cause a temporary governmental stalemate by preventing any swift executive action unless the legislative and executive branches cooperated with each other.

The required conciliatory spirit is not likely to prevail often in Latin America, since a large segment of the population is not fully integrated into the national society and has not been able to develop a strong civic sense. On the other hand, nations cannot be built or modernized without shaking an archaic but still strong economic and social structure. This in turn conflicts with the beliefs and interests of strong minorities and sometimes even of the majority of the population. No government could possibly function effectively if the legislatures fully used the freedom provided by the constitutions to paralyze the president's policy by withholding needed legislation. The problems in Latin America are so urgent and serious that even a temporary standstill on the part of the government would cause a revolutionary situation. Even in a country like the United States, whose national integration has been completed and where democracy has existed for so long, the presidential regime has been dangerously paralyzed when, because of the numerous interests and prejudices involved, the racial problem must be dealt with. The mishaps of the Reconstruction Era after the Civil War during Andrew Johnson's presidency, and those stemming from the Versailles Treaty, show the difficulties caused in emergencies by conflicts between the executive and the legislative branches.

In practice, the proper operation of the presidential regime

in Latin America has required giving up attempts to achieve a
perfect balance of powers between the president and the legislature. The constitutions specifically empower the president to
initiate legislation and give him a reinforced veto that broad-
ens his authority. Besides, in most countries, the legislatures
are relatively meek. Whenever they stand up to the president,
the stage is set for a coup d'état.

In addition to the executive power, a Latin American president needs an over-all power to govern during his term in
office. Congress can criticize the manner in which he governs
and prevent him from abusing his power. Presidential dominance coupled with weakening of the checks and balances
inherent in the traditional presidential regime has produced in
Latin America a regime similar to both the true presidential
regime of the North American type and the ministerial regime
which, in England, was derived from the old parliamentary
regime. The Latin American countries departed from the original ministerial regime for entirely different reasons than did
England; the major reason was not the importance of party
discipline, as it had been in England. The trend, somewhat as
in England, has been toward a gathering up of the various
powers in the hands of the chief executive, or if this definition
overstates the case, toward a collaboration with the legislature
under the president's guidance. Thus, Latin American legislatures are empowered to discuss rather than frame the laws.
This does not mean, any more than it does in England, that the
legislature is a useless tool: Parliament's power to discuss and
criticize has made England a model of political democracy to
this day. In Latin America the legislature's power of discussion
has endowed authoritarian rule with some measure of democracy, under economic and social conditions quite unfavorable
to political democracy.

The Latin American regimes do not try to limit the president's authority effectively by means of a balance of powers.
Instead, they make strenuous efforts to preserve the democratic character of the regime and prevent the president's dominance from becoming a dictatorship by strictly enforcing a
time limit on his term of office. Almost all the constitutions
forbid immediate reelection of the president, and Mexico forbids him ever to run again. The presidents enjoy very broad
powers, but they can exercise them legally for six years at

most. This is the compromise that Latin America aims at, by molding the presidential regime to meet two conflicting and equally compelling needs. On the one hand, the chief executive must be given very broad powers because developing countries need this form of government. On the other hand, his powers must be restricted because Latin American countries will not resign themselves to arbitrary rule. Instead of enabling the legislature to check the substance of the president's power, as in the true presidential regime, the Latin American regime of presidential dominance tries to set a very strict time limit on the president's authority.

No appraisal of the democratic and liberal character or operation of a regime of this nature should be based on the effectiveness of congressional checks on the president's broad powers. Such a criterion, which is valid for the United States, is not for Latin America.

The danger of the president's becoming a dictator looms very large in Latin America, but it does not derive from his broad powers. In developing countries this type of regime could not function properly in any other way. The essential requirements, if the regime is to remain democratic, are free elections and a definite limit of four, five, or six years on the presidential term. Then the president, regardless of his personal qualities and popularity, must relinquish his power without having the means to impose his successor on the country.

It can hardly be expected that such a regime will always operate smoothly and that the president will invariably refrain from seeking reelection. The shortcoming is the temptation to remain in office. A similar situation arose in France in 1851. the Prince-President, after failing to obtain revision of Article 45 of the 1850 Constitution forbidding his reelection, engineered the coup d'état that produced the Second Empire. The president's continued stay in office or the fear of it causes a great deal of the political unrest in Latin America.

An impending presidential election always heralds danger. In the most representative countries, however, it is not too serious. In Mexico, Brazil, Chile, and Colombia most presidents in the present period relinquish their functions when the time comes, and, notwithstanding frequent assertions to the contrary, opposition parties have won elections. In Mexico the official party's candidate is bound to win under the single-party system, but even the party itself is not monolithic, and has its own left, center, and right. This has enabled widely differing groups to gain power.

The Third Way in Latin America

In countries where a change of presidents endowed with very broad powers but limited by short tenure has been assured, presidents have seldom acted arbitrarily. In those countries today, opposition parties are usually tolerated and enjoy freedom of expression. Special judicial bodies supervise elections, and these elections are certainly fairer than the losers claim. The courts are sufficiently independent to ensure observance of the law.

The real shortcoming of these regimes is not the fact that the president has too much power, but rather that too many presidents have not dared use their power to impose necessary reforms. In any event, there is no reason to believe that the preservation of relative political freedom and great individual freedom has been achieved at the cost of slowing down economic development. Considered over a long period—from the end of World War II until 1959—a few Latin American countries succeeded in combining political freedom with relatively rapid economic growth. For instance, the annual rate of growth was 6.2 percent in Brazil, 5.7 percent in Mexico, and 4.3 percent in Colombia. Elsewhere such a fast pace could not be maintained, but the countries that sacrificed their freedom did not seem to fare better than the others.

In the period immediately following independence, many Latin American countries were tempted to copy indiscriminately the political institutions of North Atlantic nations, whose problems were not the same. Other countries, such as Cuba, today are influenced by the example of authoritarian people's democracies. But many nations of Latin America under regimes of presidential dominance are trying to work out a third solution, between the poles of the liberal democracy of the fully developed countries and the authoritarian socialism of the underdeveloped countries. There is no certainty that their efforts will be rewarded, but the political experiment of a Latin America that keeps stubbornly trying may not be dismissed, whatever the results turn out to be.

PART I

General Features of Latin American Social Structure

Faced with a Latin America whose twenty independent nations all have a common ancestry of Romance languages and cultures, Europeans and North Americans tend to overlook any differences between those nations. Besides, from a distance Latin America seems more united than she really is because so many of her features are the opposite of those found in the other America—the English-speaking United States and Canada.

There is no doubt that owing to the common Iberian background of the Spanish and Portuguese colonizers, and even more so to their similar methods of colonization and government, the various countries of present-day Latin America have inherited related political problems. Their common past has also imparted certain similarities to the political ideologies and the approach to political problems. From the day they became independent, the Latin Americans themselves helped to strengthen the belief in a united Latin America by proclaiming their solidarity in the face of the Anglo-Saxon world. From north to south and east to west, Latin America has always eagerly held up the ideal of solidarity.

Although some generalizations are justified, they are of very little value if they embrace twenty countries, especially if this means lumping together countries in both Central and South America, some with a tropical climate, others with a temperate climate, some rich, others poor, some large, others small, and disregarding the nature of the population—that is, whether predominantly European, Amerindian, or African. Furthermore, some of those countries' cultures were handed down to them by Spanish colonizers, others by the Portuguese, and in the case of Haiti, by the French. Despite the community of language and colonial past, therefore, the idea of one Latin America is far from corresponding to ethnic, economic, political, or even geographical facts.

Generalizations cannot be avoided, however, unless a mere list of the political institutions of the twenty countries is to be drawn up. Generalities are useful only if differences as well as similarities are taken into account, and then it becomes evident that few generalizations are valid for Latin America as a whole. This is why the countries of Latin America must be sorted by type into a small number of groups, each of these comprising a number of countries with characteristics in common.

1. Classification of Latin American Countries

The twenty Latin American countries cannot be classified accurately according to their level of development, especially if social and political factors as well as economic ones are to be considered. The numerous indicators cannot coincide perfectly, since they reflect cultural traits of a different nature.

The following criteria may be applied in order to divide these twenty countries into three groups: Is their social structure of a developed national type, an archaic one of small closed communities, or a dual one? It is fairly safe to assume that in 1965 the combination of an illiteracy rate of over 50 percent, a per capita income under $250, a birth rate exceeding 40 per thousand, and a majority of the active population engaged in agriculture means that most of the population is still shackled by a very archaic economic and social structure and can be but dimly aware of belonging to a national society. That is the index of a true state of economic and social underdevelopment. Conversely, when 75 percent or more of the population can read and write, less than 35 percent are employed in agriculture, and the birth rate is under 25 per thousand, it may be inferred that the majority of the population has already broken its close bonds with the *patrón* or master, the immediate neighborhood, and the extended family in order to integrate itself into the mainstream of national society. Between these two groups are the unevenly developed countries with a dual social structure.

An archaic structure is still very widespread in most of the countries, but these are also the least populated, and their combined populations are only a small fraction of the total for Latin America. In those countries a modern way of life prevails only in a few islands. The second group consists of the very few more important countries. Their advanced structure is so extensive that the term "underdeveloped" may be used only in a very relative sense, to indicate that they are less wealthy and industrialized than the United States or the most advanced countries of Europe. In these countries an obsolete social structure exists only in a few islands. In the third group—the largest by far in terms of population and territory—a dual structure predominates. The population is divided almost equally between archaic and developed forms of social organization.

These groups include only the twenty countries commonly regarded as constituting Latin America. The territories still under European control, Puerto Rico with her ties to the United States, and the two newly independent members of the Commonwealth, Jamaica as well as Trinidad and Tobago, have been left out. Of course this classification is valid only for political study. In an economic analysis, for instance, such factors as geographic regions and territorial continuity could not be overlooked, and Nicaragua could never be placed in the same category as Bolivia. In other surveys, the ethnic variable would have to be given precedence and the linking of Mexico and Brazil, as done here, would not be acceptable.

Finally, even granting that all generalizations are arbitrary to some extent, a few countries in Latin America do not fit into any group.

Exceptional Cases

COSTA RICA. Costa Rica, a small country, is the most difficult to place, for it is an exception in every respect. None of the indicators of economic and social situation coincide. This exception does not matter too much, since in 1960 Costa Rica's population was only 1,171,000 inhabitants. The very low per capita income, estimated at no more than $140 by the United Nations for the 1952–54 period (but which according

	Developed countries
	Unevenly developed countries
	Underdeveloped countries
	Exceptional cases

0   1000 Miles

TABLE 2
Classification of Latin American Countries

	Area in Thousands of km² [a]	Population in Thousands, 1963 [a]	Density per km² [a]	Crude Birth Rate in 1963, [a] Percent	Rate of Natural Increase 1953–1962 [a] Percent per Year	Per Capita Income, 1961 [b]	Percentage of Land Under Cultivation (1950) Occupied by Estates of 2500 Acres or More [c]	Percentage of Individuals over 15 Who Are Illiterate [d]	Percentage of Middle-Class Occupations Among the Active Population [e]	Percentage of Agricultural Workers Among the Active Population [f]	Number of Inhabitants per Physician [g]
Relatively developed countries:											
Argentina	2,276	21,584	8	21.8	1.6	799	74.8	13.6	25.9	24.7	760
Uruguay	186	3,914	16	22.5	1.4	560	83.2	15	33	21.7	850
Total		25,498									
Unevenly developed countries:											
Brazil	8,513	77,521	9	40+	3.4	374	50.8	50.6	15.2	61.5	2,500
Mexico	1,969	38,416	18	45	3.1	415	79.4	43	16.9	57.8	2,500
Venezuela	912	7,872	9	42.8	3.4	644	78.6	47.8	18.2	41.2	2,950
Colombia	1,138	15,098	13	44.1	2.2	373	26.4	37.6	21.9	55.4	2,900
Chile	741	8,200	11	34.2	2.4	452	41	19.9	21.4	29.8	1,900
Total		147,107									

TABLE 2 (*Continued*)

Underdeveloped countries:										
Peru	1,285	11,511	9	45	2.7	268	66.5	53	10.5	58.8	4,500
Ecuador	270	4,726	17	44.2	3.2	222	37.4	44.3		50.9	3,600
Bolivia	1,098	3,549	3	45	1.4	122	91.9	67.9	7.6	63.3	4,000
Paraguay	406	1,903	5	45	2.4	193	93.8	34.2	14.2	58.3	2,000
Dominican Republic	48	3,334	66	39	3.6	313	24.2	57.7	3	69.7	5,200
Haiti	27	4,346	157	43.6	2.8	149	none	89.5		77.4	11,000
Guatemala	103	4,095	37	47.7	3.2	257	40.8	70.6	7.6	74.8	4,700
Honduras	112	2,008	123	47.3	3.5	251	20.5	64.8	4.5	75.7	2,600
El Salvador	20	2,810	11	48.2	2.5	267	19.9	60.4	10.5	64.2	2,600
Nicaragua	148	1,606		42.9	3.5	288	32.8	61.5		69.7	2,800
Total		39,888									
Exceptional cases:										
Costa Rica	50	1,333	25	49.9	4.4	361	36.1	20.6	22.3	56.4	2,400
Panama	74	1,139	31	40.1	3.4	371	12.2	30.1	15.2	59.4	2,800
Cuba (before revolution)	114	7,203	62	35	2	516	36.1	22.1	23.3	43.8	1,000

* United Nations: *Annuaire Démographique*, 1963, and *Population Index*, January, 1964.
* ECLA, *Economic Development of Latin America*, 1964, p. 51 (dollars at current prices).
* Panamerican Union, *Tipología Socio Económica de los Paises Latino Americanos*, 1964, p. 158. (The figures are not always comparable.)
* UNESCO: *World Illiteracy at Mid-Century*, 1957. (The percentage of illiterates has decreased substantially since then, but the respective places have not markedly changed.)
* *Tipología Socio Económica de los Paises Latino Americanos*, 1964, p. 145, from data provided by Gino Germani, Carlos Rama, and J. Iturriaga.
* *FAO Production Yearbook*, 1958.
* United Nations, *Statistical Yearbook*, 1956.

to ECLA had risen to $361 by 1961) places Costa Rica among the least developed countries. The pre-Malthusian fecundity (a birth rate of 55.4 per thousand inhabitants in 1961) would seem to indicate that the underdevelopment is not merely economic. On the other hand, the low illiteracy rate—approximately 20 percent—and the broad participation of the population in an orderly democratic political life place Costa Rica on a par with the most developed countries of Latin America. This does not mean that one should blindly accept the idea that Costa Rica, in contrast perhaps to the rest of Central America, is a perfect Arcadia whose inhabitants have found peace and happiness in their acceptance of mediocrity. This would mean overlooking the fact that 1,300 people were killed in the 1948 civil war. It should be noted, however, that most of the inhabitants have had some elementary schooling, land ownership is less concentrated than in South America, and the elections since 1948 have been peaceful. In that year, without arousing any opposition, President José Figueres simply dissolved the army and turned the main barracks into a fine arts museum. Normally, none of this fits in with a per capita income of $140 and a birth rate of about 50 per thousand.

PANAMA. The case of Panama is less interesting, but that country is equally difficult to classify. Panama is an artificial state carved out of Colombia in 1903 for the sole purpose of giving the United States the right to the Canal that the Colombian Senate had just refused. The living conditions and activities of the inhabitants, who in 1960 did not exceed one million, elude classification because the exogenous influence of the Canal Zone is too strong.

CUBA. Cuba is also difficult to place because before the Castro revolution the disturbing influence of the United States was too marked—in the form of tourism, gambling, and a mixture of exploitation and favoritism linked to the sugar industry. Since the revolution, the situation has been changing too fast to warrant any conclusions regarding its long-term characteristics and effects. At present, the turmoil originating in Cuba is affecting almost all of Latin America.

Countries with a Developed Homogeneous
Social Structure: Argentina and Uruguay

Only two countries, both in the southern part of the continent and in the temperate zone, fully belong in this group: the Republic of Argentina, a large country with 21 million inhabitants, and Uruguay, which had less than 4 million in 1963.

These adjoining countries are very similar and were separated only by the incidents of the independence movement. Their populations are of almost pure European stock. In both of them, the small Indian population disappeared as colonization progressed. The land was first used for extensive cattle-

TABLE 3
ETHNIC COMPOSITION IN THE RIO DE LA PLATA COUNTRIES

	Whites, Percent	Mestizos, Percent	Indians, Percent
Argentina	86	12	2
Uruguay	88	10	2

raising that required little manpower. When the time came for a true settlement of the land—which was only in the last years of the eighteenth century—the present territory of Argentina and Uruguay was almost empty, and the countries were opened to mass European immigration not only from Spain but from Italy, Germany, and even France and England. The immigrants submerged the colonial population with its strong admixture of Indian and African blood, which at the time of independence did not exceed one and a half million inhabitants. Owing to a complete renewal in population (for instance, at all times between 1870 and 1914 almost 50 percent of the inhabitants of Buenos Aires were foreign-born) not only are there practically no Indians left, but even the mestizos are in a very small minority. The Rio de la Plata region of Latin America is more purely European than is the United States.

The immigration, which continued after World War II, was at the same time a cause and a sure sign of the advanced stage of development of these countries. Although some of the immigrants came from European countries with a relatively high standard of living, they did not come to assume leading positions, as in underdeveloped countries, but were scattered among all social classes including manual laborers in agriculture and industry.

The swift transition of the overwhelming majority of the active population from the primary sector of the economy into the secondary and tertiary sectors and its rapid urbanization also indicate the high level of economic and social development in that part of Latin America. The percentage of the active population engaged in agriculture is only 21.7 percent in Uruguay and 24 percent in Argentina—about the same levels as in Sweden and Canada. Actually, the tertiary sector is inordinately large—45.5 percent in Argentina—and this is not due, as is sometimes the case in underdeveloped countries, to a proliferation of domestic services, but to a deliberate social policy that creates employment in the civil service, nationalized enterprises, and all the service industries. As in young countries of the Australian type, the population becomes concentrated in very large cities. For instance, Buenos Aires and Montevideo each account for 30 percent of the total population, 65 to 70 percent of which is urban.

Such concentration of population in very large cities is incompatible with the survival of an archaic social structure based on neighborhood, kinship, and dependence upon a chief, or patrón, which can persist only in a few backward provinces. A level of literacy comparable to that of western European countries also testifies to the relatively high homogeneity of an advanced culture. Thus in 1950, 90 percent of the Argentinians and 85 of the Uruguayans could read and write. The small percentage of illiterates resulting from the low population density still prevailing in rural zones, together with an archaic form, the large estate, is rapidly disappearing.

The general spread of public education is helped by the favorable age distribution of the population, which stems from demographic behavior typical of cultures dominated by middle-class attitudes. Thus, in both countries the present birth rate is under 25 per thousand while the life expectancy, probably around 65 years at birth, is comparable to that of the western European countries.

A social structure that in many respects resembles that of western Europe makes for similarities in political life as well. It is true that the present political unrest in the Republic of Argentina and the resulting constant interference by military is somewhat reminiscent of the state of affairs in the least developed countries of Latin America. But in this case appearances are misleading: the demands expressed in the Peronist movement come neither from backward peasants seeking a place in national society nor from a wretched, uneducated urban proletariat. They emanate instead from an organized working class and even more from a middle class increased by hypertrophy of the tertiary sector. Both these classes are vainly struggling to keep social gains obtained earlier than the economic development of the country warranted.

Until the Peronist revolution in 1943, the aristocracy of the big landowners and the professional men closely allied to them wielded very strong economic and even political influence. But today personal allegiances based on family ties and the dependence of rural populations on the gentry no longer distort the operation of the representative system. As soon as the political parties were free from these personal and local influences, they were able to organize on a national scale on the basis of political interests and ideologies. There now exist a right and a left, although in Argentina the distinction is somewhat blurred by strong vestiges of Perón's justicialism.

The very broad social gains cannot be maintained without seriously hurting the economy, especially in Argentina where the Peronist regime was highly demagogic. The welfare state is more solidly rooted in these countries than anywhere else, although agriculture has been bypassed. The populations are still not highly industrialized, but are highly urbanized and have strong trade unions. They value social benefits above wage increases and have gained them, although the level of productivity did not warrant maintaining them at the level gained, let alone raising them. This problem is particularly acute because Argentina and Uruguay owe their great advance over the rest of Latin America to agriculture and cattle-raising. Particularly favorable conditions and the positive role of the aristocracy in this respect accounted for these successes. But now the urban majority of the population takes no interest whatsoever in agriculture and livestock, while heavy industry is not yet sufficiently developed to compensate for their decline.

As a result, since the end of World War II, Argentina and Uruguay have suffered stagnation if not recession, as shown by a slightly negative rate of economic growth—respectively − 0.4 and − 0.2 percent per year between 1945 and 1960.[1] In Argentina especially, where the people succeeded in preserving and increasing social gains, they found that these were outstripped by currency depreciation. In Uruguay a very strong democratic tradition mitigated the political effects of an equally difficult economic situation, but in the Republic of Argentina Perón's paternalism with its overtones of Fascism was still missed.

Under these conditions, Argentina and Uruguay are not like underdeveloped or developing countries, but rather like developed ones which are struggling to maintain a standard of living already won. Although Argentina and Uruguay are still well ahead of the other Latin American countries in all respects, the margin is narrowing. Whatever index is used, the situation immediately following the 1929 economic depression comes to mind. Some economists who believed it to be permanent or lasting called it *secular stagnation* or *maturity*.[2]

THE SPECIAL CASE OF CHILE. In some respects Chile is related to the group of relatively developed countries. Although it is separated from Argentina and Uruguay by the Andean chain, it is their neighbor in the southern part of the continent. As in the two Plata countries, the literacy rate is high—around 80 percent; the percentage of agricultural workers among the active population is only 29.8 percent, and the population tends to concentrate in the cities, where the tertiary sector is overdeveloped. A large middle class and an organized proletariat have secured control of political life. As in Argentina and Uruguay, the social gains of the urban population have on the whole exceeded the level compatible with the state of the economy—which is much less productive in Chile.

[1] Jorge Ahumada, *Economic Development and Problems of Social Change in Latin America*, United Nations Economic and Social Council, 1960, p. 4.

[2] Paul M. A. Sweezy, *The Theory of Secular Stagnation*, 1943.

Since World War II, the rate of economic growth has been only 0.6 percent per year, which is not enough to maintain Chile's margin over other Latin American countries.

On the other hand, some aspects of the way of life in Chile indicate that the high degree of development is not as widespread as in the other two countries and that social dualism still persists. The rural aristocracy has lost its hold on national political life but still retains power in some rural areas. Despite a start on agrarian reform, land ownership is still relatively concentrated and the methods of cultivation are very archaic. Agrarian communities untouched by a money economy, and ancient relationships with the patrón, still exist on the large estates. Chile is still one of the many Latin American countries where part of the population suffers from malnutrition. The obsolete social organization existing in some areas is reflected by a birth rate of about 35 per thousand, a rate lower than in the underdeveloped Central American countries but much higher than in Europe or North America. The life expectancy of about 50 years at birth, reached in 1952, was very low for an advanced society.

Chile differs from the Plata countries in its ethnic composition, although the political consequences are minor. Very shortly after independence, Chile received an influx of immigrants, including a large number of Germans in flight after the revolution of 1848, but the population is not of pure European stock. Today pure-blooded Indians are very few, perhaps 5 percent, and it is fairly safe to assume, although it is not certain, that pure Europeans average about 30 percent; mestizos, whether they account for 60 or 80 percent of the population, are probably in the majority. While there is a widespread admixture of Indian blood, its proportion is small. Since it is not accompanied by any cultural differences, it poses no racial or social problems and does not affect political conditions.

Chile may be placed either in the category of the most advanced Latin American countries together with Argentina and Uruguay, or in that of unevenly developed countries like Brazil or Mexico. In either case, the group of countries with a developed social organization cannot be regarded as representative or serve as a basis for generalizations about Latin America. Excluding Chile, its combined population is only 25 mil-

lion inhabitants, and with Chile, 34 million—that is, barely
10 to 13 percent of Latin America's total population.

Countries with a Preponderantly Archaic Social Structure

At the opposite end of the scale are many countries as yet
untouched by economic and social changes except locally—in
the towns and sometimes only in the capital. All of them are
small countries, at least with respect to population (except
Peru). This group, where an archaic form of social organization still predominates, includes four countries in Central
America—Guatemala, El Salvador, Honduras, Nicaragua—and the two island countries of Haiti and the Dominican
Republic; in South America, Peru, Ecuador, and Bolivia. Paraguay might be placed in that group despite certain special
features of possible importance for its future.

In its ethnic composition, the underdeveloped portion of
Latin America is not predominantly European. In Peru, Ecuador, Bolivia, and Guatemala the high proportion of Indians
makes it an Indian rather than a Spanish America. In El
Salvador, Honduras, Nicaragua, and Paraguay interbreeding
has been so widespread and the proportion of Indian blood so
large that this is an Ibero-Indian America; in Haiti and the
Dominican Republic, African blood is predominant, almost in
a pure state in the former, mulatto in the latter. Figures on
ethnic makeup are very imprecise and, according to the source
used, often vary by as much as 100 percent because some of
them are based on physical appearance and others on language or way of life. Furthermore, identical criteria are interpreted and applied in different ways. Whatever the source and
the criteria, however, there is agreement on the fact that,
except for the Dominican Republic, where the percentage of
Europeans is said to be around 15 percent, in none of the
other underdeveloped countries do individuals of pure European extraction exceed 10 percent of the population.

Some of the imprecision in the figures of table 4 results from
the fact that, according to the 1950 census in Bolivia, Indians
did not exceed 46 percent of the population, although it was
stated that 70 percent of the inhabitants spoke Indian languages.

As a rule, ethnic prejudices in Latin America have applied to a non-European way of life rather than race. Hence they have not markedly outlived assimilation. What matters in the political life of the country is not the actual number of Indians, Africans, or mestizos but the fact that a fairly large segment of the population is still bound by a way of life and a social organization that keep it outside the mainstream of society. This is the case in Bolivia, Ecuador, and Peru, where the

TABLE 4

ETHNIC COMPOSITION IN THE UNDERDEVELOPED
PORTION OF LATIN AMERICA [a]

Country	Whites, Percent	Mestizos or Mulattoes, Percent	Indians, Percent	Africans, Percent
Guatemala	3	40	57	—
Peru	10	36	54	—
Ecuador	8	44	48	—
Bolivia	10	44	46	—
El Salvador	8	52	40	—
Honduras	10	50	40	—
Nicaragua	10	45	40	5
Dominican Republic	15	70	—	15
Haiti	—	5	—	95

[a] Figures obtained from various sources.

Indian communities (*ayllus*) still remain strong because of communal ownership of land. In Guatemala as well, vestiges of the pre-Columbian era are still numerous. In those four countries, entire regions still include Indian populations completely isolated from the rest of the country whose customs and language they have not accepted.

Social dualism already exists, but the developed segments of society are narrowly circumscribed; progress has barely touched the rural populations, which are by far the largest. In none of these countries is less than two-thirds of the population engaged in agriculture. Very archaic forms of economic and social structure predominate.

Middle classes have arisen in a few towns, and the political influence they now wield, together with the embryonic workers' proletariat, is inordinately strong considering their size. This is so because the rural populations take no effective part in the political life of a national society alien to them. Advanced urban groups tend to replace the decadent aristocracy in government positions and are selfishly ruling the country people of whom they have virtually no knowledge. This urban domination resembles colonial rule because in that part of America most of the peasants are Indians. So widespread is this phenomenon that the term *campesino,* or peasant, has become synonymous with Indian. A similar derivation, although operating in reverse, has occurred in Brazil where the word *caboclo,* an Indian-Portuguese mestizo, now means peasant.

There is no shortage of examples of the extreme differences between the living conditions of a small urban society and a large rural one. The following one regarding the distribution of medical personnel will suffice: around 1953 Tegucigalpa, the capital of Honduras, had 93 physicians for its 108,000 inhabitants, that is, one physician per 1,160 persons, while in one of the departments in the interior of the country there was one physician for 99,000 persons, and in another whose population was 64,000 there was not a single doctor.[3]

None of these countries of the West Indies and of Central or Andean America was in a position after independence to open its borders to immigrants from Europe, except for a few specialists. All these countries have a surplus of underemployed native manpower with a very low living standard, with which European manpower cannot compete. In no country of this group does the percentage of persons born in Europe markedly exceed one per thousand; in most of them there are not even half as many. For instance, in El Salvador Europeans are in the proportion of one per five thousand and in Haiti of one per ten thousand. The small influx of immigrants is of the colonial type, since they come with the sole purpose of filling leading positions in the country.

[3] Ramon Villeda Morales, *El Problema social de la medicina en Honduras,* Publicaciones del Colegio Médico de Honduras, 1955.

The continuing existence of an essentially agricultural economy characterized by great estates and powerful landowners did not enable any of these countries to exceed a per capita income of $150 until 1952. In several of them, according to United Nations estimates, it was under $100. Everywhere part of the population suffers from malnutrition if not undernourishment. Some of these Indo- or Afro-American countries are already overpopulated, not in relation to what the land could yield—except possibly Haiti—but to what the level of development enables it to yield. This is certainly true of El Salvador and the Dominican Republic. At present it is also true of Peru and Bolivia, and will remain so as long as the Amerindian population is bound to its pre-Columbian communities and poor lands. The people are accustomed to the altitude of the high plateaus and hence cannot settle on the vast territories east of the Andes. These areas are still empty but lack means of communication, and besides, their equatorial climate is deadly to the mountain people.

The situation is aggravated by the fact that in those countries, although the prevailing archaic culture has prevented any attempts at birth control, the death rate has started to decline. It is difficult to obtain precise data on birth rates because the social organization hardly allows for regular registry of birth. It does seem, however, that on the whole the birth rate is not under 45 per thousand and in some countries hovers around 50 per thousand. Despite a life expectancy that remains fairly low, about 50 years, this fecundity results in an extraordinarily rapid population increase. Except in Bolivia, where the death rate is still abnormally high, the rate of population increase should cause the population to double in 20 or 30 years.

The underdevelopment of this Indian and African America is reflected in very high illiteracy rates. The proportion of illiterates recorded about 1955 generally varied between 60 and 90 percent, and in all likelihood is actually even higher. Progress is slow despite serious efforts. Even as the proportion of illiterates declines, their actual number continues to grow as the population increases. Around 1956 to 1958 only 20 percent of the children finished the sixth grade of elementary

school in El Salvador, 12 percent in Nicaragua and Guatemala, 9 percent in Honduras, and far fewer in Haiti.[4]

THE SPECIAL CASE OF PARAGUAY. In many respects,
Paraguay belongs in the group of countries with an archaic
social structure, since it is also very underdeveloped economically as well as socially: in 1952–1954 the per capita income
was still under $100. As in the other countries in this group,
only a very small minority of the population is of pure European stock. Paraguay did not have an advanced pre-
Columbian civilization with a resulting dense Indian population; not many Africans were brought in, nor was there a large
influx of European immigrants. In 1950 the number of inhabitants was 1,199,371. The popular spoken language has remained *guaraní*, an Indian language.

An accident of history enabled the primitive Indians to
survive: in the colonial era, for a century and a half starting in
1610, the Jesuits succeeded in maintaining a theocracy of a
collectivist type which kept Europeans out of Paraguay. When
the Jesuits were expelled in 1767, the Indians were victim-
ized, but shortly after the country became independent a paternalistic dictator, Francia (1811–1840), took them under
his protection. He went to great pains to keep Europeans from
immigrating, and expelled some of those who had already
come. At present, the population of Paraguay is a mixture of
races, with the Indian element predominant.

Paraguay's situation is different, nevertheless, from that of
the other Latin American countries at the same level of development, and its future appears more promising. First of all,
thanks to the low population density, Paraguay, unlike the rest
of Ibero-Indian America, can resort to European immigration
in order to develop the country, even agriculturally, by using
new settlements as starting points. The government is fostering
such immigration. The presence of Indian communities in
Paraguay poses no assimilation problems because they have
retained only the language from their very primitive heritage.
The cultural level of the masses is low, but this makes it easier
for them to assimilate the national culture of European origin.

[4] United Nations Economic and Social Council, *Las clases medias en
Centroamérica*, October, 1960, p. 19.

In addition, Paraguay is landlocked within the most advanced part of Latin America—Argentina and southern Brazil—and cannot fail to benefit from such proximity. Finally, some of the Paraguay's dictators have promoted public education so that, according to the statistics at any event, close to 60 percent of the adults can read and write—a very high percentage for a country whose economic development is so embryonic. Paraguay has never had for any length of time a regime that was not a dictatorship. At present it is a military dictatorship, but in any case it has always been one-man rule.

The countries in the Indo- and Afro-American underdeveloped group are numerous—about ten, that is, half of all Latin American countries. They are not, however, any more representative of Latin America than are the two developed countries of the southern tip of the continent. The combined population of these ten countries is about 40 million. It is no more legitimate to generalize on the basis of the least developed populations, which represent 17 percent of the total, than on the basis of the most advanced, which at most represent 13 percent. The temptation to generalize is stronger because the backward populations are distributed among more countries, but both extremes are in the minority.

Unevenly Developed Countries with a Dual Social Structure

Insofar as it is possible to make tentative generalizations about Latin America societies and political conditions, it is wise to limit these to states in an intermediate position between the extremes (the most advanced, of the Argentinian type, and the most backward, of the Andean or Central American type). The unevenly developed countries have the largest combined population in Latin America. Brazil has 78 million inhabitants and Mexico 38 million. Thus, these two countries alone contain slightly over half the population of Latin America and occupy almost half the area, but these figures are greatly increased if Colombia with its 15 million inhabitants and Venezuela with about 8.5 million are included. (As we said earlier, Chile, with its uneven levels of development, can also be included in this category.)

The group itself, however, is far from being homogeneous except for its intermediate stage of development between the two extremes and the almost even distribution of the population into two segments, one having the characteristics of developed societies, the other of archaic societies. In several respects, it is paradoxical to place Mexico and Brazil in the same category when they are completely different in their geographic environment, ethnic structure, and culture (Spanish in one, Portuguese in the other).

THE SPECIAL CASE OF MEXICO. Geographic factors place Mexico in a special situation because a large part of her territory—the most developed as it happens—is in a semiarid zone. She therefore lacks some of the agricultural assets of Brazil, Venezuela, or Colombia—three countries whose population densities range from 22 to 33 inhabitants per square mile, and must certainly still be regarded as underpopulated. Mexico does not have over 45 inhabitants per square mile, but the dryness of the most accessible zones of the country does not allow for a very high population density. Population growth is extremely rapid in all four of these countries. This may spell only trouble for Mexico; in the other three countries, the present drawbacks of too young a population and too many new recipients sharing the profits of economic growth may be compensated later by better use of natural resources.

On the other hand, geographic conditions in the arid zones have been a great asset to Mexico. In a large part of the country, village settlement created social conditions very different from those in the other three countries, where the dispersion of rural populations prevented the village from becoming an active social center. It was also easier to overcome rural isolation in the dry zones of Mexico, not only because the population was less spread out, but also because travel was easier over dry land. In Brazil, Venezuela, and Colombia the tropical and equatorial rains are a more formidable obstacle than mountains to the building of roads and railroads, and also paralyze traffic for part of the year.

The basic difference between Mexico and the four other countries lies in ethnic composition. Brazil, Venezuela, Colombia, and Chile have a complex population with widespread interbreeding. But except for a few small areas in Colombia, there had been no highly cultured pre-Columbian population organized as a state. A few Indians do remain in some remote regions but are merely an ethnographic oddity. The Indian element survived only through the racial mixing that was very common in Colombia, Chile, and Venezuela, and less so in Brazil. There, on the other hand, the presence of a large number of Africans resulted in a high percentage of mulattoes.

The very rough estimates of table 5 indicate the complexity of these countries' ethnic structure. In addition, in Brazil especially, there are a few Asians. But this has not entailed any mixing or clash of cultures. There was no native culture, apart

TABLE 5

ETHNIC COMPOSITION IN THE UNEVENLY DEVELOPED COUNTRIES

	Whites, Percent	Mestizos and Mulattoes, Percent	Africans, Percent	Indians, Percent
Brazil	60	22	15	3
Colombia	26	68	4	2
Venezuela	15	72	7	6

from the imported Portuguese or Spanish culture, to which the mixed population could have remained attached. The primitive Indian, therefore, had no choice but to assimilate or die. The fact that the populations were small enabled these countries, upon independence, to take in European immigrants when they so desired. Many of these arrived in Brazil as soon as slavery had been abolished there and made the states of southern Brazil almost as purely European as those of the Plata region. After World War II, Colombia and, even more, Venezuela tried to attract European immigration. Like Argentina and Uruguay (but only partly and in circumscribed areas), Brazil, Colombia, and Venezuela as well as Chile are new countries and, taken as a whole, their culture is entirely European.

Mexico, on the contrary, is Indian ethnically just as much as Peru, Ecuador, or Bolivia. Like them, she is experiencing problems arising from contact between native culture and imported culture, as well as the difficulties of assimilation. But unlike them, for half a century she has committed herself to assimilation. There remains in Mexico a sizable percentage of Indians who have retained most of the traits of pre-Columbian culture and many mestizos who resist assimilation. Mexico is promoting their assimilation by encouraging a minimal combination of cultures. This allows the assimilated Indians to keep their pride in their pre-Columbian past and presents the new culture as a blend of European and Indian cultures, rather than as a purely European one. In particular, Mexico has tried to adapt the communal forms of pre-Columbian land ownership, *ejidos,* to the needs of modern agriculture instead of wiping them out. The impassioned Indianism that has permeated Mexican graphic arts and sociological and political literature since the revolution expresses aims rather than achievements. Nonetheless, its value in promoting national integration is undeniable.

Mexico's ethnic composition is particularly difficult to analyze precisely. The 1960 census did not record over 11 percent pure Indians because the term Indian had been given an essentially linguistic connotation. But Iturriaga [5] suggested the figure of 27.91 percent, and Carrancá y Trujillo,[6] 37 percent. The discrepancy stems from the use of different criteria in assessing the remnants of pre-Columbian culture. The only established fact is that Mexico, whose population has not been renewed by any recent immigration, has very few pure Europeans, perhaps 10 to 15 percent. The overwhelming majority of the population is Indian or mestizo, while the African element is infinitesimal today.

Mexico resembles Brazil rather than Peru in her high level of economic and social development. In all likelihood this is due primarily to the dynamism of her Indian population which, beginning in the pre-independence period, played an essential role in all the revolutions and did not allow itself to be ignored. It also stems to a large degree from Mexico's

[5] José E. Iturriaga, *La estructura social y cultural de México* (Mexico City, 1951), p. 103.
[6] Raúl Carrancá y Trujillo, *Panorama crítico de nuestra América* (Mexico City, 1950), p. 126.

geographical position, which saved her from isolation and fostered contacts with the developed countries of North America rather than with the rest of Latin America. These contacts made for a dangerous national life, for since Mexico is in the United States intervention zone and shares a long common border with the United States, she has suffered more from these interventions than any other country until the Good Neighbor Policy was launched just before World War II. While South America, secure in her isolation, slumbered in memories of the past, the disturbing influence of the United States forced Mexican society to change in order to survive.

Proximity certainly fostered Mexico's progress and so did U. S. investments of capital in industry and agriculture, tourism, and the seasonal employment of agricultural workers in the United States. The political dangers of proximity also indirectly helped Mexico, where the responses to danger were a hastened national integration and the transforming of xenophobia into patriotism. Thus the United States' victorious wars in the middle of the nineteenth century to gain portions of Mexican territory, her repeated interventions to protect her economic interests, and the attempt of Napoleon III to intervene in the civil wars and impose a foreign sovereign upon Mexico combined to arouse national awareness within broad segments of the population. In the rest of Latin America, wherever there was a comparable level of economic and social development, such awareness was only embryonic.

EQUILIBRIUM BETWEEN THE ARCHAIC AND DEVELOPED SEGMENTS OF SOCIETY. Political and social problems assume different aspects in each of the four or five countries of this group. They are nevertheless similar in nature because they are problems of societies that are divided fairly evenly into very archaic and developed areas, the one type rural and the other urban. It is impossible to give for each country an accurate estimate of the population in the respective areas. It is fairly safe to assume, however, that in each of these countries the developed area includes over one-third of the population and that in none of them does it include more than two-thirds. In all of them, of course, the archaic segment is rapidly shrinking. It is the vestige of the past, whereas the developed segment is the image of the future. In the meantime, there are two Mexicos, just as there are two Brazils, closely intertwined with each other.

The numerical ratio of the two segments changes within a few years, but in 1960 out of Brazil's 70 million inhabitants, probably 25 or 30 million in the southern states and in the large cities all over the country belonged to a developed, organized society. The others still retained the traits—almost intact in certain rural areas—of an archaic culture that vanished from western Europe several centuries ago. The contrast can be seen in the mud or sod peasant huts in the countryside and the twelve-story concrete workers' dwellings in the towns. Even within the towns, modern, large urban developments coexist with shacks made out of branches, dried mud, or sheet iron. These form the squalid slums that immigrants from backward areas rebuild faster than they can be torn down. Because they sprawl all over Latin America, many names have been invented for them: *favelas, villas miseria, villas malocas, quebrados, barrios clandestinos, poblaciones de latas, poblaciones de ratas, poblaciones callampas,* and *charnecas.* In the countryside, nothing shows the gap between the two societies more strikingly than the small airfields of the interior where, for lack of roads, discharged cargo must be hoisted onto mules or placed on an antiquated Iberian cart that five pair of oxen painfully drag along a rutted trail.

REGIONAL DIVERSITY IN BRAZIL. Within each country of this category, all the diverse situations existing throughout Latin America are present, together with their distinctive problems. This is particularly true of Brazil, where vast distances and isolation sharply outline regional differences.

In the southernmost zone of Brazil, including almost the entire states of Rio Grande do Sul, Santa Catarina, Paraná, and Guanabara, most of the state of São Paulo, and a few zones of the states of Minas Gerais and Rio de Janeiro, the per capita income is relatively high; almost all the inhabitants can read and write; the middle classes are large and diversified and are beginning to appear even in the countryside; and life expectancy is approaching that of western Europe. This part of Brazil, like neighboring Argentina and Uruguay, presents the characteristics of a developed society. It is less developed than Argentina, however, since archaic sectors remain in the countryside and the overly rapid migration to the cities reproduces these sectors there.

The opposite is true of the northeastern states—Paraíba, Rio Grande do Norte, Ceará, Piauí, and even northernmost Pernambuco, as well as in the west—Amazonas, Pará, and Mato Grosso. There the living conditions of the ignorant, uneducated, and diseased rural masses hardly differ from those of the underdeveloped populations of Andean and Central America. Fecundity is equally high, life expectancy and per capita income as low, and illiteracy equally widespread. The archaic social structure is predominant in the Brazilian Northeast, and the modern way of life is so narrowly circumscribed to a few large cities like Recife that its sole effect upon the preponderant archaic society is to begin its breakdown.

Finally, between the two extremes there is an intermediate zone extending over the largest parts of the states of Rio de Janeiro and Minas Gerais and a small portion of São Paulo. In this zone, where change is at its swiftest, the large cities and a few prosperous rural areas showing all the characteristics of an advanced stage of social and economic development adjoin other rural areas where the colonial social organization and agricultural methods of past centuries are firmly rooted.

OPPOSING CHARACTERISTICS OF THE TWO SEGMENTS OF SOCIETY. In Mexico, Brazil, Venezuela, and Colombia—four countries torn by social dualism—the percentages of illiterates and of those with a minimum of schooling are roughly equal. But regional surveys show that illiteracy prevails mainly in the backward regions, especially among rural populations. In the large cities and the modernized regions, many migrants from the archaic society provide their own remedy; one remarkable characteristic of the developing areas is that the number of those who can read and write is larger than the number of those who have attended school.

Of the three sectors of economic activity, about half the active population in these four countries is engaged in agriculture. The 1950 percentages were 60, 58, and 54 respectively for Brazil, Colombia, and Mexico; the percentage is markedly lower for Venezuela, not so much because of a higher level of industrialization but because of the growth of a parasitic tertiary sector fostered by the squandering of taxes and royalties on oil.

The major role played in some areas by the tertiary sector has already given rise to very large middle classes, especially within urban society. But to the illiterate, wretched inhabitants of the underdeveloped sections of the country and to the fringe populations crowded in the hovels of the capitals, almost all the regularly employed population of the developed areas must appear as the middle class, so great is the difference in living standards, way of life, and levels of education. It is in that indirect sense that some specialists on Latin America, for instance John J. Johnson,[7] use the expression "middle classes" or preferably "middle sector." They include in it the regularly employed workers' proletariat which owes its existence to partial industrialization. Even if its wages are not very high, it nevertheless has a living standard three or four times higher than that of the rural population.

Except in Venezuela, where high income (1952–1954) had little relation to the level of domestic development, these unevenly developed countries had per capita incomes that were still low—220, 230, and 250 dollars respectively in Mexico, Brazil, and Colombia. Incomes are very unevenly distributed between the developed and backward areas, as well as among the various strata of the population. In Brazil in 1960 the differential was 7 or 8 to 1 between the populations of developed states such as São Paulo and of backward states like Piauí. In Colombia (1953) it was 11 to 1 between the departments of Cundinamarca and Chocó. In Venezuela, 12 percent of the population holds half of the income; in 1957 the average per capita income in the country was estimated at about 3,700 bolivars, but 80 percent of the rural population did not earn over 125 bolivars. In Colombia 5 percent of the population receive 41 percent of the income, and in Mexico 16 percent of the inhabitants have 56.5 percent of the in-

[7] John J. Johnson, *Political Change in Latin America: The Emergence of the Middle Sectors* (Stanford, 1964).

come.[8,9] These figures show that the living conditions of the two segments of the population differ in every respect. But the figures themselves should not be assumed to be wholly accurate, for the differences between the two ways of life are such that the respective incomes of the two societies within one country are as difficult to compare as those of two different countries. It may be added that the favored group does nothing to bridge the chasm.

RAPID EVOLUTION OF THE UNEVENLY DEVELOPED COUNTRIES. The countries in this group are still very unevenly developed, but they are changing more rapidly than any others in Latin America. In Brazil and Mexico, the rate of annual increase in the national product between 1945 and 1959 was respectively 6.2 percent and 5.6 percent.[10] These rates of growth are similar to those of Italy and Germany for the same period. It is true that their effect was mitigated by the population increase—3.4 percent per year in Brazil and 3.1 percent in Mexico. The situation is not as favorable in Colombia where the increase in the national product declined during that period to 4.3 percent, partly because the economy is more dependent on coffee prices than anywhere else, partly because of the continuing existence of banditry in the archaic society, and possibly, in the developed part of the country, because of social legislation that slows down productivity. In Venezuela, until 1959, the increase was extremely rapid, 9 percent yearly, but it is difficult to assess its meaning because it is too closely tied to the rise in volume and value of oil exports during the Suez crisis and until the end of 1957.

It is often deplored not only that Latin America is generally

---

[8] "Economic Growth and Social Policy in Latin America: The Seventh Conference of the American States Members of the ILO," *International Labour Review,* July, 1961, pp. 50–74.

[9] United Nations, "Economic Developments in Venezuela in the 1950's," *Economic Bulletin for Latin America,* March, 1960, p. 23 and n 9.

[10] Jorge Ahumada, "Economic Development and Problems of Social Change in Latin America," United Nations, mimeographed. Reproduced in UNESCO, *Revue internationale du travail,* July, 1961, p. 57, and in *Aspectos sociales del desarrolo economico* (1962), p. 129.

very underdeveloped but that her progress is very slow. This is true of most Latin American countries but, at least from 1945 to 1957, not of a small number of countries that include the large majority of the population. Of the three most important countries, inhabited by two-thirds of the Latin Americans, one, Argentina, is already developed socially even more than economically; the two others, Brazil and Mexico, have developed haphazardly but have advanced very rapidly since World War II. Although the rate of increase in the national product slowed down markedly in all of Latin America after 1957, in Brazil, Mexico, and Venezuela it nonetheless remained around 5.6 percent between 1955 and 1961.[11]

[11] United Nations, *The Economic Development of Latin America in the Post-war Period* (1964), p. 6.

2. Political Effects of Independence

Latin America's political problems are common to all developing countries. The particular forms they assume in Latin America, however, result from a combination of features inherited from Iberian colonization and from the conditions under which independence was won. Remnants of colonization are more or less marked depending on which of the three stages of development defined earlier a particular country has reached. But they are present in all of Latin America, even in those countries that differ most from one another in ethnic composition, natural resources, and stage of development. The effects of colonization are still felt after one and a half centuries of independence because its advent was not accompanied by the immediate rejection of colonialism.

Early characteristics of Spanish colonization in America that have remained dominant were shaped by methods used in the two regions with a large native population, a sizable portion of which was civilized—the Viceroyalty of New Spain, set up in Mexico City in 1535, and the Viceroyalty of Peru, set up in Lima in 1542. In the few years between the landing of Cortés in Mexico in 1519 and the assassination of Pizarro in 1541 the Spaniards and Portuguese took over almost all of America from California to the Rio de la Plata, but a large portion of the huge territory which was thinly populated by primitive peoples was neglected until much later and assumed some importance only in the eighteenth century or even only after independence.

Thus the Spanish colonies were always to bear the mark of the social conditions that prevailed in Europe in the sixteenth century, of the social background of the conquerors, of the motivations that animated them, and above all, of a large native population subjugated by no more than a few thousand men. In Mexico around 1570, for instance, probably not more than 30,000 Spaniards faced the 3,500,000 Indian survivors of ill-treatment and epidemics, and in the Andes the ratio was not much different—about 40,000 Spaniards and two million Indians.

In the Antilles, where the native population had been rapidly decimated by ill treatment and epidemics, and in Brazil, which never had a large indigenous population, similar conditions were created through African slavery. Colonization methods were firmly rooted by the time regions with a scarcity of forced laborers started developing. The Viceroyalty of Buenos Aires was organized only in 1776 on the eve of independence, when there were still very few Spaniards in the area, with little Indian manpower. Colonizers were more numerous in the Antilles because high-yield plantations made it worth their while to resort to African slavery.

Comparison Between Iberian and English Colonization in America

Inevitably, owing to its origin, Iberian colonization was bound to differ considerably from English colonization in North America. The spirit of the New England colonists was to be the major factor in shaping North America, since the plantation owners in the Carolinas and Georgia, whose form of society was not quite so different from that of the Spaniards and Portuguese, lost the Civil War. The two periods of colonization were different as well as the goals of the colonists with their opposite temperaments. The patterns of settlement of the indigenous peoples were also quite dissimilar, and the relationships between the colonists and their home countries had nothing in common. These were indeed the prototypes of "exploitation" and "settlement" colonization.

The first Spaniards who rushed into Mexico and Peru almost immediately after the discovery of 1492 were not emigrants. They had not left their country permanently, and were merely adventurers without families who, depending upon their social status, meant to get rich quickly by looting or to carve out principalities for themselves. In North America, on the contrary, the first New England settlers—who started coming only after 1620—were emigrants who did not intend ever to go back but had decided to establish a new society in America. While the Spaniards were the efficient if troublesome and unruly servants of an absolute monarchy, the Puritans had come with their families in order to realize the ideal of self-government in a republican New England.

In both cases, the religious factor played an essential role, but in opposite ways: in New England, there were dissidents fleeing from religious oppression; in Spanish America (apart from the looting of the adventurers) the conquest was a religious crusade undertaken by Spain's Catholic sovereigns to force conversions.

In Spanish America, the natives were subjects, to be mastered and brought to service, although the colonists also wished them to assimilate and multiply. In English America, the natives were foreigners, to be kept at a distance. Diplomatic relations were maintained with them under a treaty, or they were expelled from their lands by force or exterminated.

The paramount difference between the two types of colonies lay in the fact that the Castile and Aragon monarchies of the early sixteenth century were still very close to the Middle Ages, while the Puritans' conflicts with the English monarchy a century and a half later foreshadowed the eighteenth-century revolutions that marked the beginning of the modern era. Thus one society that had not repudiated feudalism brought it to America in a degraded form, while the other ushered in liberal capitalism and found in North America a fertile terrain for its growth.

The conditions under which the Latin American societies were thus first shaped—so different from those in English-speaking America—have left their marks to this day and slowed down the economic, political, and social evolution of that part of the world.

Persistence of the Colonial Structure
After Independence

Nowhere else have the initial forms of colonial domination left such a strong and lasting imprint on countries that have been independent so long. The fact of a national origin founded on the exploitation of territories and population for the benefit of the mother country produced almost grotesque results. These effects have been preserved almost intact in the least advanced parts of Latin America and are still substantially present even in the most developed.

The fact that the colonial period started so early and lasted so long (and that its effects persisted even longer) gave Latin America certain advantages that should not be underestimated. The first was interbreeding, which alone could prevent racial antagonism and allow populations of such complex ethnic composition to achieve national unity; another was Christianization, very widespread if not complete, which combined with the very wide dissemination of the Spanish and Portuguese languages, provided the basis of cultural unity. By the time nationalism reached the Latin American masses in the twentieth century they had sufficiently assimilated the culture of the settlers so that national unity was not threatened by separatist drives. There are reasons to fear that backward countries of Andean and Central America have missed their chance for such assimilation. But in all the other countries the results of sixteenth-century Iberian colonization resemble those of Roman rather than of nineteenth-century colonial expansion. There are today Brazilians, Colombians, Venezuelans, and Chileans as well as Mexicans who are no longer Europeans, Amerindians, or Africans, just as there are Frenchmen who are no longer Gauls, Latins, or Germanic peoples; in the veins of most of them the blood of the victors blends with that of the vanquished, and they can have the same feeling toward their ancestors as a Frenchman has toward Vercingetorix, Caesar, and Clovis.

The present economic and social evolution is shaped by the various traits of European culture, and is greatly helped by the fact that most of the Latin American population belongs to that culture. A single example suffices: public education is very difficult to achieve in underdeveloped countries with an excessively high birth rate. It is difficult everywhere, but even more so wherever many languages are spoken. The Andean countries, where the pre-Columbian tongues have survived, are faced with this problem. Even when people learn to read and write, they have less to gain if no literature exists in their language. But except for a few countries of Indian America, Spanish or Portuguese is known to all and provides contact with the outside world.

Education would have been much harder to achieve if the influence of European culture had not made it easier for women to teach. In Latin America primary education is almost completely in women's hands. In Brazil, for instance, in 1954, out of 147,955 elementary teachers, 137,348 were women. This figure also disproves the myth of a Latin America that, like so many other underdeveloped countries of non-European culture, frowns upon women working outside their homes.

On the other hand, the colonial era, which started too early and lasted too long, gave Latin America an economic and social foundation, forms of ownership, and in many cases, an elite psychology that fulfilled the needs of the home country instead of the colony; to some extent these factors linger on to this day.

The colonial structure left its lasting mark on the pattern of settlement—a vacuum in the interior of the continent—and on the direction of the communications routes on which the products of the various regions were carried for shipment overseas. To this day, national borders conform to the divisions established by accidents of conquest or for the convenience of the colonial administration. The division of the continent between Spanish America and Portuguese America, resulting from papal arbitration and the Treaty of Tordesillas signed on June 6, 1494, between Spain and Portugal, was substantially altered to Brazil's advantage, but this was before independence. In Spanish America, the splitting up of territories resulted partly from the tendency of each seat of a viceroyalty, captaincy-general, or *audiencia* to turn into the capital of a state when independence was achieved. Even in Brazil, on the whole, the present states of the federation match the feudal principalities, or captaincies. This is quite remarkable, considering that these lasted only a few years: they were set up in 1533 and by 1549 had already lost some of their autonomy owing to the broad powers granted to Tomé de Souza over all of the country. As a result, in Latin America, as in Africa today, even arbitrary administrative divisions set up by the colonizers have tended to foster strong nationalism.

Even more remarkable, because limited to Latin America, is the fact that within each independent state the colonial economic and social structure has persisted to this day, although it was doubly archaic: not only had it been part of colonial society, but the colonization that produced it dated back to the beginning of the sixteenth century. Whereas in the former European colonies in Africa and Asia emancipation has been accompanied by the drive to eliminate all economic and social remnants of colonialism, not only have the independent Latin American countries retained them, but for a long time they continued to strengthen and extend them to new areas and new populations.

The most obsolete social forms of organization persisted mainly because, as in the United States, independence resulted from a rebellion of the colonists against the mother country and not from a revolt of the natives against them. Hence the rebellion was not meant to decolonize Latin America, and at first merely altered the political tie between America and the European home countries.

The Creoles had always tended to rebel against the mother country, and one of the fundamental causes of the independence movement in the eighteenth century was the colonists' dissatisfaction with imperial economic policy. Furthermore, among the elites there had been a sensitivity to the ideologies of political freedom and nationalism. However, the independence movement was mainly the result of the weakening of the Iberian ruling countries during Napoleon's hegemony, at a time when no yearning for independence was generally felt.

Only in Haiti, which had thrown off French domination as early as 1804, did the slaves at that time revolt against the colonists. Another exception in Spanish America was Mexico, where the first insurrections were supported by the indigenous populations. Two priests, Hidalgo and Morelos, led an Indian social revolt aimed as much against the Creole masters as against Spain herself, but it was put down before 1815 by the Creoles allied with the Spaniards. Independence was finally won in 1821 and proclaimed by Iturbide, who for a short time was the emperor of liberated Mexico. (He had previously helped to crush the native uprising.) Outside Haiti, the political revolutions concerned only Europeans. They were matters to be settled between the colonists or Europeanized people and their own governments at home, not between the colonists and

TABLE 6
DATES OF LATIN AMERICAN INDEPENDENCE

1804	Haiti	1821	Central American Con-
1811	Paraguay		federation—dismem-
	Venezuela		bered in 1839 to form:
	Ecuador		El Salvador
			Guatemala
1813	Colombia		Honduras
1816	Argentina		Nicaragua
1818	Chile		Costa Rica
1821	Peru	1822	Brazil
	Mexico	1825	Bolivia
	Dominican Republic	1898	Cuba
		1903	Panama (carved out of Colombia)

the natives.

The oppressed in general, and, more specifically, the Indian populations, usually stayed aloof from struggles that concerned only their masters. They took part in them only because they were forced to, or because they were attracted to warfare. They cared little about whose side they fought on. In Argentina, Güemes helped San Martín, the liberator of the south, at a crucial moment by having his followers, semisavage *gauchos*, intervene in his behalf. In Peru, on the contrary, the viceroy armed the Indians and with their help countered Bolívar's first moves. The turn of events in Venezuela was even more characteristic of the attitude of the indigenous or semi-indigenous populations: the *llaneros*—the gauchos of the equatorial regions—first took up arms on behalf of Spain under the leadership of a chief named Boves and in 1813, defeated Bolívar. Then, after 1816, after finding another chief, Paez, they helped win the final battle for Bolívar. The uprising of Tupac Amaru in Peru in 1780 is even more significant: a mestizo, he believed he could unite the Indians and the Spanish Crown in order to shake off the tyranny of the Creoles.

Independence won under such circumstances brought no immediate change in the condition of the natives or the rural populations in general. The most archaic social structures remained in a changed political setting. Some of the liberators had been sincere in fighting for political democracy, but did not believe it was applicable to the natives. Few of the reforms could benefit those populations who did not take part in politics. The opening of the country to international trade affected only some of the well-to-do Creoles. The ending of the Inquisition concerned only the Creoles and mestizos, for in 1575 it had been agreed that the Indians were not answerable to the Inquisition tribunals. The progress of anticlericalism and the measures against the religious orders were a setback to the Indians, who had been protected by a segment of the Church. The opening of Latin America to immigration had very little effect on the countries with a large indigenous population or widespread slave systems. Only the suppression of head taxes benefited the Indians.

Worsening of the Natives' Plight After Independence

Even the reform that should have helped the Indians most—the proclamation of equality before the law—at first turned against them. When the Indians' special status that sealed their inferiority was abolished, so was a meticulous legislation which, although discriminatory, aimed at protecting these inferiors against excessive exploitation by the colonists. The result of this strictly legal egalitarianism unmatched by social reality was somewhat like egalitarianism in the United States one century later. Thus, for a while, the United States courts declared that labor legislation infringed upon basic human rights by branding workers as inferiors incapable of knowing their interests and of defending them themselves.

The abolition of legal racial discrimination helped the mestizos who were already integrated into the colonists' society, but the Indians only suffered from it at first. For the Creoles, political freedom also meant being free to finish enslaving the Indians economically and to split among themselves a large part of the land that Spain had endeavored to preserve for them. Actually, after independence, and in some cases for a long time thereafter, until the twentieth century, the Indians were worse off than before. The Creoles' independence, instead of starting to decolonize Latin America by freeing the natives, only helped to subjugate them completely.

The economic development of the Latin American countries, which accelerated in the second half of the nineteenth century, was dreadful for the Indians. Everywhere they were robbed of the lands still left to them after the Crown's earlier land grants to the liberators as a reward for their services. In Mexico, the policy of the *científicos,* who in 1892 started to modernize Mexico, was particularly cruel to the Indians. In Chile in 1880, the Araucanians who had managed to remain in the southern part of the country were finally subjugated. In Argentina in 1879, General Roca finished exterminating the Pampa Indians. In Brazil, the movement that at the turn of the century opened up a new territory in the north of the state of Paraná also meant complete elimination of the Indians living in the area. The westward movement, to which the foundation of Brasília has given new impulse, is dreaded even to this day by the few surviving primitive people.

Only in Argentina and Uruguay did the archaic and hierarchic social structure based on ownership of land and the patrón's authority over those who cultivated it begin to weaken before the twentieth century. It has always taken a long time for the ideal of democracy, although established in the political field, to have any social impact. The colonial society created in the sixteenth and seventeenth centuries was still being strengthened in the middle of the nineteenth century, and Latin America must quickly shake off its remnants if she is to go on developing. These remnants of colonialism assume extremely varied ideological, technological, and sociological forms. They have common roots in an institution that prevails all over Latin America—the very large estate where traces of

serfdom still persist. Nowhere else in the world is the ownership of land concentrated in so few hands, and nowhere else
has this concentration had so many and such dangerous consequences. As Latin America becomes more aware of her problems, the more she must see that they are all linked to the need
for agrarian reform—the most pressing and difficult of all.

It would be an oversimplification to state that the particular
form of large estate which has for so long dominated all of
Latin America and still prevails over most of her territory is
the determining cause of her delayed evolution as compared to
English-speaking America. Nonetheless, the fact that this lasting archaic form of large estate has had so many varied consequences makes it worthwhile to investigate it as a starting
point for an analysis of the many causes of delayed development.

3. The Latifundio: The Large Estate in Latin America

Nothing has had a more widespread and lasting effect on Latin America's social and political history than the large estate. In the rural areas, lands were divided into overly large estates where, after the abolition of forced labor, relationships of personal dependence persisted between the freed agricultural workers and their former masters. In Latin America the term *latifundios* is used to designate this antiquated form of land ownership, as opposed to other, newer forms of large estates whose function is more specifically economic. The latifundios were defined by a Latin American seminar that met in Brazil in 1953 [1] as "large estates operated under archaic methods and only partly put to use." It is in this technical sense that the word *latifundios* instead of *latifundia* will be used here.

Under the name of *hacienda* in Spanish America and *fazenda* in Portuguese America, these latifundios were the fundamental institution of Iberian colonialism. The hacienda was not merely a form of land ownership, but primarily a form of social organization capable of fulfilling needs of all kinds. But even though the remnants of the hacienda system are so harmful today, it should not be forgotten that during the colonial era it was the only means of providing an elementary community life to a rural society isolated from the outside world.

[1] *Problemas de tenencia y uso de la tierra.*

Whatever the usefulness of the latifundio may have been in the past, it has become utterly anachronistic. The problem now is not to adapt to complete isolation by forming small self-sufficient communities but, on the contrary, to break that isolation to ensure a division of labor in a national and international market, and to allow interaction among individuals in society at large.

In colonial times distant governments were weak in a world where means of communication were lacking. Hence, the masters of very large estates, who imposed forced labor on natives and slaves, came to wield economic and political power over small communities under their direct authority. These were the basic characteristics of a feudal regime. The landowners of Latin America became barons, and some of them still are.

As the latifundios spread in the sixteenth and seventeenth centuries, a quasi-feudal system began to arise in Latin America at the very time when it was on the wane in western Europe. When in the nineteenth and in some cases even in the twentieth century, capitalism was introduced in Latin America in very advanced forms, it clashed with a still young and strong feudal society. The two forms of society, one urban, the other rural, were forced to coexist for a long time, not always peacefully. Two forms of social organization, two stages of evolution that in western Europe were separated by centuries of history, are contemporaneous in Latin America. In the presence of rapidly changing urban societies, the latifundios, owing to their power to resist change, were a major factor in dividing society into two very different segments.

The economic and social changes which have been particularly rapid in most of Latin America since 1930 have seldom left the archaic rural society untouched. Furthermore, this society no longer shapes national policy to a degree commensurate with the size of the population it still controls. Locally, however, the social structure shaped by the latifundio still embraces a large part of the population, in some places even the majority. The latifundio is largely responsible for the fact that, while Latin America is ripe for political democracy, centralization, and overriding state authority, political power in the rural areas has not yet been divorced from land ownership.

Growth of the Large Estate

In all of Latin America, land was so concentrated into very large estates that there was no room for the small or medium-sized farm. Even to this day, except in the few countries where land reforms have been carried out, only very small plots can exist side by side with the large estates. The equally dangerous counterpart of the latifundio is the *minifundio,* a patch of 2 to 12 acres, as compared to estates exceeding 2500 acres that cover most of the land. The latifundios are too large to be operated efficiently, and the minifundios (which are in the majority) are not large enough. In Bolivia, where estates exceeding 2500 acres covered 92 percent of the territory when land reform began in 1953, 60 percent of the farms were under 12 acres. It should be kept in mind, however, that in the mountainous regions of Bolivia, Peru, and Ecuador, the dry zones of Mexico, and the almost uninhabited regions of the Amazon or Orinoco basins, the size of farms cannot be compared to those in Europe. However, even if 2500 acres do not necessarily mean that an estate is very large, one wonders what minifundios under 12 acres are to be called.

Aside from the small countries of Central America—El Salvador, Costa Rica, Honduras, and the Antilles of course, where the relatively small expanse of land coupled with a relatively high population density has limited the size of the latifundios—Colombia is the only country where estates over 2500 acres are the exception. There they cover no more than 26 percent of the area, but include all the best farmland. In Mexico, where the concentration of land continued until the end of Porfirio Diaz' stay in power in 1910, 836 large landowners held an area of land which, depending on the source used, was regarded as ranging between 85 and 97 percent of the total. Even in 1965, half a century after land reform, very large estates had not disappeared in Mexico. Argentina and Uruguay are the two most advanced countries in Latin America, economically and socially; yet just after World War II, with urban populations enjoying living conditions similar to those of western Europe, estates exceeding 2500 acres occupied 73 percent of the agricultural and cattle-raising lands in Argentina, and in Uruguay, almost the entire cattle-raising

zone in the north and west. It is true that in both countries
these large estates have been partly modernized and hence are
no longer unproductive latifundios.

In 1960, even after radical agrarian reforms in Mexico,
Bolivia, and Cuba, and after the start of land reforms in Chile,
Colombia, Ecuador, and Central America, over 65 percent of
Latin American territory was still said to be occupied by
estates exceeding 2500 acres representing only 1.4 percent of
the total number of farms. These figures do not show the full
extent of land concentration. The nature of the latifundios
becomes more obvious when it is learned that at the start of
Mexico's land reform, one of the first estates to be split up,
Fazenda Huller in Lower California, measured 13,325,650
acres. In the state of Coahuila, the property of *licenciado* De la
Garza covered 11,115,000 acres, and in Bolivia, an estate
of 7,410,000 acres was confiscated. In 1956, a census in
Paraguay recorded that 534 estates exceeding 12,250 acres
covered 73.53 percent of the occupied land, while the
103,633 minifundios under 25 acres included only 2.34 percent of the occupied land.[2] This was after the Paraguayan war
(1864–1870), when most of the land became state property.

Latifundio Formation

The main causes of excessive growth of large estates and of
the archaic form they have retained date back to the colonial
era. Two causes were paramount: too few immigrants came to
the Spanish and Portuguese possessions during that period,
and they were able to make forced laborers out of the natives
or the African slaves.

The conquest of Latin America was premature and too
swift, so that it could not be combined with immediate settlement by Europeans. The few who did come were too scattered.
The discovery of Brazil was a mere accident that did not
immediately distract the Portuguese from their real purpose,
which was to expand the newly established trade with Asia. As
for Spain, the first territories conquered and organized had a
relatively large indigenous population and hence did not lend
themselves to settlement by Spanish peasants.

[2] Manuel Benítez González, *Situación de la agricultura en el Paraguay* (Asunción, 1964).

In any event the conquest came too early to be followed rapidly by a large immigration. In the beginning of the sixteenth century, Portugal probably had hardly over one million inhabitants, and Spain, with her six or seven million, first had to settle the home territories just won back from Islam. The absolute monarchies of that period were as reluctant to let their subjects scatter all over the world as they were to admit foreigners. Even the other European countries had few potential emigrants, since the discovery of America preceded the great European population increase by at least two centuries. The essential fact is that Latin American institutions were firmly rooted before the end of the sixteenth century, at a time when so few Spaniards faced so many natives.

In Brazil, where the natives were few and their civilization too primitive for any organized land ownership, a few thousand conquerors were able to seize the land without encountering any opposition, and the process is still going on as settlers continue to move inland. In Mexico and Peru, with a denser population of civilized agriculturists, the Spanish monarchy tried to maintain ownership of land by the Indian communities. In some places, they were partly successful. Thus, when Mexico won independence a few Indian communities still owned communal lands—lands that were taken away from them in the nineteenth century. In Peru, Bolivia, and Ecuador, the *ayllu* is a form of communal ownership of land by a village or clan under which about two million Indians are still living. It is felt in some quarters that it is no asset to them, because these lands—among the poorest in Latin America—are periodically redistributed among a too rapidly growing number of recipients, and since they adjoin latifundios, they cannot be expanded.

The well-meaning if often clumsy policy of the Spanish sovereigns was of little avail since the first conquistadors started out by carving very large estates for themselves, and later had to be given title to them. The communal forms of farming in the pre-Columbian societies, with lands earmarked for the emperor, the priests, and the clans, enabled the Spanish masters to take over the entire structure from the natives without appearing as glaring usurpers. Far from stopping with independence, the seizure of native lands went on at a faster pace as the natives were deprived of the little protection they had been receiving from the government in Europe. In Mexico, a few powerful figures confiscated the huge Church domains (allegedly half the good land in the country) in the second half of the nineteenth century. Since the urban reformers took no interest whatsoever in the peasants, public lands continued for a long time to be distributed as latifundios. The case of Argentina is striking, for between 1880 and 1890, while the country went into debt in order to build railroads for expansion, the squandering of lands reached its height.

Forced Labor: Indian Ecomienda and African Slaves

This concentration of land ownership provided the necessary basis for the setting up of feudal regimes. The long practice of forced labor introduced by the first colonizers gave those regimes their political attributes. The first Spanish and Portuguese conquerors had no intention of becoming farmers. At the time of the conquest, Spain more than any other country believed in the ideal of a noble life and regarded manual labor as demeaning. The sailors, soldiers, and priests who accompanied Columbus and later Cortés and Pizarro did not want to till the soil and were not even capable of doing it. Not all of them were *caballeros,* but they all yearned to be.

On his second voyage (1493–1496) Columbus took along to Hispaniola twelve or fifteen hundred—caballeros, soldiers, artisans, and priests. A few years later, especially when Ovando arrived with his 2,500 companions, a twofold problem arose—that of supporting the Spaniards established in America and that of obtaining the gold required to make the conquest profitable. The only solution was forced labor by natives, and the first thing the invaders did was to impose slavery. Although the Spanish sovereigns were against enslaving the Indians, they could not prevent their being drafted as forced laborers. In order to make it easier for the indigenous subjects to pay their tribute money, Spaniards in America were permitted by their monarchs to have Indians allotted to them as laborers, at a fair salary.

This system, called the *repartimiento,* spread very rapidly. The instructions dispatched on March 20, 1503, to Ovando, the governor who had just replaced Columbus, specified that in order to obtain gold, the Christians could use Indian labor, but that these Indians must be regarded as free men who were obliged to work but had to receive decent pay. The *cédula,* or decree, of Medina del Campo of December 20, 1503, legalized this form of forced labor, and an order of March 3, 1509, outlined its specific provisions; that is, civil servants and *alcaldes* who were married could use the labor of 100 Indians, the married hidalgos 80, the squires 60, and the simple farmers 30.

This made the repartimiento a legally organized institution. The distribution of Indians, originally meant to be only temporary, was revised at regular intervals and tended to become hereditary, and the duties of workers and their masters were specified. The Spanish monarchs, to whom Las Casas consistently reported all abuses, closed their eyes to the true nature of this serfdom and professed to believe that the Indians had been entrusted for their own good to protectors who, besides watching over their temporal welfare by forcing them to obey the law of labor, would ensure the salvation of their souls by converting them to Christianity.

The body of rights and duties that accompanied the now established repartimiento produced the fundamental institution of the first hundred years of the colonial period, the *ecomienda.* The ecomienda delegated part of the sovereign's powers to individuals, the *ecomenderos,* and gave rise to mutual personal duties on the part of the masters and their dependents. This system has left marks upon all the Spanish-American societies which have proved more lasting than those of a strictly patrimonial slave system. It was the first element of feudalism, and the Spanish kings' advisers continually referred to feudal law in order to establish the institution and justify its existence.

Relationship Between Encomienda and Latifundio

From Hispaniola, the encomienda was brought to Mexico by Cortés and from there into all of Spanish America as more territories were occupied. It did not embrace all the Indians, but throughout Latin America it did include many—all those who were not isolated but were assimilated and who now, after interbreeding, form most of the rural population. As the institution endured and spread to new regions, its feudal character hardened. The personal power of the encomendero gradually became tied to the ownership of the large estate, and this created the latifundio.

The basic purpose of the repartimiento had originally been to supply labor in the mines to provide gold and silver to the Spanish treasury. A pre-Columbian variety of forced labor, the *mita*, a singularly cruel practice, had been used in the Peruvian mines. In the mines, the condition of the Indians working under an entrepreneur was far more similar to outright slavery. As the population grew and Creoles permanently settled in America carved out estates for themselves, the encomienda increasingly turned into a form of feudal serfdom.

In Mexico Cortés, who was not a mere adventurer but an empire builder, was worried that too many Spaniards were coming to America for a few years just to make a fortune, not to settle. In order to promote colonization, he tried to make the allotment of forced laborers dependent upon land ownership, and also promised that the encomienda would be permanent. The institution thus became tied to land ownership. Since there were large indigenous populations in Mexico and Peru, some encomenderos were entrusted with entire communities. The encomienda granted to Cortés in 1529 in the valley of Oaxaca encompassed a population of 100,000 and the estate that exceeded 23,000 square miles. This was exceptional, it is true, but evidence that there were many very large encomiendas is found in a provision of the Statute on Good Government of 1524, which required the encomenderos to provide a priest when they were responsible for more than 2,000 Indians.

The encomendero became a full-fledged feudal lord when he was directed to support armed men to take part in the colony's defense.

Everywhere true slavery, which the Indians had been spared, befell the Africans. But it was only in the Antilles and Brazil, where the Indians either had been decimated or had never been numerous, that slavery played a role as crucial as the encomienda in shaping society. Slavery and the encomienda had similar effects and depreciated the status of agricultural workers in the same way. As a general rule, all those who worked on the land were subject to forced labor during the colonial era.

By the time the various forms of forced labor were officially abolished, they had been in general use for so long that personal dependence of the workers on the landlords continued to exist within rural society. However, even before independence, personal obligations of the Indians to the former encomenderos had lost their legal basis. The enslavement of Africans was abolished fairly soon after independence (in Brazil, however, it lasted until 1889), but the large estate remained and the relationship between the master and those who lived on his land did not, in fact, change very much.

Instead of being broken up after independence, the latifundios continued to grow. They monopolized the land and, until quite recently, when work in the cities became available, most of the former serfs or slaves and their descendants had to go on cultivating the land as free laborers. Since the landlord was usually too poor and the estate too large for agrarian capitalism, the large estate kept its manorial character and the owner remained a lord. That is the latifundio, an antiquated remnant of the colonial past in contemporary America.

Persistence of Manorial Economy in the Latifundio

The overly large estates, liberally granted or seized with impunity, could not be fully farmed, especially after the abolition of serfdom and slavery, since the population was still small. Besides, the difficulty of transportation in the hinterland provided no incentive to estates far from the sea to produce much in excess of their own needs. In contrast to the United States, where the pioneers were relatively slow in appropriating land and did so only when they could farm it, land in Latin America became private property before it could be used. Land, therefore, the owners could afford to waste, since their capital was infinitely smaller than their estates.

The wasting of land brought nothing but evil and caused the latifundios to retain their archaic character. From the technological viewpoint, the latifundio enabled the landowner to pick only the best farmlands for cultivation, even if he had to abandon them later after they were exhausted. To this day on the latifundio, the practices of shifting to fresh land, burning, and leaving land fallow for long periods have not completely stopped. Primarily, excess land on large estates causes the regrettable form of land leasing typical of the latifundio. When, long before independence, forced labor by Indians and slave labor by Africans were no longer possible, the masters of the latifundios, who had more land than capital, had to devise a way of farming without paying wages. In order to do so, they retained only a small portion of their land to farm themselves. Tenant farming was not a practical solution for the land that the master gave up cultivating himself, for it would have been even more difficult for the tenant to pay his rent in cash than for the landlord to pay wages. The essential feature in the organization of the Latin American latifundios is that, even to this day, they live as much as they can outside the money economy.

Generally the owner of the latifundio leaves a large portion of his estate unfarmed, or uses it for very extensive cattle-raising. This is how 80 percent of the farmland is used in Brazil, Colombia, and Venezuela. In Bolivia where, it is true, a large part of the territory is unfit for agriculture, it was estimated that, before the agrarian reform of 1953, no more than 1.2 percent of the land on the large estates was cultivated. In many other countries the percentage is only slightly higher. Under these conditions the master can allow anyone to remain on his land—Indians formerly under the encomienda regime, freed slaves, and newcomers. He helps them to build cabins and makes available to them the few community services he maintains for his own farm. Thus, by increasing the number of people on his estate, even if only on sufferance, the landlord is assured of abundant manpower for his own cultivation.

The system permits any number of variations since, despite developing protective legislation, relations between the landlord and those living on his estate are subject to the landlord's will more or less mitigated by custom, instead of being governed by contract. Sharecropping (*aparcería*) is in fairly wide use. On the surface, it is profitable for the tenant, who is alloted a small parcel in exchange for a payment which seldom exceeds one-third of the crop. But in most cases, the plot is too small to permit the tenant farmer to eke out a living. He is given the concession only to keep him on the estate and he must, in addition, work for a certain number of days on the landlord's private farm if he wants to go on living there. Another variation, probably even more widespread, is the concession of a plot of land sufficient to support the laborer and his family plus grazing rights. In exchange, he must work for the master for a given number of days without any pay, or for a very low one.

In either case, the system whereby the cash nexus is only subsidiary whereas forced labor—unpaid or paid very little—is the tenant's main duty, is akin to serfdom. It is the type of personal dependence of the *inquilinos* in Chile, of the *huasipungeros* in Ecuador, of the *colonos* in Brazil or Bolivia. Sometimes this status of the agricultural workers is called peonage, but this term leads to confusion because the landless day laborer or, in an even more general sense, the unskilled laborer is also called a peon.

Persistence of Personal Dependence in the Latifundio

Legally, the tenants enjoy full freedom and many have a small farm of their own, though on precarious terms. This enables them to eke out a living and to avoid being landless peasants. As long as they remain on the large estate, however, they also remain in a state of quasi-serfdom. Modern Latin American legislation is fighting this, for instance by demanding the drawing up of contracts to define each party's obligations and stabilize the workers' status. But in the absence of agrarian reforms, legislation has little effect and most labor legislation does not apply to agricultural workers. Tradition, the peasants' ignorance, the aristocracy's domination over local politics—all contribute to forestall any government action.

The precarious land tenure of the tenant farmers over their personal plots subjects them to complete dependence upon the landlord, who remains a master. In recent times and until land reform, such a situation seems to have prevailed to an extreme degree in Bolivia. The colono was granted 12 to 25 acres for his family's needs, but the land was very poor. He was also allotted a cabin and grazing rights for a horse and a cow. In exchange, he owed three to five days' work per week on the master's private farm, as well as one or two weeks of service a year in the master's town or country house. He also had to transport the produce of the large estate—and this could mean his being on the road for several weeks. As for his own produce, he could sell it only through the patrón. But generally, his plight is not quite as bad as that. In Chile, a relatively developed country, around 1952 the inquilino—and most of the rural population were such—was allotted a house and land. Each head of the family received annual wages, three-quarters of which could be paid in kind. In exchange, the inquilino and all members of his family were under obligation to contribute a given number of days of work. On many decadent old Brazilian estates, the obligations of the colono are being lightened: in exchange for a patch of land he is only required to give a few workdays for small pay. He finds them too few, for they bring him most of his cash. In many cases, part of the latifundio is occupied by squatters. The master may not know about them, or else he tolerates their presence. He asks nothing of them but evicts them whenever he needs the land.

Sometimes the tenant farmers' dependence is aggravated because, despite attempts at agrarian social legislation (which does not exist everywhere, and is seldom enforced when it does) the tenants go into debt to the landlord for advances of cash. This situation occurs frequently because even when the truck system is banned, its substitute on estates remote from any commercial center—the single storekeeper—is no improvement. The storekeeper must abide by the wishes of the landlord, who merely tolerates him on the estate. Everybody has to resort to his services for all sales and purchases. The landlord or the merchant may own the sole means of transportation—truck, draft or pack animals. The storekeeper may, in fact, be the landlord's agent. When the manorial system starts to disintegrate, he may substitute his own personal domination for the owner's and his actual monopoly further worsens the rural laborer's condition.

Of course, the colono is free to escape this paternalistic rule by leaving. In feudal societies, too, the serfs, many of whom were only bound to the land, could withdraw from serfdom by abandoning the land. But this also means leaving a family plot to which, poor as it may be, these peasants have been tied for generations. Sometimes they are also prisoners of their debts, and, even though it is forbidden by law to retain them forcibly when they own no property fit to be seized, out of solidarity no master is willing to take in men who are indebted to their former employer. Their only way out, then, may be to escape to distant regions where agriculture has been modernized, if these exist. In such areas, the shortage of manpower supersedes any employers' solidarity. But in most cases, flight to the cities is the only way out, whether jobs are available there or not.

In the system of social relations that bears the mark of ancient bondage, the rural laborers—whether they are Amerindians, Africans, mestizos, or of European stock—are relegated to a very low social position. Instead of being citizens of the nation, they are subjects living under the local authority of a lord. For this to happen, the laborers do not even have to be dependents or employees of the large estate, because the seignorial system does not tolerate free land tenure. Faced by the latifundio, the owners of minifundios cannot be independent. They too are subject to the social and political authority of the large estate and are not entitled to any protection, as its direct subjects are. They need the large estate's community services, its means of transportation; they also need day-to-day employment to supplement their income. The condition of the minifundio owners is often much worse than that of the colonos because their plots are too small. In Bolivia, where the colonos had only 12 to 25 acres for themselves, the minifundios represented 60 percent of the independent farms and their average size was 3½ acres. It has been found that, as a result, it is mostly the minifundio owners who flee to the cities.

Archaic Latifundios and Modern Plantations

Not all large estates in Latin America are latifundios, however. Some very large tracts of land are fully and efficiently operated with large amounts of capital. Their productivity is high and they provide, or could provide, reasonable wages for their workers and at the same time high incomes for their owners. Thus, in Brazil, the famous coffee fazendas in São Paulo and northern Paraná have erosion control programs, distribute fertilizers liberally, and even use planes for insecticide spraying. Some estancias in Argentina and Uruguay are equally efficient. They produce baby beef for refrigeration plants, in high demand in England, and also grow cereals using fleets of combines. Irrigated sugarcane plantations have been established throughout the Antilles as well as in Central and South America by sugar refineries, while the United Fruit Company operates fruit farms in the small Central American republics.

These large, modern productive farms are often thought of as representative of Latin American agriculture because they account for its wealth. They attract attention because they stand out in the developed society—the only one that foreigners and Latin American city people know—whereas the latifundios are hidden in an archaic society that everybody would rather shun. The large modern farms also concentrate on a single crop for export—the kind that has made Latin America famous and brings the countries lacking oil and minerals the bulk of their foreign currency. Brazil, Colombia, Cuba (before the revolution), the Dominican Republic, Ecuador, Guatemala, Honduras, Nicaragua, Uruguay, and even Argentina owe over half the value of their exports to these large farms, which are not latifundios.

Since very large estates are widespread throughout Latin America, it is extremely difficult to assess the respective numbers of large modern farms visible to observers, and of latifundios isolated in the hinterland. The best means of estimating their respective sizes in terms of population is to analyze the nature of the legal relationships between owners and workers. The large modern farm with large capital investments cannot afford to waste land. Since wages are paid, manpower cannot be wasted either, whether the workers are paid by the day or month or are on piecework, as in the Brazilian coffee fazendas. There each family is paid a lump sum for tending a specific number of plants. After the harvest they are paid an additional sum depending on the yield. When the owners of modern farms do not operate the farms themselves they prefer to rent them—a system demanded by experienced agricultural workers. The latifundios, on the contrary, waste land and try to avoid paying wages. The farming of the large estate through an exchange of services in kind (concession of a small plot under sharecropping or in exchange for services) is the criterion for detecting the latifundio.

Official statistics on the use of manpower tend to overestimate the proportion of workers receiving wages, for in most cases the days of work demanded in exchange for a concession of land are combined with payment of wages, generally at a very low rate. Thus, workers who are paid irregularly as an incidental remuneration are listed as wage earners, and it is precisely the incidental character of the cash wages that accounts for the extraordinary low rates sometimes recorded. For instance, it was noted that in a few regions of Guatemala the archaic latifundios were paying ten cents a day in 1955. It should be kept in mind, however, that the bulk of the payment was in the form of land, food, and various services.

Although statistics overestimate the number of wage earners, they also disclose[3] the preponderance of payments in kind, which is incompatible with rational farming and means that remnants of serfdom are present. Only in Uruguay, Argentina, and in a few circumscribed developed regions of other countries are most of the agricultural population renting land for money or receiving wages.[4] Land concessions, sharecropping arrangements providing for various personal services, the obligation to work for a specific number of days in exchange for payment in kind—all the arrangements that do not require actual use of cash—prevailed widely in Mexico and Bolivia before the land reforms, and still do to this day in Peru, Ecuador, Brazil, Paraguay, Venezuela, Panama, Guatemala, El Salvador, Honduras, and the Dominican Republic.[5] It is also estimated that over 35 percent of these tenants had only

[3] *L'agriculteur sans terre en Amérique latine,* Organization Internationale du Travail (1957).

[4] Gino Germani, *Estructura social de la Argentina* (Buenos Aires, 1955).

[5] Berta Corredor and Sergio Torres, *Transformación en el mundo rural latinoamericano,* FERES (Bogotá, 1961).

precarious rights to their farms in Venezuela, 48 percent in Paraguay, and 67 percent in Panama.

It seems, therefore, that the archaic latifundios are still the dominant form of large estate in Latin America and that the rural populations, which are still in the majority throughout Latin America, are generally subject to the political as well as the economic authority of their former lords, or are left to their own devices; in either case, they are cut off from national society.

4. Responsibility of the Latifundios for Lags in Social Development

In most of Latin America the rural societies are much too far behind the urban societies. Many factors account for this lag, which almost everywhere accompanies rapid change—isolation, transportation difficulties, lack of capital, and especially the resistance of the existing social structure and rural society to any drastic change. In Latin America, however, the action of these factors is intensified and perpetuated by the existence of the latifundios.

Hoarding of Land and Agricultural Underemployment

The Latin American countries, like so many other underdeveloped countries, suffer from agricultural underemployment except in the southernmost developed regions of South America, around the cities, and in a few areas where new lands are being developed. It is typical that the masked underemployment prevailing in two-thirds of Latin America's territory stems not from the shortage of arable land but from its overabundance. Underemployment did not spread as a result of rural overpopulation and an attendant surplus of agricultural manpower. In many cases it is due to the fact that excessively large estates monopolize lands of which they can farm only a small portion, using methods that do not allow for full use of the available manpower.

It is true, if paradoxical, that wherever the latifundios predominate—in Brazil, Venezuela, Colombia, Peru, Chile—it has been established that insufficient agricultural production causes part of the population to suffer from undernourishment or malnutrition; the shortage of agricultural manpower prevents the use of perfectly good farmlands, or badly run estates have a surplus of agricultural manpower but cannot use it for more than a few days a year.

Even when the latifundio owners do not use all the manpower available, they seldom complain of an excess of laborers, since they do not have to pay them. The extra land enables the owner whose capital is short to maintain a cost-free reserve of manpower on subsistence farms on his idle land. Thus, in case of emergency, he is conveniently assured of a massive labor force. One owner who had let about a hundred families settle on his estate without working for him explained they would be very handy to have around in case of a fire on the land during a drought. He added that these families had been there so long he did not have the heart to evict them. (The case is exceptional, to be sure, but significant nonetheless.)

True, some latifundio masters were tyrants who oppressed their subjects, but an institution should not be judged solely by its shortcomings. Considering the archaic social relationships within the rural Latin-American world, the authority of the big landlord has generally been paternalistic rather than tyrannical. Otherwise, the latifundio could not have survived through all of Latin America's revolutions. Land reforms are necessary mainly because the latifundio keeps its subjects outside the mainstream of political and economic life and gives them no incentive to improve their condition, rather than because it is cruel, oppressive, or hated. The antiquated large estate demands personal loyalty rather than work and productivity. It accommodates itself very comfortably to its subjects' semi-idleness. It provides a shelter for those who have neither the desire nor the initiative to seek anything else. Provided the patrón is not a tyrant, his traditional mission toward his perennial dependents includes many social obligations but too few economic demands. If he is conscientious about the functions assigned to him by a paternalistic society, he must protect and help those who depend upon him and must always take their side even against the law and the state. In exchange for blind loyalty he owes them relative security at the poverty level.

Contrary to frequent allegations, the social problem caused by the concentration of land in the latifundios is not that the peasants are landless but rather that by accepting less than full freedom they are granted the use of patches too small to deliver them from squalor but which they are understandably reluctant to give up, since they are their family farms. It is also typical that, if certain reports are to be believed, even the Latin American agricultural laborers who are closest to serfdom, the *huasipungeros* in Ecuador, are not wholeheartedly in favor of agrarian reforms that would free them, for fear their freedom would mean the loss of the small plot the master lets them have. It is also typical that in Brazil many of the poor colonos on the decadent fazendas of Rio de Janeiro or Minas Gerais hesitate to give up the relative security of the latifundio in order to take up work in northern Paraná for wages two or three times higher. Modern coffee plantations, after hiring all available Italian immigrants, had to seek out laborers fleeing from the drought in the remote states of the Northeast. The latifundio is at the root of the social problem in Latin American agriculture, while the minifundio is responsible for its economic problem. The reason is that, in addition to the minifundios recorded in censuses as belonging to peasants, many more minifundios situated on only partly developed large estates are farmed by peasants under precarious tenure.

At the cost of personal subjection, the latifundio gives its subjects relative security as well as the satisfaction of enjoying some freedom in the work itself. It gives freedom not to work beyond what is needed to avoid starvation. Above all, it leaves the peasants free to refuse change and to remain outside a society that is changing too fast. The latifundios are always economically inefficient, but they are cruel only when the masters are bad. This happens all too often today. Some landowners refuse to behave like feudal lords and have given up their social role, leaving their estate in the hands of a manager. Other landowners want money more than power and seek profit from the estates. Their farming methods make this possible only if they oppress the workers. Whether the latifundio owner wishes to be a good master or not, in the second half of the twentieth century his paternalistic role, which tends to perpetuate an irrevocably doomed archaic society, is antisocial.

Premature Destruction of the "Frontier"

At the same time that lingering feudalism encourages its subjects to resist change, it tends to forbid them the forms of mobility for which they would be best fitted. Premature appropriation of more territory than could be farmed and the resulting land-hoarding harmed Latin America. It deprived her of the asset of new thinly populated countries—namely the clear-cut division between an already developed zone with land available for purchase, and a still uninhabited zone open only for development where land was allotted free of charge. This division has been called "frontier" ever since Frederick Jackson Turner [1] showed its full importance for the economic and social life in the United States.

Most of Latin America outside the Inca and Aztec empires was so thinly populated, and by such primitive Indians that, like North America, it was a new world. Like the United States, it might have had a frontier to be opened for private appropriation when this became economically and socially useful. In Brazil, Venezuela, Colombia, Chile, and Argentina, however, the entire territory became public domain as soon as it was conquered and a large part remained in that state until the middle of the nineteenth century.

In North America, the westward movement and land appropriation were slow partly because belligerent Indians prevented immigrants from living in isolated outposts. In the middle of the nineteenth century, there still existed an immense public domain untouched and relatively nearby that was distributed in small lots as soon as the political hold of the proprietors of slave plantations was broken. The family homestead was a powerful magnet for the pioneer immigrants who first shaped the United States. Before the United States was industrialized, the homestead fostered its economic and social development.

[1] Frederick Jackson Turner, *The Significance of the Frontier in American History* (New York, 1920).

Latin America, on the contrary, resembled the suburbs of cities lacking a rational town-planning program and a socially minded real estate policy. Speculators in such areas are able to monopolize land they do not wish to develop immediately, thus compelling the city to extend costly lines of communication through vacant lots and build its new sectors much too far from the center. The results of land-hoarding are the same whether it is farmland or urban lots, but when the evil consequences spread to the entire country, they are far more serious. Even in countries as huge as Brazil or Venezuela, which have retained a frontier, the large estate has moved it so far away that, if the new land were to be given to prospective farmers, it could be made accessible only by pushing the transportation network beyond huge empty regions; the returns on this would be very low because, although intervening land is already appropriated, it is not yet developed.

Under these conditions, the frontier beyond which the new country lies is not accessible to the pioneer, who would find himself cut off from civilization. It is a "big man's frontier" which, until the government makes it habitable, is available only to the large estate. New latifundios spring up in this area. A paradoxical situation is thus brought about, and two examples are to be found in the westward expansion in Brazil and in the agrarian reform in Venezuela at its start. These were poor countries compelled to squander precious capital to establish the infrastructure required for the opening up of remote territories while large tracts of idle or badly used land with the needed infrastructure were already available and agricultural workers were idle. This is one reason why land reform is necessary in countries like Brazil, Peru, or Venezuela, where the unused public domain includes thousands of square kilometers, as well as in Central American countries, where no more vacant land is available.

The latifundios, which throughout Latin America use only—and inefficiently at that—a small fraction of their land, 10 or 15 percent at most, find an additional incentive for dangerous land-hoarding in the extremely rapid natural population increase, which is bound to increase real estate values. In the meantime expense-free, extensive livestock-raising and tenant farming enable the owners to pretend they are using the land. Indifference on the part of governments because these are dominated by the urban middle classes who care little about rural problems has enabled latifundio owners to use their influence to prevent taxation on fallow land or partially farmed estates. In many cases this alone would have made agrarian reform unnecessary by penalizing land-hoarding. In 1965 Castelo Branco's government in Brazil suggested a means of coping with the problem which might be of crucial importance, namely making the national government responsible for taxation instead of the local governments where the real estate lords are the masters.

Misused surpluses of manpower on the latifundios are difficult to employ in agriculture despite the wealth of unused lands and insufficient production. Departure toward too distant virgin lands is an adventure but also exile, and the latifundio subjects are ill-fitted to undertake it because the paternalism of the manorial estate did not help them to acquire the techniques or the initiative.

In some instances, however, the large capitalistic estate has been a useful educational stage in training men for the responsibility of independent farming. This is a role that the United Fruit Company plantations may be playing as the firm now has started to split up its lands and distribute them to its former laborers. The São Paulo coffee fazendas in Brazil performed the same function, probably unintentionally, when they trained qualified agricultural workers for the rich virgin lands in north Paraná.

It appears that, when free accessible land has been available and the governments and developers have opened it to families for farming, the frontier in Latin America has been as useful as in North America in allowing an enlightened peasant middle class to rise.[2]

Rigidity of Social Structure

It is widely recognized that, in complete contrast to the developed countries of Europe or North America, whose social structure is complex and flexible, Latin America—like all underdeveloped areas—seems to be dominated by a very rigid,

[2] Pierre Monbeig, *Pionniers et planteurs de São Paulo* (Paris, 1952), p. 363.

simple form of hierarchical society. Because of the lack of large diversified middle classes, social mobility is almost impossible. It is thought by certain analysts that this situation prevails in Latin America even at levels that are no longer truly underdeveloped. The Latin American aristocratic tradition and lack of social spirit are held responsible.

As an acknowledged generalization, this is not wholly untrue. But as far as Latin American urban societies are concerned, a number of reservations are called for. As a matter of fact, large middle classes have existed in the cities for a long time. Even during the colonial era not all Spaniards and Portuguese were big landowners. Very few of the poor immigrants settled on the land, and Spain and Portugal tried to attract artisans to the cities. Together with the small businessman and the lower civil servants, they formed a large segment of the urban populations, and were joined by many mestizos. These middle classes were sufficiently large by the end of the eighteenth century to play a crucial role in the independence movement.

Lack of Rural Middle Classes

Any careful analysis of Latin American societies as they are at the present time instead of thirty years ago shows that the aristocracy's hold over the nation has been forever broken. In the cities, where industry is only beginning to develop, an overgrown tertiary sector has arisen, consisting of civil servants, shopkeepers, professionals, middlemen of all kinds, military men, and students who have no ties with the former ruling classes. These aggressive middle classes are gradually taking over political leadership or restraining the aristocracy. Where the aristocracy has succeeded in staying in power they are forcing it to adapt national policy to their own special needs. These groups may be called the middle classes or, even better, the "intermediate sector." In any event, individuals from various strata who belong neither to the proletariat nor to the ruling class are extremely numerous in Latin American cities. This intermediate sector exerts a political domination—not only in Argentina and Uruguay but in Chile, Brazil, Mexico, and Venezuela as well—which is more absolute than elsewhere because the rural masses are still outside society while the industrial proletariat is not yet large enough or well organized enough to wrest the leading position from the middle classes. Many people and groups today speak in the name of the proletariat, but most spokesmen, and the students in particular, are members or future members of the middle classes.

Despite allegations to the contrary, it has not been demonstrated that prospects for upward social mobility are more limited in these urban societies dominated by the intermediate sector than in Europe or the United States. Numerous surveys on social mobility, although incomplete, show that it is difficult to rise from a lower to a higher economic and social level, as is true everywhere. Within the intermediate sector, however, mobility is easy; the reverse would have been surprising since the men in this sector shape national policy.

While it is quite incorrect to state flatly that in all of Latin America the middle classes are small and social mobility is lacking, this is entirely true of the archaic rural societies, where the intermediate sector is almost nonexistent and the possibilities of rising on the social scale are very limited. As long as Latin American rural society is dominated by the large estate, it will in this respect remain quite different from western European societies.

In western Europe and in some old Asian societies, long before the present period, rural society included a large class of independent or relatively independent farmers. Parceling of the land and flexible forms of leasing permitted diversification. The rural structure was made even more flexible through its link with the village and its independent artisans and tradesmen. Between the condition of the day laborer, who is disappearing from western Europe, and that of the big landowner there are numerous intermediate classes that have permitted active social mobility within rural society. Only lack of perspective and the patronizing attitude of the city dweller, as well as his ignorance of the rural way of life, prevent him from noticing the extreme complexity of the hierarchy. Possibilities for social rise are dimly perceived because they usually lie outside the path of university degrees, the only path known to sociologists.

It has happened, although rarely, that a fairly flexible rural society developed in Latin America in areas where the great estate was not established systematically, or was split up afterward. This has occurred in some parts of Argentina, Uruguay, and in the southern states of Brazil. This is the exception, however. As long as rural organization is dominated by the large estate it is too structured and too rigid. The forms of ownership and land tenure are not varied enough to allow middle classes to develop, and even trade and crafts provide few openings for a change in social status without a complete break with rural life. On the large estate all are dependents, be they paid workers, colonos, or peons forced to make deliveries in kind which prevent them from efficiently using the plots allotted to them. Even owners of small farms who have wedged themselves between large estates need too many services to withdraw from the protection of the patrón.

The simplicity and rigidity of this society bring about an extreme concentration of wealth and power. The wealth of the lords in a very poor society is entirely relative. In terms of money, most of them would appear quite poor compared to big city industrialists and businessmen. But between the master with his relative wealth and the wretched mass of his dependents there are too few intermediate stages for any communication to be possible. There are no steps between two utterly different social levels, and furthermore, the number of higher positions available is limited since these are tied to the ownership of an estate and tend to be hereditary.

Since the birth rate is still very high, even among the rural aristocracy, the size of property keeps shrinking so that in the archaic rural society it becomes possible only to go down, never to rise. Ambition is useless. Breaking away from a static society which does not foster initiative was and still is the only way for people to change their social status. If they do not, resignation to their fate is wisdom.

The Role of the Village and Small Town

A rural society where social position is hereditary offers great resistance to change; there are no opportunities to take advantage of and no incentives to bring it about. Admittedly, it is quite difficult for economic development in the countryside not to be slower than in the cities, but this does not mean

that stepped-up economic development in the areas best suited
for it must prevent social progress from spreading throughout
the nation. The impulse for change almost always comes from
the city, but its benefits can be disseminated throughout the
country to avoid an excessive gap between the two societies.

In France, for example, more than in any other European
country, the prime mover in the evolution has been the capital,
and this has hampered economic development south of the
Loire—one reason why the population of the southwest was
illiterate, diseased, and backward in the past. It has been
found, on the contrary, that certain noneconomic indices of
social progress—rate of infant mortality and literacy rate—are
particularly favorable in some departments of the center and
the southwest which are allegedly underdeveloped, and certainly are economically so. The French country people have a
lower income than the city people, but they all live in a modern society.

In Europe the social by-products of change have successfully spread to the countryside because the latter is very seldom really cut off from the city. In comparison with Latin
America, the country populations of western Europe are sub-
urban rather than rural. There are very few country dwellers
who have not had direct, sustained relations with the inhabitants of some small town. In exceptional cases, of mountainous
regions, for example, where this has not occurred, the populations have suffered serious lags.

The small towns and even the large villages engaged in
commerce or handicrafts and fostered the early rise of middle
classes who kept close ties with the countryside. The small
town was the useful intermediary between progressive city
dwellers and rural societies. It helped in the rapid diffusion of
changes originating in the large center. It was also very active
politically and helped to bring the country dwellers into national political life. The French peasants were fully able to
make themselves heard by governments in the nineteenth century—all too well, it was thought in some quarters. In Latin
America at that time the aristocrats were the only countryside
dwellers who could make themselves heard; their dependents
were voiceless in political matters until the second half of the
twentieth century.

All nineteenth-century French literature, which is predominantly urban, is pervaded with irony toward the small town and its attempts to imitate the ways of the capital. Little did the writers perceive the useful role of the small town, which was to complete the unification of the nation in a period of rapid economic and social upheaval. Thanks to the small town's efforts to keep up with the big city, there was seldom a problem of a gap between western European urban and rural societies. The city's influence was felt everywhere. It was more advanced, but any innovation soon reached the countryside. If the small town was still too remote from the country proper, the village served as a relay. To describe a social process in economic terms, it was admirably balanced national planning that made each canton a nucleus for political and social development.

Deepening Rural Isolation

In Latin America the danger of a break between the rural and the urban society is far greater now than in Europe in the nineteenth century because change is more rapid and urbanization is concentrated in the very large cities. In seven countries—Brazil, Mexico, Bolivia, Peru, El Salvador, Panama, and the Dominican Republic—the urban population increased by 53.4 percent in the ten years from 1945 to 1955. In Cuba, Chile, Venezuela, and Uruguay, the average increase was 44.4 percent, and in all of them it was felt mainly in the national capitals and the largest cities. Since 1955, the rate of concentration of population in cities has accelerated. Thus between the censuses of 1950 and 1960, the Latin American urban population increased at an annual rate of 4.5 percent (it might double in 16 years) while the population in cities of over one million inhabitants increased at the rate of 6 percent (it might double in 12 years). Despite a fairly low level of industrialization, by 1970 over half of Latin America's population will be living in the cities.

The possibility of employment in industry has been a negligible factor in this urban population growth in Latin America. In the most industrialized countries, the proportion of the urban population employed in industry did not exceed 8 percent in 1950, and in the least industrialized it was only 3 percent. Between 1950 and 1960 these percentages decreased even further. The country dwellers in flight from the large estates only increase underemployment in the cities.[3]

In all countries except Brazil and Colombia, the population of the capital city is larger than the combined population of all cities of over 100,000 inhabitants. In 1960, half of Uruguay's population lived in Montevideo, one-third of Argentina's in Buenos Aires; in Chile, Cuba, Panama, one-fourth of the inhabitants lived in the capital, and in Peru, Venezuela, Paraguay, and Costa Rica, one-fifth. In extreme cases like Peru there is no real urban society outside the capital. Under such conditions, although Latin America is highly urbanized—excessively so, considering her level of development—urbanization is narrowly circumscribed. The concentration in large cities magnifies the characteristics of urban societies and their adaptability to change, while in the countryside isolation perpetuates the complete alienation of the rural way of life. The large estate has its share of direct responsibility for this, along with the facts that the rural population is too small and scattered and transportation is lacking. Actually it is responsible even for the scattering of the population and the shortage of roads because by wasting land it has vastly increased the distances to be covered.

Nothing has fostered isolation and an archaic way of life more than the manorial aspect of the latifundios. They tend to imprison their subjects within a rigid social structure that fills all needs provided they are the needs of a past age and remain on a primitive level. At the estate center, around the master's large house, stand the heavy agricultural equipment (if there is any), the draft and pack animals, a sugarcane mill, a still, and the truck (if there is a road). Sometimes there is an electric generator, and all those who live nearby have electricity. The artisans receive wages from the landowner; the storekeeper (if there is one) is his dependent. Some owners have built a school on the estate center and have provided living quarters for a teacher, either because it is required by law or because they feel it to be their moral duty. Schooling is of little use because

[3] United Nations, *The Economic Development of Latin America in the Post-war Period* (1964), p. 77.

in this society lessons have no practical application and hence are soon forgotten. The lord or his overseer are equipped to give first aid and legal advice. There is a small supply of drugs on the estate, and sometimes the big house takes in a passing priest.

As long as the latifundio discharges its social function and its subjects ask for nothing more, it fulfills so many needs—and these are so primitive—that the village and the small town have never had much opportunity to develop. The large estate usurps their function. At the same time its limits are too narrow, and its activities not diversified enough, to truly replace the village and town. Thus, by assuming a role it cannot effectively fulfill, the estate completely isolates its peasants from urban society instead of being an intermediary between the country and the city.

Social and Political Need for Agrarian Reforms

The form of feudalism that the latifundios established in Latin America was an inferior one since it lacked the hierarchies of true feudal societies: the big landowners were lords, but they had no overlord. It was difficult for national governments later to reunite authority that had been so dispersed. The task has not yet been completed, and it will be a difficult one if thorough agrarian reforms do not take place.

This is why the need for land reforms in Latin America is so urgent, for political and social reasons even more than for economic ones. It is doubtful that distribution of land to peons or colonos used to a subsistence life, without capital, uneducated and ill-prepared to assume any responsibilities after having lived always under a paternalistic system, can in itself improve the economic condition of rural populations and increase the production of foodstuffs, which are in such short supply that a large part of Latin America has become a land of malnutrition.

The risks that must inevitably attend agrarian reforms, no matter how inadequate they may be, are minimal, however, since by definition the latifundios are estates farmed through antiquated methods, and their yield is so low that splitting them up among poor, ignorant peasants cannot substantially

decrease their productivity. Besides, the latifundios are operated in such a way that a very large portion of the lands is
already in the hands of these poor, ignorant peasants. It is only
the ownership of the land that is concentrated, not the farms
themselves. Appearances notwithstanding, the fact that half of
Latin America is occupied by estates over 2,500 acres does
not make it a land of large farms; neither is it a single-crop
land. Most of the peasants grow food crops—corn, cassava,
sweet potatoes, beans, and sugarcane—on very small patches
of land using hand methods almost exclusively. Between the
hoe of the latifundio and the tractor of the modern plantation,
the plow has seldom found a place.

The latifundio combines the shortcomings of the too large
holding with too little exploitation: the farms are too small and
the people too backward to make them produce; land tenure is
too precarious for full use of its potential.

But inadequate reforms, limited to the splitting up of large
estates, could merely deprive the peasant of services maintained by the master's paternalism. These services are social
rather than economic. They lost much of their effectiveness
long ago, and are further deteriorating as the feudal organization disintegrates. Too often, though, no other services have
taken their place. The most elementary community services
accompanying a land reform would be better than the present
ones. After distribution of land to those who wish to farm it,
the peasants should be helped to give up their pre-Columbian
or African farming methods, which were satisfactory on the
latifundio, for newer ones. They also should be helped to break
the isolation brought about by the latifundio.

Neglect of Rural Populations by the Urban Society

Resistance on the part of the feudal lords to agrarian reforms is abetted by far too many city dwellers. Those who seek
to industrialize their country are only too happy to forget the
peasant masses. It has been found, for instance, that not only
most national governments but also the Economic Commission for Latin America (ECLA), which does so much to
promote economic development in that part of the world, for
long avoided the problem of agrarian reform. Many economic

planners were not convinced that local survival of feudal social relationships hampered economic development. They knew that some day they would have to face the problem of integrating populations left outside the mainstream of the nation, but until the peasants stirred they preferred to concentrate on the cities, which were clamoring for attention.

All Latin American countries are striving for rapid economic development, and in order to set it in motion they must earmark a large portion of their scant revenue for economic investment. It is impossible, however, without resorting to totalitarianism, to deny the urban population some immediate social benefits deriving from economic growth. City dwellers demand immediate wage increases, better housing and education, health services, and recreation. With the disastrous demographic growth in most Latin American countries very little money would be left for economic development if these costly advantages were granted to the bulk of the rapidly increasing population. Restricting housing, schools, hospitals, and social security to the purely urban segment of the population reduces the cost of development. Attempts to achieve a better balance are given up, and only the privileged urban minority enjoys the gains.

The only way this can be done without risk is to avoid overexposing the rural populations to the amenities of urban life. The bulk of the country people are segregated in communities able to fulfill their wants as long as these remain primitive, and isolation prevents new wants from arising. This permits social development and consumer goods to be restricted to the advanced sections of the country.

The archaic nature of manorial society tends to minimize pressure for immediate improvement in living conditions. The day laborers on modern farms are stirring and the beneficiaries of agrarian reforms have some ambitions, but the peasants on the latifundio had been quiet for a long time. Urban society uses the social dualism and persisting anachronisms of the latifundio to further its own economic and social advancement. Its policy consists in tolerating the latifundio, and the motives for this are naturally repressed into the subconscious. Reformers never fail to condemn the remnants of feudal forms of property and social organization, but up to the last few

years, except in Mexico, they have done their best to put the
problem out of their minds. The selfishness of urban societies
in Latin America (which is common to most underdeveloped
countries) was mentioned in a 1957 United Nations publication [4] in which regret was expressed that the governments of
Latin America have limited their concern to the urban populations and abandoned the rural populations to their fate.

The few urban dwellers who are aware of the problem are
prompted by wishful thinking to believe that these backward
people are happy with their mediocre way of life under the
paternalistic authority that shelters them. They succeed in
convincing themselves that it would be useless if not downright
unkind to interfere with the peasants' peace of mind by prematurely foisting upon them the worries of a society in constant
flux. This is made even easier by the obvious squalor of the
rural migrants who crowd the Latin American cities. Rather
than worry about the survival of the latifundios, the city people tend to complain about their premature disintegration.
Illiteracy, irresponsibility, often idleness as well, are the
built-in shortcomings of the archaic society. It is easy enough
to idealize them as long as they remain hidden, but let them be
exposed in the large cities and become mass phenomena, and
they are found intolerable.

To city people, rural populations are merely an inexhaust-
ible reservoir of manpower which, until they acquire new
wants, costs nothing to train and support. The developed society can dip into the reservoir as required by the process of
development, and in the meantime does not feel obliged to
share with the country people the slim benefits of its own early
efforts. Leaving part of the rural masses locked in a very
remote past is the same as eliminating them, for in this way
they are forgotten. If this situation could last long enough, the
latifundio would function as a perfect cold room where the
most backward part of the population would hibernate until
the country was wealthy enough to attend to it. It would also
solve the problems of a too rapidly growing population: seal-

[4] United Nations, "L'Urbanisation en Amérique latine," chap. IX in
Rapport sur la situation sociale dans le monde (1957).

ing off a fraction of it in the latifundio satisfies the national pride in a large population and does not cost anything.

Agrarian Revolutions

The wishes of those who think only of immediate economic benefits and the rate of increase in national income for the following year might have been fulfilled if the two societies could have remained completely watertight. But the manorial society is rapidly disintegrating, with or without prodding. The latifundio is still present but it is in its death throes. Everywhere the patriarchal authority of the former barons is contested, either because the growing power of the civil service has undermined it or, more often, because the rural populations, aware of the urban ideologies and ways of life, have stopped accepting it; possibly, too, because landowners who no longer believe in a social role whose returns are steadily dwindling have given up playing the part.

The slow death of manorial society is not enough to ensure integration of the rural populations into the mainstream of society. The mere decomposition of the small group formerly ruled by the master only leaves its members more wretched and disoriented. The rural Indian, African, mixed, and even European populations must be integrated immediately, at any cost. The only way of achieving this integration is first to reform the latifundios because, while they can no longer benefit the people, they can still do them considerable harm.

The problem is most urgent in the developing countries, since the advanced segments of society are large enough and their living conditions good enough for the less advanced to be aware of them and envy them. Under such conditions, they come to regard the latifundio as an unbearable remnant of the past. If land reforms do not reorganize rural society, too many people will flock to the cities before jobs are available, and those left behind will be too miserable. Both groups will become asocial and conditions will be rife for random peasant uprisings instead of constructive revolutions. Natural deterioration of the large estate is the most dangerous type of agrarian reform.

To this day, no real agrarian reform has ever been carried

out in Latin America without a revolution, but Mexico's experience with ways of dealing with the latifundios, and the results of this type of reform, have been particularly fruitful and lasting. The reform followed the 1910 revolution, and its principle, "The land belongs to the nation," was stated in Article 27 of the Constitution of 1917. It was the oldest of the great agrarian reforms since, in its principle at any rate, it preceded the post-World War I eastern European reforms. The Mexican agrarian reform, which has been going on for over half a century, did not abandon its beneficiaries to their own devices. The land was not to be given to individuals but returned to the Indian communities from which it had been taken away. This communal property is the *ejido,* but today the collectivist-oriented ejidos are a small percentage of the total number of plots. Most ejidos have given up the ejidal form of ownership in favor of individual property in small family plots. The reform has not yet been completed, and some very large estates still remain in Mexico. New ones are being formed even now, but year by year the reform is extended, and land was rapidly distributed between 1958 and 1964 during the presidency of López Mateos.

Although after the first few years the reform was conducted cautiously and the ejido peasants received leadership and guidance, for a long time it was doubtful whether the reform had improved the lot of the Mexican peons. Even at the present time most of them still have to use wooden plows. However, very few observers deny that the reform was socially beneficial and started to integrate the Indian rural masses into a national society from which they had been alienated. The former peons are not much better off yet, although for the past few years Mexico's agricultural production has been increasing faster than in any other Latin American country. It is now easier to educate the peons because they are no longer both oppressed and sheltered by the paternalistic power which imprisoned them in overly narrow societies. They are no longer subjects and are becoming citizens. They have not yet reached the level and way of life of the advanced segment of the population, but they are now aware that they belong to society at large, and the nation has been forced to acknowledge their presence.

The political impact of the agrarian reform has been most

important, since it has cut the bonds of personal dependence that tied men to their lords and isolated them from the state. The rural masses no longer owe allegiance to individuals who used it to perpetuate a static society that gave them political privileges enabling them and their clan to stay in power. Their allegiance now goes to the official party, the PRI (Partido Revolucionario Institucional), which cannot afford to overlook them completely if it expects to remain in power. Whether this occurred spontaneously or as a result of the context made possible by the agrarian reform, Mexican political life, despite particularly difficult conditions, has been for the past three decades one of the most orderly in Latin America, with rapid progress being achieved in all fields. Even the fact that the revolution has been taken over completely by the middle classes has not made it completely useless for the rural population.

The other two sweeping agrarian reforms, also the outcome of revolutions, are harder to assess. The Bolivian land reform, instituted by the decree of August 1953, was hastened by the spontaneous occupation of land by the Indians. Despite the government's efforts, it followed a disorderly course. It was also hampered by the extreme poverty of the *altiplano* lands, the only ones which the Indians accustomed to a mountain climate were able to use, and it does not seem to have been very successful. In 1960 Bolivia was still importing 50 percent of her foodstuffs.

The Cuban agrarian reform, ordered by the law of May 17, 1959, was a radical one since it specified that no estate over a thousand acres was to be left, unless its yield exceeded the national average by 50 percent. This reform is being carried out under changing conditions because of the collectivistic evolution of the regime. It is in its critical stage, and the effects cannot possibly be judged yet.[5] Another land reform has been started in Guatemala, also by a revolutionary movement. In 1952, President Jacobo Arbenz arranged for expropriation of large estates, in particular those of the United Fruit Company.

[5] However, for an evaluation of its technological impact on agriculture, see René Dumont and Julien Coleou, "La réforme agraire à Cuba: ses conditions de réussite," *Etudes Tiers-Monde* (Paris: Institut de Développement Economique et Social, 1962).

The distribution was interrupted by the counterrevolution in 1954, but a start had been made.

In all other Latin American countries, agrarian reforms remained in the planning stage until 1959. Even the left-wing parties made no serious efforts to carry them out when they were in power. The few parties with a clearer notion of the realities in Latin America had tried to change the structure of rural society, but did not find sufficient support among the urban segment of their followers to succeed in pushing them through. In 1938 the Chilean Popular Front and in 1945 the Apristas in Peru and the Democratic Action group in Venezuela came up against this problem.

By the middle of the twentieth century the Mexican Revolution was old and had settled down considerably, but many people overlooked the fact that it was enabled to do so in part because of Cárdenas' insistence on rapid distribution of land between 1935 and 1940.

Awareness of Rural Problems after the Cuban Revolution

The Cuban revolution of 1959 changed the situation entirely. All Latin America felt it, either as a threat or as a hope. The revolution succeeded only because the peasants had supported the intellectuals against a dictatorship interested solely in the urban proletariat. For the first time, everyone paid attention to the peasants who were beginning to stir, if only sporadically. Weary of the indifference of the advanced urban society and its governments, knowing that their demands would never be met through the normal process of representative democracy, the peasants started to occupy the large estates and split them up. The agrarian league movement in Northeast Brazil led by the deputy Julião is the best known, but similar ones have been active in other parts of Brazil as well as in Peru, Colombia, and even some areas of Mexico.

Many times in the past peasant movements had sprung up in Latin America, but most latifundios had their subjects well in hand. The usual response had been to repress the agitation rather than meet the peasants' demands. However, in a Latin America where the building of roads and above all the introduction of loudspeakers are beginning to cut through the peasants' isolation, such revolts are no longer local incidents, and the Cuban example has shown that they can produce a radical social change. The advanced city dwellers can no longer display a scornful aloofness toward the rural world. Whether they are liberals or conservatives, they have become aware of the revolutionary potential of the peasant movements, and it has dawned upon them that they must concern themselves with these backward people, whether to prevent revolutions or to hasten them.

Concern was felt in many quarters. For instance, the ranking hierarchy of the Church, which had for a long time been linked to the most conservative forces, no longer hesitates to censure the latifundios. Colombian and Chilean bishops have advocated reform of the latifundios. In 1962 and 1963 the National Conference of Brazilian Bishops spoke in favor of basic land reforms and so did the Latin American Bishops Conference (CELAM). The United States, which earlier had strongly opposed land expropriations in Mexico, is using all her influence on the conservative elements to induce them to split up the large estates. The Punta del Este Charter of August 5, 1961 (Alliance for Progress) makes such a reform incumbent upon the contracting parties and contains the promise that "unjust" forms of property will be eliminated and the latifundios and minifundios replaced by family holdings of reasonable size. For the first time the problem of agrarian reform was raised by international organizations at the Food and Agricultural Organization (FAO) regional conference held in Rio de Janeiro in November, 1962.

A few years earlier the mere concept of land reform was regarded as subversive, whereas since 1960 very few people have dared to come out against it. This does not mean, of course, that those who profit by the present agrarian structure do not oppose the actual carrying out of reforms even while they pay them lip service.

All over Latin America, laws, if not the constitutions themselves, specify that the right of property is to be respected only inasmuch as it is exercised in conformity with its social function. Outside the three countries which by 1960 had already carried out an agrarian reform through revolution, there are hardly any that have not enacted land reform laws, as shown by table 7.

Uruguay did not vote a law supporting the principle of reform, but a National Colonization Institute has started buying up land to sell in small plots. Argentina is so completely urbanized that agrarian problems are not of foremost importance.

Almost all Latin American countries very recently voted in favor of the principle of agrarian reforms; but outside the three which carried out reform by revolutionary means, the new legislation has had very little practical effect up to now and no

TABLE 7
DATES OF ENACTMENT OF LAND REFORM

Mexico	1915	Colombia	1962
Bolivia	1953	Honduras	1963
Cuba	1959	El Salvador	1963
Venezuela	1960	Costa Rica	1963
Haiti	1962	Nicaragua	1963
Panama	1962	Paraguay	1963
Dominican Republic	1962	Brazil	1964
Chile	1962	Ecuador	1964

psychological impact whatsoever. More than one agrarian law was passed as a measure of appeasement. It was a matter of proclaiming a principle rather than of actually meeting the people's demands. In an even larger number of countries reforms consisted of distribution of remaining public domain lands instead of division of latifundios, whose owners would have had to be compensated.

This does not mean, however, that the entire legislation was useless. In Venezuela, Costa Rica, El Salvador, Ecuador, in Peru with President Belaúnde's regime, certainly in Chile after President Frei Montalva's victory, and possibly in Colombia as well, the governments are trying to carry out carefully planned agrarian reform laws or to get bolder ones enacted. But because these laws have been so meticulously worked out, their impact will be relatively slow and results may seem punv in relation to the cumulative effects of lags in development. The most frequent procedure is the setting up of Agrarian Reform Institutes, whose task is to conduct a census of land, decide which estates must be expropriated because their yield is too low, and provide for their redistribution and the organization of community services. These services are intended to enable poor, uneducated peasants to make good use of the land they receive. Thus the carrying out of an agrarian reform is time-consuming and also requires very large investments. If it is too slow, however, it loses some of its psychological impact; those who doubt that the governments are in good faith may well contend that, since the application of the law is forever being put off, the peasants have no other recourse but violence.

Since Latin America has kept for too long very obsolete forms of rural organization, it is faced today with two conflicting and equally compelling needs. On the one hand, to avoid disorganizing the entire economy and social fabric, to prevent the peasants' condition from deteriorating, and to enable them to become integrated into the nation, any agrarian reform must be selective and gradual. On the other hand, in order to strike the imagination in a prerevolutionary situation, which cannot be prolonged, reform must be swift and sweeping.

The problem is far from solved, but in the 1960's it has been posed throughout Latin America. Latin Americans have become aware of the urgent need for radically changing the agrarian structure. This will certainly not go unopposed in many quarters, and for the next few years the problem will remain in the forefront of Latin America's political life.

5. Survival of Motivations Peculiar to an Aristocratic Colonial Society

Considering the mores of the sixteenth century and the fact that the mother countries had no way of putting some of their good intentions into practice, the shortcomings of Iberian policy toward indigenous populations have been exaggerated. That policy enabled the natives to survive and to some degree prepared for the reconciliation of colonizers and colonized. It is no small achievement to have given birth to nations that both groups regard as their own. On the other hand there is no gainsaying that criticism of Spain's and Portugal's economic policy is fully justified, for it left Latin America poorly prepared for twentieth-century economic activities and bound by social hierarchies based on the latifundio.

The Iberian Colonial System

Being precocious colonizers, the Spaniards and Portuguese applied the mercantilist colonial system. The home countries regarded their colonies merely as a means of accumulating wealth through importation of precious metals and colonial agricultural products and, to a lesser degree, as a market for the industries of the mother country. The entire functioning of the conquered countries was organized to serve the direct needs of the home country, while their own internal development was not even considered. The colonies were restricted to mining and agriculture, and were forbidden to make any manufactures that the home country could provide. They were also forbidden to engage in direct trade with foreign countries or among themselves. This concept of colonialism prevailed for a long time, by England and France as well as by Spain and Portugal.

The Iberian colonial policy was remarkable not for its selfishness, but rather for its effectiveness and duration as compared with that of other countries. In Anglo-America the type of people who immigrated in order to develop a world and make it into a homeland were opposed to a lasting policy of economic domination by the home country, although the Southern planters would have readily accepted it. In Latin America, on the other hand, immigrant conquerors who came to exploit the labor of natives and imported slaves allowed the mercantilist policy to continue for a long time. After independence, Latin American countries pursued a policy similar in its spirit and effects, the only difference being that domination was exerted by economic instead of political centers and that the middlemen who reaped the profits were Creoles (those of Iberian ancestry in America) instead of European-born Spaniards and Portuguese.

For two centuries, beginning in 1543, in order better to enforce Spanish monopoly, the Casa de Contratación in Seville, which supervised the colonies' relations with the outside world, limited them to an annual convoy that was allowed to land only in Seville, then in Cadiz. It is true that the monopoly was never complete, and a contraband trade which grew with the decline of the Iberian maritime power considerably widened the markets. Although the English, French, and Dutch made extensive use of this contraband, it was only a makeshift arrangement during the colonial era. Free trade was established among the colonies only after 1778, and even then it did not extend to Mexico or Venezuela. The convoy system was completely abolished in 1789, although it had long before stopped being effective.

Portugal pursued a similar policy after her temporary union with Spain in 1581. Having regained her independence in 1640 Portugal continued enforcing the policy until the monarch sought refuge in Brazil in 1808. The Portuguese monop-

oly was far less effective than the Spanish, however, because
when Portugal threw off Spanish domination, her weakness
forced her to make concessions to her English protectors.

Weakening of Economic Incentives
by the Colonial System

The colonial system which had endured for so long created
enough dissatisfaction among the Spaniards settled in America
(the Creoles) to be largely responsible for their embracing the
eighteenth-century ideologies of political and economic freedom which eventually led to independence. As a result of
colonial policy, however, the ruling classes that started governing the emancipated colonies were poorly prepared for economic development along the lines opening up in the nineteenth century. The freedom they yearned for was the freedom
to act like the Spaniards, but for their own benefit. The fact that
the nationalism of the masters of Latin America remained
strictly political for a long time—until World War I—was one
cause of her economic lag in comparison with Europe and the
United States. Freed from the monopoly of the home country,
Latin America sought new, richer, and more varied sources of
trade and did not refuse to be dominated by them.

During the protracted colonial period, the Creoles had been
barred from any major industrial activity. Large-scale commerce, strictly regulated from Spain by the Casa de Contratación, had been dominated by the *Peninsulares* (Iberians from
the home countries). Hence, in Latin America only artisans
and small businessmen had any scope for their activities.
Portuguese, Spanish, and mestizo artisans amassed some
wealth and formed embryonic middle classes which later
played a major role in the independence movement. But such
activities held no attraction for leaders of an aristocratic society who, however, could not occupy profitable and dignified
government posts because Spain, which distrusted them with
good reason, reserved important public functions for men sent
from the home country.

Mining could not bring wealth to everybody, so the Creole
higher classes turned their ambitions toward the land itself.
The conquest had made this easy, since large estates were

freely distributed and their possession was enhanced by almost sovereign power over the men who farmed the land. Thus in the seventeenth and eighteenth centuries a society was formed whose values were those of a landed aristocracy. At that time these aristocracies were declining in Europe, while in North America their influence was over. Latin America entered the century of industrialization and entrepreneurs with newly developed medieval economic structures and values.

In the past, in all countries, the landed aristocracy has always scorned trade and industry. The concepts of risk and profit which underlie modern economic development are rejected by this type of society: not only do commerce and industry—import-export trade excepted—prevent man from leading a noble life, but even in agriculture the landowner plays a social and political rather than an economic role.

The fact that just after independence political incentives prevailed over economic ones was partly to blame for the failure of attempts at Latin American unification and for the splitting up of the Spanish empire. In North America after independence, the Federalists used the strong economic motivations of some of the English-speaking population to unite the thirteen colonies under a strong central government despite the powerful individualistic tendencies of the pioneers in the West. Hamilton, skillfully using the lure of a large domestic market to foster commerce and industry, ensured the success of a federation which most of the population probably disliked. By mustering its small forces and opening its territory to the incoming flow of men and capital, the United States was able to start the rapid rise which, in a century and a half, was to propel it toward economic and political leadership.

In Latin America economic incentives of a common market and a strong central government could exert little influence over a patriarchy of big landowners who had everything to fear from a strong government that would deprive them of their political powers. They had nothing to gain from a large domestic market, since their production was geared to consumption on the estates or export to Europe. The small ruling class which dominated political life for most of the nineteenth century would have accepted an even further fragmentation of the

Spanish empire, since this would have increased the number of available government posts from which it had previously been barred.

Lack of economic incentives also proved to be harmful when the era of landed estates gave way to the entrepreneurial era. The landed aristocracy was ill suited for providing entrepreneurs, and all too often allowed new immigrants to assume functions that it neither could nor would fulfill. When the aristocracy understood that economic development only weakened it, it was sometimes prone to reject it. Among the middle class as well, the prestige of land ownership for a long time diverted the interest of the elite from major economic activity. Even at the beginning of the twentieth century businessmen and artisans who had acquired education and wealth regarded the acquisition of a latifundio as the culmination of the social climb. This in their eyes imparted the twofold prestige of the noble way of life and of local political influence. The prestige of the latifundio endured long after it stopped having any basis in reality.

Aristocratic Ideal of Culture for Its Own Sake

In Latin America, as elsewhere, the scale of values of the landed aristocracy favored the development of a general culture which, while it was of some value, had no direct economic or other practical use for American society. This form of culture, which was restricted to the aristocracy, coexisted quite comfortably with complete ignorance among the masses.

The contrast in this respect is striking between Latin America and the United States. Anglo-America—not the Southern plantations but the Middle Atlantic states and the Midwest, to which the future belonged—cared little about general culture for a long time, but took great pains to promote basic education. Until an industrialized United States rediscovered culture and harnessed its wealth to serve it, the North American masses ignored or looked down upon the intellectual with his sheepskins. On the other hand, from the earliest days a practical elementary education had been promoted with utmost zeal. The one-room little red schoolhouse where a dedicated, self-educated instructor taught reading, writing, and arithmetic to parents as well as to children might symbolize North American pioneer society.

The Spaniards and Portuguese of Iberian America lost no time in opening universities. The first was created in Hispaniola as early as 1538, and the two great and still active universities of Mexico and of San Marcos in Lima were opened respectively in 1551 and 1553. When Latin America won independence she already had twenty-six universities, although some of them existed somewhat more in name than in fact. The figure is extremely high, nevertheless, for a still very small Creole population. These universities were intended to serve the ruling classes and gave them a traditional background in theology, law, and literature; the still semi-illiterate mass of the population revered its masters' knowledge and their degrees. The title of doctor might symbolize an Iberian America which cared very little about teaching the people to read and write.

The universities in Latin America were organized on the traditional European medieval pattern, that is, into four faculties. The law faculties gained the ascendency and retained it until the middle of the twentieth century. In colonial society and the independent society which succeeded it, university degrees, culminating in the doctorate, were symbols of a truly superior social status. Part-time professorships were avidly sought by priests, judges, high civil servants, and people of leisure because they were regarded as the highest honor. The liberal professions made accessible through university degrees enjoyed great prestige; those who belonged to them and did not have to earn a living thanks to their income from other posts or from their estates could practice them as professions instead of as mere occupations. The noble way of life meant not only that one was free from the need to perform manual work in order to live; it also meant that one had attended the university.

Many of these characteristics of culture and teaching persisted in Latin America until World War II: for instance, the tendency of the people to call the gentry "doctor," which really means "gentleman"; the desire of wealthy aristocrats to teach a few barely paid courses in the university or even secondary schools; the unwillingness until quite recently to regard univer-

sity teaching as a full-time occupation and a means of liveli-
hood. Many sociological investigations have disclosed that occupations are rated according to prestige, and the liberal
professions head the list. Only now have technological developments brought some prestige to engineering.[1]

Alienation of the Elites

Considering the stage of development Latin America has
been going through in the last half-century, these advantages
could not be acquired without cost. Brilliant as it may be, a
purely aristocratic culture cannot be a national culture when
the mass of the population—which is still illiterate—has no
share in it. As long as culture in Latin America was the
privilege of a few thousand or a few tens of thousands, it was
bound to remain a colonial culture. The individuals who possessed culture were too few to make it independent. They only
could, and did, contribute to the achievements of intellectual
centers in other countries; they also had to transfer their allegiance to these centers. They would have been forced to do so
if only because it is difficult to disseminate a culture through
the printed word alone when readers are too few. After the
Iberian mother countries weakened and their ties with Latin
America were loosened, the Ibero-American cultures tended
to become extensions of French culture. This continued during
the entire nineteenth century and even until World War I.
Because the Latin American intellectual elite was so highly
cultivated amid uneducated masses, it remained for a long
time a cosmopolitan, alienated aristocracy more involved in
European than in domestic issues.

Since the 1930's Latin America has tried to make her
culture democratic and national. This cannot be done without
second thoughts and qualms, nor without great sacrifices. Culture cannot be made national and democratic without suffering a temporary setback in quality, and intellectuals are bound
to suffer by it. A large segment of the Latin American intellectual elites had derived their wealth mainly from their estates

[1] Latin America undoubtedly has gained a great deal from the prestige
of general culture. She early had brilliant groups of writers, historians,
and jurists. Despite her low level of economic development, she has
today great architects, painters, and musicians. [Ed.]

and had thus been able to seek culture from the best sources. Aristocrats with a passion for literature or science could afford to spend years in Paris, Oxford, Vienna, or Heidelberg, build up huge libraries for themselves, and return there periodically for study.

The large middle classes seeking an education today have to get it at home in their native language. Teaching institutions yet to be organized cannot immediately reach the same level as those in Europe or the United States. Above all, the culture adapted to a landed aristocracy cannot satisfy the needs of masses who wish to increase their productivity, raise their standards of living, and improve their life. Nor can the same teaching methods be used.

Latin America today must build an educational system adapted to the needs of forward-looking national societies, and this is a hard task for countries which are poor, where 40 percent of the population is under 15, and half of the remainder is still illiterate.

PART II

Contradictions in Political Life

Statements to the effect that nowhere else are political disorders as frequent as in Latin America tend to be glibly made because the contrast with Anglo-America is so striking in this respect. The military *pronunciamentos,* the succession of caudillos who seize power merely out of selfish motives and care little about changing the political regime or the social structure, the many coups which never seem to produce any enduring results, the strictly political and totally useless revolutions have given rise to the cliché of comic-opera republics.

The cliché is not untrue, but, like all generalizations, it distorts reality so that overly simplistic judgments have to be tempered by a few qualifications.

First of all, the sheer number of Latin American countries is conducive to some exaggeration as to the frequency of political turmoil in each of them. In some countries which have been independent now for one and a half centuries, there have been long periods of constitutional rule that more than one European country might well envy. The Argentine Republic experienced 72 years of relative political stability from 1853 to 1925. Despite unrest in 1891, Chile had 92 years of peaceful rule between 1833 and 1925, Brazil 68 years from 1821 to 1889, Costa Rica 69 years from 1871 to 1940, and Colombia 46 years from 1902 to 1948. After 1934, when Cárdenas became president of Mexico and the gains of the revolution had been secured, subsequent presidents have taken office following normal elections. Permanent political turmoil has occurred mainly in about ten countries whose combined populations do not exceed one-quarter of the total for Latin America. It is no more legitimate to apply the same standards to the political life of Chile or Brazil and Bolivia or Haiti than it would be to group together England or the Scandinavian countries with the Balkan countries.

It also should be kept in mind that many political irregularities which have been labeled revolutions in Latin America were quite peaceful and stem from a form of presidential regime which otherwise answers imperative needs of countries of the Latin American type. When (as has often been the case) a duly elected president has had to accept the evidence that it would be better for him to stay in Paris for a while (the bureau of foreign exchange never failing to provide him with the needed hard currency), this arrangement could certainly not be termed the most perfect example of constitutional procedure. On the other hand, under the regime of presidential dominance which is the usual one in Latin America, it is so important to guard against the tendency of the president to remain in power after the expiration of his term of office that overly stringent measures have some justification. If the successor of the president who had been forcibly expelled or persuaded to leave the country were also compelled to leave under similar conditions a little before or after the expiration of his term, but if none of this altered the country's political life, it would be an overstatement to call it a revolution. In an archaic social structure where only a small fraction of the population participates in elections whose meaning it does not properly understand, the very artificial character of political democracy tends to produce most unconventional ways of handing down power. Comic-opera republics they might well be if presidents change several times a year, but in that case one might also mention another kind of comic-opera republic outside Latin America where the façade is that of perfect legality but where cabinets have on occasion lasted three months or only three days.

With these reservations, it is true that as a whole Latin America underwent a period of recurrent political turmoil immediately after independence. This happened in all the countries except Brazil. Since 1930 such disorders have recurred very widely and in some countries, particularly in Central America, they have never stopped. Suffice it to recall that the first constitution of Venezuela, adopted in 1811, has been followed by 21 others, and within 150 years that country has suffered 136 years of dictatorship. Ecuador had 13 constitutions in one century, the Dominican Republic 6 between 1872 and 1879, and within 14 years Nicaragua had a succession of 23 presidents. In the 12 months from September 1960 to October 1961 there were, aside from the continuous student uprisings, two military coups in El Salvador, a dictator's assassination in the Dominican Republic, the violent upheavals of the Cuban revolution, a defeated revolution in Nicaragua, another in Guatemala, and military revolts in Bolivia. These disorders, which did not stop after 1962, even spread to large countries whose life had been more peaceful in the past. In Brazil military intervention forced Congress to amend the constitution and ended by forcing the president to resign in 1964. In Argentina, before they forced president Arturo Frondizi out of office, the military made him reshuffle his cabinet several times and alter his policy to suit the generals and admirals. After Frondizi was unseated the military pressure on his successor, President José Maria Guido, became more forceful and incoherent. Altogether, in the two years of 1963 and 1964 there were six successful military coups in Guatemala, Ecuador, the Dominican Republic, Honduras, Brazil, and Bolivia.

The political instability of a large portion of Spanish America and also of Brazil since 1930 is a well-documented fact. Nowhere is there greater awareness of this fact than in Latin America itself. Latin Americans have devoted an extremely extensive literature to the search for the causes of the instability peculiar to their countries.

One theory, which was very fashionable in the nineteenth century and has never been completely abandoned, is that the crucial factor is the racial heritage of the Iberian populations, compounded by that of the Amerindian and African populations. The proud Spaniard was alleged to be an intractable individualist on whom discipline could be imposed only through sheer force. The passive Indians, used to the communal despotism of the pre-Columbian societies, and the Africans, accustomed to slavery, were thought to be able to live only under an authoritarian regime. The blend of these races through interbreeding would doom Latin America to an alternation of anarchy and dictatorship, or even to their coexistence. Some pessimists, even among Latin Americans, who believe that nothing can mitigate the results of this racial inheritance, also think that dictatorship is a social necessity in Latin America because governments can never attain a lasting equilibrium under political democracy in its classic form.

Unless one accepts the idea that only northern peoples are capable of governing themselves and all others have to be governed—a theory that has often been propounded—the explanation based on race psychology is suspect if only because it has been suggested for so many different peoples. The peculiar features of a country's political life stem from highly varied causes, and any explanation may hold some truth. It is very possible that Latin Americans are constitutionally ill suited to stable political regimes, but there are no ways of proving it. It is not even necessary to bring in genetic factors, since social factors suffice to explain political instability. It is obvious indeed that the social history of the Latin American people poorly prepared them to govern themselves under orderly democratic processes. Many features of Latin American political life stem from the history of Latin American societies, the social structures it has left them, and the way it molded the people and their leaders.

Even if political instability does assume certain forms peculiar to Latin America, the fact is that revolutions and authoritarian regimes—especially of the military type—are to be found today outside Latin America as well, for instance, in most of the developing countries whose archaic economic and social structure is rapidly changing under the influence of technology and ideologies copied from more advanced countries. Dictatorship and political instability seem almost inseparable from the present pattern of transformation of underdeveloped countries.

It seems wise, without overlooking the extreme complexity of the factors that may have affected political life, to emphasize those whose existence may be demonstrated and whose effects are always similar. It is obvious, for instance, that at the beginning of the nineteenth century when Latin America became independent, deep contradictions existed between the archaic economic and social structures inherited from Iberian colonial policy and the spirit of the political institutions of representative democracy which were gaining ascendency in Europe and which exerted a powerful influence on the Latin American elites. Comparable contradictions, although different in some respects, exist in countries that won their independence only after World War II. In Latin America these contradictions persisted for a long time after independence because of the ignorance and poverty of the rural masses, isolation, and the obsolete forms of property represented by the latifundios. In some areas they still exist.

Political maturity is often mentioned as if it were a psychological concept involving special gifts, experience, and wisdom on the part of a people and its leaders. Actually, political maturity requires mainly that the desired institutions harmonize with the social structures to be preserved. Political maturity can be said to exist only in relation to a given type of political regime. As far as regimes of political democracy are concerned, Latin America was certainly not mature when she became independent. Even now it is only in the most advanced countries that the needed harmony is becoming sufficiently established to enable democratic institutions to function properly.

Obvious contradictions between the form of the institutions and the social structures, the resulting presence of political forces pertaining to different periods and having to deal with unrelated problems, suffice to hamper the functioning of political institutions designed for more homogeneous societies.

There are three main types of contradictions whose effects on political life have been very far-reaching in the past and cannot be resolved as long as a large part of Latin America is so unevenly developed.

(1) Contradictions between different cultural traits. The ideological elements of the Latin American and North Atlantic cultures have never been dissociated. They developed jointly and at the same pace. On the other hand, in Latin America, technology (in agriculture at any rate) and, above all, the

social structures resulting from the circumstances of colonization and the presence of backward indigenous populations
were far more archaic from the beginning than those of western Europe. They remained unchanged for a long time while
changes occurred in the North Atlantic part of the world. As a
result, many Latin American countries with ideologies belonging to the nineteenth and twentieth centuries demanded corresponding political institutions. Over a large part of their
territories, however, the social structure retained the hierarchies of feudal or even slave societies. These countries have
not yet reconciled their progressive political ideologies with
their archaic structure, and the combination is conducive to
pronounced instability.

(2) This situation breeds contradictions between the results expected from the methods of government and administration in a society they were not meant for, and the actual
results. Wherever the traditional and personal authority of
local chiefs persists, the law appears only as a declaration of
intention on the part of the government. An administration
that cannot reach individuals is helpless to enforce the law.
Not only does this helplessness hamper the country's development, but the contrast between the ideal proclaimed and the
facts that belie it creates a frustration that also feeds political
instability.

(3) The most serious contradiction stems from the fact
that society is divided into two different segments because of
its very uneven economic and social development. The social
processes are not the same in both, and the two sectors of
society cannot be governed in the same way. When both forms
of society nevertheless coexist within the same state, they have
to be subjected to the same government and institutions if
national unity is to be maintained and strengthened. The
urban and rural populations which, for the purpose of this
survey, may be said roughly to correspond to the advanced
and backward populations, belong to two societies utterly different in nature as well as in size. One category regards the
nation as one and indivisible, the other as a conglomeration of
small communities belonging to the tribe, the estate, or the
neighborhood. Thus, within the independent Latin American
nations, the problem is the same now as in the colonial period,

when the mother country had to decide whether to apply its own institutions to archaic societies where they could not operate, or leave these societies with their customary institutions, thereby giving up the task of developing them.

The national institutions which were coming into being in Latin America in the nineteenth century could only be at that time institutions of representative democracy. While they were needed by one of the two segments of society into which most Latin American countries are still divided, they were incomprehensible to the other. The very different operation of the same political institutions in societies of a different nature also made for great instability.

The result of these various contradictions is the same everywhere: the acts of the government seem ineffective to some people, the height of injustice to others, and legality does not seem commendable to either group. Hence, there is a constant temptation to resort to illegality. Revolts and coups are regarded as necessary and even legitimate political methods.

6. Contradictions Between Advanced Political Ideologies and Backward Social Structures

These contradictions arose immediately after Columbus landed in America. They were inherent in the goal of Iberian—especially Spanish—colonization whose sovereigns were seeking an impossible reconciliation between selfless proselytizing of the Indians and selfish acquisition of precious metals. These monarchs who hoped to save the souls were not willing to give up exploiting the bodies.

The principles and methods of Spanish and Portuguese colonial administration were similar, although the administrative institutions imposed on Brazil by Portugal differed in their details from those imposed on the rest of Latin America by the Spaniards. The differences deepened especially after independence because of the long period of monarchy in Brazil. Both systems were much alike nonetheless, particularly because, at the time Portuguese colonization grew in scope, between 1580 and 1640, Portugal was united with Spain. In Brazil, however, there were few natives and only very primitive ones, and the mines were only belatedly discovered at the end of the seventeenth century and were far poorer than those in Spanish America. The conflict between the desire to treat the natives well in order to convert them and the temptation to oppress them to obtain gold and silver was milder and shorter-lived than in Mexico and Peru. The idealistic missionary goals of the Spanish rulers also inspired part of the clergy in Brazil, especially the Jesuits, but the Portuguese sovereigns were also less zealous in this respect. Contradictions between ideals and the profit motive were sharper in Spanish America and must be studied there.

The Spanish Policy of Good Intentions

For a Spain emerging from the Middle Ages, the discovery of America in the fifteenth century also meant the discovery of a diversity of cultures as well as the savage himself. Until the nineteenth century "the savage" was modeled on the American native. For the first time Europeans established close permanent contacts with primitive peoples as well as with people who had not been under the influence of Greco-Roman civilization or Semitic religions. Spanish theologians were not even quite sure that the inhabitants of the New World, whose existence was not mentioned in the holy texts, were actually humans. At the same time the suddenness of the conquest required a choice of methods to govern these millions of mysterious beings. There was no pattern to follow in coping with such a novel situation.

In Santo Domingo, Peru, and even more in Mexico, two opposing tendencies arose at the very start and persisted until independence. The first was that of the Spaniards who had settled in America in the hope of acquiring wealth and power—who favored utmost exploitation of native labor through slavery. The second was that of the Catholic sovereigns and a segment of the Spanish clergy, particularly the regular clergy (those belonging to orders), who aimed at winning souls for the Catholic religion, and in order to do so wished to shield the Indians from harsh treatment by the colonizers. When America was discovered, Isabella and Ferdinand, who had just completed the reconquest of Spain from Islam, were still burning with the crusading spirit. The instructions on the conversion of the natives which they gave Columbus when he embarked on his second voyage in 1493 clearly reflect this. Charles V and Philip II also were inspired with missionary zeal. Once the Spanish sovereigns were convinced that the natives really were humans, they assumed the task of converting them. Converting them to Catholicism also meant converting them to Roman-Christian civilization.

Faced with this policy, which in principle at least called for assimilation, the Creoles complained that the situation was not understood at home and charged their government with trying to issue rules on problems of which they knew nothing. Endless arguments ensued between the supporters of the colonizers and those of the natives, each side finding theologians to rekindle the doubts of the Spanish monarchs and persuade them that the Indians must be left free and treated well, or on the contrary to play upon their greed and convince them that the Indians were inferior beings fit only for slavery. During the sometimes violent struggles, Spanish America grew accustomed to illegality: either the colonists' resistance to the lack of understanding on the part of the home country nullified the law, or the home country herself altered her principles to suit her immediate interests. In either case the conflict between the ideal and the profit motive was resolved by dissociating principles from action.

Idealism of the Sovereigns and Greed of the Conquerors

It would be absurd to vindicate the Spanish conquest and deny the ruthlessness of most of the conquistadors and those who followed them. Looting, torture, and massacres were so widespread and long-lasting that entire native populations were decimated. It should not be forgotten, however, that the complete extermination of certain indigenous populations, on Hispaniola for instance, was probably due to diseases unintentionally brought in by the invaders rather than to deliberate ruthlessness on their part. It would be unfair to idealize the motives of the Spanish monarchs and blame the conquistadors alone for all the suffering inflicted on the natives. When the monarchs realized that the conquest could be secured and the mining of precious metals continued only through resort to forced labor, they resigned themselves to that fact. Religious idealism and hunger for gold and power were present among both those who ordered the conquest and those who carried it out, the only difference being that the Spanish sovereigns, unlike the colonizers, had some qualms. The fairest way of expressing this may be to state that, while the Creoles sought gold and also conversions, the Spanish monarchs sought conversions and also gold.

It is undeniable, however, that when order was established and Spain set up a colonial regime, its principles were humane considering that this was the sixteenth century—a period that was not very exacting in this respect. Spanish colonization was condemned more harshly than others because there were so many victims and because it utterly destroyed two native civilizations. Also its iniquities were better known. It was different from other conquests and foreign dominations—in North America in particular—not because of greater ruthlessness but rather because, when the acts of cruelty were being perpetrated, some Spaniards were moved by conscience to protest. When oppressed peoples cannot write, the victims' suffering is not recorded. History forgets it and it is very easy for the conquerors who describe the conquest to idealize their own role.

In Latin America the religious orders inveighed against the brutality of the conquest, and possibly sometimes exaggerated it in order to make their point. As early as 1511 in Hispaniola stubborn denunciations by the Dominican Montesinos elicited a warning from his Spanish superiors, but did not stop him. A little later in Mexico the Franciscans Zumárraga, Gante, and Quiroga, and the Jesuits everywhere strenuously defended the Indians. But the most adamant was a conquistador, Bartolomé de Las Casas (1474–1566) who, deploring the excesses he had witnessed, entered the Dominican order and devoted his very long life to protecting the Indians and denouncing the abuses to which they were subjected. In his eagerness, Las Casas even ill-advisedly recommended (he was forever to regret it) enslaving Africans, as he thought this would be the lesser evil. He was relatively effective in protecting the Indians, however. It is in his *Brevissima Relación de la Destrucción de las Indias,* published in 1552, that historians have found the basis of what Spain today, with the approval of the most reliable historians, calls the *leyenda negra*.

It is called a legend not because the facts as reported are untrue, but because Spain is blamed for what was actually done by Creoles. Besides, it is forgotten that other colonial countries have been far more inclined to cover up excesses committed by their men. Las Casas' denunciations were used in Europe and in the United States as an effective propaganda weapon in the political and religious struggles of the eighteenth and early nineteenth centuries. Countless editions of the *Brevissima Relación* were published in French, English, and German, and their tone is quite obvious from the title of the 1689 English edition.[1]

Societies yearning for political democracy and religious freedom could hardly be expected to acknowledge the stubborn if hesitant and helpless humanitarian strivings of an absolute monarchy and of the two most hated religious disciplines—those of the Inquisition and of Ultramontanism (the movement to assert the power of the Pope). Everything conspired to make the obscurantism of the Spanish clergy and the absolutism of the monarchy, rather than the colonizers themselves, appear as responsible for the excesses of the latter. The settlers in North America stood for the ideal of political freedom while those in Latin America invoked that same ideal against Spain. It was nonetheless the Jesuits' expulsion from Paraguay in 1768, as a result of the "enlightenment," that brought ruin and enslavement to the Indians.

Spain deserves credit for her stubborn efforts, unprecedented before our time, to introduce legislation to help the oppressed natives. Thanks especially to the ceaseless endeavors of Las Casas, protective legislation was firmly established through the promulgation of the *Nuevas Leyes* by Charles V in 1542. This body of laws, which was constantly reviewed and improved, is part of the *Recopilación de Leyes de los Reinos de las Indias*. It forbade slavery (only for the Indians) and took steps to prevent its recurrence in disguise. For that purpose it ordered the elimination of the encomiendas, forbade forcing the Indians to perform personal services, regulated the hours and conditions of work (for women in particular), provided for reasonable wages, and stipulated that the employer must settle accounts with his laborers at least every four months. Equality was out of the question, of course, and

---

[1] Lesley Byrd Simpson, *The Encomienda in New Spain* (University of California Press, 1950), p. 2: "Popery Truly Display'd in its Bloody Colours: Or, a Faithful Narrative of the Horrid and Unexampled Massacres, Butcheries, and all manner of Cruelties, that Hell and Malice could invent, committed by the Popish Spanish Party on the Inhabitants of West-India."

the Indians were even barred from many occupations. Spain, in her eagerness to preserve the purity of Spanish blood, *la limpieza de sangre*, penalized those who lacked it. On the whole, however, this was paternalism of unquestionable generosity.

Thus in the sixteenth century the Leyes de los Reinos de las Indias, although constantly broken and constantly revised, foreshadowed modern labor legislation, but within the limitations of a country and a period that ignored equality and individual freedom.

Creole Resistance to Policies of the Home Country

If the black legend was unfair because it overlooked all efforts to help the natives, it is nonetheless true that the abuses it disclosed had been committed, even if Las Casas had exaggerated them to make his point. The good intentions of the Spanish monarchy toward the Indians were undeniable, but they were carried out only where there was no wealth to exploit and when the religious orders were left alone with the Indians, as in Paraguay. In scattered spots all the way from California to Argentina, Jesuits and Franciscans set up isolated mission villages where the Indians were shielded from the colonizers. This protection through segregation had its drawbacks, for it perpetuated nuclei of indigenous populations which to this day have remained outside the mainstream of national Latin-American societies. In Paraguay the Indians were the best protected of all as long as the Jesuits were present, but Paraguay has also remained one of the least developed countries in Latin America.

The first act of the lay conquerors everywhere was to enslave the Indians, and when the mother country tried to free them, the colonizers complained about being unable to make a living because their government was forcing caballeros to perform undignified manual labor. Their resistance to enforcement of the protective laws could not be overcome. In vain did the home country reiterate its stern instructions to the viceroys and the governors and organize frequent inspections, or *visitas*. The viceroys, captains-general, and judges, eager to ensure the success of colonization could not remain indifferent when measures favoring the Indians were announced. The colonists, brought out at great expense, threatened to leave, and did so whenever any attempt was made to enforce the laws. Spanish civil servants and many members of the secular clergy, too, if they had spent any time in America, were influenced by the colonial outlook and waxed indignant at the lack of understanding of the mother country.

When Tello de Sandoval, the first *visitador,* arrived in Mexico in 1544, he had orders to enforce the Nuevas Leyes. The mere announcement of his arrival caused so many departures and such indignation among the remaining colonizers that the viceroy, Mendoza, fearing a revolt, finally persuaded the visitador to refrain from applying the law. In Peru, on the contrary, where viceroy Blasco Núñez Vela attempted to have the royal instructions obeyed and the Indians freed, the colonizers did revolt and under the leadership of Gonzalo Pizarro (a brother of the recently assassinated conquistador, Francisco Pizarro), proclaimed virtual independence in 1546. They used the classic device of appointing a descendant of the Incas the nominal sovereign of an independent state while they remained its actual masters. After the viceroy had been killed by the insurgents, the revolt was finally put down by Pedro de la Gasca, but only after he had made a new distribution of Indians to the Creoles in Cuzco in 1548. The sovereigns were obliged to overlook the matter. In principle the *Nuevas Leyes* remained in force, but in fact the serfdom they prohibited spread even further.

Spain, which had good reason to distrust the Creoles, was careful to appoint only men from the home country to government and administrative posts. But these officials could not forget the case of Blasco Núñez Vela who, when trying to apply the law, had provoked the 1546 insurrection which caused his death. Furthermore, he was repudiated by the home country and was remembered as an incompetent. On the contrary, Mendoza, who had been lax in carrying out orders (but had used more discreet means of protecting the Indians), went down in the history of Spanish America as its best viceroy. The result of the Spanish monarchy's good intentions was to hide enslavement of the Indians in the guise of the encomienda and later under the colon, inquilino, and pongage systems—that is, serfdom in various forms.

This is how the evil started from the earliest days. It is still causing many complaints in Latin America today and disrupting economic as well as political life. A proliferation of laws and reforms enacted as a token of good intentions is met only by widespread evasion of the law.

Contradictions Between Theory and Practice After Independence

Far from decreasing after independence, evasions of the law and the contradiction between principles and their application intensified at first. When Portuguese and Spanish rule was thrown off, the power of the clergy weakened and freedom of the press was instituted. The elites who had assumed power were drawn to the ideologies prevailing in countries far more advanced than the Iberian countries, namely, France, England, and the United States. Although the social organization of Latin America remained as it had been established three centuries earlier by two of the most conservative countries in Europe, her independence movements sought moral support from and ideological identification with the nations of the world that were most advanced in political freedom and democracy.

The drawbacks as well as the advantages of an aristocratic culture identified with the culture of more advanced countries then became fully obvious. No developing country can resist the compulsion to imitate advanced countries—the result of what is commonly called exposure. This is probably fortunate, for imitation as well as invention fosters progress. But the Latin American countries, more than other countries, were irresistibly driven in this direction because of the alienation of their elites. Although these elites were living in an economically and socially backward environment without having the slightest intention of forsaking the advantages it gave them, they were intellectually part of North Atlantic society.

This is why the ideas that accompanied the nineteenth-century economic and social changes in Europe and the United States immediately spread through Latin America, well before any of those changes had begun there. Even though the principles and institutions to which the future belonged could not function, they were bound to have some impact. Hence Latin America, thanks to the premature alienation of her elites, started changing earlier than other underdeveloped countries. She also suffered lasting political turmoil because the contradictions between theory and practice were multiplied. These contradictions were at their sharpest at the hour of independence itself, when the first national institutions were taking shape. During the revolutionary period liberty, equality, fraternity were ideals cherished by the very people who owned slaves or serfs and took advantage of independence to acquire more of them.

By the second half of the eighteenth century, the independence movement had forerunners who had been raised on French or English political literature. After the Jesuits' departure, neither Spain nor Portugal succeeded in effectively preventing the spread of the new ideologies. Both sections of Latin America were under the intellectual domination of the *afrancesados*. In New Granada (today's Colombia) Nariño translated the Declaration of the Rights of Man; in Buenos Aires Moreno translated the *Social Contract;* in Brazil in 1789 the leaders of the first independence movement, A Inconfidência, were under the influence of Montesquieu, Rousseau, and especially Jefferson; in Mexico, Peru, Chile, Ecuador, the cultivated segment of the aristocracy and the middle classes, who were concerned with the struggle against obscurantism, hailed the American revolution and the early stages of the French revolution.

Influence of the French and North American Revolutions

Many leaders of the independence movement had lived in Europe and the United States, and some of them had taken part in the revolutions on both continents. Only San Martín in Argentina, the purest of them all, had had only a European, essentially Spanish, training. The overlapping of the revolutions in Latin America with the democratic revolutions in France and the United States is well shown by the career of the Venezuelan Francisco de Miranda. Although Miranda had begun so early that he did not live to see his cause triumph, he was one of the great men of Latin American independence. To an equal degree, however, he was one of the great men of the French Revolution. Present wherever the battle for political freedom was being waged, he fought first for the independence of the United States, then was one of the best generals of the French Revolution, which made him second in command of the army sent into Belgium. In France he was unjustly discredited after the treason of Dumouriez. He made a first unsuccessful attempt at a revolution in Venezuela in 1806. He was again defeated in 1812, was turned over to Spain by Bolívar, and died in prison in 1816. Bolívar, the man who symbolizes Latin American independence, turned away from the French Revolution to seek more effective support in the English-speaking world, but he had lived in Europe for a long time, had been in contact with the *philosophes,* and had become a high Masonic dignitary.

Despite the reaction that followed independence, prompting those who feared the spread of democratic ideologies to wish for monarchy, Latin America was never severed from the political movements in Europe. When Europe, changed by industrialization, replaced franchise based on property with the political democracy of universal suffrage, Latin America also wished to reform her institutions, although her economic and social development had not kept pace with that of the North Atlantic world. Latin America never lagged when it came to guarantees of individual freedom, declarations of economic and social rights, affirmation of the principle of universal suffrage.

Until the twentieth century (slightly earlier in the Argentine Republic), when thanks to urbanization the cities contained a large educated and politically conscious population, reforms were merely theoretical. They had some impact, however, for by proclaiming as early as the nineteenth century the principle of reforms that most of the populace was not yet dreaming about, the elites precipitated a desire for these reforms among the masses. Even today the contradiction is profound between the modern forms of institutions and the backwardness of a large part of the societies where they exist.

Such contradictions are not of course peculiar to Latin

America. Suffice it to recall that many of those who in the United States proclaimed lofty principles of freedom in the Declaration of Independence or in the Constitution of 1789 found nothing odd in having African slaves or European indentured servants. Contradiction between facts and principles exists as long as those who profess principles benefit from the opposite of what they profess. What is peculiar to Latin America (and here again the latifundio is partly to blame) is that the rural masses resigned themselves to their condition for so long. Even today the reformer who has just introduced the most elaborate provisions into legislation in order to safeguard electoral freedom finds it quite normal that his peons and colonos should dutifully demonstrate their blind devotion to him by voting for the candidates of his choice. The enlightened aristocrat who does not cringe before the most progressive ideas and returns full of awe from a visit to Mao Tse-tung's China finds it quite natural to give his morning blessing to his peons on their way to work. The lawyer, while believing that only the rule of law is worthy of a civilized nation, thinks he is nonetheless doing his duty when he steps in to shield his clients from the law.

The contradiction between, on the one hand, institutions and ideologies of the most developed societies, and, on the other hand, a partly archaic social structure that no one tries to change, produces a proliferation of reforms, laws, and regulations as well as systematic efforts to evade the law and rob the reforms of their substance. The process is cumulative. Reforms are enacted with an ease and frequency proportional to their relative futility; political life is active and agitated in proportion to its lack of effectiveness. Latin America suffers as much from the complexity of politics as from its sterility.

Blue Laws and Contempt for Law

Latin America tends far too often to indulge in wishful thinking. Many other countries have given in to the temptation to translate into legislation an ideal that no one could or would put into practice; the results have always been disastrous. The United States is an example: there were and still are laws in certain states that ban gambling, tobacco, alcohol, or even swearing. These are the blue laws, which strive to improve human society. Attempts to enforce them, such as Prohibition, bred contempt for the law and corruption of those charged with enforcement.

The Latin American societies, with the contrast between their ideology and their social structure, lent themselves to this type of legislation. The consequences, however, were far worse than in the United States because these laws embodied not only an ethical or religious ideal, but a system of necessary social reforms. The desire for these reforms had been aroused but their realization was delayed because mere words were mistaken for reality.

During the colonial era, the Leyes de las Indias were idealistic and moralistic legislation. Their source of inspiration was religious, but they endeavored to help the Indians on this earth. Since Spain had had neither the courage nor probably the means to reform the colonial structure, the Leyes de las Indias were to remain blue laws forever.

For a long time after independence the principles of political equality, universal suffrage, and exercise of legislative power by elected representatives only expressed an ideal. The absence of national consciousness among the illiterate masses and the strength of the masters' power made the existence of democratic institutions possible only in theory. As long as the principle was honored, nobody was surprised that it covered up the most authoritarian paternalism or the most despotic dictatorship. The democratic constitutions that Latin America so liberally proclaimed in the nineteenth century all too often remained blue laws, and still are in a few countries.

There is not one Latin American constitution at present that does not provide for free compulsory elementary education and specify its duration and in some cases its content. For a large segment of the rural populations, however, for whom schools, teachers, and teaching materials are not available, school legislation belongs to the realm of blue laws.

Latin American constitutions do not overlook social rights either. The International Labour Organization has on many occasions praised the eagerness of Latin American delegations in advocating progressive social legislation. But representatives of the organization have also had occasion to deplore its sketchy enforcement and the persistence, in the rural world at any rate, of a quasi-serfdom of the laborers. To this day most labor legislation bypasses the countryside, so that peasants are not covered by social security provisions. For most of the population, except in two or three countries, social legislation belongs in the category of blue laws.

Brazilian folk humor has coined a very expressive term for laws that merely pay lip service to the ideal: in the nineteenth century when British prestige was at its height, they were called laws *para inglês ver*—to show off or brag about to the English!

Theoretical Centralization of Political Institutions

During the colonial period the complete lack of realism in the centralizing policy that Spain tried to apply to her remote and widely differing colonies resulted in idealistic legislative systems. Tolerance for human foibles in the form of illegality corrected some of their rigidity. This situation continued after independence owing to the conflict between the lingering colonial structure and the ideologies copied from western Europe and the United States. Power was legally concentrated in the hands of the national authorities, while in fact local personalities retained their power over the isolated societies of the interior, particularly in the latifundios. Thus Spain gave Latin America a tradition of government centralization and absolutism, while the colonization methods left her with a social structure that paralyzed the action of any central government.

Everything conspired to drive the Spanish monarchy toward a policy of extreme centralization—the same spirit of absolute monarchy which in the sixteenth century had barely extended national sovereignty over a country where regionalism was always very strong. In Spain the tendency of the municipal bodies, the *cabildos,* to turn into regional governments had to be fought, and it was feared that these same traditions might lead to separatist movements in America. Actually, during the colonial period the striving for independence or at least for self-government never let up in Latin America, and more than once the cabildos took the lead in fostering it. It should be added that experience soon led the home country to mistrust the Creoles, whose policy of native exploitation ran counter to her own intentions.

Spain has often been blamed, especially by English-speaking peoples, for not having established self-government institutions that might have enabled the Latin Americans to acquire political experience. This reproach is quite illogical; although representative government was beginning to emerge in England in the seventeenth and eighteenth centuries, there was no trace of it in Spain in the sixteenth century; her sovereigns could not conceivably have given America a regime they denied to the mother country. Even if self-government had been possible, it would have been in the hands of the Creoles instead of the natives. The Creoles might have gained political experience, but this would have been to their own advantage; in all likelihood the Indian masses would simply have been destroyed by unbridled exploitation. The colonies had to be deprived of autonomy for humanitarian reasons, and unfortunately for the Indians the Spanish government failed in its attempts to do so.

The policy regarding America was painstakingly drafted by the Council of the Indies, set up as early as 1524. The Council, presided over by the king, included former viceroys and captains-general. Its authority extended to all fields, but economic policy was more closely supervised by the Casa de Contratación, founded in Seville in 1503. In America proper, all civil servants entrusted with major responsibilities had to be Peninsulares, that is, from the mother country. The monarch was represented by viceroys in Spanish America and by a governor-general in Brazil (after 1549). Four viceroyalties were established, the first in Santo Domingo in 1535 (shortly transferred to Mexico City) and the second in Lima in 1542. Two others were created, in Bogotá in 1717 and in Buenos Aires in 1776. Since they were too large, they were subdivided into captaincies-general, whose heads reported directly to the king, wielded powers substantially equal to those of the viceroys, and were in fact independent from them. Some territories detached from the viceroyalties constituted *presidencias,* whose heads were more closely subordinated to the viceroys. The provinces were administered by governors supervised by the viceroys and captains-general. In the eighteenth century, this administrative system was radically changed when the Spanish Bourbons set up *intendencias,* which had so effectively centralized power in the hands of the French monarchy. But by the time this reform was extended to the entire territory in 1790, it was too late for it to have any deep impact.

The huge distances and difficulties of communications—often interrupted by corsairs and pirates when the Iberian powers were no longer the masters of the seas—made it necessary to grant broad powers to the viceroys and captains-general. This involuntary lessening of administrative concentration was in no way decentralization. The officials, who were closely supervised and called to account, were reluctant to act on their own; their state of uncertainty was obvious when the French occupation of Spain left them to their own devices.

A skillful control system extended to all administrators. First, the clergy, subjected to royal authority by the *Real Patronato de Indias,* granted by a papal bull in 1508, formed a second administrative hierarchy. Besides, all viceroys, captains-general, and some of their subordinates had to face the *audiencia,* a body which was at the same time a tribunal and a council. There were fourteen audiencias by the end of the colonial period. In addition to their judicial duties, their members had the task of protecting the Indians and enforcing ecclesiastical discipline. They also had fiscal functions and constituted a kind of legislative council. Only Peninsulares could belong to the audiencia.

The audiencia had another function which gave it some power over the representatives of the Spanish government. When these men relinquished their posts, the audiencia investigated their past performance. The most remarkable institution in the Spanish colonial system, however, was the *residencia.* A judge invited all persons who had any complaints about the conduct of a man who was leaving office to come forth and state them. This was far from being an empty threat, and it weighed heavily on the administrators. Seldom did even the highest officials escape investigation, and to many of them no indulgence was shown. The practice may have served too often to vent grudges. All results of the investigation and the recommended sentences were made known to the Council of the Indies, with whom the final decision rested.

Control by the home country was further reinforced by the inspection system of the *visitas*. The Council of the Indies periodically sent investigators to inquire about the conduct of administrators, study any special problems, and make sure that its instructions were being obeyed. In Brazil the mother country was less systematic in her control, but the governor-general, the judges, and especially the fiscal administration were closely supervised. Here also there was no official place for self-government.

Actual Decentralization Resulting from Social Structure

In view of the complete absence of self-government, the ineligibility of Creoles for any high administrative or judicial posts, the meticulousness of the legislation drafted in the home country (over 6,000 of these laws have been preserved in the Recopilación de Leyes), it has often been stated, seemingly with good reason, that Latin America has been smothered by centralization. Many North Americans in particular, accustomed to self-government and the extreme decentralization deriving from federalism, regard centralization as a major cause of the lag in Latin American development and her political instability. It is claimed that Latin America achieved independence without being prepared for political responsibilities; hence it was inevitable that, accustomed to be governed, she should become a victim of anarchy when called upon to govern herself because everyone would seek power for his own or his clan's benefit. (Today more than ever, according to this thesis, Latin America is suffering from her inherited tradition of centralization.) As a result, when the time was ripe for economic and social development, local communities and in general all those who were to form the elites were not fit to help themselves and take the necessary initiatives, being accustomed only to obey the central government.[2]

This analysis of the effects of absolutism, centralization, and

[2] Asher N. Christensen, editor of the survey *The Evolution of Latin American Government* (New York, 1955), pp. 53–59. A. C. Wilgus,

the monopolizing of high posts by men from the mother country may seem logical. However, it is based on legal appearances rather than social reality. There was a major difference
between theory and practice, for when the Spanish government issued an order it was seldom faithfully obeyed. In
theory, the colonial administration was completely centralized,
but the social structure offered such resistance that the administration had little effect upon local communities largely administered by their own chiefs. Latin America suffered much
more from the helplessness of governments and the lack of
discipline of the local authorities than from absolutism and
centralization. The evils that the colonial system imparted to
Latin American political behavior stem from a lack of realism
on the part of the government at home, which continued to
issue orders it was powerless to enforce. Latin America was
not the land of almighty officials, but on the contrary the land
of unruly caciques and caudillos.

To speak of centralization in Latin America and of the
barring of Creoles from all political or administrative authority means first of all overlooking the fact that even in the home
country, sixteenth-century Spain, absolutism did not prevent
an active municipal life. The municipal bodies, the cabildos,
remained very powerful, particularly in Castile, until 1521,
when the revolt of the municipalities and their *Santa Junta*
were crushed. The town councils were transplanted to America, where the municipal administration was in the hands of
councillors, the *regidores,* who originally were elected by the
segment of the population that enjoyed political rights. (The
Indians but not all of the mestizos were barred from voting.)
The regidores themselves selected the town magistrates, the
alcaldes, who wielded very real powers in police, fiscal, judicial, and even defense matters. Thus true municipal freedom
existed and Latin America even retained traces of a direct
democracy which had rapidly disappeared elsewhere. For instance, in certain circumstances, decisions on the municipal
level were taken in *cabildo abierto,* an open assembly in which
all people of standing participated.

"The Chemistry of Political Change in Latin America," *Annals of the
American Academy of Political and Social Science,* July, 1962, p. 43.

It is true that the regime deteriorated in Latin America, just as it did in continental Europe when the system of the sale of offices was instituted in 1620 and the local government lost its representative character. It did turn what might have become democracy into oligarchy and may be partly to blame for the growth of corruption, but not for the suppression of local freedom. Neither did it prevent people of standing from learning the business of administration. On the contrary, the sale of offices has always enabled those who bought them to remain independent. A far worse trend toward centralization in Latin America as elsewhere stemmed from poor financial management by the local administration, which gave Spanish officials the occasion and the need to intervene.

Most Spaniards lived in the cities during the colonial period, while most of the Indians and mestizos lived in isolation in the countryside. Instead of being subjected to the authority of Spanish administrators, they were controlled by their Creole masters or, in some cases, by their Indian chiefs. Under the regime of the large estate and isolation Latin America was left prey to feudal lords, and while feudalism has never been a very democratic type of social organization, it has always been particularly effective in causing decentralization.

Creoles were never appointed to any major government posts by the mother country, and the big landowners very effectively ruled the populace. Hence it seems debatable that centralization robbed the landed and even the urban aristocracy of all political and administrative experience. It is true that their experience was too narrow—within the limits of the estate, town, or region—but that was because Latin American social activity was thus limited. Awareness of belonging to a state and a nation did not develop because power was fragmented, as was obvious immediately after independence.

During the entire nineteenth century, certainly during its first half, the main task of the governments was to contain the separatist tendencies throughout Latin America which disguised themselves as federalism and strove to break Latin America into as many small local sovereignties as there were local political chiefs.

To blame colonial overcentralization for having created a state of mind that led individuals to expect everything from the central government—a trait hampering Latin American development to this day—is paradoxical. It is all the more so since the same authors also state, with greater justification, that the separatist tendencies of the regions and towns, the fact that local populations are not integrated into the nation, added to narrow-mindedness and selfish parochialism, all hamper development and account in part for Latin American political instability.

Central Government's Areas of Direct and of Weakened Action

It is legitimate to claim that Latin American countries are centralized only if judicial evidence of institutions of local self-government is sought, and its absence held as proof of this assertion. Although some countries under United States influence have tried to institute some form of federalism, many of them, steeped in the legal tradition of continental Europe, have tended to lean toward methods of administration closer to the French than to the North American pattern. In view of the archaic social structures still prevailing in a large portion of Latin America, it is wise to discard the formal concept of centralized versus decentralized governments in favor of a sociological concept of an *area of direct action* of the administration, as opposed to an *area of weakened action*. There are very few Latin American countries where these two areas do not coexist and the central government's operation does not widely differ according to the area.

Whatever the powers enjoyed by a central government in Latin America and its desire to use them, authority is difficult to maintain wherever isolation and a social organization of small closed communities persist. Authority can assert itself fully only in the modernized areas of the country—in the cities and the few rural regions reorganized through the splitting up of the large estate or the relaxation of its control. This breaks down groups whose members maintain direct contact only with one another and brings the state into direct contact with individuals. Only a developed section of a country is an area of direct action of the government and can really be administered.

Wherever local communities have not yet been broken up,

wherever people still live in a closed economy, give their allegiance to traditional chiefs, and place the ties of neighborhood or personal loyalty above national solidarity, the authority of the state does not reach individuals directly. This is an area of weakened action of the law and administration. In such an area, however tyrannical the most authoritarian dictator may be—and very often in Latin America bloodthirsty caudillos have committed the most arbitrary deeds—the power of the dictator cannot be totalitarian. It may tamper with the person or property of some individuals, but it is unable to impose its authority permanently upon all individuals.

A striking example, even to this day, of the helplessness of the central administration to extend its power beyond the area of direct action is the difficulty of trying to set up national statistical services. The only exceptions are two or three countries where developed social structures predominate. This is of major importance, for it is quite obvious that today no administration can be effectively centralized without having statistical knowledge of the society it claims to govern.

Beyond the immediate borders of the segment of society where the government wields direct power—the only one that foreigners usually are acquainted with, and certainly the only one that businessmen and industrialists have to cope with—the effects of regulations are weakened by the indifference of a population that does not need the government. In addition, the customary authorities who are much closer to the population than the remote government act as a buffer.

In contemporary Brazil, as in many other countries, the formalities of birth, marriage, and death are meticulously prescribed by law. Everybody needs a personal or professional identity card with more photographs and fingerprints than in any other country. The city dweller is helpless without one, but the man of the interior has never been registered anywhere and manages very well. The regulations on marriage and the body of civil law are uniform over the entire territory, but the man of the interior sets up a household without getting married and has no contracts to draw up, nor property to protect. The government prescribes the duration and curriculum of public education, but the man of the interior does not go to school. Commerce and industry are subject to detailed regulations, and so is agriculture, but the man of the interior lives outside the market economy and does not use money. The law protects the peon and the colono, but the peon and the colono are used to asking the master to shield them from the law.

Should the central government's officials be tempted to step in, they would be ill advised to do so against the master's wish. As long as rural communities have not disintegrated, their traditional chiefs, who used to wield physical power, still wield enough electoral power, buttressed by the loyalty of their subjects under the present regimes of representative democracy, that the governments usually prefer to make some compromise with them.

Within the archaic social structure preserved by the large estate, very effective if quite improper means of defending local freedom are disobeying or, even better, not knowing the law. Local freedom is not enjoyed by the people but by the notables, who act as buffers between the state and their subjects. When Latin America won independence she was by no means liberated from a form of feudalism. Hence, she first had to undergo the violence that accompanies recreation of central power. Because this process has not been completed, the attempt to centralize the nations by means of political institutions is at the same time so necessary and so often disappointing. Spanish colonization's legacy to Latin America is the lack of national administration. Latin America did not inherit centralization from Spain. The struggle today is not aimed at freeing Latin America from the shackles of an overly centralized administration but, on the contrary, at compelling unruly groups to integrate into the nation and giving the new nations a unity that Spain and Portugal were unable to bequeath to their colonial empires.

7. Contradictions in Political Life Within Dual Societies

It is a paradox of Latin America's political life that few peoples in the world are so attached to the ideal of political democracy while few have lived for so long under dictatorial regimes. Actually, Latin America as a whole has lived longer under dictatorships than under democratic regimes. Her only democracies, except in Uruguay and possibly Costa Rica, have been *limited democracies*. She has not, however, rejected democratic principles for any length of time, except possibly in Paraguay—a nation prepared by the paternalistic theocracy of the Jesuits to accept totalitarian regimes. These regimes, of Francia and the two Lopezes, lasted uninterruptedly from 1811 to 1870. Haiti also seems never to have had democratic regimes.

Nevertheless, for a short time, when Fascism and National Socialism appeared close to victory in Europe, a few elements in Latin America were tempted to imitate those regimes and reject the principle of political democracy. They were the *Integralistas* in Brazil, the *Nacistas* in Chile, the *Sinarquistas* in Mexico, the MNR of Paz Estenssoro in Bolivia, and the Peronistas in their original form in Argentina. They parroted the Fascists in denouncing the concept of democracy (and in Latin America this was certainly a concept rather than a reality). Even cautious President Vargas of Brazil announced in 1940 that democracy was no more than a remnant of the past and that the future no longer belonged to it. Once again, however, Latin Americans responded to events in Europe, and the decline of European Fascism shortly put a stop to these repudiations of democracy. The rapid change of heart of those who had momentarily rejected political democracy was interesting. Thus, a substantial number of leaders of the most progressive political movements in Latin America received their political training in the forties from semi-Fascist movements or fringe groups. This was true of Perón, of Vargas in his first government, and of many others.

This was only an interlude. Contrary to what is happening today in the developing countries of Africa and Asia, Latin America has a very strong tradition of attachment to political freedom, as old as that in western Europe and the United States, from which it was never severed ideologically. There is no Latin American regime, however despotic, that does not need to pay lip service to the principle of free elections and people's sovereignty. Perón in Argentina, Batista in Cuba, or Trujillo in the Dominican Republic found it impossible to avoid doing so for any length of time. As a matter of fact, it was not utterly useless, since the care taken to respect certain forms did limit the arbitrary aspect of many authoritarian regimes in Latin America, at least after the most archaic forms of caudillismo had disappeared.

Resistance to the Processes of Representative Democracy

Despite the past and present prestige of democratic institutions, these can seldom operate as they are meant to, even when governments are most eager for them to do so. Latin America has had many reluctant dictators who imposed their will arbitrarily only because they had no alternative. The best known of them, a man whose sincere democratic convictions are unquestionable, was Juárez in Mexico. The constitutions, most of which were modeled on the United States Constitution, cannot produce the same results in the unevenly developed Latin American societies as in societies for which they were intended. This is true even when constitutional legality is scrupulously respected, when the presidential regime appears to operate normally, when freedom of information is respected, and the ruling groups abstain from exerting pressure on the voters. It is true even when—as frequently occurs—independent magistrates limit the authority of the other two branches of government and apply the equivalents of the Anglo-Saxon writ of habeas corpus and appeal procedures, namely the *amparo* in Spanish America and the *mandato de segurança* in Portuguese America.

If all this is true, it is because Latin American countries are not politically mature; immaturity in this case means that society is divided into two segments so different that national political institutions cannot operate harmoniously. Two contrasting obstacles hamper representative democracy in the archaic and the developed society. Democracy is premature in the archaic society, whose members are not sufficiently integrated into the nation. The developed society, on the other hand, already on the path of state planning and socialism and eager for very rapid progress, may have outgrown classic democracy. Unless institutions are adapted, they cannot fully fit either society, and certainly not both at the same time.

The system of representative democracy to which Latin America is clinging rests on the existence of a public opinion concerned with national problems. In a dual society this indispensable basis for the regime is fragile because the problems arising in the two segments of society cannot be solved by the same authority. Public opinion is different in each of these two societies and does not function in the same way.

In the developed society, which is mainly urban, public opinion is certainly deeply divided; but even if the aims of the respective sides are incompatible, they are national in scope and the national authorities are competent to solve the problems. Even though a split between the partisans of authoritarian communism and those of liberal capitalism may weaken a country or lead it into civil war, it nonetheless testifies to national political integration. Each side seeks to impose its own way on the nation as a whole by political methods used on a national scale. In this society, insofar as conflicts of opinions and interests can be resolved nonviolently, they are likely to be settled through the electoral processes of representative democracy, by helping one of the opinions to become a majority opinion.

In an archaic society (until it has disintegrated) the situation is entirely different. This society consists of a multitude of communities cut off from one another and from the nation as a whole. Problems are communal in scope and must be solved within each community. Since the communities are outside the market economy and outside the law in many respects, their members can expect very little from the national government and ask very little of it. A manorial society is a closed society, not only economically but politically as well.

There is a public opinion within these small groups as well as in the largest countries, but it does not need the procedures of representative democracy to express itself. The chief or chiefs of the community—the men who impose their decisions and who, depending on their personality, may or may not consider the group's opinion—were invested with authority by custom in the Indian communities, and by the fact of property ownership in the latifundios. Election of representatives to national assemblies is a mere formality as long as this type of society persists, and its only object is to allow the subjects to affirm their loyalty toward their chiefs.

Public opinion operating only on the level of multiple small closed communities is of no immediate use in national political life. The two public opinions in the two different societies cannot meet, and the result is divergence and perpetual frustration. It is almost inevitable that efforts to provide a point of agreement so often result in purely emotional propaganda—playing up xenophobic nationalism, the United States being the favorite target. All the parties resort to this negative approach: it helps to push real problems into the background. Its most obvious effect is to enable the Communist parties to draw support from populations as yet untouched by Communist ideology, and even from groups otherwise quite hostile to it.

Either the people have become resigned to the fact that government statements are merely declarations of intention not meant to be carried out fully or immediately, or these statements reach a large portion of the population in a weakened form, or societies of varied types react to them in unexpected ways. In any case, the inevitable consequence is that the government's authority is undermined, corruption is fostered, and the governed as well as the governing are led astray from the normal paths of political democracy.

The most immediate consequence is probably that in this period of economic planning the best plans may be useless if they are not effectively imposed upon the nation or if they can only partially be carried out. A conscientious administrator may regard it as his duty to temper some regulations. He cannot conceive that anyone would wish these to be carried out literally, upsetting a centuries-old situation. He may regard their strict application as tantamount to shirking his duty, somewhat like those officials who show their dissatisfaction with the government by being overzealous in order to tie up administrative machinery. The people and the administrators themselves see the immense gap between the legislator's stated intentions and reality. Being accustomed to regard laws as declarations of intention only, they are prone to think that it is up to them to find some trick to alter or soften the law when it is too difficult or unpopular to enforce. *Dar um jeito,* they say in Brazil.

Economic planners in Latin America increasingly tend to think that their countries' economic development requires a change in the governments' attitude and methods. Very often they blame high officials for their lack of understanding of and concern for economic problems. The remedies would be simple if this were the case. It is not fair to blame the officials; the problem is far more complex because the social structures themselves, which cannot be changed painlessly or smoothly, paralyze or distort government action. Today many important men in government do care a great deal about their countries' economic development.

Corruption or Belief in Corruption

The fact that enforcement of the law may be and in some cases has to be tempered and official orders disobeyed brings about many other untoward consequences. Public opinion cannot with impunity become used to the idea that the law may be flouted and that officials find it normal to help flout it. People who are skeptical about the government's good intentions in the first place may decide that, since there are ways of evading the law, it is almost normal to pay those who help them do this or who look the other way. If civil servants are often understanding toward those who wield political power, they may also be tempted to be understanding toward those who may not have the power but have the money to pay for favors instead.

There are widespread complaints about corruption in government agencies and even among high officials; this is said to be a continuing flaw in Latin American political life. It remains to be proved that this is true. It is probable that it is another case of hasty generalization and that the more advanced countries are grouped with the underdeveloped ones under the pretext that they all are Latin American. It is certainly true that there have been (and still are) Latin American chiefs of state and ministers whose only concern was to make money. The extortions practiced by Trujillo in the Dominican Republic, Perón in Argentina, and many others are no myths. Too many dictators have retired abroad after they made a fortune and too many politicians have made a fortune without having to leave the country. Latin America has had badly paid officials who accepted bribes, but she also has had statesmen and administrations of the utmost integrity. There never has been and never will be any objective investigation proving that there is more corruption in that part of the world than elsewhere.

Actually, a government does not have to be corrupt to be held in disrepute by the population and thereby weakened. Belief in corruption is sufficient. It is true that in countries where the law cannot be applied equally to all citizens, opportunities for graft are much greater, and this breeds belief in its prevalence. Whatever the motives for which some people escape strict enforcement of the law, the interpretation is always the same—corruption. The widespread belief that corruption is rife is as dangerous to good administration as is corruption itself. Officials who are subjected to too much temptation tend to yield to it, and, what is even worse, the people develop fear and contempt toward the state. Thus the people are prone to welcome the savior, especially the military savior, who at the price of dictatorship promises to restore integrity.

Red Tape

The administration's helplessness and fear of corruption also hamper its freedom of action by forcing it to increase paper work. The administration that is unsure of being obeyed when economic planning is at stake multiplies its regulations, but sees them lose their effectiveness as they pass down the ranks. The helpless administration leaves a section of the country underregulated while those who submit to its control are smothered under the sheer weight of regulations. This is one more incentive for them to seek their way out through bribery.

Red tape—the inevitable by-product of fear of fraud and attempts to forestall corruption—is generally agreed to be the vice of Latin American government agencies. Even on that point, however, complaints should be verified, for red tape is not the bane of any particular government but rather of an economic and social setting that complicates and increases government functions. It is not certain whether foreign businessmen are inconvenienced by red tape because it is so much worse than that in North America and elsewhere, or because they are less familiar with it. Conceivably also, before the rise of nationalism too many foreign firms had become accustomed to avoid red tape through questionable means whereas now the extra paper work may be a weapon deliberately used to harass foreigners.

Whatever the case may be, the resulting state of mind weakens the government. It is necessary to hire more civil servants whose productivity is lowered because the country resists them, as much from the fact of its social structure as from its people's distrust. The proliferation of civil service results in low pay, which increases the risks of bribery or crushes the needy population under the burden of a costly bureaucracy. Besides, civil servants have a standard of living so much higher than the rural masses that they cannot understand the people they are to control. The creation of an overgrown tertiary sector, a large portion of which is occupied by the civil service, is a well-known phenomenon in Latin America. The causes are quite varied: the prestige of public service dating back to the colonial period, the attempt to satisfy would-be voters and university graduates, premature migration to the cities of rural unemployed people. In addition, administrative work has become so intricate that more men are constantly needed.

The combination of burdensome administrative work and a largely illiterate population further complicates matters by compelling many people to hire middlemen to help them in their dealings with government agencies. Customs brokers are a commonplace everywhere, but in Latin America such agents are used for all government agencies. Besides informing people of requirements and preparing cases, they follow them up through the various offices, prod officials into action when the file has lain on one desk too long, and tell clients how to hasten administrative procedures. These *despachantes* are not disliked by government officials, who thus receive files in proper order and avoid contact with uneducated people who have to be helped even to sign their name.

These agents may be quite honest and many of them probably are, but their activity is of a nature that makes corruption easier. They are in a position to know who is corruptible, and the fact that they have to be hired at all spreads belief in universality of corruption—all the more so since the dishonest middleman may pad his bill by invoking the need for bribes.

Another drawback of the almost unavoidable resort to paid middlemen for the slightest formality is that the very poor masses who do not dare approach a government office directly for fear of the cost are prone to abstain from complying with any regulations and thus are driven to live outside the law. A typical example is the very high percentage of poor people who are not legally married and often do not register births and deaths. This is one reason why the percentage of illegitimate births around 1958 was 58.6 in the Dominican Republic, 73.9 in Panama, and 56.4 in Venezuela. This is due partly to family instability, but some marriages which are quite stable are not registered for economy's sake.

Demagogy and the Urban Population

Another consequence of the long-standing custom of using legislation to show good will without too much thought as to whether the social condition of the country warrants its immediate realization is the premature promise of social benefits. Whenever promises are not kept, the resulting dissatisfaction leads to political turmoil; when they are kept, the national economy is overtaxed. In many countries where a modern society exists, the administration is able to act in that part of the society. Social reforms that are too advanced for the over-all level of national development development are granted liberally and are beginning to be carried out in the government's areas of direct action. These reforms can be carried out quite effectively, since the beneficiaries already have the necessary organization.

The result of government regulations that can be effective in the administration's area of direct action (the developed section of the country) but not in the area of weakened action, (the backward regions) is to deepen the gap in living conditions between the advanced and the archaic society. The contrast is particularly striking in Brazil between the South and the Northeast, and between cities and countryside generally. The contradiction between a progressive ideal enacted into national legislation and an archaic social structure that denies its benefits to some parts of the country because of evasion or ignorance of the law in turn brings about further contradictions between the two levels of culture. The result is that one culture progresses rapidly while the other remains at a standstill or even regresses.

Disillusionment with Democratic Processes

Emotionally, Latin American countries are almost unanimously in favor of representative democracy. Castroism and its authoritarian methods of economic development are only now beginning to lure away some intellectuals and urban workers. Almost inevitably, however, the institutions of representative democracy turn out to be disappointing. If they are used in good faith they can do no more than reflect present-day society. But the problem in virtually all Latin American countries is that there are two societies instead of one. These societies are very different and know very little about each other. Neither recognizes itself in the confusing blend produced by the operation of the democratic processes. Each, believing it has been deceived, yearns for a change of government or of regime.

The basic process of any modern democracy—elections, in particular through universal suffrage—is perverted by the lingering archaic society that confronts developed society. Elections have no meaning for the archaic society and cannot solve its local problems. For the developed society elections are disappointing because they bring into national political life the most conservative backers of the anachronistic situation persisting in the rural areas.

The association of two radically different societies in the political life of a nation is a source of disturbance and impotence. The advanced populations, even more than the backward ones, disappointed by the results of elections which they find so incomprehensible that they believe them to be fraudulent, tend to resort to violence and to accept the promises of would-be dictators.

PART III

Political Forces and Political Parties

In contrast to western Europe and the United States, political life in Latin America is characterized by multiplicity and the heterogeneous character of its political forces. If simplicity of structure prevails in completely archaic agrarian societies, this is not true of developing societies which are changing by imitating more advanced cultures. Latin American societies in which the cultural advances and lags are especially pronounced are certainly not simple.

Because of the dualistic nature of the society, in the great majority of Latin American countries there are two hierarchies of classes which are completely separate from one another. The developed society includes the classes found in industrial countries of the Western world: a ruling class, middle classes which are already large because of the overdevelopment of the tertiary sector, and a proletariat which is very heterogeneous in view of the large recent migration from the areas of archaic culture. With the exception of these recent migrants, who do not immediately become integrated into a completely different world, almost all of urban society might seem like a middle class when compared with rural society, where the simple hierarchies consist of a small aristocracy and a subject mass.

The acceleration of history caused by the spreading of innovations from outside Latin America has enabled the political forces of the past to exist side by side with those of the present. This phenomenon often has been pointed out. The Peruvian

Haya de la Torre gave it an important place in the doctrine of APRA, the political party that has been trying to adapt non-Communist marxist theories to the particular needs of Latin America. This, too, is what led Morazé to call his book about contemporary Brazil *The Three Ages of Brazil*.

Even today political forces of a very distant past can be found quite alive in Latin America. Aside from the pre-Columbian indigenous societies which still survive but which, as long as they have not disintegrated, remain outside political life, the political forces of a feudal type of society manifest themselves through the persisting influence of large landholders who have not given up their efforts to prolong the existence of manorial property and its attendant social organization in the countryside. The local political chiefs who, as a reminder of the pre-Columbian era are called *caciques* in Spanish America and whom the Brazilians prefer to call *coroneis*, inject into modern democratic electoral processes a personal authority which is generally patrimonial in nature.

More recent political forces can be found in Latin America although elsewhere they are already outmoded—forces whose appearance coincided with the beginning of the industrial revolution. Primarily they express the requirements of the entrepreneurs. These men believe so firmly in the greatness of their economic mission that they have no doubt that the government's sole reason for being is to guarantee them freedom to make a quick profit. They also are so convinced of their power to prepare a better world that they cannot worry in the meantime about the suffering of the rural proletariat or the disarray of the urban proletariat created by their activities. In Latin America the day of the robber barons is not past, the day of the *condottieri* of industry who, a century ago, on the eve of the Civil War, paved the way for the economic and social development of North America while plundering the country. For the robber barons of Latin America, too, the role of a good government is to be a business administration whose main task is to facilitate their activities. It seems quite natural to them to pay for such government cooperation. They do not regard corruption as unethical as long as it works.

These political forces of budding industrialization include a crystallizing proletariat whose members have broken away too recently from the traditional framework of rural society to know how to build a new one by orderly and efficient trade-union movements in the city. The migrants from rural Latin America are seeking personal protectors, just as the newly arrived Italians and Poles did upon landing in the United States at the end of the nineteenth century. Instead of building a true trade-union movement, these new Latin American city dwellers submit to the tutelage of an urban *caciquismo* which is not unlike rural caciquismo. The boss of the foreign sections of North American cities of the nineteenth century, translated into the Latin American cities of the twentieth century, is the cacique or coronel of a society in the process of industrialization.

Finally, political forces of the same type are beginning to emerge in the countryside, even in the backward areas. In many places, the authority of the upper classes, especially of latifundio owners who take no active interest in their property and are losing the confidence of the masses, is beginning to break down. The rural masses who no longer belong entirely to the archaic society but have not yet been integrated into the national society feel disoriented. They constitute a potential political force more readily available for riots or for the personal pursuits of demagogues than for the responsibilities of political democracy. Here too, the traditional, conservative cacique is only making way for the demagogic boss who inherits his followers.

In addition, at least in the more advanced Latin American countries, the wealthy and educated political forces of an industrial society, the forces of the era of the organizers, are arising. These new, essentially urban, political forces are those of the middle classes and of an embryonic, stabilized proletariat. While united in a common desire for rapid economic development and fired by intransigeant nationalism, their members disagree over the choice between the liberal methods of the Western democracies or the authoritarian methods of the peoples' democracies. Thus, side by side with surviving old political forces are new ones found in countries long since developed.

There are several reasons why these heterogeneous forces are difficult to discipline for an orderly political life. Not only does their very number multiply the chances for disagreements, but even worse, these political forces, created at different periods, are dealing with different problems and often even operate in different social groupings. They have a hard time coming directly to grips with one another. Because these political forces are divergent rather than antagonistic, because each opposes only its counterpart in the same society and the same period, political life is incoherent. The most unlikely conflicts and alliances can appear and change abruptly according to whether the internal conflicts within each society or the conflicts between the diverse societies take precedence.

The large number of possible combinations makes political life extraordinarily active, but forces that are too divergent tend to paralyze one another. None is powerful enough to seize power for any length of time through regular democratic means. Each must enter into purely tactical alliances, none of which is rational, but none of which is impossible. These forces tend to avoid rather than confront one another. Victories, which under the existing democratic institutions can only be won by coalitions of the moment, are immediately challenged by other coalitions, and none of the fundamental economic and social problems are really resolved by peaceful means.

This impotence of political forces operating through the normal channels of elections and parliamentary majorities offers the opportunity for and raises the temptation of illegality. Misuse of presidential power, conservative or revolutionary dictatorships, and, even more often, military intervention are the various forms of illegality.

8. Caciquismo and Caudillismo

After independence, in the nineteenth century the national sentiment that inspired the liberators could only spread very slowly in Latin America since the populations were too dispersed, too ignorant, and were composed of races and cultures that were too heterogeneous. Within the former Spanish and Portuguese empires, the social organization consisted of a scattering of little groups, closed in on themselves, whose chiefs enjoyed a large amount of de facto autonomy. The only thing that had united them was their common submission to authorities sent over from the mother country. Once independence had been achieved, there was nothing left to unite them other than their common resentment of those who had dominated them. Doubtless, attachment to Spain and Portugal, kindled by the closeness of the United States, constituted a tie for people who were, or thought they were, of Iberian stock, but this link had no meaning for the oppressed masses, who were mainly of Amerindian, African, or mestizo origin. It was not the Latin American countries which became independent between 1810 and 1825, but prominent figures and small communities—first of all the cities, where the citizens meeting in assemblies had repudiated Spanish sovereignty, but also large landholders, heads of clans, and leaders of gangs.

Unleashing of Political Forces During the Critical Period

During the colonial period, the home government had, somehow or other, counterbalanced the anarchic tendencies inherent in a society whose constituent elements were too isolated and too self-sufficient. But the distant monarchy had not been as efficient in America as it had been in Europe in controlling a different form of feudalism. The authority of the home country, which disappeared with independence, left only a multitude of aristocrats. In the void created by the disappearance of this authority, all of Spanish America went through a period when centrifugal forces tended to provoke an endless parceling of territories into small sovereignties. It was a "critical period" in the sense in which the term might be used in United States history to refer to the period from 1782 to 1787, when it seemed that the thirteen independent but disunited colonies were going to founder in an anarchy which, to the isolated pioneers of the West, seemed instead to be true liberty.

Portuguese America escaped that critical period because the fabric of the state had not been destroyed. Independence did not do away with the monarchy but on the contrary brought it closer to the people by "brazilianizing" it. Brazil in 1822 was not a nation any more than the Spanish American territories were, but it did have a Brazilian political organ. It was not a matter of creating Brazil, for the borders existed, but rather of keeping it from disintegrating—a much easier task which was helped by the existence of a definite administrative groundwork, a relatively structured one as compared to the Spanish territories which surrounded it. The centrifugal forces were as strong as elsewhere but they had not been released in the same way as in Spanish America.

Several of the liberators of Spanish America had well understood the value of monarchy in bringing together divergent political forces and making them participate in building the modern countries they dreamed of. In Argentina and Mexico, thought was given to selecting kings, but the American climate of the nineteenth century was not receptive to monarchy and the attempts were not successful, either with the people or with the possible candidates.

The administrative structures needed to extend the central sovereignty were also lacking. The most tempting territorial units were those provided by the main colonial administrative divisions: viceroyalties, captaincies-general, audiencias. These generally corresponded to natural geographic boundaries or at least to the zones of influence of the cities—Buenos Aires, Lima, Bogotá, Mexico City. But these structures, in which the independence movement had been organized, were not recognized by the people because they were not accompanied by any national spirit.

In the end, by and large the divisions followed natural borders and colonial administrative structures despite the efforts of some individuals to gain sovereignty over domains of their own. Some audiencias and natural regions were divided, and one man put his stamp on a country, as Artigas on Uruguay, Francia on Paraguay, and Carrera on Guatemala. Many other ambitions were frustrated, generally because they collided with stronger and cleverer ones. In Argentina the provinces of La Rioja under Facundo Quiroga and of Santa Fe under Estanislao López might have become independent states like Paraguay or Uruguay had their leaders not come up against Rosas, an abler adversary. Attempts at regional independence occurred in Colombia and Mexico. Quito and Guayaquil in Ecuador had the greatest trouble in remaining united, and even in Brazil, Rio Grande do Sul and perhaps São Paulo toyed with the idea of secession.

Under these conditions, the nationalist ideologies which exercised a powerful attraction over the liberators who led the independence movement were not a sufficient counterbalance to the centrifugal drives resulting from the social structure, for the reason that nationalism had no basis in either territorial or demographic structure. The independence movement professed allegiance to nationalism because it arose at the beginning of the nineteenth century in a society whose elites were part of all the intellectual movements of the North Atlantic world. Since in Latin America there were no nations as yet, this abstract nationalism was in search of a body in which to materialize.

Premature Ideal of Latin American Unity

The example of the United States helped lead this disembodied nationalism to the idea—certainly an unrealistic one at that time—of a great Latin American or at least Spanish American nation. Nationalist ideology, by aiming at such a mammoth structure, lost its effectiveness. This left more freedom to the divergent forces which aimed at subdividing Spanish America into estates and free cities under the cloak of a vague federalism. Bolívar, the liberator who tried to be the least doctrinaire, was one of the least realistic in this respect and stubbornly tried to realize his dream of a Latin American nation. The Confederation of Great Colombia in which he attempted, from 1821 and 1830, to unite Ecuador, Colombia, and Venezuela, foundered almost as soon as it was put together. The small Central American Confederation, which corresponded to more genuine needs, lasted only from 1821 to 1839.

The ideal of Latin American solidarity as expressed by a federation has not been abandoned since independence. It is a powerful ideal which has always played an important role in the behavior of the Latin American nations toward foreign countries, particularly the United States. Up to now, however, it has had no practical effects within Latin America itself. Today it is no longer impossible that plans for Latin American integration are on the way to fruition. This is because the common market agreed upon in Montevideo has appealed to the same economic motives that made the United States federation possible, but which were alien to purely agricultural Latin America in the first half of the nineteenth century. At that time, it was not a matter of achieving the federation of Latin American nations, but of creating these nations in the first place. The surprising thing is, not that the Spanish territories split into so many sovereign states when they became independent, but rather that the parceling stopped where it did.

Prenational Political Forces at Independence

The first task for Spanish America was to create states. These had to be built with political forces that dated back to a period when the states did not exist. Almost all of these forces aimed at breaking up society:

(1) The strongest and most widespread political forces, and probably also the most dangerous, were those of a multitude of feudal domains, namely the latifundios. The landowners, who already enjoyed de facto autonomy, often ex-

pressed their desire for order but were not at all disposed to submit to authority.

(2) The political forces of the cities were the only ones likely to promote national integration because they were unwilling to accept the splitting up of the country for the benefit of the rural feudal lords. They were even less willing to accept this than the medieval European cities had been five centuries earlier, because these nineteenth-century Latin American cities were the outposts of a vigorous foreign capitalism.

(3) There were also indigenous communities which had preserved their pre-Columbian organization in villages or in clans, although, except in Mexico, they played only a sporadic role in the nineteenth century. These were forces that generally resisted rather than acted, but more active forces were able to use them for their own political ends.

(4) Finally, there were very powerful forces in the asocial groups that arose because of isolation. These consisted of adventurers of all kinds—Indians, Africans, half-breeds who were unwilling to accept servitude—and above all the herders of the regions of extensive cattle-raising, the gauchos in the south and the *llaneros* in the north. There were also soldiers of the armies of the first half of the nineteenth century. All semi-bandits living outside the law, they were to Latin America what the nomads were for the sedentary peasants and townspeople of the Near East. These were the barbarians of Latin America who often pillaged and imposed dictators.

All these political forces of independent America, with the occasional exception of the urban forces, followed lines dictated by personal loyalties. Each group blindly obeyed its hereditary or self-appointed chief. Despite their different backgrounds and use of power, the latter depending on whether these political chiefs were people of substance or adventurers, they are usually called caciques, a title the Spaniards gave to the Indians chiefs. In Brazil the term *coroneis* (colonels) is preferred.

Caciquismo and Coronelismo

Caciquismo in Spanish America (coronelismo in Portuguese America) is the underlying phenomenon that controlled all of Latin America's political life in the nineteenth century. Although it is now on the decline, caciquismo has nevertheless left traces in the archaic segment of the dualistic society where it is closely tied to the isolation and continuance of the latifundios. These remnants still influence national political life except in a few countries, such as Argentina and Uruguay, which are too urbanized for the caciques to retain great authority. It is impossible, even today, to understand the nature of Latin American political problems without taking into account the effects of the long reign of the caciques.

During almost all of the nineteenth century Latin America, with the exception of Argentina, remained essentially rural, and the rural populations were directly or indirectly under the authority of the latifundios. Outside the cities, the real economic, social, and political authority was a personal one exercised over a village, a piece of land, a clan, a gang, or even an army. For professional soldiers lacking any national feeling and in the service of weak states, the general was often a cacique whose personal authority was all that counted. Feudal caciques on the latifundios, tribal caciques among the Indians, condottieri-caciques in the armies and also among the outlaws, all made free use of their followers for their own personal ends and those of the group. The cacique owed his followers protection and his followers owed him loyalty, whether he called on them to revolt or to vote for him.

In this prenational type of society the supreme social virtue was not patriotism, but loyalty toward the chief; rather, patriotism in that society took the form of loyalty to the group and its chief. Moreover, the cacique who wanted to be sovereign in his domain did not lack the means of forcing obedience and punishing those who refused it. The history of Latin America is full of atrocities—the punishment of treason against the political chief—as well as of acts of generosity by the chief toward his faithful followers. Even today local political chiefs sometimes entrust their henchmen with summary executions in order to remind their followers to be faithful, and in some countries either the weakness of the government or its remoteness allows them to do so with impunity.

As long as caciquismo prevailed, the recognized effect of the conquest of power, whether through violence or by election, was the exploitation of this power for the benefit of the victorious group and its chief. When conquest was achieved by violence, this meant looting by the victorious troops. When power was gained by election it meant free dipping into the public till. Of course that form of personal power did not exclude enlightened despotism, and it would be easy to name numerous rulers who came to power in Latin America thanks to the loyalty of their personal following, but who rose above their selfish interests and steadfastly worked for their country's economic development and national integration. But even in such cases, a power founded on the rights and obligations of personal followers excluded efficient and honest administration in the sense in which it is understood in the modern nation-state. The enlightened and disinterested cacique could overlook his personal interests, but not those of his following. His intentions might have been honest, but he had to pursue them by means which, in a national society, are dishonest.

The effect of caciquismo was inevitably to weaken the authority of the state, and unless a strong force was capable of controlling caciquismo, it tended to split up authority just as feudalism had done in Europe. *Caudillismo,* the dictatorship of a cacique who was stronger than the others, has generally been an effective if brutal and clumsy instrument which started imposing national control over the caciques.

From Caciquismo to Caudillismo

Nowhere in Spanish America could central authority regain control of the land without the intervention of a caudillo at some point. Only Brazil, thanks to the monarchy, escaped caudillismo on the national level. Nevertheless, it did experience it on a regional level, particularly in the state of Rio Grande do Sul, whose political life was influenced by the proximity of Uruguay and Argentina. That Brazilian state had the same customs that were part of the way of life of the unruly gauchos.

No aspect of political life in Spanish America has been subjected to more surveys than caudillismo, the dictatorship or merely the dominance of a man who leans on a personal following. In the past, even the recent past, caudillismo has triumphed so often that many analysts regard it as the most salient political characteristic of Latin America. It is enough to recall the case of Venezuela—almost a caricature, it is true. From 1830—the date of the dissolution of Great Colombia, which opened the way for Venezuela's existence as a nation—until 1935, one caudillo was always immediately replaced by another. Páez, who ruled the country from 1830 to 1846, was replaced by the Monagas brothers (1846–1861), then Páez again (1861–1863), Guzmán Blanco (1870–1887), Crespo (1887–1898), Castro (1899–1908), and finally Gómez (1908–1935). In the course of a century the regime of the caudillos was interrupted only during the seven years from 1863 to 1870, but these were seven years of civil war.

In their search for an explanation, most students of this form of personal power have tended to ascribe it to the specific temperament of Spanish Americans. It does not seem, however, that caudillismo is a political phenomenon peculiar to Spanish America; rather it is the Spanish American form of a general phenomenon. In fact, wherever feudal structures were not brought under the control of the hierarchy and legitimacy of monarchy, private wars and the ambitions of the *condottieri* have spread unrest. During the first seventy-three years of Uruguay's existence until the advent of José Batlle y Ordóñez in 1903, the interminable civil wars were typical private wars, even though they were disguised under the then fashionable labels of liberalism versus conservatism. The caciques used those labels to cover their personal rivalries. What is peculiar to Latin America is that the condottieri and the feudal lords fighting for power have often tried to claim affiliation with democratic ideologies.

As an excellent observer noted in 1895,[1] caudillismo results from the political immaturity of Spanish American societies in the nineteenth century rather than from congenital political incapacity. Under the influence of the political ideologies prevailing in Europe in the nineteenth century and the prestige of representative democracy, Latin America was forced to base legitimacy of power on the will of the people as expressed through elections, although she was not yet freed from feudal structures and allegiances. The legitimacy that the govern-

---

[1] William Dalton Babington, *Fallacies of Race Theories* (London and New York, 1895).

ments invoked was not recognized by all segments of society. In the prenational structure, which has persisted long after independence, this imported legitimacy has been convincing only for the small elite that borrowed it from abroad, and this only to the extent that such legitimacy has been profitable for it. Elections show only how homogeneous each group is, and how loyal the members are to their leaders. Hence, elections are not likely to make either the defeated groups or their leaders accept the results if these are prejudicial to their interests or their ambitions.

Political struggles occur between domains, clans, villages, and gangs which can count on the blind allegiance of their members. Their only purpose is to show the power of these groups and their leaders and to ensure that political power will be exploited in their own interest. Because there is still no national consciousness in the budding state, internal political struggles are akin to dissensions among nations rather than among citizens of one nation. Since the supreme interest is that of the group rather than of the state, defeat in the conventional form of combat, namely election, does not mean that the group that believes it is the strongest must eschew other weapons. It is almost a patriotic duty toward the group to use every means to obtain victory, and if the results of the election prove or are likely to prove unfavorable to the group's vital interests, resort to brute force to challenge them is used without further ado. If it is necessary to resort to violence, there is certainly no dearth of pretexts for contesting the validity of the elections, such as pressures and electoral frauds which have interfered or might interfere.

The use of force to secure power, then, has long seemed as legitimate as the ballot. For a long time too it has been facilitated by the absence of a truly national public force and by the tendency of personal followers to turn into private armies. The unsophisticated combatants could understand the nature and objectives of battles far better than those of conventional election procedures. Immediate rewards, such as cutting the enemy's throat and looting his property, were also much better appreciated.

In an open test of strength the condottiere, whether man of substance or adventurer, who had distinguished himself by courage or ruse, could extend his personal influence over a vast province or the entire country. This gave him the authority of a lord, leader of a gang, or chief of a tribe, quite different from that of the elected politician. He could exercise his authority as arbitrarily as he had formerly done over his small territory or gang. The cacique became a caudillo, and the republic of notables gave way to caesarism.

The mechanics of the transformation from cacique into caudillo have often been described since 1842 when Sarmientos wrote his classic work, *Facundo,* about the Argentine caudillo, Facundo Quiroga, the ally and unlucky rival of Rosas. Quite the opposite of what is often imagined, the caudillo is not necessarily a soldier, and few of them have been professional military men. Regardless of his background, the caudillo must be capable of leading his followers in battle, and for that reason more than one landholder, lawyer, and more than one bandit as well, has come to power with the title of general, won in a revolution.

Nature of the Caudillos' Power

The caudillo is a revolutionary leader to whom others have submitted only for the purpose of overthrowing the existing government; hence he is rarely in full control immediately after seizing national power. Until those who helped him take power have been eliminated, or unless they are satisfied with their share of the spoils, the reign of the caudillo is beset by intrigues. No domination has been more absolute than that of Rosas over all of Argentina, but this was true only after the assassination in 1835 of his chief ally Facundo Quiroga, the gaucho caudillo, master of the provinces of La Rioja and Córdoba, who never resigned himself to taking second place. Porfirio Díaz ended up by governing Mexico without any rivals from 1876 to 1910, but to reach that point he first had to gain the allegiance of the local caciques by distributing honors and bribes. He used the police to compromise those who refused to submit, or he even had them summarily executed. Cipriano Castro, after imposing his dictatorship on Venezuela in 1899, was unwise enough not to get rid of Gómez, who had been his chief ally. In 1908, while the caudillo was in Paris, Gómez seized the opportunity and let him know that he was not to return to Venezuela. Gómez was wiser. He ruled for twenty-seven years until his death, trusting in no one but his relatives and his faithful following of half-savage herders, the llaneros.

The illegal origin and the very nature of their power almost inevitably force caudillos to resort to even more violence in maintaining power than in obtaining it. Even the best of them have tended to become tyrants. It has been all the more difficult for caudillos to avoid making themselves feared, since democratic ideology in nineteenth-century Latin America prevented them from holding absolute power by institutional sanction. Generally to gain power in the first place, the caudillo has to affirm his desire to reestablish the genuine interplay of democracy politics subverted by his opponents. He has taken up arms in the name of freedom, he claims, because legality has been violated, the elections have been rigged or are about to be, or the officials are corrupt. The first job of the dictator, then, must be to reestablish democratic institutions in all their purity and to promise to insert into the constitution the most meticulous guarantees against the exercise of personal power and against the infringement of the rights of man.

Porfirio Díaz thought it wise to profess such respect for constitutional forms that, when his first term ended in 1880, he refused to run again. He had Manuel González named in his place. This, however, did not keep him from ruling Mexico himself for another thirty years. The use of straw men is a necessary formality to keep from breaking the rule against immediate reelection, a rule which exists almost everywhere in Latin America. The cleverest caudillos are careful to avail themselves of such devices. Close relatives and intimate friends are the safest, and Trujillo did not fail to use them in the Dominican Republic. But there are not always relatives close enough or followers loyal enough to make it safe not to keep an eye on them. The separation of powers called for by the constitutions, which are almost always presidential constitutions, must also be respected. Favorable elections and obedience on the part of elected representatives are also indispensable if executive power is not to be curtailed by congress.

The caudillo has to pay lip service to the forms of representative democracy. Hence his authority depends on the use of illegal means of coercion over the very people with whom he must pretend he is sharing power. It is difficult not to resort to corruption, but corruption itself is rarely enough to reduce opponents to impotence and force the faithful to obey. Caudillismo then ends up by resting on the despotism of an omnipresent police force and often, too, on henchmen, whom it is easier to disown. Rosas' gauchos in Argentina and Gómez's llaneros in Venezuela knew very well indeed how to make anyone who disobeyed disappear without leaving any doubt about where the punishment came from, but also without anyone's being able to prove anything.

Although caudillismo always leads to despotism and often to terror, it is still not possible to condemn outright its role in the national evolution of Spanish American countries. Caudillismo is a general social phenomenon, the result of social structures and ideologies that prevailed in all the Spanish American countries at one time, although each caudillo is a personality distinct from all the others. Thus it would be useless to sketch the portrait of the typical caudillo and paint it black or white. Latin America, which has had so many of them, has had all types. Different because of their racial or social background, different in their ideologies—progressive or reactionary—wise men or illiterates, some caudillos were agents of progress for their countries, others ruined them; still others, the greater number perhaps, did their countries a great deal of harm but at the same time a little bit of good.

All the social strata of Latin America have been represented among the caudillos: Francia (1811–1840) in Paraguay was a cultivated, paternalistic aristocrat; Santa Anna (1828–1844) in Mexico was a wealthy Creole, charming and volatile, who dreamed of military glory; Santa Cruz (1829–1839) in Bolivia was a professional officer, honest but conceited, who believed himself heir of the Incas through his mother's line; Portales (1830–1837) in Chile was a rich businessman, concerned with order and prosperity; Rafael Carrera (1838–1865) in Guatemala was a mystical and illiterate Indian; Juárez (1857–1872) in Mexico was also an Indian, but highly educated and liberal; Melgarejo (1864–1871) in Bolivia was an illiterate, alcoholic mestizo; García Moreno (1869–1875) in Ecuador was a very learned and pious professor; Rufino Barrios (1872–1895) in Guatemala was a general, but Fulgencio Batista (1934–1959) in Cuba was a noncommissioned officer in revolt against the generals; Guzmán Blanco (1870–1890) in Venezuela was a cultivated gentleman, but Cipriano Castro (1899–1908), who succeeded him, was an illiterate cowboy.

Some of these caudillos were nothing but bloody bandits who brought only pillaging and death to their countries. The perfect example is the Bolivian Melgarejo. The second of the Lópezes (Francisco Solano) who ruled Paraguay from 1862 to 1870 was a cruel megalomaniac; and more recently, it would be hard to discover in Estrada Cabrera's government in Guatemala (1898–1920) anything but extortion of all kinds. Juárez on the contrary, although he may have become an authoritarian dictator in the last years of his life, was the defender of the Indians and the liberator of Mexico, where he has remained a national hero. So has Artigas (1810–1820), the gaucho founder of Uruguay, although his role and especially his methods are debatable.

Although the very nature of their power may have led the caudillos to confuse the patrimony of their nation with their own, there have been thoroughly honest caudillos. Nor are examples of the most cynical corruption among them lacking. When Gómez's long dictatorship in Venezuela ended in 1935, it was said that he, who had begun life as a cowboy, had left over a billion dollars to the ninety children born out of wedlock whom he had legally acknowledged. There are also hundreds of millions of dollars that the members of the Trujillo family divided among themselves after his assassination in 1961, not to mention the lands he had bought or confiscated and the interests he had held in all the important business concerns. It is wise not to place too much faith in the figures on misappropriations published after a dictator's downfall. Nevertheless, public funds do tend to be treated as legitimate spoils when power is seized by the head of a clan or gang and when he and his followers place their own interests above those of the state. This is the way Zelaya (1893–1909) in Nicaragua and Machado (1925–1933) in Cuba cynically enriched themselves during their stay in power.

But it would be unfair to generalize, and the various caudillos differ widely from one another with respect to honesty. It is said that Guzmán Blanco took his personal cut on all transactions but exacted the most scrupulous honesty from others, and he gave Venezuela a remarkable administration. Vargas, on the other hand, who had been a caudillo in the state of Rio Grande do Sul before becoming a labor party leader when the 1950 Brazilian election returned him to power, made systematic use of corruption as a means of weakening the opposition and buttressing loyalty to his cause, but carefully refrained from taking anything for himself. Lastly, certain caudillos used their power to stop plundering by the previous government. García Moreno may certainly be blamed for having turned Ecuador into an intolerant theocracy, but no one can dispute that he sought to foster economic development without drawing any personal profit from it. Ubico (1931–1944) may be reproached for despotism, but he is acknowledged to have given Guatemala one of its best fiscal administrations.

Caudillismo's Reaction Against Upper-class Conservatism

No uniform political coloration may be ascribed to caudillismo, and neither should it be regarded as an instrument of conservatism or of social reform. In Guatemala, the dictatorship of Rafael Carrera was blindly conservative and certainly retarded political and social evolution, just as the Francia dictatorship did in Paraguay. Quite often, on the other hand, the caudillos have been great reformers. Juárez is the prototype of the enlightened revolutionary caudillo who freed his country from a conservative clerical government. Tomás Guardia (1870–1882), one of the few Costa Rican caudillos, put an end to the hegemony of the upper class. O'Higgins (1817–1823) tried prematurely to fight against clericalism in Chile. In Venezuela, Guzmán Blanco removed education from Church control and tried to liquidate the huge holdings of the Church. Rufino Barrios (1871–1895) did the same in Guatemala. Even a caudillo like Santa Anna, who made questionable use of his power, abolished slavery in Mexico at a time when the United States was still trying to extend it; it was also a caudillo, Ramón Castilla (1855–1862), who put an end to slavery in Peru.

It has often happened that caudillos who seized power to restore the threatened social order and who imposed very conservative regimes eventually paved the way for the transformation of their country through their policy of economic development. That was most certainly the case with García Moreno in Ecuador, who stripped non-Catholics of their rights as citizens, reestablished ecclesiastical courts, and accorded more privileges to the Vatican than Philip II had done, but who also modernized agriculture, built roads and schools, attracted foreign business, and thus began to draw Ecuador out of the Middle Ages. Porfirio Díaz in Mexico is an even more striking example. He took from the Indians all the advantages they had acquired under the Juárez government, but left economic policy to Limantour and his group of positivist engineers, thus paving the way for the modernization of Mexico and the social revolution which was to drive Díaz from power in 1910. To a lesser extent, this was also true of the recent Trujillo dictatorship, which was particularly cruel and corrupt but under which the Dominican Republic made unquestioned progress in the economic sphere.

Although some caudillos have been conservative and others reformist, caudillismo is nevertheless most often characterized by its opposition to government by the upper class. This form of caesarism is not necessarily progressive, but with a few exceptions it is almost necessarily demagogic. Local caciques would not have turned into national caudillos if they had not possessed a powerful appeal for the masses, especially the more disinherited who formed their following and provided their soldiers. It should also be noted that the extortion which a number of caudillos practiced to gain power, perpetuate it, and enrich themselves and their followers generally affected only a small segment of the population. The victims were the landed aristocracy and the liberal professions, persons of wealth or education who participated in political life. Technocracies such as the one established during the regime of Porfirio Díaz, in which the engineers, imbued with the mystique of economic growth, lacked patience with the ignorance and indolence of the Mexican Indians, were an exception. As a rule, the wretched peons were not the ones who had their goods confiscated or who were deprived of freedom of speech or thought, since their own masters restricted it more effectively than the most authoritarian of dictators. Nor were they deprived of political freedoms they had never possessed.

Rebellion against the despotic power of the caudillos has come from the upper class more often than from the masses; wherever traces of caudillismo are found today, those who rise against it are generally members of the middle class, particularly the students, and sometimes the military. Thus, caesarism in Latin America has met the same fate as under the Roman emperors, when neither the common people nor the aliens complained of imperial despotism, but only the patricians. The masses in Latin America often regarded themselves as better off under the despotic but demagogic domination of the caudillo than under the legal liberal government of the conservative upper class.

Role of Caudillismo in the Formation of Latin American Nations

Insofar as it seems possible to discover a general trend in the diverse effects of caudillismo, it may be stated that in every country of Latin America except Brazil the caudillo played a necessary role at a given moment in history. He was the one who reunited territories. His role was not unlike the one the monarchies played in Europe, extending central authority during the feudal era and laying the foundations of nation-states. It is also similar to the role that dictators, official parties, and military juntas play in the developing countries today.

Brazil, where the emperor-philosopher came of age in 1840, avoided the era of caudillos because of the monarchy, but all the other countries of Latin America experienced it after independence. An arbitrary power was needed to force the formation of nations whose birth had begun in the name of freedom but was rarely completed in freedom. In essence, caudillismo was a centralizing force. Often enough, in order to find allies who would permit him to take power, the caudillo had to invoke democracy and become the defender of local liberties which were at that time identified with democracy. As soon as he was installed in power he had to subdue the feudal elements and set up a strong central government to preserve this power.

Rosas is the most typical example: he could never have become the national caudillo of Argentina without presenting himself to the regional caciques, whose backing he needed, as the staunch defender of local autonomy against the centralizing ambitions of the middle class of Buenos Aires then trying to dominate national government. "Long live the federation! Death to the savage, loathsome unitarists!" was a war cry that Rosas never disavowed. But once in possession of power, Rosas had to subdue the local caciques and the regional caudillos to whom he had promised freedom. When he was finally overthrown in 1852, there was an Argentine Republic united in its present form. What was left of federalism was a system of decentralized administration, but it was no longer a threat to national unity. Although Rosas, the modern Caligula, may have been the most stupidly ruthless of the caudillos, historians hesitate to condemn him outright because he did create an Argentine Republic.

García Calderón [2] and many others firmly assert that caudillismo was a necessity and a factor in progress. Caudillismo was at its height from 1830 to 1860, at a time when the leaders of independence had just disappeared from the political scene and when the weakness of what they had created was most obvious. Just as Rosas did in Argentina but without his ferocity, Portales in Chile (1830–1837), Santander in Colombia (1832–1836), Páez in Venezuela (1830–1837), and Santa Anna in Mexico (1828–1844) were caudillos who gathered the scattered fragments of the former Spanish empire into vast states and forced divergent political forces into national structures.

Almost all the countries of Latin America had to go through the caudillo stage in order to become nations, and the upheavals of that period were not completely senseless. The Latin American states were not wrought out of feudal anarchy without a great deal of violence and extortion. But because this was the nineteenth century, the violence was anachronistic and a lasting discredit to Latin American political behavior. However, just because the elimination of feudalism and the

[2] Garcia Calderón, *Les démocraties latines de l'Amérique* (Paris, 1912).

extension of national sovereignty began five or six centuries earlier in Europe, it should not be forgotten that the modern states of western Europe owe their existence to violence no less cruel and longer lasting.

These first years of independent political life should not be judged from the point of view of the North Atlantic countries. Instead, they should be evaluated in terms of the very archaic economic and social structures inherited from Iberian colonization. It then seems amazing that the process of forming a modern state, which took several centuries in Europe, could have progressed so far in thirty or forty years, at least in several large countries which contain the greater part of the Latin American population. Moreover, in other parts of the world many of the territories that gained independence in the twentieth century have been unable to unite their heterogeneous social groupings into nations by any method other than dictatorship. Even when these regimes hide under the machine of a single party or claim socialist legitimacy, they are nothing more than the equivalent, a century later, of the regimes of arbitrary personal power of caudillismo.

End of the Caudillos

The caudillo system has occupied such an important place in the political life of Latin America that in the presence of dictatorships that have sprung up there again and again, observers often continue to talk about caudillos. But the time of the caudillos is past. Chile, Argentina, and Colombia were the first Latin American countries to emerge from that era, around the middle of the nineteenth century. Uruguay did not really leave it until the end of the nineteenth century and then did so very quickly, when José Batlle y Ordóñez became president in 1903. The death pangs of caudillismo were particularly long and painful in Mexico, which was dominated by it until the revolution of 1910. Caudillismo, particularly that of the condottieri, lingered there within the revolutionary movement until Calles was eliminated in 1934. Even after 1950 in the Dominican Republic the Trujillo dictatorship had many of the characteristics of caudillismo, and so does the dictatorship of the Somoza family in Nicaragua in a less crude form.

9. Survival of Prenational Political Forces and the Traditional Political Parties

In exceptional cases, decadent forms of caudillismo have been known to recur in small countries where armies of a few thousand men—police forces, really—were one individual's private domain and were used by him to impose his dictatorship. This seems to be so in Haiti now and in some other countries in recent years.

On the whole, however, national integration of Latin American countries is too far advanced to permit caudillismo's survival in its older forms, solely on the basis of allegiance from servants, the clan, or the gang. The emergence of national feeling, the broadening of the body politic through the growth of the middle classes, the progress of public education, and the urban proletariat's fresh awareness of social problems no longer allow a caudillo and his allies to dominate national elections and assume power by peaceful means. Neither can a caudillo, helped only by his armed followers, seize power by force. In the twentieth century, physical power is in the hands of the regular officer corps instead of caciques. Private armies no longer exist, and the regular national armies are too securely organized to allow a caudillo to turn them into a personal army.

The dictatorships that have replaced the caudillos can no longer remain purely personal in modernized states whose problems are national in scope. Concentration of power in a single person in present authoritarian Latin American regimes comes about because of conflicts between parties, social classes, and ideologies. These regimes are the product of new political forces in developing societies, whereas caudillismo was the product of archaic political forces. Present-day dictatorships are mainly the result of contradictions between these new political forces and the lingering, weakened old ones.

The Legacy of Caudillismo

The era of caudillismo may be over, at least in most of Latin America, but old customs have left lasting traces in the political life of countries it dominated for so long.

In all likelihood, the long rule of caciquismo made it more difficult to dispel the belief prevalent in Latin America (rightly or not) that too many politicians regard the acquisition of wealth as the normal by-product of power. It is very difficult to detect how much truth there is in these assertions, since politicians everywhere tend to be accused of corruption. Without even mentioning Trujillo, it does seem that the new brand of dictators, like Perón, invariably made fortunes while in power in a manner that is exceptional elsewhere.

It is also probable that the caudillo tradition increased the need to give personal character to political struggles. Even to this day, in countries as advanced as Brazil, Argentina, or Mexico, ideas and programs tend to be presented in a personal form. Perón's regime in Argentina was never called *Justicialismo* as its partisans wished, but *Peronismo*. Vargas' in Brazil was dubbed *Getulismo* (Getulio Vargas) before it was renamed *Travaillismo*. Later, *Janismo* (Janio Quadros) was very popular in Brazil. In Mexico, the official party (PRI) is divided into two factions personified by Alemán and Cárdenas. Even in Cuba, where the Communist way of thinking has asserted itself, the regime is personified—it is Castroism rather than Communism. The claim that personalization of the regime is typical of Latin American political life does seem an exaggeration, nonetheless. There are too many striking examples of it elsewhere at the present time, not only in the various developing countries, but even in those where high stages of development were reached long ago.

Remnants of Caciquismo

The persistence of archaic political forces in present-day Latin America manifests itself primarily in the large role that caciquismo is still playing, even in countries sufficiently advanced to prevent personal dictatorships by caudillos. Today caciquismo is only a local vestige of the past in backward rural areas, although in many countries these areas contain a large part of the population.

In the archaic segment of society of the unevenly developed countries where dualism is present, rural landowners often retain their hold over those who have remained their subjects. Thus, latifundio owners can exert very strong pressure when most of their dependents have only precarious tenure over the land. Wherever caciquismo lingers on, electoral processes are bound to be distorted, and they give the chiefs a greater political authority than their actual strength would warrant. Universal suffrage, especially, enables caciquismo to perpetuate itself locally, although it is doomed to disappear with social evolution. The importance of the vestiges of caciquismo in the countryside is the subject of a new classic survey by Victor Nunez Leal.[1]

Reaffirmation of Upper-Class Electoral Power Through Universal Suffrage

In an advanced society, the middle classes and an increasingly sophisticated proletariat represent millions of individuals eager to take part in political life. In an archaic society, on the other hand, only a few thousand aristocrats are politically active. Universal suffrage, however, enables these rural aristocrats to win the majority of votes locally and to constitute large minorities nationally, thanks to their personal following. The result is the same as if the aristocrats, blindly followed by their supporters, actually had a large margin of votes. Their authority is seldom wide enough or secure enough, it is true, to enable them to gain power nationally; but in many countries local remnants of caciquismo are sufficiently widespread to

[1] Victor Nunez Leal, *Coronelismo, enxada e voto: O municipío e o regime representativo no Brasil* (Rio de Janeiro, 1948).

compel the political parties opposing them in the national assemblies to make deals with these dispensers of rural patronage. Even the most progressive parties may be forced to stop demanding reforms of the social structure, in particular the elimination of the latifundios, even though reforms are needed for the country's development.

The urban classes, even though they are still a national minority, do not question their right to govern because they know they represent the future. The results of universal suffrage tend to disappoint them; its advocates believed it was a tool of social progress as well as of political freedom. The urban classes see that it can be used instead to delay the liquidation of remnants of the past.

The resulting disenchantment is bound to hamper democratic institutions. Those who have been affected by propaganda from totalitarian regimes are prone to believe that representative democracy cannot hasten the transformation of archaic structures. Or, more often, advanced urban populations, still attached to democratic principles but unaware of the archaic nature of rural society, are convinced that, in order to produce such unexpected results, the elections could only have been dishonest. In either case, a revolution may seem desirable, either to end democracy, or to make it work.

Latin Americans are not the only ones to reach this conclusion. Many foreign observers, North Americans in particular, cannot understand how free elections under universal suffrage can possibly perpetuate the power of men they regard as reactionary exploiters whom everyone must hate. They wholeheartedly believe the contentions of the losers—that nothing but fraud can account for defeat. Belief in the value of the institutions of representative democracy, regardless of the structure of the societies in which they operate, has more than once led the United States astray in her policy toward underdeveloped countries. She has seen corruption in what was merely the true reflection of a society very different from her own.

The fact that in Latin America universal suffrage has often favored the most backward political elements in elections does not necessarily mean that the elections were dishonest. Conversely, if universal suffrage is to produce the same results in both developed and archaic societies, and within Latin America in both the backward countryside and the modern cities, pressure and some limitations of electoral freedom would be required. It is quite probable that if the official party had not controlled elections in Mexico there would have been many attempts by the reactionary voters after 1928 to bring the caciques back into power, while the most advanced elements would have resorted to force to prevent it. In the past few years, many peasants in Latin America have been rebelling against the power of the rural gentry, and things are beginning to change.

Rural Elections under Caciquismo

There is an old joke still going the rounds, and it is not always left in the past tense. It is about the political boss who before the elections hands out shoes for the right foot and promises the others only after the returns have come in. The decline of caciquismo, rather than its hold over the people, makes such a precaution necessary. Corruption in the form of selling votes to the highest bidder accompanies the disintegration of closed, isolated groups and the weakening of personal loyalties. A vote is for sale only if it is free. The homogeneous archaic communities provide the best opportunities for electoral fraud when they start disintegrating. The cacique can no longer depend on personal allegiance, but the state has not gained it completely as yet. It has to be bought with money or, more often, with promises.

As long as the cacique remains the real master of his domain and political parties have to abide by his wishes, he has little to worry about because his dependents have everything to gain from his victory. The cacique does not have to buy his clients' votes himself, but he is well placed to negotiate with the different parties about delivering the votes of the community he controls.

This does not mean, of course, that at election time the cacique does not offer gifts in kind or in cash. In the advanced society where national allegiances are supreme, this would indicate fraud and corruption; but in the archaic society it is only a legitimate token of the personal ties between the chief and his following. The cacique is not buying the votes; they are

his anyway. As a chief, he is merely running a community project. The gifts do play a role, but no more than they would on
the occasion of a wedding, a birthday, or Christmas.

The characteristics of an election campaign today in areas
where caciquismo still lingers—in this instance, Brazilian coronelismo—have been accurately described in a special issue
of the *Revista Brasileira de Estudos Políticos* [2] devoted to the
1958 elections. The authors of the various articles note that in
a large part of northeastern Brazil—Piauí, Sergipe, Ceará,
Pernambuco, Rio Grande do Norte—the latifundio owners
still control most votes although their authority has been
shaken, especially in the state of Pernambuco, because the
large city of Recife is a center of revolutionary ferment. Since
1958 the anti-landowner agrarian leagues of Francisco Julião
have gained great influence in Pernambuco, where a progressive party won the 1962 elections. But in the hinterland of
northeastern Brazil, caciquismo still persists and elections reflect this.

Francisco Ferreira de Castro in one of the articles of the
above-named journal [3] lists the coronel's commitments to voters:

The political bosses in the interior are burdened with the permanent expense of subsidizing the voters before, during, and after
the elections. Much of the assistance they provide personally
should in fact be dispensed by public powers in the form of welfare services. But in many *municípios* such services either do not
exist or are not properly run.

Some of the election expenses are for voter registration and
food and clothing deliveries, in addition to the expenses of the
precinct workers for the purchase of harmonicas, rifles, carbines,
sewing machines, and agricultural equipment.

Voter registration entails additional expenses besides the cost
of photographs that the electoral branch of the judiciary is supposed to pay for but cannot be depended on to do. It is axiomatic
that the voter feels obliged to vote for the man who arranged for
his registration. Therefore, the parties spend large sums for registration—sometimes over 100 or 200 cruzeiros per person. [At
the time the per capita income in those states ranged between

[2] *Revista Brasileira de Estudos Políticos,* April, 1960.
[3] "A campanha eleitoral de 1958 no Piauí," *Revista brasileira de
estudos políticos,* April, 1960, p. 28.

1,500 and 3,000 cruzeiros, but in the rural zones in the hinterland it was only a fraction of this.]

Transporting voters to the polls makes elections much more expensive today because motorized vehicles have to be used. Horses, and even walking in groups, were once acceptable. Now the voters expect trucks or jeeps, and this costs an average of 10,000 cruzeiros per day of election. Food for the voters and those who accompany them—an average of three persons per voter—is a large expense.

Clothing and shoes in varying quantities according to the municipality also cost a great deal.

This expensive service to their followers would be an unbearable burden for the caciques if they could not charge part to the public treasury in case of victory. Since the rural district controlled by the cacique cannot afford to pay out of its meager budget, the national government is called upon to do so.

Northeastern Brazil—the topic of the *Revista Brasileira* article—provides a striking example of the disastrous consequences of diverting public funds to pay off the voters. The region described is the dry zone of Brazil, subject to periodic famines which force part of the population to move away. The federal government has earmarked very large funds for drought control, dams, and reservoirs. All too often, political bosses have used the money instead to reward their followers by securing for them the equivalent of pensions for work of questionable value in drought control, allegedly performed on a regular basis. One major political problem in the region at the end of 1961 resulted from the federal government's attempt to take over the drought control program in order to avoid the diverting of funds and efforts. The local political bosses, on the other hand, were intent on remaining free to distribute the funds as they saw fit. The rejection by the Brazilian Senate of a law depriving drought profiteers of this privilege showed how influential the coroneis were in national political affairs as late as 1961. The same men were responsible for defeating the equitable, moderate agrarian reform bills drafted by the economist Celso Furtado.

Futility of Representative Democracy

In countries like Brazil, the preponderant type in Latin America, caciquismo survives only in the backward regions, and even there the cacique's power is being contested. It is still very strong nevertheless, not only directly in local politics but indirectly in national politics. Press notices, given the prominence of major news items, still appear occasionally during national election campaigns and announce that a certain family is supporting one of the parties; these are clear evidence of the strong ties among the families, clans, and voters.

National political life in Latin America is usually focused on urban problems. The numerical strength that caciquismo still has in representative democracy may remain relatively neutral in these matters. The caciques defend the most archaic, conservative interests, but they can do this only locally in a rural society of no interest to the advanced regions. Current social changes in the developed segment of national society do not immediately disturb the archaic communities. The caciques—who represent the remnants of feudalism—only ask the national government not to meddle in their own domain; in exchange for their neutrality in national politics, the caciques want the government to help them satisfy their personal clients by letting them share the spoils of political victory.

Political democracy based on universal suffrage cannot by itself hasten the evolution of archaic communities. Economic development is so narrowly circumscribed in Latin America that it takes too long for its benefits to reach the entire countryside. Hence the archaic social structures that preserve the caciques' power have to be attacked directly, first by dealing with their bulwark, the latifundios. It is difficult for the governments to make changes without limiting somewhat the classic forms of political democracy. Devices which seemingly most respect the forms do not necessarily correspond most closely to the spirit of those institutions, nor are they always the most effective.

Deals and Schemes

One arrangement allows the electoral process in each segment of society to run its course undisturbed. Elections produce different results according to the environment, but the forms of representative democracy are preserved and the constitutional requirements scrupulously obeyed. This is done by a tacit agreement between the political forces of the respective societies whereby each group is left in control of its own sphere. The political forces of the advanced society carry out the reforms they desire and are even supported in their endeavors by conservative rural political bosses. The advanced political groups only have to abstain from extending these reforms to the archaic society that is left under the authority of its traditional chiefs. The fact that these chiefs are elected serves as proof of legality. This is the most frequently used scheme. Despite its outward fairness, it is the least democratic in spirit and the most dangerous for national unity. Using it means accepting a dual society instead of trying to unite the two segments of society under a single authority. Far from being drawn together, each segment is left with its own institutions, thus perpetuating and intensifying the differences. One segment has progressive, often demagogic, governments; the other is ruled by the cacique and is a perfect example of conservatism. (See also chap. 4, the section on "Deepening Rural Isolation.")

Disenfranchising the Illiterates

A more obvious expedient, which might be justified in the name of democratic principles, is the literacy requirement. If strictly applied, this can be very effective in weakening the strength of the chiefs of the archaic society. Illiterate populations do not exactly correspond to the rural populations still ruled by landed gentry, but the two categories almost completely overlap, so that the populations not directly integrated into national society cannot take part in its political life, either. Disenfranchising the illiterates deprives the political bosses of archaic communities of their constituents' votes, thus increasing the margin of the advanced segment of society.

The new political forces may be given even more weight by lowering the voting age—which is often done. In countries such as Brazil where literacy is required for voting, 18-year-old secondary school students may be able to vote while countless countryside people, even heads of large households, are disenfranchised.

The extent to which the scales are weighted in favor of the advanced society is reflected by the picture in Brazil in the 1958 general elections. The population of voting age numbered 31 million, but since school attendance is rapidly increasing, illiterates were most numerous among the voting age group, and 17 million Brazilians over 18 years of age were barred by the literacy requirement. This of course was chiefly in the backward rural regions, where only 20 to 25 percent of the adults may thus be admitted to the polls. Such discrimination produces results similar to those of the first Soviet voting laws, which gave city dwellers a higher ratio of representatives than country people. Outwardly, the Latin American method is fairer, but in fact it is more discriminatory.

The disenfranchising of illiterates gives an appearance of legitimacy to the elimination of a large part of the electoral body. Even the staunchest advocates of universal suffrage in the advanced countries cannot object to it. But they do not stop to think that in societies where most countryside dwellers are illiterate and no attempt had been made to educate them, this method is tantamount to robbing them of citizenship.

Besides, the procedure is difficult to enforce honestly, and favors electoral fraud. It is known to have permitted discrimination against Negroes in the South of the United States. Literacy is always difficult to define, and any provisions against fraud—for instance, an independent electoral judiciary often used in Latin America—cannot always prevent the political boss from having his clients registered if he has taught them to trace their name, while those of his opponents are subjected to a stricter test. The government is then tempted to interpret the literacy provision according to the groups whose victory it desires.

Such discrimination, if strictly enforced, can restrict voting to members of the advanced society, and the formidable drawback of the method is to foster indifference of urban populations and governments toward backward countryside dwellers, who are treated as subjects rather than as citizens. When domination of the advanced society over the archaic society becomes legal, social dualism is allowed to continue. This hampers national integration, which requires assimilating the backward populations instead of barring them from national life.

Excluding backward peasants from national society by disenfranchising illiterates creates a new danger. The peasants become aware of the fact that they are being abandoned by the governments and also increasingly, by their political bosses, who have little incentive to spend money on clients who cannot vote anyway. This drives the peasants to resort to violence, since they cannot make themselves heard by voting.

Single or Official Party System

To give the vote to backward peasants who are accustomed to obey local chiefs and who still live outside the mainstream of society is to jeopardize national development. Either the peasants use their vote to help the ultraconservative gentry or, if freed from their traditional dependence, they use it to help the demagogues of the urban parties who pursue different goals. To deny the vote to backward peasants for these reasons is not only unfair but also dangerous, because the governments are only too prone to disregard their welfare.

A safer and more reliable method can be used to achieve the necessary hegemony of advanced society without neglecting development of the archaic society. This is the single party or the privileged official party system. Apart from Cuba, which is under a dictatorial regime, Mexico has been using it since 1929 and Bolivia since 1952. One party which enjoys official or actual monopoly substitutes its own control for that of the upper class. The vote of the Mexican countryside dweller, often an illiterate Indian lacking any notion of national politics, is guided by the officials of the PRI (Institutional Revolutionary Party). Although opposition parties are tolerated, individuals whose votes can be freely manipulated by the official party are so numerous that the party cannot be deprived of its actual monopoly.

This method of superseding the traditional chiefs of the archaic society curtails the proper operation of political democracy in Mexico more than it does in Brazil, where illiterates are completely or partly barred from voting. In one case the principle of free suffrage is violated; in the other, the principle of equal suffrage. The advantage of the Mexican method, however, is that, since the political power of the official party rests primarily on the peasant vote, the government dominated by that party cannot overlook the peasants. If the goal is to unify the country into a nation with a homogeneous culture, it is certainly better to bring the backward peasants into the political life of the nation, even under some guidance, than to exclude them from it completely.

The main danger, however, is that the official party, assured of victory, may forget that its role is merely educational. Its task is to integrate the backward populations into the mainstream of the nation. The existence of the peasants is its only justification, and it should exist only to prepare for its own disappearance. History, however, knows of few instances of official or single parties that have abstained from perpetuating themselves and of persecuting actual or potential opponents in order to retain power.

The official party system as it is applied in Mexico today may seem a tolerable device to resolve the political contradictions of a dualist society and prepare the country for more democratic regimes. On the whole, the Mexican PRI has abstained from using the convenience of dictatorial arbitrary rule too often. Nevertheless, the possibility of abusing this power is inherent in the official party system.

This single party can be effective and induce rather than force the backward peasants to vote for the government only if agrarian reform has been carried out previously and the peasants have emerged from the isolation of the latifundio and have been freed from its bonds. This has been done in Mexico and Bolivia. Latifundio reform is thus invariably the prerequisite for a more orderly political life. It is not a remedy in itself, but no remedy can work unless preceded by such reform.

Caciquismo and Government by the Gentry

The remnants of caciquismo are still bedeviling political life in the developing countries of Latin America. In the past, caciquismo was also a source of turmoil because it lent itself too well to the dictatorship of caudillos. In those days, however, it was not anachronistic, and after Latin America became independent it produced a few relatively stable governments that gave impetus to economic development; their legacy is not entirely unfortunate. Caciquismo gave rise to the liberal rule of the upper class as well as to the arbitrary one of the caudillos. A segment of the population still yearns for the return of this liberalism, although it cannot be brought back.

But to this day, nostalgia influences political life where old traditional parties still play an important role.

As long as most of Latin America's population was still completely subjected to the personal authority of the upper class, effective political regimes outwardly compatible with the principles of representative democracy could be based on caciquismo. Substantial economic progress was achieved under such governments, which were well entrenched in a few countries at the end of the nineteenth century and the beginning of the twentieth.

Actually, the institutions of representative democracy so highly regarded in western Europe and the United States could quite well give a veneer of democratic legality to the domination of feudal lords over national government. Many of the most enlightened and respected latifundio masters, and members of the professions who were their close allies, had studied in France or England, and their political ideology had been inspired by the literature of the two countries. They were also well acquainted with United States institutions. The Latin American gentry had retained the archaic authority of the cacique beneath their European education and the political ideology of the civilian *doctores*.

Firmly believing that the rule of law is the only civilized rule, that, in order to ensure it and avoid the continuing threat of caudillismo, representatives elected by the people must supervise the executive branch, the upper class tried to transpose to Latin America the liberal regimes of the monarchies of Queen Victoria and Louis-Philippe in the form of the presidential regime. They had not the slightest intention, however, of changing the archaic social structure that enabled them to control the rural populations. Even on this point, the example of the Virginia aristocrats who played such a large role in shaping the presidential regime in the United States but found nothing wrong with taking advantage of slavery, was most convenient in allaying any qualms.

As long as the upper classes were in agreement, they were entirely satisfied with the representative system because their members were, so to speak, the born representatives of their followers, and elections were no more than a formality. They did not even have to restrict the franchise to the propertied classes to ensure their victory as mid-nineteenth–century Europe had had to, for universal suffrage was even more reliable.

Instead of leading to democracy, the representative regime in Latin America has often served the landed gentry, just as it did in England, the birthplace of the representative regime, until the 1832 electoral reform—the move toward greater democracy. In Latin America, the rural society's social structure prevented the central government from directly controlling the entire country—which it did not intend to do in any event; hence, each cacique remained the master of his own domain. Thus, under the appearance of democracy, the gentry had little difficulty in retaining power in Brazil until 1889, but the wise guidance of Emperor Pedro II gave them an element of discipline. With somewhat greater difficulty the regime of the landed gentry lasted until 1930 under the old Republic. In the Argentine Republic, a relatively orderly government respectful of constitutional forms lasted from the downfall of Rosas in 1852 until the rise to power of the middle classes under Irigoyen in 1916. In Chile, after the initial turmoil of independence, which lasted until 1830, the aristocracy, whether liberal or conservative, ruled unchallenged until 1891. In Colombia, the liberal or conservative gentry provided long periods of political stability. This was the period when foreign observers regarded Brazil, the Argentine Republic, Colombia, and Chile as models of liberal moderate democracies.

Legacy of Gentry Government

The republic of the gentry already belongs to the past, but in its heyday it was the only form of the rule of law that Latin America enjoyed until revolutions spread following the 1929 depression. Just as did caudillismo, government by the upper class left traces in the political life of those countries it dominated for any length of time.

Political scientists, whether Latin American or foreign, do not as a rule sufficiently emphasize the lasting mark that a long period of government by the upper class has left on some Latin American countries. They devote their full attention to caudillismo, which they long regarded as a specifically Latin American phenomenon, and dismiss government by gentry as a

Latin American form of the regime that in Europe helped to achieve the transition from monarchies to democracies. Among underdeveloped countries, however, this limited democracy—government by the gentry—has been peculiar to Latin America, whereas all underdeveloped countries have gone through stages of caudillismo.

During the nineteenth century all Latin American countries were forced to control the centrifugal forces of caciquismo. Some of them partly succeeded, by accepting the discipline of gentry government; Chile, Brazil, the Argentine Republic, and Colombia are in this category. Other countries—Venezuela, Peru, Eduador, Bolivia, and all of Central America except Costa Rica—succeeded only by submitting to caudillismo. All these countries can be divided into the same two groups on the basis of their present-day political characteristics. Countries formerly governed by the gentry now enjoy a relatively orderly political life. Even their dictatorships are mild; the governments abstain from using harsh methods, and fundamental freedoms are usually respected. The picture in countries ruled by caudillos for too long is entirely different.

Since the few countries where government by the gentry was long accepted are by far the most populated, government by gentry rather than by caudillismo should account for the differences in the political life of Latin America as opposed to that of other developing regions. The after-effects of this basically conservative but sometimes enlightened type of government were the same in Latin America as in Europe. The system may have had many flaws, but its respect for legality, independence of the judiciary, freedom of opinion, individual freedom, and even the freedom of opposition deserve credit. In Latin America, as elsewhere, though perhaps to a greater extent because they had greater latitude, the gentry used their power to serve their own class; but there, as in other countries, they generally stopped short of ruthlessness in pursuing their goal.

These regimes were representative, but the society they represented and sought to perpetuate was a very archaic one. The form of their institutions made them democracies, but only in the sense that the patrician republics of antiquity may be called democracies. The citizenry consisted of a very small rich or educated minority. Good rapport between the rural feudal lords and the urban professional men (or most of them) and a sincere respect for legality ensured political order and some economic progress. They could not, however, integrate the scattered political forces into a nation. In societies where legality amounted to immobilism and the institutions of "limited democracy" (Gino Germani's phrase) led to domination by the aristocracy, it is easy to understand how caudillismo provided a counter balance to government by the gentry and helped prepare for change.

These aristocratic regimes cloaked in the forms of representative democracy therefore deserve credit for preparing the people to use these forms as soon as the economic and social structure permitted, although they delayed any change in those structures. Obviously, aristocrats could not be expected to change a society when they were the privileged class.

The Latin American gentry of the second half of the nineteenth century and the beginning of the twentieth played an entirely different role than did the gentry who governed the North Atlantic world in the first half of the nineteenth century. The ruling class in the limited democracies of that period in Europe and the northeastern portion of the United States belonged to the industrial and commercial capitalist bourgeoisie. That ruling class not only tolerated but demanded the destruction of the archaic rural structure because the economic development that was making the capitalists wealthy could continue only if rural populations were integrated into the national market. However conservative they may have tried to be or thought they were in their social outlook, these bourgeois were prime movers of social change because they were revolutionaries in the economic realm. It is they who gave impetus to a movement whose social consequences they could not foresee or continue to control.

The Latin American upper classes were not capitalist bourgeois but feudal lords whose wealth and power rested on the same activities that had inspired colonization. They had remained colonists despite independence, and their survival as aristocrats depended on the perpetuation of the mercantilist system and the archaic rural structure.

It would be unfair to say that government by the gentry in Latin America consciously delayed national economic development. But they did neglect it, just as the North American plantation owners neglected industrial development in the United States because they were more interested in the prosperity of the English textile industry.

Archaic Political Forces Within
Traditional Political Parties

Caciquismo has survived only in the archaic segment of the dual society—a segment that is shrinking throughout Latin America and no longer tolerates true gentry rule. Within the rural society, nonetheless, caciquismo has retained a fairly important position because the gentry's political strength is still one of the basic elements of present-day political life.

Until very recently, political parties in Latin America reflected only the drives of the gentry. Whether the parties were conservative or liberal, federalist or centralist, clerical or anticlerical, they were certainly not peoples' parties. In order to win elections, they needed the backing of the caciques, who brought in their own following. Today new political parties have emerged that are growing stronger and are trying to muster the reform-minded political forces of the advanced society. Traditional conservative parties have not disappeared, however. Their old political machines are still strong. Despite the gains of the new parties, the old ones still have the votes of the rural lords' followers.

The archaic political forces in the rural world have not united within a single conservative party to counteract the new political parties. Instead, they are scattered among the traditional parties according to family traditions and local interests. Since the political elements of the advanced society are not gathered in a single party either but are divided and opposed among themselves, no government can be formed without a coalition. Hence it is very tempting for any political party, instead of seeking alliances with its immediate competitors in the same segment of society, to make deals with a party whose strength lies mainly in the opposite segment of society. The ability to throw their weight behind one of the new parties and enable it to gain power gives the rural caciques enormous leverage, even though their following is very limited. Hence, the political role of the archaic political forces is quite incommensurate with their true strength.

10. Rise of Modern Political Forces in the Cities: The Labor Movement

Although Latin America remains essentially rural, only the urban populations, except in very rare cases, have adapted to the new political and social structure. As a result, even when well-meaning governments wish to comply with the form and spirit of representative democracy, they scarcely heed the demands of the rural masses. This seems to be a common phenomenon in all developing countries. In Latin America, however, it is still present after more than a century of formal democratic practice, and it makes Latin American political life extremely different from that of the countries that developed slowly before the twentieth century.

In Western Europe and even more so in the United States, the representative regime grew increasingly democratic thanks to true universal suffrage in the nineteenth century, by which time most peasants were already freed from domination by the gentry. The free peasants still held most of the votes, and, even when the former lords still enjoyed such prestige that the peasants elected them, they had to voice the demands of the rural population.

These European and North American peasants or farmers, who were fully integrated into political life, knew how to use their voting power to defend their interests. Since they generally held the majority of the votes, they could depend on the regime to listen to them even if they could not be policymakers. Even today, when peasants or farmers are often in the minority, their former position has generally enabled them to retain political power. Suffice it to mention the rural character of the Senate in France under the Third Republic and, in the United States, the strength of the farmers' lobby as well as the difficulty of achieving a more equitable representation for the cities.

Because of the political strength of the rural population at the start of industrialization in the United States and Western Europe, the budding capitalist and urban middle classes allied themselves with the heads of large farms in the formation of representative governments, and these alliances were socially conservative. The Republican party in the United States and the English Conservative party are examples. One result of these alliances between the privileged group in the city and the peasant or farmers was that industrial workers were the victims during the initial stages of industrialization in the North Atlantic countries. During the period from 1810 to 1830, a difference of 36 years in the respective life expectancies of workers' children in Leeds (7 years) and for Hereford peasants (43 years) testifies to the sacrifice.[1] Barred from voting, or in a minority when they enjoyed the franchise, and having lost faith in the processes of representative democracy, workers in the North Atlantic world could voice their demands and improve their condition only by resorting to trade-union pressure and revolutionary acts or threats.

In the second half of the twentieth century, when industrialization started in Latin American, the balance of power in that area was just the reverse. Although the rural masses were numerous and still often in the majority, governments were not accustomed to taking them into account, but were in the habit of reckoning with the urban proletariat. If the peasants are to make themselves heard now through the legal processes of political democracy, they will need to build up political strength. The time is not propitious because industrialization appears to be the choice remedy for underdevelopment, and widespread nationalism tends to equate the defense of agricultural interests with a concession to neocolonialism.

[1] *Abstracts of the Answers and Returns to an Act Passed in the Eleventh Year of the Reign of His Majesty King George IV*, 3 vols., 1831.

When nineteenth-century political life in Latin America was molded to conform to representative regimes, the agricultural laborers, many of them Amerindian or African, were too close to serfdom to be able to carve a political place for themselves. Peasants were not yet citizens. Usually being ineligible to vote, they were legally excluded from political life. Insofar as they were able to take part in it, they did so only indirectly, through their political bosses. The lingering latifundios actually excluded the rural populations from direct participation in political life until the middle of the twentieth century, and many of the consequences are still being felt today. The only rural interests represented directly and very effectively have been those of the latifundio masters. Hence the rural masses had nothing to expect from national politics except power and prosperity for their lords, from whom they might reap some indirect benefits.

Thus, particularly after 1930, when the rural notables no longer were alone in dominating political life, alliances were often made between the feudal lords and the middle classes or even the urban proletariat. The peasants were thus sacrificed in the takeoff stage of economic and social development. This is shown by the fact that the life expectancy at birth of the peasants of Northeastern Brazil was lower by 10 to 15 years than that of the middle classes and the São Paulo workers. Overlooked by political parties and ignored by governments, the Latin American peasants who now are seeking a place in national society must resort to revolutionary action if they want to be heard.

Weakness of Peasant Pressure Groups and Trade Unions

The rural workers now have pressing demands that can be fulfilled only by decisions made at the national level. They want to own land or secure less precarious tenure over it, they seek personal independence and, above all, education and integration into the advanced society. These demands are not likely to be satisfied by the masters who have represented them politically up to now.

Thus progressive rural popular political forces are arising in Latin America. They could be strong if they knew where and how to use their power, but so far it is a latent power that is useless until the masses are organized. Traditional leadership is weakening or has even vanished, and the peasants are not experienced enough to build up their own leadership. They are no longer willing to be led by their former masters, but they are accustomed to being led and are ready for revolutionary action if no other solution is available. The disorganized Latin American rural society is in a transitional stage during which the withdrawal of the anachronistic and beleaguered power of caciquismo is leaving it without useful representation in national, urban-dominated politics.

It is true that very effective pressure groups exist in the small segment of Latin American agriculture that grows the main export crops. For instance, the wealthy pressure group of the coffee planters, who bring the governments the largest portion of needed hard currency, can never be ignored for any length of time by the Brazilian or Columbian governments. All over Latin America the large fruit farms and sugarcane plantations (and, in Argentina before Perón, the livestock producers' and wheat growers' associations) are in the same position. The demands of these groups, which are listened to, are the demands of capitalists who are usually at the head of large enterprises. Although they are agriculturists, they are certainly not peasants.

It is also true that in these capitalist enterprises—seldom on the coffee plantations, but frequently on the sugarcane plantations and fruit farms—day laborers' trade unions have been established, and they exert a relatively effective pressure on governments. Organization of these unions was helped by the concentration of manpower, and their demands were heeded chiefly because many of the concerns were in the hands of foreign firms.

In any event these are small minorities. Trade unions have made little headway in Latin American rural society. Governments that had always cared more about latifundio owners than about their dependents not only refrained from promoting agricultural trade unionism, but usually hampered it. While, on the whole, Latin American governments have been very favorably inclined toward the industrial labor movement (often, it is true, in order to subjugate it instead of respecting its independence), they have tried to impede or hamper the formation of peasant trade unions. As late as 1961 the *International Labor Review* [2] listed the legal obstacles encountered by agricultural workers' trade unions. In Guatemala and Nicaragua only those laborers who could read and write were allowed to unionize, thus eliminating almost all of them. Even in Chile, where the industrial labor movement is particularly strong and influential, agricultural trade unions were not allowed to unite in a federation.

Even in the absence of legal impediments, however, the nature of the Latin American rural environment itself is seldom propitious to trade unionism. Except in the few areas where large capitalist enterprises employ salaried day laborers, Latin American rural society, although very poor, is not an agricultural workers' society. This is because the prevailing system of labor remuneration based on the latifundio calls for payment in kind—a proportion of the crops or a bit of land instead of, or as part of, the salary. The Latin American peasant is a hybrid. The fact that he frequently is partly salaried and is always in a precarious condition likens him to the day laborer. On the other hand, the patch of land given him, small as it may be, likens him to the farmer. If economic interests are to be defended in a society of peasants who are not solely wage earners, governments must do more than refrain from hampering the labor movement; they must help to organize it. Above all, the peasants must be educated, to a degree reached only lately in even the most developed countries. Thus, for the time being, riots are possible but not long-range trade-union action.

Absence of Peasant Political Parties

In the nineteenth century, in all the North Atlantic countries, the system of political parties was such that, while no party was concerned exclusively with peasants' problems, all the political parties competed to appear as their advocates, in order to win the rural electorate. Latin America has had very few political parties that claimed to defend the peasants; when-

[2] "Recent Trends in Labour Legislation for Hired Agricultural Workers in Latin America, *International Labour Review*, July–August, 1961, pp. 101–111.

ever such parties existed their efforts were to no avail, and they rapidly abandoned their task. The old traditional political parties, even when they are liberal, are dominated by caciques in the rural areas. The new people's parties organized in the cities do not care about the peasants, and find it easier and more rewarding to deal with the rural political chiefs, who ask only that they not trouble themselves about rural society.

Peasants in Latin America have often in the past pressed their demands, but generally by rioting and not through political parties or trade unions. Latin America has had a rich history of ruthlessly suppressed peasant uprisings. Their economic and social content has not always been perceived because they have often had a religious undertone or, as in Colombia today, have been associated with certain forms of banditry.[3] The agrarian league movement in Brazil, which was led by Julião, a lawyer, and all the land expropriation movements that have been growing in the last few years in most latin American countries have had many forerunners.

The three social revolutions in Latin America—in Mexico, Bolivia, and Cuba—were peasant revolutions for a while, but after victory they were taken over to some extent by the urban populations. Far oftener, peasant revolts have remained local incidents because they were not organized on a national basis.

On the whole, until recent years the Latin American rural populations have not been strongly influenced by Communism, possibly because they were not sufficiently integrated into the mainstream of national society to conceive of any other goal than the right to the land they were cultivating. The reason might have been also that these were peasant as well as proletarian populations; or perhaps the Communists despised them, as did the other urban parties, and did not bother organizing them until they began to riot.

At the present time, however, the helplessness of representative democracy to give a fair political share to the rural populations in Latin America is providing extremely favorable opportunities to turn peasant uprisings into social revolutions. The Cuban revolution started as a peasant movement, whereas the Communist workers' trade unions had no qualms in com-

[3] Rui Facó, *Cangaceiros e fanáticos* (Rio de Janeiro, 1963).

ing to terms with Batista. But this background makes Castroism, which enjoys great prestige, a useful tool in Communist infiltration of a rural society that had not responded to its direct propaganda.

Rise of Workers' Political Forces in the Advanced Society

Since World War II, urbanization of Latin America has greatly accelerated. In 1960, 46.2 percent of the population were already living in centers exceeding 2,000 inhabitants. Part of the urbanization—that of the very large cities—has been due to industrial development, and as a result Latin America's working class has also rapidly grown. In Brazil, for instance, while the total population increased by 26 percent between 1940 and 1960, the number of workers in manufacturing also rose by 26 percent. Although the cities and the number of workers have grown, the size of the rising working class should not be overestimated. Urbanization proceeds independently of industrialization. (See chap. 4, the section on "Deepening Rural Isolation.")

In many countries most industrial workers, who represent only 5 to 6 percent of the urban population, are employed in tiny craft enterprises that do not provide the concentration of manpower required for the emergence of the trade-union spirit. In the little-developed Central American or Andean countries in 1950, out of the workers employed in industry the proportion of those in craft enterprises varied from 85 percent in Ecuador to 70 percent in Peru. Even in the most advanced countries—Argentina for instance—it was no lower than 40 percent, while in Mexico, Brazil, Cuba, and Chile it was around 50 percent.[4]

These people, who are still not very numerous, have only recently joined the working class, and very few are sons of workers. Most of them are migrants from the countryside, and many have been living in cities for less than ten years. Such a new working class, coming from a very archaic rural background, suffers many of the cultural lags of that society. It

[4] ECLA, *Estudio sobre la mano de obra en América latina* (La Paz, 1957), p. 373.

does not provide a favorable terrain for a labor movement independent of personalities, parties, or government.

Despite its lack of education and its small size, this working class is at present very powerful because it is highly concentrated in a few industrial areas which are often close to the political capitals. In Brazil, for instance, almost half the industrial workers are in São Paulo and its surroundings, and half the remainder are in the neighborhood of the former federal capital, Rio de Janeiro. The concentration is even greater around Buenos Aires, and in Mexico around Mexico City and Monterrey. In other countries such as Chile and Bolivia, the concentration of workers in a few large mining industries also fosters trade-union action.

The strong popular political force now organizing trade unions in the cities does not represent the small, unorganized working class as much as an overly large tertiary sector that has characteristics of both the middle class and the proletariat. The weight of these organized urban groups is all the greater as the scarcely integrated peasant masses play only a minor political role.

In western Europe in the nineteenth century political life developed in such a way that between the ruling classes and the workers' proletariat there always existed an arbitral force—the rural masses who already owned land or had the right to farm it. They did not usually favor the workers. In Latin America, where political life is dominated by urban society, only the middle classes, whose most active elements are the students and the military, can arbitrate between the upper class and the workers. They are far less inclined to defend the existing order than are conservative landowners or the heads of large farming enterprises. The beneficiaries in Latin America are the middle classes, but they have not always been able to avoid sharing the profits with the politically strong urban workers.

Difficulties in Building a Free Labor Movement

The labor movement was finally established in Latin America before the end of the nineteenth century. It began as a European import in the few countries which had a large segment of emigrants from Europe. The trade-union movement was established in Argentina around 1880. It was imported into an environment where immigrants were not only managers, as in the rest of Latin America, but also white- and blue-collar workers who retained their working status in their new country. The first solidly organized trade union seems to have been that of the typographers, founded in 1878 in Buenos Aires. In Uruguay, so closely tied to Argentina, the situation was the same. In Chile, settled by German immigrants and always influenced by Argentina, trade unions started organizing around the same time, but they found different conditions in the northern part of the country, where the mines employed far less educated and more concentrated manpower.

In any event, these first trade unions were restricted to European Latin America, which was also the developed Latin America. Like European trade unions, they were independent, and the governments were hostile rather than sympathetic to them. Politically the unions were divided into those with anarchosyndicalist and those with socialist tendencies. Independent trade unions did not have mass support. Their members were recruited among a few highly specialized occupations, such as the typographers and employees of the public utilities, which were often foreign concessions. Argentina and Uruguay did not have a well-developed mining industry. Manufacturing did not lend itself to labor action because the enterprises were not large enough (except in the textile industry, whose workers have never anywhere been among early trade unionists).

In the rest of Latin America the labor movement started growing only after World War I. The Confederaçño Geral dos Trabalhadores do Brasil was founded in Brazil in 1929; unions were established in 1928 in Colombia on the foreign capitalists' plantations, and in Venezuela in 1936 after the downfall of the dictator Gómez. The trade-union memberships in these countries were much larger and less educated, but the unions were still not a mass movement. They remained vulnerable and usually tied to political movements. The General Workers' Federation in Brazil was influenced by the revolution of the "lieutenants" in 1922 and remained loyal to one of its leaders, Prestes, as he moved toward Communism. In Brazil, Venezuela, Ecuador, Bolivia, and Colombia these trade unions, between the two world wars, were divided into orthodox Communists and dissident Marxists and were more concerned with the revolution than with improving working conditions. Their membership was limited to a very small segment of the workers.

At present trade unions are deeply rooted in Latin America, including a large portion of the urban workers and miners. But the labor movement has been strongly promoted by the governments themselves, in particular by the semi-Fascist governments which at one stage of World War II were in power in several Latin American countries. In many of the most important countries, labor organizations grew because membership was made compulsory by governments who completely controlled them. Undeniably, this government domination of the trade unions was quite beneficial to the workers; but even after the downfall of the semi-Fascist regimes, the Latin American labor movement continued to seek the protection of the government, or at least of a political party. Even in countries like Argentina, with a strong tradition of independent trade unionism, the unions are finding it difficult to become reaccustomed to freedom after Perón's downfall. The trade unions have become a major political force, the strongest perhaps, but not an independent one. Rather than enabling the proletariat to exert pressure on management and government, the unions are being used as a tool to manipulate the proletariat by the government or by a party that had been in power before it was in the opposition.

Robert J. Alexander has listed trade-union memberships in the various countries. The figures cannot be vouched for and they vary considerably depending on whether the government supports or is hostile toward organizations that are not always fully independent. Out of an active Latin American population of about 64 million, trade-union membership is placed at about 6.5 million, distributed as shown in table 8. Subsequent estimates are twice as large as Alexander's, but trade-union headquarters are prone to pad their rosters.

Mexican Trade Unions

The Mexican trade-union movement deserves special consideration. It also sprang from the government's desire to have

TABLE 8
TRADE UNION MEMBERSHIP [a]

Argentina	2,500,000	Bolivia	100,000
Brazil	1,000,000	Uruguay	75,000
Mexico	1,000,000	Ecuador	75,000
Cuba	800,000	El Salvador	25,000
Chile	300,000	Honduras	25,000
Venezuela	250,000	Costa Rica	25,000
Colombia	150,000	Panama	15,000
Peru	200,000	Guatemala	15,000

[a] From Robert J. Alexander, *Politica* (Caracas), June–July, 1961.

trade unions it could control, but the governments involved were the products of a people's socialist revolution that started in 1910. In this case, government control was not copied on the Fascist methods in vogue after World War I.

In Latin America, Mexico was a pioneer in social reforms after the 1910 revolution. She was the first country that tried to promote trade unions in order to use them as a branch of government. When in 1920 Obregón started organizing the revolutionary society, he made wide use of Luis Morones' services. Morones was a labor caudillo whose organization, the Confederación Regional Obrera Mexicana (CROM), became an unofficial branch of the government. Morones was allowed to call upon the police and the army in order to force enterprises to obey him. This tie with the government enabled CROM to increase its membership between 1920 and 1924, during Obregón's presidency, from 50,000 to 1,200,000. The agreement continued under Calles, the new president selected jointly by Obregón and Morones. CROM, with growing government backing, claimed a membership of 2,250,000 by 1927.

The extent to which such organizations depended upon the state soon became evident. In 1928 President Calles, whose term in office was about to expire, decided to establish an official political party, the Partido Nacional Revolucionario (PNR), and withdrew government support from Morones, whose personal power was becoming dangerous. CROM soon dropped to a minor position. One of Morones' former associates in 1935 founded a new labor organization, the Mexican Labor Confederation (CTM). President Cárdenas, who was elected in 1934, supported its leader, Lombardo Toledano, and the new organization soon superseded CROM. By 1938 its membership exceeded a million. Although Cárdenas was extremely well disposed toward the labor movement, he refrained from giving CTM the monopoly that Obregón had granted CROM. Besides, the labor movement was shaken by ideological struggles exacerbated by Trotsky's presence in Mexico and his assassination. Lombardo Toledano increased the difficulties by stubbornly following the Stalinist line. In 1940 Toledano was removed from a position where he could directly influence the Mexican labor movement by being elected to the leadership of a large international labor body, the Latin American Labor Confederation (CTAL). Toledano tried in vain to engage in Mexican politics by founding an opposition party, the Partido Popular (PP), but it was never able to undermine the official party. The labor movement remained under the control of the government which encouraged divisions within the labor movement after Alemán's presidency (1946–1962).

Exploitation of the Labor Movement by Demagogic Dictatorships

Mexico is a special case because of its revolution. In the other countries the mass labor movement developed chiefly in the period from 1936 to 1946 and at that time the methods used were inspired by Fascism and National Socialism. A relatively large proportion of the workers, employees, and civil servants are unionized at present because the governments assumed the task of collecting union dues. In a labor movement of this type, the governments control its income and are able to manipulate it to a large extent.

This system was used most systematically and successfully in Argentina. The military dictatorship established in 1943 tried to destroy the old independent labor movement, which was divided into anarcho-syndicalist, socialist, and Communist factions. Perón, who started his political career as Labor Minister under the dictatorship, tried on the contrary both to promote and subjugate the labor movement by appointing his own men as union leaders. Later, with the skillful help and demagogic methods of Evita Perón, he made the trade unions into such an effective tool that in October, 1945, he even won a quarrel with the military by calling upon the *descamisados,* the shirtless, to rise. By the end of Perón's regime in 1955 the General Labor Confederation (CGT), which was completely subservient to him, had attained a membership of 6 million out of a total economically active population scarcely exceeding 7 million. Despite the fact that Argentina had a stronger and older union tradition than other countries, the labor movement did not recover from government control and regain its former spirit of independence.

The Peronist labor movement outlived the regime that had produced it. It withstood the pressure of a hostile government, but, inured as it was to political rather than to union activity, it confined itself to political opposition. The masses still yearn for government patronage. The newly freed labor movement is divided into Peronist trade unions (62, that is, the majority); the old socialist and anarcho-syndicalist unions, which are trying to rebuild but consist mainly of cadres (they number 32); and the 18 Communist unions, which are dissolving so that their members may infiltrate the Peronist unions. As elsewhere in Latin America, there are also the new Christian trade unions, the Acción Sindical Argentina set up in 1955.

In Brazil the labor movement, strongly influenced by the Communists, remained very weak until 1937, when Vargas' dictatorship openly veered toward Fascism and a corporate regime was set up. Vargas banned the old trade unions and enrolled all workers, employees, and civil servants in a pseudo-labor movement whose leaders were actually public officials. After being freed from the corporate regime the Brazilian trade unions tended to remain close to Vargas' old labor party just as the Argentine trade unions remained loyal to Perón's Justicialism. A Christian trade-union movement is emerging in Brazil.

In Brazil the March, 1964, events have clearly shown the strong and weak points of a labor movement controlled by the government or by a political party represented in the government. During the presidency of Goulart, who was the head of the labor party, trade unions closely associated with that party were able to hold seemingly irresistible mass street demonstrations. When the chiefs of the armed forces decided to oust President Goulart, the trade unions, robbed of government backing, posed no resistance whatsoever.

In Cuba the special conditions stemming from the proximity of the United States and control by North American economic interests had favored early development of a workers' movement. Batista's first dictatorship (1940–1944) fostered trade-union growth. A very close alliance had continued under the pro-socialist administrations of Grau San Martín and Prío Socarrás from 1944 to 1952. Cuban trade unions, strongly infiltrated by Communists, were backed by Batista during his second dictatorship, but they were unable to help any regime that supported them whenever it fell victim to a coup d'état or an insurrection. A last-minute reversal rallied the unions to Castroism, but it was not from the labor movement that Castro received his crucial help.

Trade-union subservience to the government was most glaring in Bolivia. The labor movement in that country grew powerful after the war with Paraguay, when Colonel Toro took power in 1936 with the help of officers sympathetic to National Socialism. Trade union membership was made compulsory under a corporate regime. Later the National Revolutionary Movement (MNR), which in its first stage was strongly influenced by National Socialist ideology, also promoted trade unionism. When the MNR, which later moved very far to the left, took power in 1952, the miners' union led by Juan Lechín, the strongest union in the labor movement, became in fact a branch of the government. In this case the government became a prisoner of the movement to which it had given too much power. The situation changed only when the head of the government, Paz Estenssoro, succeeded in temporarily freeing himself from Lechín influence. In this case the trade unions were so powerful mainly because in a revolutionary situation they had armed militias. Lechín's authority over the government was in many ways that of a revolutionary caudillo. Paz Estenssoro's victory was short-lived. The revolution that ousted him was started by Lechín's miners and the students, but Barrientos's army was needed to end it.

There are many more instances of dictatorships, inspired by

Perón's example (but not so successful), which tried to use labor movements to promote authoritarian regimes. These alliances of trade unions with dictatorships—military dictatorships especially—were helped by the attitude of the Communist parties during World War II. Communists had influenced some labor movements in the period between the two world wars, when many of them were still independent. Lombardo Toledano's strong personal influence and that of his inter-American organization, the CTAL, were used to maintain the status quo in Latin America, thereby supporting the North American war effort. The simplest way to prevent labor troubles had been to support the Latin American dictators. It is true that during that period the U. S. State Department also often backed them, but the Communist parties are hardly in a position to blame it since they helped the State Department wholeheartedly and continued to support those regimes after the State Department stopped. Behind a façade of hostility, Perón, Vargas, Batista, and others of their kind had found in the Communist party and Communist-influenced trade unions varying degrees of overt support and of lasting loyalty. The custom of the labor movement to have a sponsor—government or party—did not make it any easier for it to gain independence.

The Christian Labor Movement

The Christian labor movement is a new factor. It began in Argentina as well as in Mexico as early as 1910, but at that time the clergy was still such a staunchly conservative political force that the Christian labor movement was in an awkward position, and instead of growing it dwindled rapidly. Only "workmen's circles" and paternalistic welfare organizations survived in Argentina, Brazil, and Uruguay. In Mexico, on the other hand, the religious persecutions waged by the Calles regime completely crushed the Christian labor movement. Only in 1960 did the Christian trade unions start developing. At the present time a Latin American Confederation of Christian Trade Unions (CLACS), which claims to be independent of any foreign political influence, exists, side by side with two other organizations, the Communist-influenced Latin American Labor Confederation (CTAL) and the Inter-

American Regional Organization of Workers (ORIT), which has ties with the United States labor organizations.

The CLACS consists of twenty-six organizations in Latin American nations or territories and in 1964 claimed a membership of 5 million workers, employees, and peasants. If the padded figures given by the various trade-union headquarters are accepted, total union membership throughout Latin America, would range between 12 and 15 million for all the groups. In Chile the Christian labor movement seems to be the main one; in Peru it claims to be in second place over-all, and in first place for agriculture; and in Venezuela it is said to be in the same position. Elsewhere Christian trade unions are only now being set up.

These quasi-revolutionary trade unions are developing in Latin America particularly among the peasants and seem to have assumed a major role only because they are tied to the rise of Social Christian political parties. Following the stand adopted by the clergy in several countries, especially after the elections in Chile, it appears that Social Christian parties have become a foremost political force in a few countries and may become so in many others. If the success of Christian Democratic parties in political life is confirmed, Christian trade unionism might find the government backing needed to make it an effective labor force in Latin America.

It is easy to understand why, under the circumstances, most Latin American countries, while expressing their sympathy for trade unionism, were reluctant to ratify the international convention on free-trade unions. By June, 1964, the convention still had not been ratified by Bolivia, Brazil, Colombia, Chile, Ecuador, El Salvador, Haiti, Nicaragua, and Venezuela. Even though it was ratified by Uruguay, Mexico, Honduras, Guatemala, Costa Rica, Argentina, Cuba, Panama, Paraguay, and Peru, it does not mean, except in Uruguay and Costa Rica, that the trade unions are safe from government interference.

11. The New Political Parties, Populism, and Christian Democracy

As a rule the moderate parties in Latin America, whether they belong to the conservative or to the nineteenth-century liberal tradition, have remained traditional parties of the old type even if they have been created recently. This is because no matter how strong their following is today among industrial and business circles in the cities and the segment of the middle classes that fears change, these moderate parties also need the votes brought in by the rural political bosses—the feudal lords. In order to rally such heterogeneous supporters, these parties of archaic inspiration must avoid facing the problems of the hour, and instead must wage their campaigns on issues pertaining to the past or face even deeper clashes on problems of personalities.

In the past few years, confronting these traditional parties that are based more on clan and personality than on class interests, are new political parties that have been trying to rally the urban populace through programs of social reforms and by appealing to nationalism.

Reformist Socialist Parties

The new parties that claim to uphold the interests of the proletariat are generally far different from their counterparts in countries where the proletariat is more sophisticated politically. There are in Latin America some socialist parties of the European type, but very few of them have succeeded in gathering large numbers of loyal supporters. Only in Argentina and Chile have socialist parties played any political role. In Argentina the existence of a working class, part of which was of recent European origin, enabled a socialist party and an independent labor movement to arise. The Argentine Socialist party enjoyed great prestige because of the personality of its leader, Alfredo Palacios, rector of the University of La Plata. The party never acceded to power, but it was influential in political life. Its courageous opposition to Peronism, which won over large masses with its demagogic slogans, seriously undermined the socialist party. In Chile there is also a Socialist party which was close to power in 1938–1942 as part of the Popular Front that elected Pedro Aguirre Cerda to the presidency. Many other Latin American parties call themselves socialist, but the name is often meaningless. Thus the Brazilian Social Democratic party (PSD) is at the extreme right, while the Bolivian Socialist party was semi-Fascist.

Communist Parties

Communism in Latin America is a strong political force. It has imposed itself on Cuba and exists in almost all the other countries. Most of the parties, however, have only small memberships and their political influence seldom manifests itself directly. Lieuwen [1] gives an estimate of Communist party memberships in the various countries in 1957. According to these figures there are relatively large Communist parties in only two countries with small populations, namely in Cuba with 30,000 members and Chile with 40,000. In absolute figures the largest Communist parties were in Argentina and Brazil, each with 50,000 members, but this was not very high for populations of 20 and 60 million, respectively. The Brazilian Communist party formerly enjoyed great prestige throughout Latin America because the personality of its long-time leader, Luiz Carlos Prestes.

These figures do not do justice to the real power of Communism in Latin American countries. It is true that the Communist parties themselves rarely played any direct political role

[1] Edwin Lieuwen, *Arms and Politics in Latin America* (New York, rev. edition, 1961), p. 54, n. 18.

between the two world wars. In Chile the Communist party was part of the 1938 Popular Front, which its own intrigues helped to break up. In Bolivia, the PIR (Partido Izquierdista Revolucionario) was a Communist party that participated in the coalition headed by the MNR, which in 1943 installed Major Villaroel as dictator. Since then some countries have banned Communist parties outright, while others merely have barred them from running their own candidates at elections. The real power of the Communists does not emanate from the parties but from their activity within the labor movement and within some political parties that are very powerful at present all over Latin America. These parties do not claim to represent a specific class, but they successfully aim at rallying broad popular support by playing up a few very simple themes. The most widely and effectively used theme is nationalism.

These heterogeneous populist parties and some demagogic dictatorial regimes provide a particularly fertile field for the Communist boring-from-within technique. Thus in 1950 in Guatemala, where the Communist party membership apparently did not exceed 500, its considerable influence on Jacobo Arbenz's government provoked the United States' indirect intervention and the government's downfall. In addition the Communist parties maintained complicated relations with many populist-inspired dictatorships which had multiplied just before and during World War II. Having supported these dictatorships to maintain order and thereby support the United States war effort, the Communist parties never broke with them completely. There was constant bargaining with Batista in Cuba, the many military dictatorships in Bolivia, the Peronists in Argentina, and Getulio Vargas in Brazil. The Communist chief Prestes, who had been arbitrarily imprisoned by Vargas, appealed to the people from jail, urging them to support the very president who was holding him prisoner.

Communists find it easier at present to carry on their work within the populist parties because their main objective is nationalist-inspired agitation against the United States. The populist parties, with their heterogeneous memberships, must appeal to groups of people most of whom have very little education. Populist platforms are very vague. They rely primarily on emotional propaganda in an environment where the strongest and most widespread feeling is distrust of the United States, and the struggle is directed against its economic control.

A few populist parties are trying to eliminate Communist influence. The Mexican Institutional Revolutionary party, which is in a special category because it was produced by a revolution and is a single party under strict discipline, was relatively successful in doing so. But the situation is quite different in political parties that arose out of semi-Fascist dictatorships during World War II and later became popular parties committed to structural reforms. They did not succeed in shaking off Communist influence. This was true of the Peronist movement in Argentina and of the Brazilian labor party. In Bolivia, on the other hand, Paz Estenssoro, who had attempted to withdraw the National Revolutionary Movement from Communist influence, was ousted in the 1964 resort to force.

Until now the parties that claimed to strive for thoroughgoing reforms, particularly land reforms, by democratic means (that is, majority support) found it extremely difficult to break completely with Communist fellow travelers. The reason is that Latin American Communists, who so far lack mass support, must show that only through revolutionary methods can change be achieved in the existing archaic social structure. This is why political parties that try to alter the archaic structure through reforms are the Communists' worst foes. The United States has understood this too and is now trying to help these reformist parties carry out substantial reforms, particularly land reform.

The problem is that the reformers find it all but impossible to keep any of their promises, because in the national assemblies they are staunchly opposed by the blindly conservative feudal forces that dub any reform programs revolutionary. At the same time they are fought by the Communists and all revolutionaries, particularly the students, who proclaim that the projected reforms are insufficient and deceiving. The helpless reformers are in constant danger of being discredited. If they are not discredited fast enough, as in Venezuela in the case of the Acción Democrática party under Betancourt's presidencies, recurrent insurrections force these sincere would-be reformers to seek alliances that turn them into conservatives.

Parties of the Populist Type

Since about 1930 the Latin American political scene has not been dominated by the traditional conservative parties or by modern parties of the socialist or Communist type. Instead, parties running on reform platforms but opportunistic in their actual policy have been in the lead. They tend to rally a heterogeneous backing around a prominent figure who has acquired the reputation of defending the underdog but whose only ideology is nationalism.

Some men have used the urban proletariat, especially the marginal proletariat in the shanty towns, to climb back into dictatorship after being ousted. The have done this by winning over to their own person the political allegiance of their erstwhile followers. In the process, the parties behind them have become to some extent the representatives of a proletarian political force. Such parties, bearing the strong personal mark of a political figure, are called populist parties, a name given them in Latin America, which helps differentiate them from the left-wing parties of the European type.

The forerunner of this type of movement was Hipólito Irigoyen, who assumed power in Argentina in 1916 with the Radical Civic Union, a party he had turned into his tool to such an extent that a splinter group called its own organization the Union Cívica Radical Antipersonalista. Irigoyen then renamed his party, which returned to power in 1928, Union Cívica Radical Personalista. Irigoyen's regime was characterized by a strong reaction against the cosmopolitan outlook of the Argentine oligarchic regime, which had given free rein to foreign, especially English, concerns. His Argentine nationalism manifested itself first by his neutrality during World War I. Another trait of the regime—a basic feature of populism —was ostentatious sympathy for the little man and a show of contempt for the wealthy and the powerful. Irigoyen is alleged to have made all high-placed figures wait outside his office while municipal sweepers and shoeshine boys were ushered in to state their grievances, which were often corrected.

On the other hand, Irigoyen was less demagogic in promoting early labor legislation, and he did many favors for the trade unions. But he helped them only when they were submissive, and ruthlessly crushed all strikes he had not authorized.

It is difficult to assess the effects of a very demagogic regime. On the one hand, during his first term of office, which started in 1916 under very auspicious circumstances, Irigoyen did not carry out a single important structural reform. No land reform took place, and the large national and foreign concerns that dominated the country generally obtained whatever they wanted from the president's less incorruptible subordinates. On the other hand, there is no doubt that the regime gave the Argentine masses a confidence in their power that changed the conditions of political life and made it impossible for an oligarchy to make any lasting comeback. After Irigoyen the Radical Civic Union became a middle-class party and the Peronists became demagogic populists in its place.

After the many revolutions that attended the 1929 depression in Latin America, a large number of similar regimes emerged. They were somewhat different at first, it is true, because social structures were less advanced and because the prestige of Fascism and National Socialism prompted those regimes to adopt the terminology of the corporate system and the methods of Fascism. One of the best examples was the development of the labor party in Brazil which gave a lasting shape to Getulism, the demagogic regime derived from President Vargas' dictatorship. The popular revolution of 1930 gave birth to President Vargas' dictatorship. When it grew solid roots in 1937, it modeled itself on Fascism. Later, after Vargas was toppled in 1945, he prepared his return to power through the Labor party's popular appeal. Like Irigoyen in 1916, Vargas in 1930 found a country dominated by the oligarchy, and, also like Irigoyen, he appealed to nationalism against the cosmopolitan outlook of the former ruling classes and presented himself as the advocate of the little man. Vargas personally was as incorruptible as Irigoyen, but his entourage was not, and powerful economic interests easily accommodated themselves to lofty but ineffectual declarations. Like Irigoyen, Vargas promoted labor legislation and encouraged a workers' movement that he successfully controlled, but he did not carry out any meaningful basic reform. Vargas' regime, like Irigoyen's, deeply changed the conditions of political life and precluded any outright return to oligarchy.

It may be said of both of those populist regimes that they built very little but destroyed a great deal. This may be their function. They were probably no more than the awkward tool of new forces that were shaking the traditional structures of those countries. The major (and significant) difference between the two regimes is that Irigoyen always acted, or believed he did, in the name of political democracy whose forms he did respect, while Vargas assumed power through a coup and probably never believed in democracy. Both regimes, however, enjoyed equal popular appeal. The Labor party founded by Vargas was the most dynamic element in Brazilian political life until 1964, just as radicalism had been in Argentina until it was similarly supplanted by Perón's Justicialism.

Perón's regime more than Vargas' was inspired in its early stages by National Socialism. It took (and retained) a much more brutal dictatorial character. After the defeat of National Socialism, however, when the military basis of Perón's authority was gone, he directed his appeal to the people by granting real benefits to underprivileged city dwellers and by demagogic methods of unequaled cynicism. He turned Peronism into a political force that lost none of its power after Perón's ouster by the military. Even more than Irigoyen's radicalism or Brazilian Getulism, Peronism destroyed a great deal but did not rebuild anything.

Paz Estenssoro's National Revolutionary Movement in Bolivia developed directly from a coup engineered in 1943 by a group of young officers who believed themselves to be National Socialists. This is somewhat similar to the rise of a populist party within a dictatorship forced to seek grass-roots support. The dictator carried to power by the 1943 coup, Colonel Villaroel, immediately sensed the need to promote a government-controlled labor movement and to enact labor legislation. He also abolished *pongage* (the system of Indian serfdom), if only in principle. After the defeat of National Socialism in Europe and the fall of the military dictatorship in Bolivia, Paz Estenssoro tried to turn the National Revolutionary Movement into a true populist party. After it took power in 1952 its policy was unlike that of the other populist movements in that it was not indifferent at first to the peasants' plight. This was because the formation of too-well-armed workers' militias induced President Paz Estenssoro to seek the backing of the Indian peasants, who were content with a splitting up of large estates in the absence of methodical land reform.

Economic Role of the Populist Regimes

The populist parties that succeeded the aristocratic governments, especially after 1930, have dominated Latin American political life since then. Their most earnest and systematic efforts have been aimed at economic emancipation by means of industrialization. Until they assumed power, Latin America had by and large accepted economic domination by Europe and the United States. The oligarchic regime had been cosmopolitan in its outlook, since the economic interests of the ruling class depended entirely on the exportation of agricultural products, and its culture was that of the European capitals. The populist governments wished to alienate neither the entrepreneurs nor the workers, and especially not the middle classes and the military. Nationalism was the one theme on which all of them could agree. At that point in Latin America's foreign relations, nationalism, which was primarily economic, meant above all industrialization and nationalization of the large foreign enterprises. Although this economic nationalism often inspired measures of demagogic rather than economic value, populist governments undoubtedly started the era of economic development. In many countries populism heralded economic decolonization and created some of the conditions for economic takeoff.

It cannot be denied that the populist parties and the semi-Fascist dictatorships that created some of them made the urban workers aware of their political power and forced the Latin American governments to heed them. The populist regimes broadened the Latin American body politic. Since the populist politicians, whether dictators or democrats, had organized the workers in parties or trade unions in order to secure their help in wresting power from the upper class, they had to favor them. This is why they had to start major social reforms, at least on behalf of the city dwellers.

Political and Social Role of the Populist Regimes

Unfortunately all too often some of the populist parties without a definite program were unable to rise above empty demagoguery. The lack of any economic experience, particularly among military dictatorships of populist inspiration, rendered the best meant programs utterly ineffectual. The fact that they were being bestowed upon the countries by paternalistic rulers instead of having been obtained through struggle or collective bargaining only added to their futility.

For instance, any social policy dictated by opportunism consisted first in courting supporters by multiplying job openings, particularly in occupations most easily controlled by the party and the government: civil service, public utilities, nationalized industries. It is under the populist regimes that the tertiary sector in the Latin American cities has grown so large.

In order to bring about and justify the proliferation of posts and show their social usefulness, the populist governments have given in to the temptation to orient labor legislation in a direction that slows productivity. Thus the workday has been shortened, featherbedding promoted, and the retirement age lowered. Under these conditions salaries have usually remained very low. In order to maintain their popularity among workers and civil servants, the governments have raised minimum wages excessively, the result being almost invariably an inflation that has canceled the raise. These regimes have promoted social progress through featherbedding rather than through higher productivity and salaries. Even though party supporters have been disappointed by the stagnation and in some cases the deterioration in living standards, the populist regimes have lost none of their popularity. The people's protectors had given evidence of their good intentions, and they can always blame any failures on mysterious plots of political foes and the evil scheming of international capitalism and the United States government.

Vargas in Brazil did not disdain using such demagogic

methods, but the past master was Perón in Argentina, who both gained lasting popularity and jeopardized for a long time to come the privileged position of the Argentine people among Latin Americans. In no other Latin American country was domination of the masses by the dictator and his party more complete or the social benefits granted to the urban workers more extensive. In no other country were the benefits dispensed more arbitrarily and with greater disregard for economic conditions. The whims of a benevolent actress dictated their distribution for a long time. A genial rather than a cruel dictatorship combined with demagoguery brought unconditional loyalty from the urban masses, with the exception of small, politically conscious minorities faithful to the tradition of free trade unionism. Argentina's economy was so completely ruined that the condition of the workers and middle classes, formerly by far the best in Latin America, deteriorated considerably, and the governments that succeeded one another after 1955 were unable to break the habit of resorting to Peronist demagoguery.

The greatest harm done by the populist regimes throughout Latin America has been to widen the chasm between a chiefly urban advanced society and a chiefly rural archaic one by carrying out reforms in only a segment of each nation. Government by the upper class had preserved archaic feudal structures in the rural areas until the end of the first third of the twentieth century. The populist leaders who have followed the oligarchy have paid no attention whatsoever to rural society and have left its feudal structure untouched, while their reforms have hastened changes in the advanced urban society, thus broadening the gap between the two societies instead of narrowing it.

Indeed, although the populist regimes have tried to be very progressive or have believed they are, they have instinctively fitted into the dual social system that they inherited from the oligarchy and the system of narrowly based democracy that it produced. Under government by upper class, the peasants did not participate directly in political life, but were represented by their lords. To urban intellectuals yearning for economic and social development and to populist dictators eager to attract supporters among the urban masses, the rural population has been too remote, too backward. It has not seemed able to take part directly in political life. It has been so passive and alien that it has not seemed worthy of the sacrifice entailed in sharing with it the advantages of economic and social development. The new regimes, like the aristocratic regimes, have regarded the process of political democracy as applying only to the advanced society. The national political life of Latin America became more democratic when the overly conservative government by the upper class gave way to the progressive governments of the populists, but it is still restricted to the advanced society.

Alliances Between Populist Urban Forces and Rural Feudal Forces

This social dualism condoned by governments that believe themselves to be promoters of reforms has more than once produced strange bedfellows. The urban progressive forces have inevitably met with opposition in their struggle for power and have never been in the majority nationally. If they want to comply with the forms of representative democracy they must seek allies in the rural society. Since they cannot directly reach the peasants who are still too dependent upon traditional authority, the simplest way is to make deals with the lords who wield the authority.

Alliances between the most modern political forces and those determined to remain the most archaic may seem extremely odd, but they occur quite easily, since political forces most likely to clash do not even meet because they operate in entirely different societies. The conflicting aims of progressive and feudal allies can be pursued simultaneously, within the separate segments of the dual society, neither feeling any impact of its counterpart's activity.

The gap between advanced and backward populations in Latin America has remained so wide that the relations between the two segments of society are not unlike those of native populations and colonizers. It has been generally noted that in the relations between native chiefs and the home governments, a North African kaid or Middle Eastern emir cared very little whether he was protected by a conservative or a liberal English or French government. It has also been noted that the Laborite prime minister in an English government or the socialist premier of a French government was no more embarrassed than a conservative in being the protector of feudal lords. Until the past few years, Latin American urban reformers were not in the least disturbed about coexisting with rural feudal lords, and as long as the reforms were to be confined to the cities, the feudal lords did not mind in the least whether they collaborated with socialist or with capitalist urban elements. Indeed, one of the tenets of political science is that each society must have the regime best suited to its own level of economic and social development as well as to its degree of political maturity.

Should any comparison with colonized and colonizers be rejected because in Latin America we are dealing with citizens of a common nation, one example from the political scene in the United States will suffice to show how opposites readily unite whenever serious cultural differences exist among the regions of a single country. Like the Latin American countries in the twentieth century, the United States in the nineteenth century suffered from lingering regional archaic structures in the southern states which had not yet recovered from the long period of slavery on the plantations. Naturally, after the victory of the advanced segment of society over the archaic one in the Civil War, the balance of power between them was far different from what it was to be a century later in Latin America. Despite this, dualism in North America was serious enough to produce similar political effects. Differences in time, environment, and methods could not obliterate the obvious underlying kinship between the alliance of latifundio feudal landlords with the progressive Labor party in Brazil, and the lasting alliance that produced the Democratic party in the United States. In United States presidential elections this alliance has brought together elements in the northeastern and western states that dislike the social conservatism of the Republican Party and elements in the southern states that refuse to accept the full consequences of Abolition. They vote with the Democrats because they have never forgiven the Republicans for Abolition.

The exact terms of these alliances are never stated, of course, but their effects are obvious. In archaic rural Latin

American society the national governments have no trouble fulfilling the chief demand of the latifundio masters—to leave the rural world alone and leave the lords free to govern their subjects as they have in the past. Let the governments carry out all the reforms they please in the advanced society, since they must satisfy their supporters among the people. As long as they do not extend the reforms to the peasants, do not undermine the local authority of the feudal lords, and avoid broaching the problems of land reform, they may act as they see fit. There is no dearth of examples of such odd alliances and their harmful consequences. For instance, it is quite typical that in Uruguay the Colorado party, in power for 93 years, has avoided clashing with the Blanco party on the agrarian problem ever since Batlle y Ordóñez was elected in 1903. The widely admired constitution inspired by Batlle y Ordóñez institutionalized this tacit agreement by providing room for the opposition within the government. Under this regime the Colorado party through its socialist-inspired reforms has made Montevideo a model "welfare state" matched by few European countries. This has not prevented the Colorados from collaborating with the Blancos, who were backed by caciques of the livestock-raising areas in the interior. The Colorados headed the national government, but they confined their reforms to Montevideo and the developed areas, and gave the Blanco caciques free rein in their own constituencies. The Montevideo area has been upheld by North American writers as a Latin American Switzerland, while the archaic structure of northern Uruguay has seemed backward even to its Brazilian neighbors of Rio Grande do Sul.

Throughout almost all of Latin America there are still some political parties dating back to or permeated by the spirit of government by the upper class, and their success hinges largely on the loyalty of rural caciques. These political bosses join one party rather than another because of family traditions, clan solidarity, or simply greater convenience at election time. Local bosses, working through their respective parties, compete to consolidate their authority over their constituency and to gain a larger share of government patronage for their followers. They are less interested in power on the national level. In a rural structure that is feudal rather than national, local issues are more important than national ones, these being a mere by-product of politics.

In Uruguay the Blanco party, in Brazil the Social Democratic party (PSD) and the National Democratic Union (UDN), in Colombia the Liberal and the Conservative parties, and in Argentina and Chile Conservative parties, all accept Latin American societies as they are and do not take a stand on any of the major present-day problems. In order to enhance personality or clan struggles, they merely rehash old issues that have left a legacy of grudges and still arouse passion but require no solution—for instance, clericalism versus anti-clericalism, federalism versus centralization, or presidential versus parliamentary regime. Such political parties frequently take no pains to conceal the personal character of the interests rallied around an influential leader and use his name as their banner—such as the National Odriist Union (UNO) in Peru.

In countries where the advanced society has become too strong, feudal lords have been barred from wielding direct power on the national level, but they have found accomplices among reform-minded political parties, thus enabling them to retain their local power. Many populist parties have asked local chiefs for support and have paid for it at the expense of the peasant populations. Furthermore, other parties, which really meant to carry out reforms and would have liked to extend these reforms to the countryside, were forced to accept the help of the rural bosses in order to resist less scrupulous opponents, and were thereby made helpless. Whatever the cause, the fact is that many reform-minded parties have been in power in Latin America for long periods since 1930, but whether their program has included agrarian reforms or has been limited to action in the cities, none of these parties seriously tried to carry out land reform and to put an end to rural feudalism. Until the past few years, the only extensive rural reforms have taken place in Mexico, Bolivia, and Cuba, but through violent revolutions rather than through the normal operation of political forces in elections. A reform was started in Guatemala between 1950 to 1954 during the presidency of Arbenz, but it may not be an exception, since the president seemed ready for social revolution through authoritarian methods.

Failure of Vargas' Populist Regime in
Brazil and the Coup d'État of Spring,
1964

The clearest example of an alliance of progressive and conservative forces with opposite policies in urban and rural societies is that of Getulio Vargas' regime in Brazil. It also shows
the failure of the populist regimes and the revolutionary situation they created by failing to integrate rural populations into
the mainstream of national political life.

In 1930 there occurred in Brazil, as in several other Latin
American countries, a revolution which, in addition to purely
political objectives, aimed at social reforms and economic
independence. It was thorough, produced lasting effects, and is
generally regarded as the divide between the old republic and
the new republic. From then until 1964 Brazilian politics was
dominated by Vargas' personality, a domination that continued even after his suicide in 1954. He became a dictator in
1937. Thus he did not remain faithful to the ideal of political
democracy that had helped him accede to power, but he did not
stray too far from his program of social reform and economic
nationalism.

The political system adapted by Vargas to the forms of
representative democracy after his ouster as a dictator, rested
on two parties. One of them, the Labor party (*Partido Trabal-
hista* or PTB) was the more progressive of the two parties
allowed to participate in the elections. It drew a great deal of
its backing from the trade unions organized by Vargas during
his dictatorship. The other, the Social Democratic party
(PSD) was supported by a segment of the urban middle
classes and by loyal followers of latifundio masters in several
states. The alliance of these two parties, which constituted the
Getulist political system, provided for a lasting national government. After having enabled Kubitschek to be elected president in 1955 the alliance was temporarily overshadowed by
Quadros, but later carried Goulart, a Laborite, to the presidency.

There is no denying that Brazil underwent major changes
under the presidencies of Vargas and Kubitschek. Industrial
development was accelerated and the rise of the urban middle

classes and the awakening of the proletariat were promoted. To the urban populations Getulism was pro-labor. On the other hand, there is no denying the fact that rural society was abandoned to its plight and nothing was done to remedy its lags. No agrarian reform was attempted; and even though the authority of the caciques started to wane because country dwellers were turning against their masters, the government was careful not to hasten the process. For the rural populations, Getulism remained an archaic regime of domination by feudal masters.

There is no doubt that Getulism was a very convenient system for Labor and Social Democratic politicians. It lasted for a long time but could do so only as long as the advanced and archaic societies remained fairly well isolated from one another. The situation has changed in Brazil just as it is changing throughout Latin America. The rural populations are no longer sufficiently isolated to resign themselves to their plight, and their reaction, which is sometimes violent, brings the problems of land reform and integration of rural populations into the national society to the forefront of political life.

Country dwellers cannot be integrated into the mainstream of the nation as full citizens until the latifundio and the remnants of feudalism have been destroyed. Hence it is useless to expect that coalition majorities resting partly on the vote of those same feudal lords whose power must be shattered can possibly endure. All through 1963, President Goulart saw the anachronistic results of a coalition of progressive and feudal forces and the ensuing failure of populism. Getulism, whose heir he was, prepared the way for national integration by giving the impetus to economic development that requires integration. The contradiction on which the system rested, however, prevented Goulart from integrating the society.

It was no use asking Congress to enact the needed reforms. An event like the Night of August 4 (abolition of feudal rights during the French Revolution, when the privileged themselves solemnly gave up their privileges) can occur only in revolutionary situations. President Goulart understood this quite well when at the end of 1963 he saw that he could no longer evade the land reform issue after his populist predecessors and he himself had done their best to put it out of their minds for thirty years. In order to reenact a Night of August 4 and force the feudal lords who were part of his majority to make the sacrifice, Goulart organized or helped organize revolutionary demonstrations. But as it turned out, the revolutionary situation, so awkwardly created by Goulart through noncommissioned navy officers, provoked army intervention instead of helping the plotters. This ended the Getulist regime—a regime that had lasted only through the political skill of Vargas and Kubitschek.

Need for Political Realignment for National Integration

Now that the problem of reforming the archaic rural structure is moving into the foreground of the political scene throughout Latin America, the various political groups will have to take a stand for or against the reform. Rural lords can no longer remain neutral in national politics while they defend only local personal interests. They are certain to lose much of the authority which up to now has enabled them to delay long-needed reforms. The caciques' political tactics resemble those of trade unions in the United States that proclaimed their political neutrality and yet delivered the votes of their membership to either the Democratic or the Republican party, depending on the benefits promised. This profitable neutrality lasted as long as the problems of concern to the two parties—states rights and grudges dating from the Civil War—did not affect specific trade-union interests. The picture changed when trade-union issues started to play a major part in national politics. Since Roosevelt and the New Deal trade unions have been neutral only in theory. Their ties with the Democratic party tend to become permanent, and as their commitment grows they lose their bargaining power in elections. Retreat from neutrality means loss of blackmailing potential.

Up to now too many political parties in Latin America, thanks to their makeup, were able to avoid taking a stand on the reforms that divided the various political forces too deeply. They have succeeded so well in evading the issue that the cumulated lags have become unbearable. Realignment of political forces with respect to these urgent problems is now necessary so as to bring about the inevitable reforms by peaceful means instead of by violent revolution modeled on the Cuban pattern. There is great awareness in Latin America of the need for new political parties, or for a new outlook in the existing ones. It is to be feared, nevertheless, that the necessary realignment will be difficult to bring about. The alliances of contradictory forces that paralyzed a regime like Getulism in Brazil have been so profitable to the politicians in power that it will be difficult to dissolve them. Similarly, in the United States Democratic politicians have up to now stubbornly endeavored to maintain the alliance of the Northeastern and Western liberal forces with the conservative forces in the South. Not until the Negro people themselves rose in revolt to demand integration was the profitable alliance shaken, but not shattered. In Latin America the backward peasants also had to revolt and demand integration. Even though the alliances were undermined it is not certain that they have been broken and that more legitimate realignments are assured.

Political Force of the Catholic Church

Paradoxically, the most hopeful sign of an effective realignment of political forces in Latin America to cope with the emergency while avoiding violent revolution is that within the Catholic Church. An ideological movement is under way in the institution customarily regarded, and with good cause, as the most conservative in Latin America.

The Catholic Church has always been a political force in Latin America. Not only has the bulk of the population remained faithful to Catholicism, but this force is a legacy of the colonial period when the monarchy used the Church as an instrument of government. At that time, the *patronato* privilege gave the sovereigns the power to appoint members of the clergy. Despite the anticlerical reaction after independence, most of the clergy in the nineteenth century were still in the habit of using their authority over the rural aristocrats and the peasant masses in political affairs. The Church is still politically strong today, and the clergy does not always refrain from interfering in elections. Except for the revolutionary regimes in Cuba and to a lesser extent in Mexico, and for Haiti where the caudillo is trying to promote voodoo against Catholicism, rulers are very sensitive to interventions by bishops, even in the many countries where separation of Church and State prevails.

As a rule the political force of the clergy has until quite recently been used for the most conservative purposes. Particularly after independence, when the struggle between the clerical and anticlerical factions dominated Latin American political life, the Church emerged as the preeminantly conservative if not reactionary political force. The Latin American clergy then earned its reputation as the least liberal in Christendom. This, however, should not preclude a subtler assessment of the political role of the Church in Latin America. It should not be forgotten that in the early centuries of the conquest, the regular clergy were the sole protectors of the Indians and that the Leyes de las Indias obtained by Las Casas in 1542 were several centuries ahead of the social climate of the sixteenth century. Neither should it be overlooked that even when the Church became decidedly conservative, the clergy were not unanimously behind it. There have been conservative bishops and chaplains in the service of the feudal landowners and some religious orders themselves became feudal powers, but more than once priests have led Indian or peasant insurrections.

Even in the nineteenth century, although the political force of the Church was always used to further conservatism, its political role may have indirectly promoted modernization, if only as a reaction to its obscurantism. After independence, the power wielded by an obscurantist clergy roused a strong anticlerical movement among populations that were otherwise deeply religious. At some time, all the countries inevitably came to grips with the temporal power of the Church, and the clearest consequence of its political and economic power was to provide political parties with a theme around which they could organize on the national level. Clericalism versus anticlericalism has been, along with federalism versus centralization, one of the two major issues that aroused the national parties. Thus, in countries that were not yet nations and in which clans and regions opposed one another, the clerical question helped promote national integration. The existence of the political force of the Church posed national instead of local problems. In this respect it was an indirect factor in modernizing Latin American political life, if modernization means a political life centering on national issues at state level, rather than on estate or regional problems.

Although the Church generally used its strong political force for reactionary ends in the initial stages after conquest, the fact that in the past few years it is revising its position on social and political problems is of major importance and may change the conditions of political life in Latin America. With increasing frequency a segment of the clergy and lay workers is preoccupied by the anachronism of the social structure still prevailing in the rural areas and the wretchedness of the fringe populations. The movement is just starting, but it is very active. Forerunners like Alceu de Amoroso Lima in the Catholic Action group in Brazil are no longer isolated figures. Many centers for social action or study organized by clerics or lay persons are expressing a progressive viewpoint.

The Cultural Action group in Colombia and its work in rural parishes, particularly through radio classes, the organizations affiliated with the International Federation of Catholic Institutes for Social and Socio-Religious Research (FERES) in Brazil, Argentina, Chile, and Paraguay, and the work of the Institute for Latin American Political Studies in Montevideo deserve attention as well. The high-quality scientific work performed by the Bellarmino Center under Father Vekemans in Chile has been particularly valuable. Catholic institutions are trying to promote understanding of the daring role that Catholic-inspired movements can play in encouraging reforms in Latin America. They are also trying to help on the international level, namely through the Economics and Humanism teams in Colombia, the Seminary for Latin America at the University of Louvain, and through action by the Jesuits of the Colombianum in Genoa and the Dominicans in Toulouse.

Centuries-old attitudes do not change overnight, and in many respects the Church's political force is still an archaic one in Latin America. But the controversy within the Church between the authoritarian and the socially progressive tendencies has resumed as in the time when Bartolomé de Las Casas was debating with Juan Ginés de Sepulveda before the "Council of the Fourteen" in Valladolid in 1550. The bishops of several countries—Brazil, Colombia, Chile, Peru, Bolivia, Ecuador—have taken the major step of advocating thorough reforms, particularly land reforms. Even though this stand antagonizes a segment of the clergy, the Latin American Episcopal Council (CELAM) approves their stand. The encouragement given by the Church to the creation of a new political progressive force is only beginning; it should increase since the reforms of the Ecumenical Council (Vatican II).

Chilean Elections of 1965 and the Rise of Christian Democracy

It is hard to tell whether the creation of Christian-Social political parties results from the change in the political and social position of the Latin American clergy, or whether the change is due to the creation of progressive Catholic movements by lay persons and foreign priests. In any event, the double victory of the Christian Democratic party in Chile signals a new factor in Latin American political life—a factor that, if the party keeps its promises, may be the most important since the Castro revolution.

Christian social movements assumed some importance in Latin America only very recently, growing and spreading to most countries between 1950 and 1960. The Latin American Christian Democratic Organization (ODCA) includes the entire continent, and Christian social parties have formed under various names in almost all countries. Within a very short time, five to ten years, several of them have acquired enough political influence to seem able to win power and, in the meantime, to encourage any governments that wish to carry out reforms. In Venezuela, the Christian Social Party (COPEI), after having helped Betancourt's Democratic Action group to resist opposition from the right and extreme left, became the second most important party with 40 deputies elected to the legislature, while Democratic Action had 65. In Peru the support of the Christian Democrats enabled President Belaúnde to win on a program of reforms that he seems determined to carry out.

The crucial event was the first accession to power of the Christian Democrats in Chile in 1964 after election campaigns in which definite commitments were made. During the 1964 presidential elections the principal opposition to the

Christian Democratic candidate, Eduardo Frei Montalva, was a Popular Front that united socialists and Communists with open sympathies for the Castro regime. Eduardo Frei asserted, just as his opponents did, that the situation in Latin America called for a revolution and not evolution. But the choice was not, he said, between a conservative and a progressive policy, but between two forms of social revolution, namely a violent revolution of the Castroist type or a revolution using the methods of political democracy.

After winning the presidential election, Eduardo Frei had his initial reform bills rejected by a Congress in which the right wing joined the left wing in opposing him. In the legislative elections of 1965, however, the right-wing opposition collapsed and Christian Democracy won an absolute majority.

Everything occurred as if public opinion had accepted the declaration of Christian Democracy, that the choice is only between revolutionary reforms carried out peacefully in a free society and a violent revolution of the Castroist type. Realignment of the parties left only two large political forces facing each other: Christian Democracy and a Popular Front of Castroist tendency. Christian Democracy has the president and the majority in Congress on its side, is assured of the neutrality of the armed forces, and therefore is able to carry out its program. If the Christian Democrats prove that the antiquated social structure of Latin America can be changed rapidly by nonviolent means and a revolution can be combined with freedom, as President Frei has said, the conditions of Latin American political life might be transformed. The success of Christian Democracy in Chile would probably precipitate needed realignment of political forces in many other countries as well.

12. Middle-Class Pressures, Student Agitation, and Military Interventions

Side by side with these heterogeneous political forces, namely the rural forces under disintegrating feudalism and urban popular forces in the early stage of industrialization—the former quite archaic, the latter still somewhat lagging—the middle classes are the most influential politically. They are still relatively small in most countries as compared to the total population, but very numerous in the cities, which dominate political life. Theirs is the only political force that is completely free and impervious to the paternalism of the old caciques and the new bosses. At present the middle classes dominate Latin America's political life, although often not by entirely legal means. Generally they provide the most active revolutionary elements.

The middle classes are most sensitive to the lags in Latin America's development. They hope to transform their countries, and take it for granted that it is up to them to use their authority to impose those changes, by force if necessary. The new elite, although less cultivated than the old landed aristocracy, is usually well educated. It detests the old ruling classes and blames them for Latin America's underdevelopment. It is hardly acquainted with the peasants, despises them, and is humiliated by their cultural backwardness.

Nationalism of the Middle Classes

Resentment of the handicaps caused by underdevelopment is most acute among the middle classes, and it is they who, with the Communists, have turned nationalism into a political doctrine. The United States is its chief target because of her brutal political interventions in Latin America during the first half of the twentieth century. The middle classes, unlike the old ruling classes, have received their education at home where the history of relations between the United States and Latin America has been strongly slanted against the former. The bulk of European assets were liquidated after World War II, and public utilities, where most of the money had been invested have been nationalized. Hence, present-day foreign economic domination is represented chiefly by the United States. The very sensitive middle classes resent having to depend on the United States for needed economic development.

The sincerity and vigor of the middle classes' anti-Yankee nationalism is to the liking of the people's movements, but it also exposes them to the manipulations of Communist organizers. No one in Latin America today can afford not to be ostentatiously nationalistic. The old landowners' and big business oligarchies are trying to erase the memory of the disrepute in which they were held because of their former cosmopolitan outlook and their readiness to tolerate economic domination by more developed countries. This is why all the members of the old oligarchy who have managed to cling to power have to display extreme nationalism. This forces them to adopt a large part of the middle-class political platform. The rural masses, still insufficiently integrated into national society, are not markedly receptive to true nationalism. On the other hand, since parochialism predisposes them to distrust foreigners, the results are about the same. The new industrial oligarchy is also very sensitive to the appeal of economic nationalism: it wants to drive out large foreign enterprises or force them to use domestic firms as a front, and share the profits. The industrial proletariat also is looking forward to squeezing out foreign concerns on behalf of domestic ones, since the latter will be under closer control of politicians in need of working-class support. The proletariat is still too uneducated politically and too accustomed to paternalism not to seek its spokesmen in the middle classes. Communist organizers, whose primary aim since World War II has been to incite Latin America against North America, find the nationalism of the middle classes a useful weapon. Thus, everything conspires to bring middle-class elements to the fore within the populist parties that make nationalism the primary issue in their platform. This also forces the other political parties to outbid populism in this respect.

The middle classes are too diversified to have a common political philosophy and, as elsewhere, they include many conservatives. However, in Latin American countries, unlike more evenly developed ones, and despite the conservatism of a segment of the middle classes, these classes provide the elements that most often instigate revolutionary agitation. Among the heterogeneous conglomeration of these middle classes or, to be more accurate, this intermediate sector formed by the regularly employed city dwellers, two groups stand out: the students and the officer corps. Those groups are sufficiently educated for political activity and sufficiently organized for revolutionary action.

Both groups were disappointed in the processes of representative democracy in Latin America. They often noted that it led to the hegemony of the rural caciques and hence of archaic society. They saw how useless political parties were that refused to or could not tackle the real problems. The middle classes, determined to eliminate remnants of feudalism and hasten economic emancipation and development, and convinced that they alone can achieve this, are easily lured by authoritarian solutions. They believe these to be the only way to force change on the masses who too easily accept their wretched plight as well as on the aristocrats who strive to retain their privileges.

Political Role of Students

The active participation of students in political life in a revolutionary direction is so widespread in developing countries that it might be regarded as a reliable index of political underdevelopment, on a par with low per capita income—an index of economic underdevelopment—or unbridled fecundity —an index of over-all backwardness. In no highly developed country of the North Atlantic area has the student movement gained wide authority, nor do students as a body play any political role. There is no politically influential students' union in the United States, England, the Netherlands, the

Scandinavian countries, Australia, or Canada. Student-instigated revolutions are inconceivable, and students are not even an effective pressure group in any of those countries. Conversely, unless a ruthless dictatorship succeeds in temporarily silencing them, there is no developing country in Asia, Africa, or Latin America where students are not the prime movers in nationalistic demands, do not claim to speak for the people, and are not the initiators of revolutionary movements.

There are many reasons why students are an unruly political group in the present stage of beginning development, just as they were in Europe in the first half of the nineteenth century. The most obvious is the lack of education and organization of the rural and even urban working people. The notion that students should claim to speak for the labor movement in North America or England is preposterous, whereas in Latin America the small segment of workers who are organized is still accustomed to seek protectors and has not yet lost its awe for the "doctors," the educated people. In countries where education is a privilege, students behave like an elite entrusted with a definite social responsibility and are largely regarded as such by the masses.

Furthermore, the small size of the body politic in Latin America, as in underdeveloped countries generally, where rural populations and even urban fringe groups of recent immigrants from the countryside are barred from real participation in political life, substantially increases the relative weight of the student group. It is misleading to take at face value statistics on education which show that, compared to more developed countries, relatively few young people in Latin America are students. Considering these students' political role, their number should not be compared to the population as a whole, but only to its politically active segment. Since on the average 50 percent of the adult population are illiterate and therefore barred officially or de facto from political life, the ratio of students should at least be doubled in order to reflect their real political influence.

The fact that most Latin American countries set the voting age at 18, which is very young, should also be taken into account. Thus, when the political role of students in Latin America is discussed, it should be kept in mind that not only university but also high school students are involved, if the voting age is 18, political activity is likely to start at 15.

The Reforma Universitaria Movement

Students freely engage in politics because many governments, eager to secure a following, have helped to organize a student movement just as they promoted a labor movement, even though it might hamper their own freedom. Not enough attention is devoted to political implications of the unusual privileges granted the student body by the so-called University Democratization movement. This movement started in Argentina after 1918 and became a political training movement within the university. A change in the philosophy and structure of many universities had become necessary because the quality and teaching methods were not up to standard and also because the governments had been trying to control them. The Reforma Universitaria, a modernization movement, strove to bring teaching methods up to date and make the university independent. Joint government by faculty and students seemed the best way to achieve this.

As the movement prevailed in several countries, the autonomous university became a state within the state. It is the one institution almost impervious to interference by government, even by authoritarian governments. The university becomes a fort where, in case of street violence, students barricade themselves in order to carry on their agitation in safety from the police.

The countries where the Reforma Universitaria movement has been most successful are Argentina, Uruguay, Cuba, Peru, and Venezuela. In the first two, the students' political activity has been minimal, since the countries' level of development was high enough to prevent the students from being the foremost revolutionary element. In the other countries, as well as in Chile, Colombia, Brazil, Mexico, and Bolivia, the new university organization did foster the students' political activity. The most extreme case of university control by the students was probably that of Guatemala under the regimes of Juan José Arevalo and Jacobo Arbenz between 1945 and 1954.

The Reforma Universitaria movement also increased political activity within many secondary schools. Some advocates of the system even contended, although such extremes were rare, that it was essential to hold the final examinations for the year within one short span, regardless of daily schedules, so as not to interfere with student strikes. They also maintained that students who failed to take the examinations or who consistently failed in their studies should not be expelled, because the university needed students who could devote themselves exclusively for long periods to political organizing.

Students usually have no ties with the rural proletariat and very few with the urban proletariat, whose standards of living are so low that they cannot send their children to high schools or the university. Today, however, education is no longer the privilege of the propertied classes. Children of recent immigrants, employees, small shopkeepers, and low-echelon civil servants regard secondary and higher education as the usual path to a higher social status. Although higher education is usually free or inexpensive, students from poor families have a hard time, and very often their life does not improve financially even after graduation. The all too numerous sons of impoverished rural aristocrats do not fare much better.

Thus, the students form a group of ambitious, usually dissatisfied young people who seek radical social reform. This group is the most accessible to Communist propaganda. Unlike the peasants and workers, they have been trained in theoretical thinking and are receptive to ideologies. Where political methods are concerned, the authoritarian ones offered by Communism strongly attract educated people who feel superior to the masses. At present, many of them have found in Castroism a model they would like the rest of Latin America to copy.

Students have their place in a recurrent revolutionary pattern starting with street agitation that at first seems to be only the usual student row. It may have been provoked by a political event (today generally a foreign policy issue) and takes the form of pro-Castro or anti-United States demonstrations. University problems also provide a good opportunity for agitation against, for example, an administrator whose political opinions are disliked, an unpopular professor, or even a rise in transportation costs or the abolition of student discounts in theaters—two highly incendiary measures.

Student parades are often swelled by people from the favellas, sporadic workers crowded in the slums on the outskirts of Latin American capitals. Then buses and trolleys are overturned and set on fire, food stores are looted, and the windows of the United States embassy and Information Services are broken. Unless the country is ruled by a ruthless dictator, the government is very reluctant to use force in restoring order because hordes of children are mingled with university students. The conditions for a revolutionary movement are present, and the organizers among the students are all set to exploit the situation. Everything hinges upon the attitude of the military, who may intervene.

Political Interventions by the Military

The most typical and best known feature of Latin America political life is assuredly the role so often played by the military. The world over, Latin America is regarded as the land of barracks revolutions, officer juntas, and dictatorships of colonels and generals.

It may seem paradoxical to describe the political role of the military as one aspect of the role of the middle classes and to interpret it as an expression of political forces in the advanced or developing society. Resort to arms to seize power occurred in the very first days of independence, and therefore its recurrence appears to many observers as an anachronism. The proliferation of military dictatorships outside Latin America today suggests, however, that they are a feature of the first stage of development, rather than of true underdevelopment. Military interventions in politics are tied to political, economic, and social immaturity, but also to the weakening of archaic economic and social structures and to attempts to modernize them.

It is true that generals, colonels, and even lieutenants never stopped meddling in politics in Latin America and using their men to seize power or control the government. But these are not the same officers or the same army as formerly, and their intentions in politics have taken on different characteristics.

Military interventions in Latin American politics have naturally differed widely. Some of them have not even been political, and have aimed only at defending the interest of the military. Nevertheless, in view of most officers' social background, education, and nationalistic ideologies, the political force they represent, like that of the students, may be tied to that of the middle classes. Although the methods have been quite different, interventions by the military have generally been inspired by similar nationalist sentiments and a determination to supersede the aristocracy. A large segment of the officer corps who dislike the former ruling classes and the remnants of caciquismo would prefer a people's progressive movement—provided it is authoritarian and does not cut the military budget—to the aristocracy's conservative liberalism. Differences in methods aside, what most clearly differentiates the political outlook of the officer corps from that of the students, is that, especially since Castro, the officers are usually immune to the lure of Communism.

Frequent as political interventions by the military may be in Latin America, oversimplified generalizations would be unwise because their frequency varies greatly, depending on the countries involved. Until very recently such interventions occurred in all countries, and they still do in most of them. Today only three countries appear completely free of them; the best proof is the substantial cutback in military budgets—an impossibility as long as the military are a political force. The three countries are Costa Rica, where in 1948 President Figueres disbanded the army altogether and left only a small police force; Uruguay where, since the abolition of the presidential regime by President Batlle y Ordóñez in 1903, the military are no longer a political force; and Mexico, which is more interesting because it is a large country. Since Cárdenas was elected president in 1934, the military has been under the control of the party born during the 1910 revolution. In none of these three countries does the share of the armed forces in the budget exceed 12 percent, whereas 25 percent is usual in Latin America.

It is too early to tell whether the single party in Cuba, which is now armed to the teeth, will achieve enduring results similar to Mexico's. The single party in Bolivia was not successful in this respect. When President Paz Estenssoro was confronted by the miners' militias he had to expand the armed forces. Their chief, General Barrientos, promptly seized power when insurrections broke out in 1964. In Chile the most brutal interventions have long been a thing of the past, although the relatively neutral army is still a powerful force. Hence the government finds it wise to heed any demands they make as far as their professional interests are concerned. In Colombia and Brazil military interventions have been less frequent than in the rest of Latin America, and whenever they have occurred the hesitant attitude of the armed forces proved that they knew they were overstepping their role. In Brazil, after several fairly discreet interventions, the military seized power outright when a serious crisis arose in 1964. The present very difficult political situation in Colombia may result in a military intervention in the near future.

With these reservations in mind, and considering only the fairly recent past, it is obvious that the military have dominated Latin American politics. In the fifty years from 1907 to 1957, Venezuela had only three years of civilian government, and the Dominican Republic six. All the Central American countries except Costa Rica have been governed by the military longer than by civilians.

Just before World War II, all except four Latin American countries had military governments. In Bolivia Colonel Toro assumed dictatorial powers in 1936, was replaced by Colonel Busch in 1937, by General Peñaranda in 1940, and by Commander Villaroel in 1943. After 1930, the Dominican Republic was governed by dictator Generalissimo Rafael Trujillo. In Ecuador a stormy military regime was in power after 1925. In Guatemala General Ubico, in Honduras General Tiburcio Carías, and in Nicaragua General Anastasio Somoza wielded absolute power. In Peru where, after 1939, there was to be a ten-year period of constitutional government under Presidents Manuel Prado and José Bustamante, Marshal Oscar Benavides still held the power he had seized after the assassination of Colonel Sànchez Cerro in 1933. El Salvador was governed by General Hernández Martínez, Paraguay by General Estigarribia, and Venezuela by General López Contreras, who in 1930 was succeeded by another officer, Medina Angarita. When the United States forces left Haiti after an occupation that lasted from 1915 to 1934, the presidential guard instituted a praetorian regime that is still in force. Cuba was different because Sergeant Fulgencio Batista's dictatorship was imposed by noncommissioned officers who had rioted against their officers. In Brazil dictator Getulio Vargas was a civilian, but his dictatorship was a product of the 1930 revolution, which in turn had been organized by the *tenentes* (lieutenants). These officers had taken all the key posts, and eventually all of them became colonels and generals. In Argentina, the regime had resumed its constitutional forms, but, since it was the product of the coup d'état engineered in 1930 by General Uriburu, it was at the mercy of the military, who brought it down in 1943. Constitutional regimes existed in four countries, but in Mexico this was the doing of a general, Lázaro Cárdenas, chosen as successor by another general, Calles; a similar situation prevailed in Uruguay, where General Baldomir was attempting to give a solid basis to civilian rule.

Such unanimous submission to military rule did not recur. After 1945, many Latin American countries reverted to civilian regimes for varying lengths of time, but these often followed military interventions. In October, 1944, in Guatemala a military junta enabled President Juan Arevalo to start his liberal presidency. In Brazil in 1945, the military put a stop to Vargas' dictatorship and reestablished a constitutional regime, whose properly elected president, incidentally, was Marshal Dutra. At the same time young officers in Venezuela enabled one of the most truly democratic parties in Latin America, Romulo Betancourt's Acción Democratica, to accede briefly to power. In 1944 in El Salvador the military, joined by students, overthrew dictator Hernández Martínez, but shortly thereafter allowed another military dictatorship to succeed his.

Since 1959, many other military interventions have occurred. In July, 1962, in Peru the armed forces refused to abide by election results and a junta replaced the government without encountering any resistance. In November, 1961, in Ecuador a majority of the military forced President Velasco Ibarra to step down and give his post to Vice-President Arosemena. In October, 1960, in El Salvador a junta ousted Colonel

José María Lemus, only to be toppled three months later by another military coup. The Argentine military, which always kept President Arturo Frondizi under tight control, toppled him in the spring of 1962, and for a year the political scene was dominated by dissensions between generals and admirals that culminated in the battle in Buenos Aires between military moderates and extremists that September. Even in Brazil, where the military are less inclined to indulge in coups, their political pressure grew after President Jânio Quadros resigned in the summer of 1961, and culminated in the coup of April, 1964. In Venezuela, President Betancourt succeeded in handing over power legally to his successor Raul Leoni in December, 1963, but only after having to put down battalion and regiment uprisings all through his term of office. The years 1963 and 1964 were particularly notable for the number and frequency of military coups and government ousters, unequaled in the twentieth century, in Guatemala, Ecuador, the Dominican Republic, Honduras, Brazil, and Bolivia.

Caudillismo and Militarism

The military have incessantly intervened in Latin America's political life. But the interventions have been of two types, and the term "military intervention" is not equally applicable to both. In one type of intervention, one man, although he bears the title of colonel or general, uses his personal armed followers for strictly personal aims. In the other type of intervention, an officer corps resorts to force or threat of force in the belief that the military should play a political role. The relatively recent development in Latin America of a regularly organized military profession whose members have been trained in military schools and have an esprit de corps differentiates the two types of coups, whose only common trait is their illegality.

In the post-independence period, Latin American armies retained the improvised character of revolutionary forces. Their equipment was most primitive, the officers of the revolution had been trained in the field, and when peace was restored many of them resumed their civilian occupations, their political activities in particular. Many of them were then replaced in the army by adventurers anxious to share the profits of politics. Latin America was still quasi-feudal, so that all these men had personal followers and were able to arm them and lead them in the battle for power. Since there was no true national spirit among the population and no regular army to serve the nation, the chiefs of the standing army or of the improvised armies could use troops for personal benefit. Both types of forces were recruited among ignorant peasants, mostly Indians, mestizos, or mulattoes. Civilian or military, the chiefs of bands all dubbed themselves colonels and generals. The revolts and coups d'état they organized, although called military, were in fact only a form of the more general phenomena of caciquismo and caudillismo.

The use of armed force persisted for varying periods. In Brazil it did not take place. In Argentina it ended in the middle of the nineteenth century with the downfall of Rosas, and in Chile only a little later. In Mexico it was in full swing when the 1910 revolution broke out, and it lingered on. When Cárdenas was elected president in 1934, despite the rising authority of the revolutionary party, generals were still competing for power among themselves. These generals of the Mexican revolution were warriors, but not professional military men. General Obregón was a cattle raiser, General Carranza a latifundio owner; Pancho Villa, who held power for a while, was only a bandit, and Zapata a warm-hearted peasant who had become the messiah of land reform. Porfirio Díaz, the dictator ousted by the revolution, had been a lawyer before playing a glorious part in defeating Maximilian and Bazaine under the leadership of Juárez, another lawyer. The military were still used for personal ambitions in the Dominican Republic in 1961 under Trujillo, and still are in Haiti and a few Central American countries where, because of social retardation, a large segment of the population cannot yet take part in political life and armies of a few hundred or thousand mercenaries can remain in the personal service of the man who pays them well.

Interventions by Military

The type of armed intervention just described is on its way out in Latin America. It is only the expression of lingering archaic political forces. The interesting fact is that today in the most advanced Latin American countries, a highly organized military profession, far from resorting to such archaic use of armed men, is preventing it. The military are now led by officer cadres trained in military colleges. The officer corps is too well organized to enable one man to use an army for strictly personal motives. Interventions must express the collective will of the officer corps or a large segment of it and correspond to their ideology or interests.

Brazil is the first country where the military became aware of their professional role. The officers were professionals who accepted the supremacy of constitutional powers and their own special mission of defending the nation. The monarchy, which lasted from independence until 1889, laid the basis for civilian control of the military. However, as the monarchy weakened, so did the relative discipline of the military, a discipline that had emerged in Brazil earlier than in the other countries. Dissatisfaction of the military, who believed they had been treated unfairly by the emperor, was a prime factor in the establishment of a republic in 1889. The success of the revolution led by General Deodoro da Fonseca, in alliance with the positivist philosophers whose propaganda had been encouraged by Dom Pedro, ushered in a period of political interventions by the military, which apparently is not over. In the first half of the nineteenth century, Brazil seemed more advanced than other Latin American countries with respect to the attitude of the armed services, but in the twentieth century this apparently is no longer true.

Rather it was in Chile that the new attitude emerged and reforms were carried out, leading to the formation of a corps of officers conscious of their professional role in the nation. Chile took the initiative of reorganizing the armed services with the help of European professionals. Her successes in the War of the Pacific (1879–1883), which enabled her to wrest from Peru and Bolivia the nitrate-rich northern deserts, moved her to maintain a modern army. In 1885 the government asked Germany to send a military mission and granted very broad powers to its head, General Koerner, who was appointed Chief of the Chilean General Staff. A military college was organized to train young officers, and a military academy to train higher officers. Their instruction was carried out by German officers and was supplemented by additional training in the German army. Koerner also prevailed upon Chile to enact the first Latin American conscription law, which deeply changed the nature of the services by bringing in other elements than the most backward and least integrated in the nation. Koerner's reforms gave the military profession a technical character and a dignity it had not had since independence.

Chile's example spread rapidly to a large number of countries. Argentina and Bolivia received military missions from Germany while Brazil, Ecuador, Peru, and Paraguay were sent French military missions. Other countries were indirectly influenced by European military missions when they detached some of their officers to train in military colleges of Latin American countries where foreign missions were operating; Chile in particular did much to disseminate German influence. In the Caribbean, during periods of military occupation by the United States, the latter tried to reorganize the armed forces in the countries involved. Despite hostility to military occupation, the United States has left her mark on the armed forces reorganized by her professionals. Little progress was achieved in these small countries, however, because of their low general level of development.

The influence of the military missions, the training geared to national defense, the technical nature of the training required by modern equipment, all have contributed to give Latin American military men a new idea of their social function. This, however, has not stopped or substantially lessened the frequency of political interventions by the military, because they result primarily from a deep concern for internal security. The international situation combined with political instability places the burden of maintaining domestic peace upon the armed services.

Internal Security Versus National Defense

Although in the nineteenth century Latin America took part in international wars—Mexico against the United States in 1847, Brazil, Argentina, and Uruguay against Paraguay's dictator Solano López from 1864 to 1870, Chile against Peru and Bolivia from 1879 to 1883—it has not lived as dangerously as Europe. After 1883, only one international war took place in Latin America, from 1932 to 1935 between Paraguay and Bolivia. Today the United States provides security from overseas threats, while the Organization of American States seems capable of imposing peaceful solutions to disputes among Latin American countries. The threat of internal subversion has long been far more serious than the danger of foreign invasion.

In Europe, political conditions never allowed the armed forces of the great powers to forget for any length of time that their role was to ensure national defense. Hence the officer corps was not trained to become involved in domestic economic and social problems, at least until the post-World War II period when the possibility of total or subversive war arose. The professional training and sometimes the social background of the typical career officer might induce him to distrust democracy and regard politicians as demagogues or as impractical men of ideas. Nevertheless he was seldom tempted to replace them and was not suited to do so. Insofar as these specialists in war took part in politics in Europe and North America, it was as a pressure group—a most effective one—concerned with the structure of the armed forces and sometimes with foreign policy.

In Latin America, on the contrary, the military are not usually called upon to ensure national defense. They are not even particularly well trained for that purpose. Lieuwen [1] notes that the armed forces in the Latin American countries are relatively small. The statistics he provides for 1955 indicate a total of 541,000 men for the armed forces of twenty countries, an average of less than three soldiers per 1,000 inhabitants, which is very low.

At present Cuba is in a different category with its militia system of hundreds of thousands, although in 1960 its population did not reach 7 million. Of the other countries, only Argentina maintains a fairly large armed force—155,000 men in 1955. The Brazilian armed services, which used to be the second largest after Argentina's, had decreased to

[1] Edwin Lieuwen, *Arms and Politics in Latin America* (New York, rev. edition, 1961).

107,000 in 1955—a small figure for a country of 65 million inhabitants. No other country, not even Mexico with its 35 million inhabitants, had over 50,000 men in its armed forces.

The size of the military in the various countries is indicated in table 9. To justify the cost of maintaining the Latin Ameri-

TABLE 9
SIZE OF ARMED FORCES, 1955 ᵃ

Mexico	47,000	Dominican Republic	18,500
Chile	41,000	Venezuela	17,240
Peru	37,500	Colombia	16,700
Ecuador	19,900	Bolivia	12,000

ᵃ Figures taken from Edwin Lieuwen, *Arms and Politics in Latin America* (New York, rev. edition, 1961).

can armed forces, which is very high despite their small size, the argument most often employed with the United States, which subsidizes them in part (317 million dollars as an outright grant and over 140 million to be refunded for the period 1952–1959) is the threat of internal Communist subversion.

Under these circumstances, except for special cases such as that of Argentina, which at times has had imperialist aspirations, officers tend to believe that the military is one of the branches of the government, next to the executive and the legislative. They often regard themselves as the branch entrusted with keeping the others in line. Hence the Brazilian joke about the Square of the Three Powers in Brasília where the government palaces stand, the aforesaid powers being dubbed Army, Navy, and Air Force.

Civilian Responsibility for Military Interventions

The role of the armed services lends itself to much misinterpretation because the military are constantly being asked to intervene in politics. All of Latin America complains about the excessive role of the military in political life, but it should be said in all fairness that all social classes and all parties try to provoke these interventions whenever they are displeased with their government. All too often under the Latin American regime of presidential dominance, presidential succession breeds political crises, either because a president whose term is about to expire tries to cling to office illegally, or because he tries to impose a successor of his own choosing. This flaw of Latin American political regimes is called *continuism*. When it occurs, the advocates of legality request the military to restore the rule of law by ousting the dictator or would-be dictator. Also, the losers in an election, who are not accustomed to accept defeat, claim that the elections were fraudulent and ask the military to seize power in order to hold better ones. This is a convenient excuse, and the military do not always need prodding. Seizure of power by a junta that promises to hold proper elections is quite customary; the Peruvian generals did so in 1962. A large segment of public opinion invariably supports the military in such a case.

An excellent example of pressure on the military chiefs by politicians and the press was the political agitation in Brazil in 1955 after Kubitschek was elected president. The losing party was the National Democratic Union (UDN), one of the two large conservative parties which is supported by the most enlightened segment of the gentry and is traditionally the most respectful of the constitution. Nonetheless it was the UDN that urged the military to prevent the elected president from assuming his functions. For a long time, public opinion was divided into *Golpistas,* who favored a coup and wished certain generals to carry it out, an *Anti-Golpistas* who wished other generals to prevent it. Brazilian military leaders needed a great deal of self-restraint to resist the urging. The fact that they themselves were divided helped to prevent the coup. In 1964, however, the military complied with similar requests because Goulart had recklessly fostered unruliness among the non-commissioned officers, and this strengthened the unity of the officers.

Political Orientation of Military Interventions

It is widely believed that most military interventions in Latin America have been reactionary, or at least have aimed at preventing popular forces from reforming an archaic society. Such a belief, however, stems from seemingly logical reasoning rather than from actual observation of facts. Even a specialist on Latin American affairs as knowledgeable as Wilgus wrote: "The officer class was composed chiefly of older sons of the aristocracy who entered the military service for the social prestige it gave them. With control of military forces, it was not difficult for the aristocracy to control the government." [2]

This comes from equating Latin America with Europe. Such reasoning, as a matter of fact, would be invalid almost anywhere outside Europe. Military interventions in Latin America would be impossible to understand if their instigators were elder sons of aristocrats. Although these interventions have usually (but not always) been aimed at governments whose form was democratic, this does not make them politically conservative. This is because in the countries involved, compliance with the forms of democracy has often led to the hegemony of the most archaic political forces.

There have also been other types of military interventions. Some of them were not political or have been very conservative, especially in Argentina, whose level of social development is closer to Europe's than to that of the other Latin American countries. On the whole, at any rate until the rise of Communism and Castroism in Latin America, political interventions by the military had aimed at change rather than at maintaining the status quo. Military interventions did much to prevent a return to caudillismo and to hasten the decline of government by the upper class.

One of the reasons for this is the officers' social background. Despite the European traditions of Latin America, the officers were recruited (at least in the nineteenth century) from other social strata than in Europe. Since most of them came from the middle classes, they usually wished to reform societies that had remained very aristocratic.

Stereotyped thinking valid only for Europe usually pictures the military profession as traditionally tied to the conservative ruling classes because respect for hierarchy is one of its basic

[2] A. C. Wilgus, "The Chemistry of Political Change in Latin America," *Annals of the American Academy of Political and Social Science,* July, 1962, p. 44.

values and because its influential members belong to those ruling classes. This image of professional military men attached to the past and to social order is not true of all European countries nor for all times, but it does have deep roots in the long tradition of monarchy that partly revived, even after the revolutions. The nature of feudalism and the stature it gave to monarchy enabled the nobility who were specialists in the arts of war to transfer into the royal army when the European monarchies extended their sovereignty. The old European ruling class, deprived of its political functions by national integration and of some of its income by the lowering of land rent, found a refuge in the army. Instead of meddling in politics, it removed itself from civilian society. Similarly, in the nineteenth century elements of the old bourgeoisie often joined the military profession to escape overly rapid social change they could not cope with.

Position of the Military Caste Within the Middle Class

In Latin America, however, military traditions are altogether different. The modern military profession only started to emerge in the nineteenth century as the product of revolutionary armies instead of traditionalist royal armies. The landed aristocracy had not yet lost its wealth or its political power. Far from it, Creole aristocracy, freed from the tutelage of the Peninsulares, was at its height in the nineteenth century. Only exceptionally were members of a wealthy ruling aristocracy attracted by the military profession. On the other hand, the masses were too ignorant and despised to be admitted to military colleges. With few isolated exceptions, they could join the services only as enlisted men.

Hence the officers were usually recruited from the middle classes. The armed forces in Latin America, far from being a haven for men barred from power by social evolution, were the stepping stone for a class on the rise and aspiring to wrest power from the aristocracy. Within the static societies with a rigid hierarchy based on latifundio ownership, there were very few ways to improve one's social status. The liberal professions provided some opportunities but were largely monopolized by the aristocracy. Industry was scarcely developed and many of the large enterprises, notably trading concerns, were in the hands of foreigners or recent immigants. Military colleges, on the contrary, provided openings for young men of little wealth, particularly if they already had some connection with the military.

Since lower-class people, whether white or colored, were barred de facto through subtle discrimination, it is not true that the officer corps in Latin America was democratically recruited. It would be even less accurate to say that its background ties it to the traditional ruling classes and that it tends to be used as a tool for the preservation of the status quo. If any generalizations are in order, the most legitimate would be that within the very diversified middle-class group which has gained power in the years since World War I, the officers have tended to form a caste equally remote from the aristocracy and from the people. The very great opportunities for advancement that the political power of the Latin American armed forces have provided, coupled with the ease with which officers' sons are admitted to military schools, have tended to make recruitment hereditary.

It would be useful to supplement rumors and personal impressions on the officers' social background with solid facts, but practically none are available. An article by José Luis de Imaz [3] provides some accurate data. Even in Argentina where, more than in other Latin American countries, the officers have on the whole intervened in political life on the side of the conservatives, the research done by Imaz confirms the absence of ties between the officer corps and the landed aristocracy, as well as most of the old-stock Argentine population. In Argentina, where a large number of immigrants arrived in the last century, out of 317 general officers, the author found only 71 descendants of old Argentine families, against 246 whose families were of recent Italian, German, or Spanish background. In 114 cases where the occupations of the generals' fathers are known, the three main categories were: businessmen, employees, and the military (69 in the latter category), whereas the number of landowners (*estancieros*) did not exceed ten.

[3] José Luis de Imaz, "Los que mandan: Las fuerzas armadas en Argentina," *América Latina* (Rio de Janeiro), December, 1964.

The large majority of these Argentine officers come from the cities. The least represented provinces in the Argentine armed forces are the most traditionalist in outlook (Córdoba, for instance, did not provide over 4 percent of the generals).

Armed services of this type could hardly tolerate government by the aristocracy, especially since in Latin America the old ruling class was generally cosmopolitan in outlook, was quite willing to put up with foreign economic domination, and cared little about industrialization. The officer corps, on the contrary, was very nationalistic, and this in Latin America inevitably brings in economic issues. For many reasons, therefore, the armed forces tended to promote change in the political, economic, and social structure rather than to preserve the status quo.

Naturally, any generalization that becomes too systematic is bound to be erroneous. The officer corps cannot be the same either in its composition or in its outlook in twenty countries as different from one another as Haiti and Argentina, and it has not remained unchanged throughout one and a half centuries. Since it plays a political role, the officer corps must necessarily represent different opinions. The different services are not recruited in the same way and do not have the same outlook. Neither do higher officers after they have become generals share the opinions of second lieutenants.

THE NAVY. The decadence of the landed aristocracy forced some of the too numerous sons of the aristocracy into the middle classes. These young men often became professional military men, a fact that may account for some nostalgia on the part of the armed services. In any event, the navy is in a special category. It preceded the other branches of the service in stressing technological progress. This factor, and perhaps also the prestige of the English in the nineteenth century, attracted student officers from higher social strata than the army and fostered greater discipline and professionalism. As a result, the navy was often apolitical, and its occasional interventions tended to favor the conservatives. At the same time it was usually more respectful of the constitution.

Argentina's case is typical: on the whole the navy stayed aloof from the Peronists, but when their opponents started to gain popular support, it instigated the revolt against the regime. In 1962, indignation about the compromises between the Radical party and the Peronists was greatest within the navy. In Brazil and Chile, the navy was more reluctant than the army to intervene in politics, and, whenever it did, it usually supported the conservatives. Outside these three countries, the navy is not a major force in Latin America. None of the other seventeen countries has a navy of over 3,700 men (the size of Ecuador's), and several have none at all.

The air force officer corps is also in a special category. Its political attitude is harder to define, but it has often been the most turbulent element among the Latin American armed services.

TENENTISMO. Many authors believe that the political tendency of military interventions depends on the leaders' position within the hierarchy. Thus, high-ranking officers are more inclined than younger men to try to preserve the status quo, and interventions organized by them tend to favor the conservatives. This is difficult to prove because groups of young officers often start a movement and, when it seems successful, the hierarchy rallies and a general lends it his name. Brazil is often mentioned as an illustration of the officers' change of heart as they rise in rank. The lieutenants who engineered the strongly reformist revolution of 1930 supported the semi-Fascist coup of Vargas in 1937 after they had become colonels, and by the time they were generals they overturned Vargas in 1954, when he again had moved closer to the masses. But the evolution of the officers' thought may have resulted from the social changes between 1930 and 1954 as much as from their riper age and higher rank. The 1930 revolution supported by the young officers was a middle-class revolution against the aristocracy, whereas the labor regime heralded by Vargas in 1954 loomed as an omen of impending proletarian revolution.

Usually, when they do intervene in politics, generals and lieutenants differ in the methods they favor rather than in the side they support. Thus, the generals try to use moderate methods, whereas the young officers lean toward ruthless ones, regardless of their respective political tendencies. For differen-

tiating between the two categories of interventions, this criterion seems more reliable than the allegedly conservative beliefs
of senior officers and the progressive convictions of junior
officers.

Types of Military Interventions

The most archaic type of intervention, a vestige of caudillismo that leads to purely personal dictatorship, is generally
carried out by the police rather than by the military. It is now
practically a thing of the past in Latin America, although of
long endurance in the Dominican Republic and Haiti. In Central America it is still a source of political turmoil that may
give Castroists the opportunity to step in. But the countries
where this is likely to happen do not account for over 10
percent of the Latin American population.

A less archaic form of military intervention consists of direct seizure of power by a junta. This is intervention by the
military as a group. In the period immediately following
1943, before Perón diverted to his own ends the action started
by the military, this was the method used in Argentina by the
Group of United Officers (GOU) led by colonels. It was also
the method selected by the military in Peru in 1962. Similar
interventions have occurred in Paraguay, El Salvador, Honduras, and other countries. The junta may take the name of a
general or a colonel or sometimes of a civilian as a front, or it
may act openly in its own right. In any event, the junta wields
the actual power and its members divide government functions
among themselves, an officer being appointed to head each
ministry. This type of intervention has very often been chosen
by young officers in revolt against the hierarchy. In Cuba in
1933 it was even used by noncommissioned officers who
ousted their chiefs and divided the higher military posts among
themselves. The junta seldom rules for any length of time.
Internal rivalries make for a stormy rule and enable one man
to use the movement to promote his own career. Sometimes
one figure manages, as Perón did, to find backers among the
civilians. Furthermore, when the junta seizes power directly,
the blatant absence of legality usually compels it to pose as a
transition regime intending to reestablish order and hold elec-

tions. These elections, it claims, will be free because the junta will supervise them.

The latest and most frequent type of military intervention is control over a civilian power, which preserves a semblance of legality. The military only exercises a veto power over the government's decision, quite openly in many cases. It demands the appointment by the president of men it trusts as heads of ministries, and almost always gets officers appointed to the armed services ministries. Often, while respecting the form of the constitution, the military appoints one of its chiefs to supervise a congress that can be intimidated by the threat of sterner measures. This happened in Brazil in April, 1964, when Congress elected as president Marshal Castelo Branco, the candidate promoted by the rebellious generals. After 1958 the military in Argentina put pressure on the constitutionally elected powers to force President Frondizi to hew to their policy. Military control over civilian powers in Argentina was particularly tight and cynical. In August, 1961, for instance, military chiefs called upon President Frondizi to learn why he had been host to the Cuban Communist Che Guevara. The president had to appease them. Throughout 1961 similar interventions occurred, and each time the president had to back down. In October, 1961, 25 officers handed him a memorandum expressing the anxiety his policy had aroused within the armed forces. The president was forced to comply with their wishes and to declare that the memorandum was "constructive" in character. The Argentine military nevertheless refrained from completely relinquishing the appearances of legality and assuming power outright. When in August, 1962, a group of generals decided to give up the pretense of constitutionality by setting up an overt military dictatorship, most of the military resisted and got rid of the men they regarded as too cynical. The majority wished to leave the government in the hands of the legal authorities but to forbid them to ally themselves with the Peronists in their domestic policy or give any support to Castroism in foreign policy.

Very few Latin American countries escape this form of military intervention. The military always control at least the management of the armed forces and are increasingly influencing foreign policy as Castroism develops into a political force in inter-Latin American relations. Only three governments, the Costa Rican, Uruguayan, and to a lesser extent perhaps the Mexican, are in control of their armed forces. Everywhere else, even in Chile, the military form a body independent from the state. The armed forces themselves determine their strength, equipment, and the percentage of the budget to be earmarked for defense, and they impose upon the government the defense ministers of their choice.

The armed forces' preference for intervention in the form of pressure upon civilian governments rather than in outright assumption of power shows a beginning professionalism within the military. In the most advanced Latin American countries, the military are no longer sure that their interference in policy-making is legitimate; when they do interfere they suffer some qualms of conscience, since they recognize the legality of elections and respect constitutionality. But just because such pressure on the government soothes the awakening professional conscience of the military, this type of intervention is becoming more frequent, even in countries where the armed forces are reluctant to use more ruthless methods. In the end, the government refuses to give in to demands that only grow increasingly insolent as the previous ones are met. At that point, the military have committed themselves too much to back down, and their only way out is to seize power. This is what happened in Peru in 1962 when President Prado held his ground, and in Argentina when President Frondizi was finally deposed after refusing to capitulate to ever rasher demands. The intervention in Brazil in 1964 was different, because a revolutionary situation brought about direct military intervention.

Effects of Military Interventions

The balance sheet of political interference by the military includes both a debit and a credit side. The debit is certainly very heavy, and it is not mainly political. Military interventions prevent the institutions of representative democracy from operating properly, but it is difficult to differentiate between cause and effect. Conceivably, the predilection of the armed forces for authoritarian regimes hampers the establishment of political freedom in Latin America. On the other hand, unsatisfactory operation of democratic institutions in societies that are changing too rapidly and too haphazardly and thus retain too many archaic traits may provoke military interventions. Actually, while the military coups d'état have often interrupted the operation of democratic political institutions, as they did in eight countries between 1962 and 1964, they also have often served to reinstate their operation, as in Brazil in 1944, in Venezuela in 1945, and in Colombia in 1957.

INSTABILITY. The greatest harm caused by military interference in politics is something that the instigators expect the least—disorder and anarchy. Although the coups engineered by the military, who only have to show their strength instead of actually using it, are usually peaceful, they often trigger a period of turmoil that completely paralyzes a would-be authoritarian government. The era of the caudillos, when individuals who were personally the masters of the armed forces tried to seize power, is past. Now interventions are carried out by a collective leadership that is never completely unanimous. Hence palace revolutions are inevitable. Different branches of the armed services contend for power among themselves, junior officers oppose their generals, some officers who try more or less successfully to remain apolitical seek to keep the intervention down to a minimum and above all to conceal it, while others want to seize power outright. It also happens with increasing frequency that military interventions lead the officer corps to be caught up in politics, and this in turn gives rise to ideological differences, just as among professional politicians. Cliques form, rallying respectively to the conservative or the progressive camp, and the two are ready to fight one another.

It is sometimes stated that political divisions within the armed forces, which arise whenever the latter go beyond defending their particular interests as a profession, are the best way to prevent military coups. The disease, so to speak, should provide its own cure. According to this theory, the responsible elements among the officer corps, in order to avoid creating and exposing their political divisions, would prefer to remain neutral. This is indeed what happened in 1961 in Brazil, when Goulart skillfully used oppositions within the armed forces to enable him to accede to the presidency after Quadros resigned. But the military are not always so wise, and in fact were not in Brazil after 1964. It often happens that internecine rivalries among the military, hushed long enough to enable them to seize power, are unleashed when the time comes to use it. The two military juntas that succeeded one another within three months as the government of El Salvador in 1960–1961 are typical. The pattern was the same in Bolivia between 1936 and 1943, when the military replaced Colonel Toro with Colonel Busch, Colonel Busch with General Peñaranda, who in turn was ousted to make way for Commander Villaroel.

In Argentina, a more advanced country, the situation since 1943 also demonstrates the instability of military governments. The 1943 coup that ended the constitutional regime had been organized by General Rawson in an attempt to force Argentina to enter the war on the Allied side. Three days later, the young officers of the GOU (Group of United Officers) who were sympathetic to National Socialism ousted General Rawson and replaced him with General Ramírez. In 1944 the military in turn forced General Ramírez to resign and replaced him with General Farrell, who was only a front man for Colonel Perón. During Perón's dictatorship there were constant conspiracies by other military groups. One of these plots did topple Perón for a short time in October, 1945, and again in 1955. Dissension among the military then resumed, one wishing for a return to constitutional government, the other intending to give power directly to the military. General Lonardi, who had seized power in September, 1955, had to step down two months later when General Aramburu, backed by young officers, took his place. At that point complete anarchy prevailed among the armed forces until the battle of September, 1962, when the most extremist military clan was defeated. In a much less advanced country, the Dominican Republic, the encounter at the end of April, 1965, between a segment of the armed forces led by General Wessin y Wessin and another under Colonel Caamaño degenerated into a bloody civil war.

Internal quarrels prevent the military from performing any government functions. Such regimes, even more than the most unstable parliamentary regimes, must devote much of their energy to satisfying officers' personal ambitions. The most obvious result of two years of military control over the government and of quarrels among the military in Argentina was the ruin of a national economy that had not recovered from Perón's erratic rule. It also caused the devaluation of a currency that before Perón had been the strongest in Latin America. Military regimes of this type combine the flaws of arbitrary rule in dictatorial regimes with the instability of the degenerating forms of democracy.

HIGH COST. These political drawbacks are compounded by purely military ones, namely the disorganization of the armed services. The short-lived victory of each group heralds purges, particularly among the senior officers. Not only does the rapid turnover of generals disorganize the services, but it is very costly to the treasury. This is because professional solidarity demands that purges take the form of compulsory retirement for the generals who must be given pensions, and these are high in Latin America compared to the low per capita income.

The debit side of the armed forces' political role is especially heavy in the financial and economic realms. Interventions take their toll whether they aim at defending the officers' professional interests (and interventions for this purpose are the most usual) or at seizing power. Although Latin American armed forces are relatively small, they are extremely costly. Whether civilian governments in their eagerness to woo the military and prevent them from meddling in politics outdo one another in catering to the officer corps, or whether the military take matters into their own hands when the governments are less benevolent, military pay is high considering the average income in Latin America, and there is a profusion of generals and even marshals. Retirement is often given prematurely with full pay. In several countries, retirement is accompanied by a lump sum enabling the recipient to take up a different occupation. In some instances, retirement is automatically preceded by a promotion that substantially increases the number of generals and even marshals.[4] Many fringe benefits are also given, such as free tuition for children, import privileges, and excessively lavish military clubs. These personal benefits, however, are not the costliest items in the budget. The main expenditure is on prestige military equipment obtainable only with precious hard currency. Cruisers or aircraft carriers given as consolation prizes to a navy eclipsed by the army in the exercise of political power have publicized these interservice rivalries.

The result is that the small armed forces in Latin America absorb an average of over 25 percent of the budget in countries whose security is scarcely threatened. The military regard this as a pittance, whatever the circumstances. It is difficult to estimate the exact percentage allocated because a good part of the military expenditures is concealed in various categories of the budget. Moreover, some of these expenditures are not shown on a full basis. For example, foreign military aid does not figure in military expenditures. In 1940, the *Inter-American Statistical Yearbook* gave percentages for the military that exceeded 30 percent for Bolivia and Paraguay, 26 percent for Chile, 24 percent for Brazil, and 23 percent for Peru. In Paraguay, when General Stroessner took power in 1954, the military budget exceeded 50 percent of the total.

Here are needy countries in search of funds for industrialization; with a large part of their populations still illiterate; without money to open schools; and with too many children because the birth rate is high. And because of the armed services' political strength these very countries must squander a substantial proportion of their assets on military expenditures. Although at present the officer corps is sincerely eager to achieve national economic emancipation, its interventions in politics have indirectly created one of the most formidable obstacles to Latin America's economic and social development.

TENDENCY TO HASTEN SOCIAL EVOLUTION. On the credit side, the political role of the military has, on the whole,

[4] John J. Johnson, *The Military and Society in Latin America* (Stanford, 1964), pp. 210 ff.

accelerated disintegration of the most archaic social structures, helped the middle classes to accede to power, and contributed to awakening the proletariat. In a static society, interventions by the military have been a factor of change. The process is costly and harsh, but not completely useless. Results can be assessed only on a long-term basis, and they must take into consideration the political and social situation in the various countries in the beginning of this century. As late as 1930 Latin America still had a preponderance of archaic social structures, and even when power was channeled through the paths provided by representative regimes, it was still in the hands of an anachronistic aristocracy. The only exceptions were Mexico, where a people's revolution had taken place in 1910, and Argentina, where Irigoyen's radical party had placed the middle classes in power. There were also the two countries in a special category, namely Uruguay [5] and Costa Rica.

Given these conditions, military interventions have had a pendulum effect, a swinging between right and left. Between 1930 and 1965, forty-four military coups d'état (counting only the successful ones) took place, as shown by table 10.

Pendulum Motion of Military Interventions since 1930

The general effect of this pendulum motion has been to help eliminate the old oligarchies from politics. Despite a few periods of reaction, the military political force, just as caudillismo had done earlier, weakened the aristocracy's authority and prepared more social strata to take part in political life. As shown by table 10, out of 28 major political interventions between 1930 and 1952, 12 were clearly directed against conservative regimes and only 2 or 3 aimed at bringing the traditional oligarchy back into power.

In the period immediately following the 1929 depression, almost all the military interventions (except in Argentina, where Irigoyen's populist regime was in power) were aimed at promoting change, at least as compared to the ousted regimes. Revolutions supported by young officers, as in 1930 in Brazil,

[5] Uruguay in 1967 returned to a presidential regime. [Ed.]

TABLE 10
MAIN MILITARY INTERVENTIONS IN LATIN AMERICAN POLITICS
FROM 1930 TO 1965

Year	Country	Nature of the Intervention	Political Tendency
1930	Dominican Republic	General Trujillo placed in power by the military	Personal—caudillo
1930	Argentina	General Uriburu ousts President Irigoyen and ends radical experiment	Rightist
1930	Brazil	Popular revolution won through efforts of young officers (*tenentes*)	Leftist
1931	Guatemala	The military install General Ubico as dictator	Personal—caudillo
1931	Chile	General Blanche Espejo ousts General Ibáñez	Rightist
1933	Nicaragua	Dictatorship of General Anastasio Somoza extended; a member of his family in power	Personal—caudillo
1933	Cuba	Sergeant Batista seizes power following revolt of noncommissioned officers	Leftist
1936	Paraguay	The military entrust power to Colonel Franco	Leftist
1936	Bolivia	The military give power to Colonel Toro	Fascist-leftist
1937	Bolivia	The military give power to Colonel Germán Bush	Fascist-leftist
1937	Brazil	The military permit the presidency of Vargas to became a dictatorship	Semi-Fascist, corporatist
1940	Bolivia	The military give power to General Peñaranda	Rightist
1943	Bolivia	Commander Villaroel places the MNR party (National-Socialist) in power	Semi-Fascist, leftist
1943	Argentina	A military junta led by General Ramírez over-	Semi-Fascist, leftist

TABLE 10 (*Continued*)

Year	Country	Nature of the Intervention	Political Tendency
		turns the conservative government	
1944	Guatemala	A military junta places a left-winger, Juan Arévalo, in power	Leftist
1944	El Salvador	Soldiers and students oust President Hernández Martínez	Leftist
1944	Ecuador	General Larrea Alba places President Velasco Ibarra in power	Leftist
1944	Brazil	The military depose President Vargas	Liberal-conservative
1945	Venezuela	The military depose General Medina Angarita, who perpetuated Gomez's long dictatorship	Leftist
1946	Bolivia	After Villaroel's assassination the military return the aristocracy to power	Rightist
1947	Panama	Colonel Remón takes actual power before becoming president	Leftist
1947	Ecuador	The military depose President Ibarra	Rightist
1948	Venezuela	A military *junta* deposes President Rómulo Gallegos and eliminates the Democratic Action party	Rightist
1948	El Salvador	Major Oscar Osorio ousts General Castañeda	Leftist
1948	Peru	The military place General Odría in power	Rightist
1951	Bolivia	A junta refuses to let the president-elect take office	Rightist
1952	Cuba	Batista deposes President Prío Socarrás and elimi-	Personal

TABLE 10 continued

Year	Country	Nature of the Intervention	Political Tendency
		nates the Cuban Revolutionary Party (*Auténtico*)	
1952	Venezuela	Dictatorship of Colonel Pérez Jiménez	Rightist
1953	Colombia	The military place General Rojas Pinilla in power	Leftist
1954	Guatemala	Colonel Castillo Armas ousts Arbenz	Rightist
1954	Brazil	The military oust President Vargas	Rightist
1954	Paraguay	The military place General Stroessner in power	Professional (military)
1955	Argentina	A junta overturns President Perón	Rightist
1957	Colombia	A junta overturns General Rojas Pinilla	Liberal
1960	El Salvador	A junta topples the government	Leftist
1961	El Salvador	Three months later a junta overturns the previous junta	Indefinite
1962	Argentina	The military depose President Frondizi	Rightist
1962	Peru	The military reject the election results and take power	Professional, rather leftist
1963	Guatemala	A junta deposes President Ydigoras Fuentes	None
1963	Dominican Republic	The military depose President Bosch	Rightist
1963	Honduras	The military depose President Villeda Morales	Rather rightist
1964	Brazil	The military depose President Goulart	Rightist
1964	Bolivia	The military depose President Paz Estenssoro	Rather leftist
1965	Dominican Republic	Military revolt followed by civil war	Leftist

profoundly changed the social structures of the countries, or at least endorsed the changes under way. The old conservative forces were never to regain direct power.

In the years immediately preceding World War II, the political orientation of military interventions was less clear-cut because they were greatly influenced by National Socialism and Fascism, and tended toward authoritarian regimes. The military still advocated reforms nonetheless, and by attempting to set the masses against the old liberal cosmopolitan aristocracy they prepared for the advent of the populist parties. Many leaders of these parties—the Peronist party, the Bolivian MNR, and the Brazilian Labor party—were trained in the semi-Fascist groups between 1938 and 1944. In aristocratic societies, Fascism should not be judged as socially reactionary.

The pendulum swung in the opposite direction at the end of the war, and military interventions aimed at restoring political freedom. They brought in new populist parties rather than the old traditional parties of the upper class. Social reforms were stepped up and reached some of the less advanced countries, such as Bolivia, Guatemala, El Salvador, and Venezuela.

Since 1954, however, the direction seems to have changed again. Out of the 13 interventions listed in table 10, 6 have been frankly conservative and not one has instituted a more reformist regime than the one overturned.

If this new line persists, it may be due to changed circumstances as well as to a new political and social outlook among the officers. The attraction of Castroism for the Latin American masses and the lurking threat of Communism have injected a new factor into Latin American politics. The officer corps in Latin America had very few ties with the landed aristocracy; in the presence of aristocratic regimes most officers, being from the middle classes, wanted reforms if not a revolution. It does not follow, however, that when the anachronistic aristocracy has been removed from power and has been replaced by the middle classes, the officers will want still more radical reforms.

In the most advanced Latin American countries, the role that the military seems to favor is that of a moderating power serving to limit the swings of the pendulum. The oscillations tend to be very violent in countries where the forces of a very archaic social state clash directly with the most radical revolutionary forces. Armies in which many officers fear the return of the old oligarchic regimes as much as the advent of Communist-inspired ones try to curtail the freedom of civilian governments by sternly imposing limits on the right and the left. The function of guardian may increase military pressures on the governments, but it enables the constitutional forms to be preserved. In more than one country, the military seem to choose such a role. It is the role that most Argentine officers (opposed by the hard-line group of Toranzo Montero's "gorillas") favored. They tried to prevent President Frondizi from allying himself with Peronist forces or making concessions to Castroists. They did not impede his governing the country within the limits they had set. In Brazil, where the military had long been skillful in their political maneuvers, interventions had taken the form of pressure, more or less disguised. Its tendency alternated between right and left and restricted the government's freedom without completely destroying it. This went on until President Goulart provoked a show of strength in the hope of shaking off military control.

There are very few countries where military control does not exist in some form. Except for the countries where the military have been eliminated as a political force, namely Uruguay, Mexico, Costa Rica, and undoubtedly Cuba, this force should be taken into account in the analysis of Latin American political institutions. It should always be kept in mind that an overt or disguised military power invariably imposes limits upon the governments' freedom of decision.

PART IV

Political Institutions

After the Latin American countries became independent, they all adopted rigid written constitutions. English political empiricism does not seem to have held great sway over countries of Latin culture. Under the twofold influence of the codifying trend of the French revolution and the prototype of rigid constitutions embodied in the 1789 United States Constitution, Latin America has never stopped drawing up solemn declarations of rights and stubbornly adding new legal guarantees to the constitutions each time they are violated.

Latin America as a whole has had countless constitutions. This adjective is not exaggerated, for each time an attempt is made to count them, the total is different. Some of the uncertainty stems from the fact that after a dictatorship has abrogated the constitution, it has been overthrown and the former constitution reinstated, sometimes with modifications. This happened in Argentina, where after Perón's downfall the old constitution dating back to 1853 was reinstated in 1957. The 1957 constitution would be counted as a new one only if the changes were regarded as important enough to warrant it.

In a century and a half there have been between 180 and 190 Latin American constitutions, not counting numerous amendments, some of which changed the nature of the regime. For instance, the 1891 constitution in Chile and the 1961 constitution in Brazil were not abrogated but amendments replaced the presidential regime with a parliamentary regime.

Presidentialism was reinstated in Brazil fifteen months later, in January, 1963.

This flood of constitutions calls for two remarks, nevertheless: (1) It occurred in part during the period before 1850, when the new Latin American countries were still working out their institutions; (2) except for this inevitable period of trial and error, out of the 127 constitutions after 1850 listed in table 11, only nine pertain to the three large countries, Brazil, Argentina, and Mexico, which contain two-thirds of the Latin

TABLE 11
LATIN AMERICAN CONSTITUTIONS [a]

Country	Dates
Argentina	1819, 1826, 1853, 1949, 1957
Bolivia	1826, 1831, 1836, 1839, 1839, 1843, 1848, 1851, 1861, 1868, 1871, 1878, 1880, 1931, 1937, 1938, 1946, 1947, 1952, 1961
Brazil	1824, 1834, 1891, 1934, 1937, 1946
Chile	1818, 1823, 1828, 1833, 1891, 1925
Colombia	1811, 1819, 1821, 1830, 1832, 1834, 1843, 1853, 1858, 1863, 1886
Costa Rica	1825, 1839, 1848, 1859, 1861, 1871, 1949
Cuba	1901, 1940, 1959
Dominican Republic	1821, 1844, 1854, 1854, 1858, 1866, 1887, 1896, 1907, 1908, 1924, 1942, 1947, 1960, 1962
Ecuador	1821, 1830, 1843, 1846, 1878, 1884, 1897, 1906, 1929, 1943, 1946
Guatemala	1824, 1851, 1879, 1945, 1956, 1965
Haiti	1801, 1805, 1806, 1807, 1811, 1820, 1843, 1846, 1849, 1859, 1860, 1867, 1874, 1888, 1889, 1918, 1932, 1935, 1939, 1944, 1946, 1950, 1957
Honduras	1825, 1839, 1904, 1908, 1924, 1936, 1957
Mexico	1824, 1836, 1841, 1846, 1857, 1917
Nicaragua	1825, 1838, 1848, 1854, 1858, 1893, 1896, 1905, 1911, 1913, 1931, 1950
Panama	1904, 1940, 1946
Paraguay	1813, 1844, 1870, 1940
Peru	1823, 1826, 1828, 1834, 1837, 1839, 1856, 1860, 1867, 1868, 1919, 1933

TABLE 11 (*Continued*)

El Salvador	1824, 1841, 1859, 1871, 1872, 1880, 1883, 1886, 1939, 1950, 1962
Uruguay	1830, 1917, 1934, 1952
Venezuela	1811, 1819, 1821, 1830, 1858, 1864, 1874, 1881, 1891, 1893, 1901, 1904, 1909, 1914, 1922, 1925, 1928, 1929, 1936, 1947, 1953, 1961

ᵃ Table of the Constitutions of Latin America given by William W. Pierson and Federico G. Gil, *Governments of Latin America* (New York, 1957), p. 161. For the period preceding 1888, Justo Arosemena, *Estudios constitucionales sobre los Gobiernos de la América Latina, con suplemento hasta 1888* (2 vols.) (Paris, 1888). Until 1932, see the historical notes preceding the text of each country's constitution in the compilation by Dareste, *Les constitutions modernes*, vol. IV (Paris, 1932); historical records of the collection of the Institute for Hispanic Culture in Madrid, edited by Manuel Fraga Iribarne, *Las constituticiones hispano-americanas; Statesman's Yearbook*, 1962.

N.B.—There are a few discrepancies in dates according to the authors. They are due in part to confusion between the date of the constitutional agreement, the date of ratification, and the date of its promulgation.

The list does not include constitutions proclaimed by revolutionary movements but never in force. In general, the constitutions proclaimed during the Wars of Independence were of this kind.

American populations, and 66 to five countries—Bolivia, the Dominican Republic, Haiti, Nicaragua, and Venezuela—whose combined population was less than twenty million in 1960.

Even the constitutions that have endured the longest—those of Argentina, Mexico, and Uruguay—have often been weakened by being applied in such a way that the letter was more or less followed, but not the spirit. Hence, it would be neither possible nor useful to try to trace the history of such a complex and stormy constitutional life. It would even be less useful to describe the political institutions in force today in each of the twenty Latin American countries, since some of the constitutions that established them existed for only a few years or a few months. Furthermore, these constitutions are so weak that they may have gone out of existence before this book is printed, while a few of them have never been applied.

It would be a serious mistake to affirm, as some analysts have done, that Latin American constitutions are only delusive documents lacking any connection with political reality— mere propaganda tools rather than instruments of government.

Possibly because in Latin America the elites have always had a predilection for the study of law, juridical form is held in high regard. Despite the number of dictatorships in Latin America, many of the dictators have made it a point to try not to violate constitutional forms. The Argentine Republic today is an example: the military are intent on imposing their will, but most of the officers would like to see this control to be exercised through the agencies provided by the constitution. In the most frequent, almost normal type of authoritarian regime in Latin America, the presidential regime operates in such a way that congress, although legally in possession of the powers provided by the constitution, is in fact subject to the president's will. Thus, the institutions provided by the constitution remain undiminished as instruments of government, but those who govern make unforeseen use of those instruments. Respect for forms does not always prevent the presidential regime from losing its representative character and becoming an autocracy. But even then this respect serves to check the autocrat's despotism, and has produced in particular some deference to the judicial power. Although some dictators have not been so scrupulous, respect for form has induced more than one of them to accept the checks on arbitrary action provided by the declarations of rights and the independence of the courts. The best evidence of this respect is the unanimous verdict by the Supreme Court in Brazil on April 20, 1965. It granted the habeas corpus to Governor Miguel Arraes, the chief enemy of an officer corps that had just carried out a military coup d'état unopposed by Congress or the masses. In very few countries outside Latin America, even those with older democratic tradition, would the courts act with such independence in a revolutionary situation. Thanks to the courts, individual freedoms are often better safeguarded than political freedom.

Episodes in Latin America's stormy political history are only of local interest, but the history itself reflects general principles embodied in the present institutions. Even if that political history is agitated, it is not incoherent. The Latin American experience is reflected in certain general traits common to the political institutions of most of its countries. These general traits constitute a most promising topic of study.

Any attempt to reduce to a few generalities a political history as confusing and as rich as that of the twenty countries of Latin America requires a number of arbitrary decisions. For instance, Uruguay has been moving toward a democracy whose institutions owe a great deal to Switzerland; Uruguay may be said to have deviated (temporarily perhaps) from the political patterns peculiar to Latin America. Cuba has also since 1959 by modeling her institutions on the people's democracies. On the other hand, a number of small countries, such as Haiti, have not yet emerged from the formative stage.

Two important traits clearly stand out in Latin America's political history. They may have some didactic value for countries that are becoming independent today because their own problems are similar to those Latin America has been trying to solve for a long time.

First is the need for an ever greater centralization despite the liking for federal or even confederal institutions that was widespread in Latin America at the time of independence. It is true that this seems to be necessary all over the world as an inevitable consequence of government planning. At the present stage of industrialization governments have to assume such a role if they are to promote economic development. But since, at the time of independence, some of the Latin American populations were very far from being integrated into the nation, true federalism would have left the different sections of each nation the masters of their own domestic policy, and would have proved to be incompatible with the very existence of these nations. The major Latin American countries, which did at first experiment with the federal system or even with confederation (called federation), had to give them up. In most cases, if they retained the original federal form, they had to correct its effects by adopting centralizing schemes. Only one country, Brazil, retained true federal institutions, but had to provide a counterbalance by giving the central government very broad powers and allowing it to intervene if necessary in matters formally within the jurisdiction of the states.

A second, far more important, trait is that developing countries whose populations wish for integration need a dominant executive power. Despite the strong tendency to broaden the powers of the legislative assemblies at the time the institutions were being organized in the nineteenth century, Latin America was able to live under parliamentary regimes for only very short periods. Some form of presidential regime had to evolve whereby either in fact or by law the president was granted far larger powers. In Latin America the normal regime is one of dominant executive power. It deserves the name of *regime of presidential dominance.*

The only exception is Uruguay where, in order to put an end to presidential dominance, executive power was vested in a nine-member governing National Council on which the presence of three members of the opposition is mandatory. The majority members of the council preside in rotation. This regime, established by Batlle y Ordóñez in 1919, was interrupted from 1930 to 1938 by the benign dictatorship of Gabriel Terra, but it is again in force.[5] A number of administrative surveys are being made of this democracy of the Swiss type. Since the situation in Uruguay is very different from that of other Latin American countries, it is not fair to hold up as an example to large, unevenly developed countries the institutions of a country of less than three million inhabitants mostly concentrated in a large city whose living conditions resemble western Europe rather than Latin America. Also, it is not certain that the economic difficulties Uruguay has had to face since 1960 will permit a regime of weak executive power to last much longer.

[5] Uruguay in 1967 returned to a presidential regime. [Ed.]

13. The Evolution Toward Centralization and Presidential Dominance

After the countries of Latin America became independent they underwent for varying lengths of time a stage of political experimentation so confused that for many of them it was tantamount to anarchy. The only major exception was Brazil whose accession to independence in 1822 did not entail any break with the institutions of the last years of the colonial period. Paraguay was also an exception in avoiding the initial state of anarchy, since immediately after independence it enjoyed a long period of stability, from 1811 to 1862, under the paternalistic despotism of Francia and the first López, Carlos Antonio. But for Paraguay the formative stage was only postponed and is under way now.

Everywhere else during the period from 1810 to 1850, numbers of provisional constitutions, provisional statutes, and confederal or federal pacts were written but were applied only locally or never applied at all. For instance, the political situation in Argentina between the declaration of independence in 1816 and the strengthening of Rosas' dictatorship in 1835 resembles the picture in the former Belgian Congo in 1960–1961. Buenos Aires, the highly developed center, was drawing up constitutions, but the hinterland ignored them. When Facundo Quiroga, the gaucho of La Rioja, received the text of the 1826 constitution inspired by Rivadavia he refused to pay attention to it and continued to govern his province as he saw fit. Even after Rosas' rise and downfall, when the measures suggested by Urquiza, the liberator of the province, seemed likely to harm the business monopolies in Buenos Aires, it was the city that seceded in 1852 and until 1861 tried to hold onto its own wealth, which exceeded that of nine-tenths of the nation.

Opposing Factions During the Critical Period

In the countries to be built, everything was food for controversy—the form of the state as well as that of the government.

A first source of conflict, particularly violent in that period because independence itself was at stake, was the opposition throughout Latin America between the federalists and the unitarists. The former supported a system of loose confederation between the different provinces or, perhaps more accurately, between the caudillos, whereas the latter wanted a unified state. The unitarists were less intent on centralization—neither necessary nor possible at that time—than on setting up a strong government so that city populations might extend throughout the country the order necessary for the development of a modern society. Primitive men who did not know the meaning of a state, caudillos who wanted uncontested authority over their following, and big landowners anxious to remain masters of their estates proclaimed their attachment to local freedom. But what they really wanted, under the guise of vague confederations, were loose agreements between towns and local chiefs that would preserve the de facto independence of the chiefs.

Added to the opposition between federalists and unitarists, another equally widespread opposition arose, which tended to blend with the first. This was the opposition between city dwellers and the rural populations of the interior. The rural people would have been quite happy without an organized state, while the city dwellers could not do without one. The polarization of the two groups was particularly pronounced in Argentina, and the first years after independence were spent in a violent struggle between the inhabitants of Buenos Aires, the *porteños*, and the *provincianos*. They clashed for the last time at Pavón in 1861. The battle was won by Buenos Aires under the command of Bartolomé Mitre.

Underlying this opposition, another more lasting one separated the conservatives from the liberals, the federalists usually being liberals and the unitarists conservative. At the time federalism, inspired by the example of the United States, appeared as the guarantee of political freedom. The opposition between liberals and conservatives was strictly political, and neither faction was much concerned about social reforms, or disturbed by the quasi-serfdom of the peasants. Most of the peasants were Indians, mestizos, or mulattoes, and scarcely any thought was given to improving their living conditions or encouraging them to participate in political life.

As far as political institutions were concerned, the conservatives would have preferred authoritarian regimes. Many of them would have accepted monarchies of the kind the Holy Alliance was then supporting in Europe. If they could not impose such regimes, they would at least have liked uncontested executive dominance. In the opposite camp were the liberals, but they also were conservative on social issues. They had been trained on the writings of Montesquieu and Jefferson; transposing to their own countries the lessons of the struggle of parliaments against absolutist monarchy in Europe, they had come to believe that the essential prerequisite for political freedom was the weakening of the powers of the head of state. These liberals wanted to repudiate not only Spanish rule, but everything that smacked of absolutism—centralization, hegemony of the executive power, and above everything else, clericalism.

Actually, the clerical issue was the crucial one in the confrontation between conservatives and liberals, and also the most enduring. When all other ideological differences had died down, this one was still alive. In the conflict between conservatives and liberals (neither faction anxious to change the social structure in its country), the issue of clericalism versus anticlericalism enabled the parties to survive. The issue was at the heart of party struggle throughout the second half of the nineteenth century. Religion itself was not at stake, since almost all of Latin America was Catholic, outwardly at least, and was not thinking of repudiating its faith. But Latin America had inherited from the days of Spanish sovereignty a clergy accustomed to playing a political role, and possessing great wealth besides. Separation of Church and State, distribution of Church property, and elimination of the clergy's political influence were the issues on which Latin American statesmen were deeply divided.

Political Experimentation in the Critical Period

Depending on which side was temporarily in power, the most contradictory experiments were carried out in the initial years.

In some countries the state was alternately confederated, federated, and unitary. The title of Argentina's first constitution, promulgated in 1811, was the Provisional Statute of the Government of the United Provinces of the Rio de la Plata. It instituted no more than a loose confederal tie; the constitution of December 24, 1826, proclaimed on the contrary the adoption of the republican representative form fused into unity of regime; this shortly gave way to the dictatorship of Rosas, who proclaimed himself supreme chief of the confederation. Chile started out with a unitary constitution in 1818, then took the path of federalism in 1826 (constitution of 1828) and reverted to unitarism under the 1833 constitution. Similar changes occurred in Colombia. In Brazil the constitution of 1824, which was unitarist and very centralist in spirit, was amended in 1834 by the Additional Act, a step toward federalism.

As has been said, many conservatives favored monarchy immediately after independence. Around 1816 Pueyrredón, who for a short while dominated Buenos Aires' political life, tried to find a sovereign, preferably a Spanish prince; Rivadavia for his part would have liked a French prince, while Belgrano dreamed of a great Inca monarchy. In Mexico, where the conservatives were also seeking a monarch, Emperor Iturbide reigned briefly from May, 1822, to February, 1823, and Maximilian from 1864 to 1867. Haiti had a king, Christophe, from 1811 to 1820 and an emperor, Soulouque, from 1848 to 1859. But, all in all, America was not fertile ground for monarchy, and only in the Brazilian empire did monarchy survive for any length of time—until 1889.

It was soon clear that Spanish America was going to be

republican, but the selection of the most desirable forms of republican regime was fuel for debate for a long while. Long after independence, conservatives and liberals alternately forced constitutions upon the various countries, aiming in turn at safeguarding political freedom by weakening and dividing the executive power, or trying to forestall disorder by disciplining the legislative power, sometimes even by legalizing dictatorship.

The Chilean constitution of 1828 tried to set up a very lax executive power combined with federalism. In Mexico, the revolutionary constitution of 1814 had provided for a collegial form of executive to ensure that it was sufficiently weak. Colombia's revolutionary constitution of 1814 did the same while also trying to introduce direct democracy coupled with the power to remove the elected representatives. In Brazil as well, the Constituent Assembly convened by Dom Pedro in 1823 to draw up the first constitution tried to limit the sovereign's authority. After dissolving that assembly the emperor was more successful, since the 1824 constitution granted him a "moderating power" that allowed him to discipline the astorship.

THE NORTH AMERICAN EXAMPLE. The liberal-inspired constitutions were generally short-lived, and in countries where the most serious threat to political freedom was the use of force by civilian or military caudillos, the surest way to dictatorship was to weaken the executive power. The United States Constitution of 1789 was of vital help in that connection. Unlike the European constitutions, it had not been intended to limit the hegemony of the executive power but, on the contrary, to break the power deadlock in the thirteen colonies during the critical period. Here was the worthy model of a constitution that repudiated monarchy and clearly proclaimed the principle of political freedom and individual rights, at the same time setting up a strong executive power. The executive was given the authority that European parliamentary regimes were trying to deny the kings. The Constitution of the United States lent authority the cloak of democratic respectability. A few countries very shortly adopted constitutions directly inspired by it—Venezuela in 1811, Mexico in

1824, the Central American Federation in 1825, and Argentina in 1826.

Some very original constitutions were not inspired by any foreign country. In the beginning of the nineteenth century the idea still prevailed that it must be possible to discover through logical reasoning the institutions best suited to govern a people well, regardless of its history, mores, and way of thinking. The best known of these constitutions was drawn up by Bolívar for Bolivia in 1826. In it this realist and foe of ideologists gave free rein to his imagination. Coming as close to monarchy as he dared, Bolívar provided for a life presidency whose incumbent could choose his successor and initiate him into the exercise of power as his associate in his own lifetime. The legislative power was divided into three assemblies—those of the tribunes, the senators, and the censors. The tribunes were to deal with matters of finance, foreign policy, and national defense; the senators were entrusted with drawing up the civil and penal laws and appointing officials; the censors were to watch over law enforcement and the proper conduct of officials. In addition to the executive, the legislative, and the judicial, a fourth power, the electoral, was provided. That constitution, which was adopted in Bolivia with some amendments, lasted only two years.

Many of the constitutions promulgated during this period were not applied at all, and none of them lasted for more than a few years. Everywhere their application was interrupted by overt or disguised personal dictatorships. Some dictators invoked the need for an authoritarian regime in order to correct disorders tolerated by a weak government; others invoked the need to end the tyranny of overly authoritarian regimes.

STRENGTHENING THE PRESIDENTIAL REGIME. The period of political experimentation was not useless. Latin America reaped some definite political knowledge from it, and its accuracy is being confirmed as time goes by. The lessons have been heeded almost everywhere, although knowing them and trying to make use of them was no guarantee of success. As early as the middle of the nineteenth century, they were put into practice in a few constitutions that turned out to be durable. They influenced all the other constitutions as well. Even when these constitutions were temporarily abandoned, the countries which had adopted them always eventually reverted to them.

The oldest was the Uruguayan constitution of 1830, which lasted until 1917. It did not, incidentally, suffice to prevent an endemic civil war caused by Uruguay's very marked dual social structure. Nowhere else was there such a striking opposition between a large progressive city, Montevideo, and a particularly archaic rural area dominated by the cattle raisers, the estancieros, and their gauchos. There have been only two parties in Uruguay, the Blancos and the Colorados, an exceptional situation in Latin America. This probably is not as conducive as is generally thought to the stability of the presidential regime. The division of the country into two segments was used profitably by Uruguay's two neighbors, Brazil and Argentina, and was a constant source of turmoil until 1903, when the hegemony of the city and its middle classes was definitely established and the defeat of the gaucho Saravia put a stop to the unrest attendant upon caudillismo.

Uruguay was not important enough and its political life in the nineteenth century was too stormy for its presidential regime to influence other countries. The three constitutions which were trail blazers for the political institutions of Latin America were the constitution of 1833 in Chile, which lasted until 1925; the constitution of 1853 in Argentina, whose principles have not been repudiated to this day and which is the basis of the present constitution adopted in 1957; and lastly the constitution of 1857 in Mexico. The revolutionary Mexican constitution of 1917 retained almost all of its political provisions and added a meticulous declaration of social rights.

Failure of Parliamentary Regimes

All these constitutions instituted presidential regimes. The major result of the Latin American experiment was to show that the parliamentary regime was not suitable for the nation-building stage that followed independence. Although Latin America wavered between the English and the United States examples, experience made her shun a parliamentarism of the French pattern. In the presence of caudillismo and interventions by the army, the crises fostered by the profusion of small parties and the personality clashes inevitably ended in coups d'état and military interventions. French influence persisted, but tended to be confined to declarations of rights.

Latin America experimented more than once with parliamentarism, and each time the attempt was short-lived and ended in failure. Periodically, some groups try to revive such regimes—always in vain. Haiti adopted the parliamentary regime in 1806, 1843, 1859, 1867, Honduras in 1925–1931, Bolivia in 1931–1937, Venezuela in 1947; even the longest experiment, in Chile from 1891 to 1925, has left unpleasant memories. Only Brazil was able to live under the parliamentary regime, but only as long as the monarchy lasted. Its latest attempt, made in 1961, is already over. In that particular case, the parliamentary regime was used only as a device to prevent civil war. President Quadros having unexpectedly resigned, Vice-President Goulart should have taken over, according to constitutional procedure. But while Goulart, who belonged to the opposition, was Vice-President, he had made a few rash statements, in support of Communist China in particular. One segment of the military opposed his accession to the presidency, while another favored it. In order to avert a civil war Congress devised a compromise whereby the constitution would be respected: Vice-President Goulart was to become head of state, but his powers were to be curtailed by a constitutional amendment under which the Cabinet was to be responsible to Congress. The reestablishment of the parliamentary regime resulted in a complete governmental stalemate, since the only achievement of Congress was to prevent the government from doing anything whatsoever. It soon became clear that the presidential regime would have to be restored, and this was decided by referendum in January, 1963.

A concession to parliamentarism made by most Latin American presidential regimes has been the adoption of certain practices that constitute a deviation from classical presidentialism—namely the appearance of ministers before congress, and sometimes interpellation, or questioning about policy. This practice might herald the beginning of ministerial responsibility. It had this effect in Ecuador, Peru, Guatemala, Panama, and in Cuba before Castro took over. This embryonic parliamentarism had a chance to grow whenever the president's personality was weak, and some cabinets have actually been compelled to resign in the fact of congressional hostility.

The controversies of the first years on the respective merits of executive dominance, legislative dominance, or true balance of powers were resolved in Latin America by the adoption of the presidential regime. It was modeled on the United States regime but usually with far broader powers vested in the president.

There has been much criticism about transposing the presidential regime to Latin America. It certainly has not prevented coups d'état and dictatorships, but it would be absurd to ascribe the dictatorships to the president's broad powers. They stem far more from the backwardness of the social structure, the insufficient integration of the population, the lack of an organized political life, and the many ensuing emergencies. In view of the social conditions that prevailed in Latin America in the nineteenth and the beginning of the twentieth century, an increase in presidential power was certainly needed, and on the whole this regime of presidential dominance seems to have given the best results that could have been expected under difficult circumstances.

14. Declarations of Rights and Court Protection

The fact that a chapter of the present survey deals with declarations of rights and their application should not come as a surprise, for political institutions of developing countries should not be judged by the same criteria as those of developed countries. The social structure of developing countries, the nature and quick succession of their problems make it imperative to give the executive power a dominance that elsewhere might seem incompatible with the spirit of political democracy. Often also, circumstances do not allow governments to comply with all the rules of constitutional legality, even when they have broad powers. The regimes must be more authoritarian than in developed countries. The extent of their democratic spirit depends far less on the degree of control exerted on the government by elected representatives than on constitutional limits to arbitrary government. These are set by provisions guaranteeing personal liberties, procedures for the defense of these liberties, and courts sufficiently independent to ensure their observance.

In these matters Latin America is often misunderstood. Since political unrest impedes proper functioning of political institutions, all too frequently generalizations are based on countries where such unrest is most prevalent; the generalities in turn lead to statements that constitutional guarantees are deceiving and that the Latin Americans' love of freedom expresses itself in words instead of deeds. This is completely untrue: the limits set on arbitrary government by private law, penal procedure, administrative law, or social law are much more faithfully respected than any limits deriving from the balance of powers. On the whole, Latin America is a land of personal freedoms, and the exercise of those freedoms is more apt to be curtailed through the helplessness of governments than by their despotism.

There have been two major stages in the setting up of constitutional guarantees, before and after 1917. Before 1917, the various Latin American constitutions were still influenced by the individualist and liberal thought of the eighteenth century and were modeled on the French Declaration of the Rights of Man and the United States Constitution. Property rights, freedom from bodily restraint, and freedom of thought and expression were emphasized. After 1917 all of Latin America was influenced by the Mexican constitution, the first in the world (since it preceded the first Soviet constitution) to be permeated with a social outlook. Promises of social justice were then inserted into the constitutions. The combination of the two declarations of rights, to which is often added affirmation of the nation's right to economic independence, holds a very large place in Latin America's modern constitutions, which are therefore long documents.

The word "guarantees" which is generally applied to the listing of the rights that governments commit themselves to respect is not meaningless, for many constitutions not only proclaim these rights but also specify procedures for their enforcement. Over half the Mexican declaration of rights (the first chapter of the constitution) lists rules of penal procedure and in the fourth chapter specifies the organization of the judicial system.

The contrast between the lengthy statement of guarantees and the resistance to their application in immature societies has led too many observers to conclude that the men who framed the constitutions merely paid lip service to lofty principles and, once they had put them into words, gave little thought to their application. The conclusion is unfair; it is not completely untrue, however, because there are enough differences among the twenty Latin American countries to justify any thesis by numerous examples.

It is true nonetheless that many countries have spent most of their independent life under dictators, some of whom were bloodthirsty despots who cared nothing about individual rights or constitutions. The declarations of rights seem even more bitterly ironical when it is recalled that Gómez, Venezuela's dictator from 1908 to 1935, bestowed upon his country in 1931 a constitution of which Title 2 listed the many freedoms to be enjoyed by the citizens and described the procedures for their safeguard. The perfect order so widely admired abroad was maintained under that dictatorship by imprisonments, executions, assassinations, and a police force renowned for its torture methods, not to mention property confiscations. In the Dominican Republic Trujillo, the dictator from 1930 to 1961, took great care in the constitution he granted in 1947 to ban capital punishment, guarantee freedom of speech, and so on. He even copied from England the habeas corpus procedure (Section I, Title II). Trujillo's foes, nonetheless, were prone to disappear without leaving a trace. One of them was kidnapped in New York and his whereabouts were never discovered. But the source of error is always the same—what occurred or is occurring in Haiti, the Dominican Republic, and elsewhere does not necessarily apply to all of Latin America.

Argentina suffered such oppression until the middle of the nineteenth century and Mexico even much later, but the situation today in the large countries is different. Brazil never knew such exactions by the national government, and they do not normally occur in Argentina, Chile, Uruguay, Colombia, or Costa Rica. Even in Peru and Ecuador personal liberties have on the whole been affected relatively little by political turmoil.

In Brazil for instance, since independence, although the constitutions have been tampered with, confiscations, arbitrary jailings, and especially executions have been very rare. In Mexico since the anticlerical drive abated at the end of Calles' presidency in 1928, the revolutionary party's monopoly and the president's supreme powers have not usually curtailed personal freedoms. In Argentina after Rosas' deposition in 1852 constitutional guarantees were secured, but the Peronist regime was a regression. Perón was most irreverent where freedom of the press and university or independence of the judiciary were concerned. It is only fair to state, however, that Justicialism was directly inspired by National Socialism. Its methods reflected the Nazi spirit much more than they reflected any Latin American tradition. Bearing this in mind it should be admitted that, despotic as Perón was, his National Socialism transposed to Latin America was remarkably moderate in its violence as compared to the German model. Justicialist despotism was far more conducive to demagoguery, corruption, and disorder than to massacre and persecution. This might be the Latin American stamp upon an alien authoritarian regime.

The fact that in the most representative portion of Latin America today even dictatorial regimes have made the most strenuous efforts to respect fundamental freedoms does not mean that everyone actually enjoys them. But if constitutional guarantees are weakened the main cause is not the nature of the institutions or deliberate action by governments. Rather it is the fact that all over Latin America, except in Argentina, Uruguay, and Costa Rica, social dualism prevails. Therefore a segment of society—in some countries the largest segment—is outside the scope of the government's protection or exactions.

The illiterate peasants live in isolation in small communities under the quasi-sovereign tutelage of the landowner, the customary chief, or the local official. They cannot claim, and usually do not even know, the acknowledged rights of citizens. Hence the promises of social justice introduced after 1917 into all the constitutions may remain useless for these peasants, even when attempts have been made to buttress the promises by legislation. Sometimes even personal freedom is substantially curtailed. The despotism of the police and the caciques weighs heavily upon these remote populations. They are deprived of all protection when the police and the chiefs combine forces.

The fact that the level of education, standard of living, and in some cases language and customs prevent a segment of the population from taking full part in the life of society within a state is not related to the form of the government. No one claims that in the United States the Bill of Rights is useless or that Wilson, Roosevelt, or Eisenhower were tyrants who flouted legality because they were unable to assure Negroes in the South the guarantees to which they were entitled under the Constitution and common law. The extreme de facto inequality in the largest part of Latin America does not stem from the deliberate intention of those who govern to subjugate people. Rather it derives from the governments' helplessness to eliminate archaic structures with sufficient speed, to administer the entire country effectively, and to raise standards of living and education. The guarantees embodied in the declarations of rights are not useless in normal times, but Latin America has not yet reached the level of development required to make every Latin American into a citizen.

Declarations of Economic and Social Rights

Latin America was remarkably precocious in introducing into the various constitutions socially inspired declarations which rounded out and modified individualistic declarations of the early nineteenth century. This was due to the influence of the Mexican revolution, the first socialist revolt to win a lasting triumph; it began in 1910, seven years before the Russian revolution. It spelled out its goals of social justice during the years of civil war and expressed them in the constitution, drawn up in 1917 by the constituent assembly of Queretaro. This constitution, which is still in force, predates the first constitution of the USSR by one year and the Weimar constitution by more than two years.

The socialist inspiration is expressed mainly through a charter of worker's rights that constitutes Title VI of the constitution: Concerning Work and Social Security. In 1917 this did not mean that a social reform program was to be carried out at that time, but it was a commitment for the future, stated as follows:

The Congress of the Union and the State legislatures shall formulate labor laws based on the needs of each region which shall apply to workers, day laborers, office holders, domestics and artisans and, in a general manner, to all labor contracts without contravening the following basic principles: . . .

In Mexico, particularly under the presidencies of Calles and Cárdenas whose mainstay was the trade unions, a strong start was made in enacting the promised legislation. Despite social lags and the conservatism of many governments, inclusion of workers' rights into the constitutions spread amazingly fast. Almost all the constitutions now include charters on working conditions, adopted in the years indicated in table 12.

TABLE 12
DATES OF INTRODUCTION OF LABOR CHARTERS
INTO CONSTITUTIONS

Uruguay	1932	Bolivia	1945
Peru	1933	Ecuador	1946
Brazil	1934	Venezuela	1947
Colombia	1936	Costa Rica	1949
El Salvador	1939	Argentina	1949
Nicaragua	1939	Guatemala	1954
Paraguay	1940	Honduras	1957
Panama	1940	Dominican Republic	1960
Cuba	1940		

Chile's constitution contains only very summary provisions on social rights because the constitution was adopted as early as 1925, but social legislation is particularly well developed in that country. Only Haiti is an exception in this respect, and in the 1950 constitution merely includes an individualist declaration of rights of eighteenth-century inspiration that is scarcely applied.

These provisions have not remained empty words; everywhere legislation has tried to keep up with the promises of the constitutions. As a whole, Latin America has very progressive social legislation. Labor codes were adopted in a number of countries—Bolivia, Brazil, Colombia, Chile, Costa Rica, the Dominican Republic, Ecuador, Guatemala, Honduras, Mexico, Nicaragua, Panama, Haiti—and in 1962 were being drawn up in the others. They embody laws that are not inferior in any way to those of the developed countries of the North Atlantic world, and sometimes are ahead of them.

Limitation of the length of the workday was introduced into many Latin American countries long before it was done in Europe, and even when it is not included in the constitutions it is prescribed by law in all the countries. Paid vacations are also mandatory. In many countries they are long, one month for example. Wherever salaries are very low and workers cannot afford to go away, they merely take another job during their vacation from the first job.

The minimum wages prescribed by the constitutions are usually enforced by special commissions. In view of general economic conditions in Latin America, however, the minimum is very low and there are marked regional differences, some countries having double the minimum of others. Unlike the situation in developed countries, the minimum wage, instead of being a seldom applied base below which it is not permitted to go, is the actual salary for most urban workers. The frequency of inflationary rises entails sharp changes in the minimum; doubling of salaries is not exceptional.

All the usual provisions are made for special working conditions for women and minors. The latter raises a serious problem in several countries. While the law forbids work by minors under fourteen, compulsory schooling sometimes does not exceed four years, and sometimes it is not possible to open enough schools to comply with such a limited requirement. The resulting period between the end of school attendance and the age of authorized employment leads to vagrancy or illegal work.[1]

Even when not embodied in the constitutions, all the countries have workmen's compensation laws. They are based on the principle that the employer is presumed guilty; to clear himself he must prove that the victim deliberately caused the accident. Social security systems covering industrial workers exist in all countries, and attempts are being made to extend them to rural workers.

Most constitutions also contain a chapter on family law, and several countries have made a start toward family allowance systems. However legitimate from the standpoint of social justice, and however low the allowances, this form of family protection has drawbacks in countries which, except for Argentina and Uruguay, suffer from the population's excessive fecundity. Conceivably, family social service methods pat-

---

[1] "Youth and Work in Latin America," *International Labour Review*, July–August, 1964, pp. 1–23, 150–179.

terned on those of Sweden rather than those of France (which encourages fecundity) would be more suitable to Latin America in view of her demographic picture.

The best enforced provisions in the area of social legislation pertain to severance pay and job security. Cuba, Mexico, Guatemala, Brazil, and Argentina have particularly strong legislation. Not only must dismissal be accompanied by severance pay, generally of one month per year of employment, but the dismissal procedure, even for a serious violation, is most complicated. In Mexico and Guatemala compensation is mandatory even if the worker leaves of his own free will because of "the lack of honesty of the employer or by receiving bad treatment that diminishes his dignity as a man." The protection is so thorough, in Brazil, where it has become virtually impossible to dismiss a person employed for many years, that it backfires. Some employers systematically dismiss their workers before they have reached full tenure, even at the cost of mandatory severance pay.

Two provisions included in many constitutions have not been supported by effective legislation, although Mexico announced to do so, starting in 1965. They are profit sharing (Title V of the Brazilian constitution) and equal pay for women (Article 123 of the Mexican constitution). Furthermore, freedom to unionize, even when promised, is seldom respected, and collective bargaining plays but a minor role. This only increases the importance of social legislation.

It may seem strange that Latin American countries, while retaining so many archaic social structures, have so rapidly introduced social guarantees into their constitutions. This is due partly to the social dualism, past and present, which creates such a deep gap between urban and rural societies. The conservative, politically influential elements used to be the landed aristocracies rather than the industrialists. They were not against social legislation as long as it was limited exclusively to city populations, since the sacrifices would be made only by large industry and business. Thus social legislation enabled the governments to gain supporters in the cities, while it helped the rural upper class to show how broadminded it was.

It would be a serious mistake to regard these declarations of social rights as never-enforced declarations of intention. Foreign industrialists established in Latin America know full well that social laws are meant to be applied, and they often find that they are as costly as they would be at home.

It is also true, however, that the social provisions cover only part of the population. In no way are they applied to rural society—usually the largest segment in the country—or to craft enterprises or to the fringe city populations that are employed only sporadically. For instance, on August 26, 1960, Brazil adopted a social security law specifically excluding 48 million rural dwellers. The Director General of the International Labour Office [2] complained that even in the most advanced Latin American countries the workers covered were only a minority: 23 percent in Argentina, 22 percent in Brazil, 18 percent in Chile, 17 percent in Mexico, and 13 percent in Colombia.

It should of course be added that whatever efforts Latin American governments make to keep the promises of social justice contained in their constitutions, the low productivity of a burgeoning industry makes it impossible to give workers more than a very low purchasing power as compared to that of the North Atlantic world. Under such conditions, the attempt to make up for low salaries by incorporating forms of featherbedding into the legislation or even into the constitutions sometimes has adverse effects on those workers who take a second job in their free time in order to make ends meet.

Individualistic Declarations of Human Rights

The model of strictly individualistic declarations of human rights—the only ones in existence until 1917—may be found in Article 14 of the Argentine constitution of 1853. The old Latin American declarations of rights were the work of urban classes that had just shaken off absolutism and wanted to be free to do everything a colonial policy had forbidden them for so long:

All inhabitants of the Nation enjoy the following rights, in accordance with the laws that regulate their exercise, namely: of

[2] "Economic Growth and Social Policy in Latin America: The Seventh Conference of the American States Members of the ILO," *International Labour Review*, July, 1961, pp. 50–74.

working and practicing any legal industry; of navigating and trading; of petitioning the authorities; of entering, remaining in, traveling through, and leaving the Argentine territory; of publishing their ideas through the press without previous censorship; of using and disposing of their property; of associating for useful purposes; of freely professing their religion; of teaching and learning.

Other constitutions included guarantees against arbitrary arrest and the inviolability of home and correspondence, and proclaimed that laws may not be retroactive. Some constitutions also affirmed the right of asylum which, considering the frequency of disorders, plays a major role in Latin America. The importance of the problem gained world attention when, after a coup by a military junta in Peru in 1948, the head of the Aprista party, Haya de La Torre, sought refuge in the Colombian embassy. The new dictator, General Odría, tried to have him extradited. Colombia turned the request down. Odría then refused to give Haya de La Torre a safe-conduct enabling him to leave Peru, and, since the International Court in The Hague could impose no other solution, he had to remain on the embassy's grounds until 1954.

PRINCIPLE OF EQUALITY. The constitutions of Latin American countries have affirmed in one form or another that men are born free and equal and, as the Uruguayan constitution puts it, differ only in talent and virtue. In all these countries where slavery prevailed during the colonial period and sometimes long afterward, it was thought advisable to stress that any involuntary servitude was forbidden. Since most Latin American nations are multiracial and legal discrimination prevailed in colonial times against Amerindians, Africans, mestizos, and mulattoes, racial equality is often emphasized as well.

The contrast between theory and practice is most striking where racial equality is concerned. For instance in the Indo-American states of the Andean region the Amerindian populations as a whole have retained, together with their pre-Columbian languages and customs, the ignorance, squalor, and bondage of the past. In Brazil the populations in cities and developed regions have a life expectancy of about fifteen years more than the inhabitants of the interior, particularly the Northeast. Preoccupation with equality seems somewhat preposterous when in some countries titles of nobility and decorations are forbidden but de facto forced labor by peasants is tolerated. But when laisser-faire economics was on the rise, neither the United States nor western Europe, whose constitutions proclaimed the principle of equality, were any more conscious of this irony.

Some constitutions affirming the principle of equality actually legalize a politically motivated exception by disenfranchising illiterates and those who do not know the national language (Article 132 of the present constitution of Brazil, for instance). From the standpoint of democratizing political institutions this measure is defensible, since it excludes from political life the individuals under the closest control of the caciques, but in reality it gives legal standing to the fact that not all Latin American people are citizens enjoying equal rights. In Brazil this measure disenfranchises half the population, which is illiterate; in Peru it formerly affected a large part of the indigenous population which does not know the language of the conquerors, now the national language. In countries of that type such a measure may ruin the very principle of equality between different races, between the developed and the backward people, between cities and countryside. In both cases, however, the cause is the lag in social evolution and not the government's wrongdoing.

FREEDOM OF SPEECH AND OF THE PRESS. Latin American constitutions guarantee freedom of speech, and most of them frown upon press censorship. The effectiveness of these provisions is what foreign observers, North Americans especially, are most skeptical about, not only because the constitutional guarantees are suspended all too often, but also because they think the government has too much control over the press even under normal circumstances. For instance, a very effective method used in Brazil by the Vargas regime consisted in importing newsprint at a special low rate and in allotting it to the various newspapers in quantities that depended on their political position.

Skepticism is not fully justified, however. The attitude of

Latin American countries toward freedom of expression should not be judged during troubled periods. Even in Europe, wartime periods should not be taken as a standard. It is not in the least paradoxical to state that Latin America is particularly attached to freedom of expression and usually knows how to defend it. One of Perón's actions that was regarded as most intolerable by enlightened opinion, and was the cause of the greatest indignation in other Latin American countries, was the expropriation and taming of the great newspaper *La Prensa*, the pride of Latin America. In Brazil Vargas was severely criticized for persecuting the Mesquita family, the publishers of *Estado do São Paulo*. The newspaper was of a high intellectual caliber, and Vargas was trying to gain control of it. It is quite remarkable that in 1965 in Brazil a government created by a military dictatorship permitted the publication of protests against its repressive methods, signed by about one hundred important citizens.

In countries such as Argentina, Chile, Brazil, Mexico, Colombia—three-quarters of Latin America—there is a strong tradition of freedom of the press. Even in the middle of the nineteenth century the imperial regime of Dom Pedro II treated the opposition press with a tolerance that might be envied by the subjects of many contemporary republics, although the press attacked the monarch as well as the institution itself. Today the situation in Mexico is typical. Although the regime has become far tamer, it still retains some of the intolerance of a revolutionary regime. Politics are dominated by an official party that brooks no effective opposition. Nevertheless, a large segment of the press belongs to the right- or left-wing opposition.

On the other hand, the Latin American press is prone to abuse its freedom. Outside the few great papers of international standing, there is a profusion of small irresponsible dailies that constantly call for insurrection and indulge in personal attacks. President Quadros in Brazil was certainly too sensitive to criticism, but it is only fair to say that the attacks in Carlos Lacerda's paper which contributed to his resignation had definitely cut him to the quick.

As to freedom of speech, it would take an extremely powerful tyrant to keep Latin Americans quiet and prevent them from airing their criticisms. It takes a Rosas, a Gómez, or a Trujillo, and in Brazil, Mexico, and Argentina the time of such tyrants is past.

FREEDOM OF CONSCIENCE AND OF RELIGION. Latin America did not enjoy religious tolerance during the colonial period. The Spanish sovereigns fully intended to force Catholicism upon the natives, and did so whenever they could. Therefore it was out of the question to tolerate religious dissidence among the Creoles. The colonial clergy was large and all-powerful, and the Inquisition established in the Spanish possessions was particularly intolerant in Mexico and Peru, lasting until independence.

After independence, there was general agreement to proclaim freedom of conscience and worship. Opinion was divided between clericals and anticlericals only on the question of Church property and the separation of Church and state. Separation of Church and state was proclaimed in many countries. In Mexico it was the outcome of the support given Maximilian by the clergy, in Brazil it stemmed from the influence of positivism on those who proclaimed the Republic in 1889, in Ecuador it was a reaction against Moreno's theocratic dictatorship from 1860 to 1875. A few countries in Central America—Nicaragua, Panama, Guatemala, Honduras—adopted the regime of separation of Church and state under Mexico's influence. It also exists in Chile, Uruguay, and Cuba.

The fact that Church and state are separate in so many countries does not imply any disagreement between them. Whether separated or not, Latin America as a whole remains Catholic. In almost all the countries the Church is still a strong political force, and the clergy is consulted by the governments. Since the clergy has been a conservative force, a segment of public opinion is complaining about lingering clericalism. It is conceivable that with the development of a Christian Democratic movement committed to radical reforms, the clergy will be condemned in other quarters for interfering in politics, as happened in Northeastern Brazil in 1964. But these protests against interventions of the Church in politics do not in any way imply that freedom of conscience and worship are not guaranteed.

The best proof of the existence of these freedoms is the fact that, in countries with indigenous communities, they have been only partly evangelized. The old Amerindian and African religions have remained underneath the Catholic religion. Hence priests of the indigenous cultures, together with those of Spiritist cults that are proliferating today, greatly outnumber the Catholic priests.

If the Catholic Church wished to be intolerant in Latin America, to control the faith of individuals and hunt heretics of nonbelievers, it would have trouble doing so effectively because it is far from being represented everywhere. Even though during the colonial period the clergy, particularly those belonging to orders, were well represented, the picture is entirely different today, despite the call for foreign priests. In 1960 Latin America did not have even one priest per 5,000 inhabitants, and priests, at any rate secular priests, like the physicians, were concentrated in the cities. Table 13, from a book published by FERES,[3] shows the distribution of the Catholic clergy in Latin America.

The most striking exception to full freedom of worship occurred in Mexico. Far from leading the attack, the Catholic Church was the target. Mexico, the most sincerely Catholic country in Latin America, also has a strong anticlerical tradition. Anticlericalists had already asserted themselves during the Reforma movement in 1859, and won a lasting victory with the revolution of 1910. The constitution of 1917 stripped the clergy of their rights and restricted public worship. Under the presidency of Calles the Church was actually persecuted and a cruel religious war was waged. It died down in 1940 under the presidency of Ávila Camacho and today has given way to toleration.

In Colombia the work of Protestant missions was hampered, an unusual case judging from the rapid progress Protestantism has made in Latin America. Hostility to Protestant missionar-

[3] Gustavo Ramírez Perez and Isaac Wust, *La iglesia en Colombia*, FERES (Bogotá, 1961).

TABLE 13
NUMBER OF PRIESTS (REGULAR AND SECULAR) IN RELATION TO
NUMBER OF INHABITANTS [a]

Country	Number of Inhabitants per Catholic Priest	Country	Number of Inhabitants per Catholic Priest
Honduras	12,530	Venezuela	5,120
Guatemala	11,050	Costa Rica	4,530
Dominican Republic	9,580	Argentina	4,530
Cuba	9,420	Bolivia	4,450
Salvador	8,290	Uruguay	4,110
Haiti	8,290	Paraguay	4,060
Greater Antilles	8,260	Colombia	3,810
Nicaragua	7,370	Ecuador	3,180
Brazil	6,380	Chile	2,980
Panama	6,380	Average for:	
Peru	5,880	Latin America	5,333
Mexico	5,380	Central America	4,820
		South America	4,990

[a] From G. R. Perez and I. Wust, *La iglesia en Colombia*, FERES (Bogotá, 1961).

ies may stem not only from religious intolerance but also from nationalistic and political intolerance: the Catholic clergy distrusts the missionaries because they are Protestant, the conservative rural caciques because they suspect them of inciting for social reform, and the progressive nationalist parties because many of the missionaries are North Americans.

INDIVIDUAL FREEDOM AND PROTECTION OF PROPERTY. Latin American constitutions have always taken care to guarantee individual liberty and promise free enjoyment of legitimately acquired property. It would be absurd to complain today, as some do, that Latin American countries no longer accept the idea that property is a right. Foreigners with economic interests in Latin America have experienced many restrictions to their activities, but limitations of the right of property and free enterprise are not peculiar to Latin America. What is more serious is that infringements of individual freedom and even threats to life are too frequent in periods of revolution or dictatorship.

As a rule, however, Latin Americans are scrupulous jurists, and in the most representative countries, such as Brazil, Argentina, Chile, Mexico, and Colombia, even very authoritarian regimes have refrained from physically attacking the person or property of their enemies. The guarantee of course is worth no more than the courts themselves. No one can question the competence of Latin American jurists, the equals of those in fully developed countries and many of them enjoying international renown. The issue is the independence, not the competence, of the judicial power.

The Administration of Justice

The value of the guarantees granted depends primarily on the available legal remedies and on the independence of the magistrates who hear the cases. This is where foreign observers usually go astray. In the past few years Latin American affairs have been painstakingly analyzed by United States experts who then express opinions on which reputations are based. However, Latin American juridical systems are difficult for Anglo-Saxon observers to understand.

Throughout Latin America the organization of the judiciary was greatly influenced by the Constitution of the United States, which served as a model for the various national constitutions. The organization of the courts, especially of the highest one, the supreme court, was inspired by the United States model. The courts have also been given functions similar to those in common-law countries. Almost all the constitutions entrust the courts with testing the constitutionality of the laws, as in the United States, and, as in England and the United States, they entrust the ordinary courts with determining the legality of administrative actions. However, this Anglo-Saxon judicial organization does not quite harmonize with the spirit of the Latin American judicial systems, which derive from civil law. The Latin American legal system is based on Roman law as it was developed by Spain; later it was influenced by French and then by Italian and Swiss law. Anglo-Saxon observers grow anxious if not indignant when they see that courts modeled on their own have a different idea of their function.

The misunderstanding stems partly from the fact that all Latin American countries, having taken the United States Constitution as a model for their political institutions at a time when John Marshall had already introduced court testing of the constitutionality of laws, have given their supreme courts the power to declare legislation unconstitutional. Some countries have gone even further than the United States. Colombia, for example, provides for action by the people (unconstitutionality petition) that allows citizens to call for a declaratory judgment of unconstitutionality in the absence of litigation. More than once an unconstitutionality petition in Colombia has met with success. In Venezuela since 1958, the states may also call for a declaratory judgment of unconstitutionality. The form in which constitutionality is tested in Mexico is very interesting; the declaration is valid only for the case being heard, but five similar declarations from a specified majority of Supreme Court justices are binding upon the government.

Latin American supreme courts have not been as daring in their use of power as has the United States Supreme Court. They are very careful to disqualify themselves whenever a question is of a political nature. They find in such a case that it is not for them to judge the constitutionality of the legislator's action, and they hesitate to acknowledge that a president is acting unconstitutionally. They tend to find that his action is based on his discretionary power. Thus the courts condone delegations of power by the legislative branch which contradict the constitutions. Similarly they tolerate very broad interpretations of the president's ordinance power. In Mexico, Argentina, and even in Brazil the courts have been very accommodating in suspending constitutional guarantees. They have been too lenient in recognizing provisional governments. They have accepted too easily improper interventions of the federal government in the affairs of the member states.

A United States observer may conclude that, if the courts are timid in dealing with the political power, they are not truly independent. A European observer, on the other hand, may think that the courts are obeying a tradition that compels them to be scrupulous in respecting the separation of powers. While he may deplore that such respect induces them to condone excesses in the president's exercise of power, he may conclude that the United States courts, following Marshall's lead, have overstepped their judicial role and have often been guilty of trying to supersede Congress and the president as well.

Court Protection of Individual
Freedoms

As a rule the Latin American courts are regarded as most effective when protecting individuals against high-handed administrative decisions. In this respect, too, the situation may seem somewhat confusing because in practice the Latin American courts have combined the methods of common law and civil law.

Latin American countries have built bodies of administrative law which, as in France, result from synthesis of doctrine. Many specialized administrative courts have also been set up. At the same time, however, almost all these countries have adopted the Anglo-Saxon system that empowers the judiciary to determine, at least on appeal, the legality of actions taken by public officials. Only Uruguay and Colombia have a hierarchy of administrative courts topped by councils of state, as in France. In Paraguay the Council of State is not a court but a government council that includes, in addition to the members of the President's executive office, the bishop, the rector of the national university, and the president of the central bank.

Almost everywhere administrative jurisprudence is the work of the supreme courts which in many cases also include a specialized division. These courts give very real protection to individuals through various procedures. The most widely used is the habeas corpus, imported from England and introduced into Latin American constitutions or practice at the dates indicated in table 14.

In many countries the habeas corpus procedure has been broadened to provide protection not only against bodily restraint and arbitrary imprisonment, but also against violation of the various individual freedoms—worship, occupation, inviolability of the home, and so on. It has also been used to offer possessory protection against government agencies. Brazil is one of the countries where the habeas corpus is the broadest.

There are also more original and remarkably effective legal

resorts. One of them, of Mexican origin, is the *amparo,* of which Mexican jurists are justly proud; the other is the Brazilian procedure *mandato de segurança.*

The *amparo* procedure seems to have originated in the 1772 *Fueros de Aragón* (customary rights). It was adopted by the constitution of the state of Yucatán in Mexico in 1841. The form under which the amparo appears in the Mexican federal constitution of 1917 (Article 103), shows the influence of the United States writs of mandamus, prohibition, quo warranto, and certiorari, as well as injunction. The amparo applies to violations of the numerous guarantees of individual

TABLE 14

ADOPTION OF HABEAS CORPUS IN LATIN AMERICA

Brazil	1832	Panama	1941
Costa Rica	1871	Paraguay	1941
Uruguay	1934	Ecuador	1945
Honduras	1936	El Salvador	1945
Nicaragua	1939	Argentina	1949
Cuba	1940		

freedoms, whether by government agencies or by the judiciary. Action may be brought by the states against the federal government to contest its laws or acts, or by the federal government against the states.

Mexico is one of the Latin American countries where presidential dominance is the strongest, because of the fact that during his term of office he is the leader of an official party which is almost a single party. Although the party today is much more moderate than formerly, it is still the product of a revolution. In no other large Latin American country is Congress more submissive to the president. Nonetheless, the best proof of the judiciary's independence is the sheer number of amparo cases before the courts. The amparo is so widely used that in 1956 several circuit courts had to be set up solely to hear amparo applications because the Supreme Court had 35,000 pending cases it could not cope with. The Supreme Court also had to introduce more stringent requirements for amparo applications, to reduce their excessive number.

From Mexico the amparo procedure very rapidly spread to other countries—Argentina, Guatemala, Honduras, Nicaragua, El Salvador, and Costa Rica—although it is not used as widely. Under some dictatorial regimes these procedures are of course a complete fraud. In Cuba, although the Castroist regime maintained all the procedures for individual protection embodied in the 1940 constitution, it suspended all guarantees by passing temporary measures, removed magistrates, and set up revolutionary tribunals. In theory the judiciary retains the power to declare legislation unconstitutional, but in fact the cabinet has been authorized to amend the constitution as it sees fit.

The Brazilian constitution of 1934 (Article 113, Section 33) established the *mandato de segurança* procedure which combines the broadened effects of the habeas corpus with other procedures based on the Mexican amparo and the United States writs. The mandato de segurança has never been abandoned, and it is as widely used as the Mexican amparo. Similar procedures exist in other countries and set definite limits on arbitrary acts of the government.

Structure of the Judiciary

With the exception of Cuba, which had a tradition of independent judicial power and renowned jurists but has no true constitution under Castroism, all Latin American countries have made it a principle to ensure independence of the courts through a system of the separation of powers. Not all of them have succeeded, but on the whole the courts rather than the legislative assemblies have benefited from this separation.

Anglo-Saxon influence (English rather than North American) is shown in the selection of judges under a procedure generally regarded as promoting their independence. There is no watertight division between careers on the bench and the bar, since all over Latin America judges and public prosecutors are recruited among lawyers who have practiced for a long time. They may be appointed directly to the highest judicial posts. The Castroist regime, however, has made judgeship a branch of the civil service.

Another feature of Anglo-Saxon inspiration is that the supreme courts fulfill many functions that in France belong to the Ministry of Justice. In most countries the supreme court not only has disciplinary power over all courts but also appoints the lower court judges (in Mexico, Colombia, Chile, Peru, Venezuela, Bolivia, Uruguay, Guatemala, Nicaragua, Honduras, Costa Rica, and Panama), or at least submits the names to the president. Thus, the judicial power is largely self-governing and recruits its members by cooperation. In principle, this leaves no room for intervention by the executive or legislative powers. Some constitutions even give the judiciary the privilege of initiating legislation pertaining to its own organization whenever the latter is not laid down by a constitutional provision.

Independence of the Supreme Courts

The entire judiciary organization rests on the supreme courts, and the independence of the magistracy depends essentially on the independence of the supreme court justices. The United States system of appointment by the president with the assent of the Senate is used by the three large countries, Argentina, Brazil, and Mexico, as well as by Panama. Many of the countries prefer to avoid any intervention by the executive power, and their supreme court justices are elected by congress. These countries are: the Dominican Republic, Bolivia, Nicaragua, El Salvador, Ecuador, Guatemala, Honduras, Uruguay, and Venezuela. Except for Uruguay and Venezuela, and barring periods of dictatorship, these are not the countries where the independence of the judges is best provided for. In Colombia and Peru, congress chooses supreme court justices from a list of several names submitted by the president. In Paraguay the name proposed by the president must be approved by the Council of State. One country, Chile, has worked out a special procedure to ensure the independence of its Supreme Court by means of cooptation; the court submits a list of five names for the president to choose from. In Cuba until 1952 the president selected a justice from a list of three names presented by a commission consisting of three representatives of the president, three of the Supreme Court, and two of the law faculty of the University of Havana.

Although in principle justices are often forbidden to belong to a political party, most appointment procedures lend them-

TABLE 15
MAKEUP OF THE SUPREME COURTS

Country	Selection Procedure	Tenure	Testing of Constitutionality of Laws
Argentina	President and Senate	For life	Yes
Bolivia	Congress	10 years	Yes
Brazil	President and Senate	For life	Yes
Chile	Court and president	For life	Yes
Colombia	President and Congress	5 years	Yes
Costa Rica	Legislative Assembly	8 years	Yes
Cuba	President—Senate (before Castro)	For life	Yes
Dominican Republic	Senate	5 years	
Ecuador	Congress	6 years	Yes
El Salvador	Legislative Assembly	3 years	Yes
Guatemala	Congress	4 years	Yes
Haiti [a]	President	10 years	Yes
Honduras	Congress	6 years	Yes
Mexico	President—Senate	For life	Yes
Nicaragua	Congress	6 years	Yes
Panama	President—Assembly	10 years	Yes
Paraguay	President—Council of State	5 years	
Peru	President—Congress	For life	
Uruguay	Assembly	10 years	Yes
Venezuela	Congress	5 years	Yes

[a] Haiti is the only country where the higher court is called Court of Cassation instead of Supreme Court.

selves to political pressure. This is true also of the United States, but there the method does not seem to hamper independence—of federal judges, at least. In England as well, political factors enter into the appointment. Whatever the case may be, guarantees surrounding tenure are certainly more important than guarantees surrounding appointment as far as the independence (if not the competence) of the judges is concerned.

Table 15, showing the appointment procedure of the various supreme courts, indicates that tenure is relatively ill provided for, since in fourteen countries appointments are temporary and some of them very short—even less than the president's term of office. Consequently supreme court justices and the entire judiciary may become dependent upon the president or congress. The temporary tenure of judges has sometimes been used quite overtly in order to secure a compliant magistracy. Thus in Mexico when President Cárdenas took power in 1934 he pushed through a constitutional amendment that reduced the tenure of Supreme Court justices from life to six years under the pretext that life appointments would make the justices too conservative. Life tenure was reinstated in 1944 under Ávila Camacho's presidency. Since the president generally controls the assemblies, even appointment for life may be no guarantee against removal if the president is determined to get rid of a certain judge.

Under these circumstances, many observers firmly believe that statements in the constitutions that the judiciary power is independent and subject only to the constitution and to the law are empty words, and that Latin American courts are at the mercy of the executive power. The generalization is not accurate. It is true that certain dictatorships had no trouble subjugating the magistracy by summarily removing any judges who resisted them, and that the courts then offered no protection whatsoever. The Dominican Republic, Haiti, Nicaragua, Cuba, Guatemala, Paraguay, and Bolivia have lived under tyrannical regimes too long to permit one to speak of the independence of the judiciary as a normal state. In Mexico also, in the past and during the revolutionary period, the judges were under presidential control, and quite recently in Argentina Perón's regime systematically purged the magistracy.

It is quite obvious, on the other hand, that any dictatorial regime that means to transform society and brooks no resistance tends to subjugate the judges. It would be naïve to think that independence of the judges could prevent dictatorships and revolutions, or that dictatorships and revolutions always respect the independence of the judiciary. Far from testifying to the servility of judges, the fact that the only way of subjugating them was to remove them, as Perón, Castro, and Paz

Estenssoro did and as Cárdenas wanted to do, proves on the contrary that the judges in their countries were traditionally independent.

If one considers the number of inhabitants instead of the number of countries in a given situation, the conclusion is that normally in Argentina, Brazil, Mexico (today), Chile, Colombia, Venezuela—and even in Ecuador and Peru when the relaxation of dictatorship permits it—there does exist a tradition of true judicial independence. It was remarkable enough that the military revolution in Brazil in 1964, which carried out a ruthless purge, did not dare extend it to the Supreme Court. Even more remarkable was the fact that all the Supreme Court justices, regardless of the risk to themselves, concurred in ordering that Miguel Arraes be set free. (And the revolution was directed against Arraes almost as much as against Goulart himself.) Still more remarkable was the fact that President Castelo Branco, carried to power by the military, immediately complied with the Supreme Court order, on April 22, 1965.

This independence of the judiciary exists on the national level in any case; when the regime is a federal one, the state courts may be of much lower quality. This is also true of certain states in the United States.

The point to be kept in mind is that while in Latin America political freedom is often endangered, as in so many other developing regions, arbitrary action is always limited in the major and most representative countries. Latin American countries differ in this respect from developing countries in other parts of the world because their courts are determined to enforce the rule of law.

15. Form of the State: Centralization, Federalism, and Local Administration

It is convenient, the better to outline specific characteristics of Latin American political institutions, to contrast them with those of the United States, since to a very large extent these institutions were transposed to Latin America. The method is useful, but it lends itself to some distortion.

For instance, under the assumption that the central government in Latin America is usually vested with broader powers than in the United States, it is alleged that Latin American countries are very centralized, that they hardly provide for local initiative, and that such initiative would be foreign to people content to await instructions from the central government. This in turn jeopardizes the use of liberal methods for achieving economic, political, and social development. The Latin American frame of mind, it is also stated, results from colonial traditions that have so accustomed the people to despotism and centralization that they were unable to give them up after independence.

This belief gives rise to the first error about the very nature of federalism, which immediately after independence exerted such a strong attraction on the large countries of Latin America. It is claimed that in Latin America, with the possible exception of Brazil, federalism was no more than an artificial structure based on the United States constitution. Outwardly similar institutions are alleged to have fulfilled opposite functions in the two continents of the Western hemisphere. In the

United States, federalism by aggregation aimed at creating a permanent tie of clearly limited scope among states that renounced part of their sovereignty. Latin American federalism, on the contrary, is held to have been only a means of decentralization attempting, not always successfully, to provide local freedoms to which the population was not accustomed.

The contrast between the two forms of federalism certainly does not correspond to any sociological reality. It stems on the one hand from equating absolutism with centralization, which was certainly not the case, and on the other hand from over-emphasizing the forms of colonial institutions without regard to the social structures that greatly influenced their application. Actually, the varied provinces of Argentina—for instance Buenos Aires and La Rioja—differed more from one another than did Massachusetts from Virginia. The state of Rio de Janeiro had little in common with states of the Northeast except for the language, and perhaps even less with the southernmost ones. The differences between the temperate valley of Mexico, with the civilization of its ancient capital, and the tropical jungle of Yucatán would be difficult to duplicate in the thirteen original colonies of the United States. Even from a legal point of view, one could hardly conclude that in 1816 the United Provinces of La Plata were united by stronger ties than the thirteen former English colonies were by the Articles of Confederation.

Historical Foundations of Latin American Federalism

In any event, the critical period resulting from the desire of each small region to govern itself has been much longer and more dangerous in the large Latin American countries which formed federations than it was in the United States. Although federalism or even unification in a unitary form finally prevailed in certain areas, the intensity of regionalism in others was enough to wreck the attempts.

In the viceroyalties of La Plata and New Spain federalism succeeded in uniting a large number of provinces and cities to form two great nations, the Argentine Republic and Mexico. In Portuguese Brazil, the survival of the monarchy and soon thereafter the establishment of de facto federalism brought the same results. In the viceroyalties of New Granada and Peru, on the contrary, federalism was unable to check the overly strong centrifugal drives, as was also the case in the captaincy-general of Guatemala. Bolívar's prestige did not prevent the Confederation of greater Colombia from breaking up in 1830 into Ecuador, Colombia, and Venezuela. Despite the efforts of Andrés Santa Cruz, the Confederation of Bolivia and Peru had to dissolve itself in 1839, and the Organization of the Central American Provinces could not prevent the former captaincy-general of Guatemala from splitting up into five small states in 1838.

Under these conditions and despite the prior existence of a colonial administrative fabric, it can hardly be denied that whenever federalism prevailed, it resulted from aggregation, just as in the United States. It made allowance for strong sectionalist drives that had to be controlled and could scarcely be ignored. It was far more difficult to blend cities and provinces into a few large nations than to federate the thirteen British colonies in North America. This was because in Latin America, the caudillos confronted the urban middle class with a far more powerful force than the western pioneers of the United States could muster against the conservative and centralizing drives of the Eastern gentry. Had caudillos existed west of the Alleghenies in 1787, the United States of America would probably not have been formed in 1789.

The initial crystallization of civic sentiment on the narrow basis of town or province has left many traces to this day, even in the unitary states. Colombia, with the rivalry between Medellín and Bogotá, and Ecuador, where the coastal area competes with the Andean plateau, are good cases in point. Lingering parochialism is not obvious to the foreign observer today because it is masked by fiery nationalism and no longer threatens a national unity in existence for over a century. Such sectionalism is strong, nonetheless, and prevents centralization patterned on European countries.

Latin American political institutions have moved steadily toward centralization—which is true of all countries in the world. It is true that whenever federalism has persisted in Latin America it differs from United States federalism in that its federal governments have been given broader powers. This is largely because Latin American constitutions have been changed often and are generally easy to amend. In most countries, Brazil for instance, an absolute majority of the legislative houses at two consecutive sessions is sufficient; in other countries an absolute majority at one meeting is enough. In Mexico, where the vote of Congress must be ratified by a majority of the states, the official party system reduces the requirement to a mere formality. When economic and social changes have made it necessary to broaden federal powers, it has been easy to amend the constitutions accordingly. In the United States, the federal government has remained in theory a government restricted to the powers granted to it in 1789 and altered by few amendments. This has not prevented a trend toward centralization, and this in many ways has been done more effectively than in Latin America.

Spread of Federalism

In Chile federalism was only a brief episode under the 1828 constitution which did not last even two years. In Colombia, where opinion has always been deeply split as to whether the state should be federal or unitary, federalism prevailed for a long period under the constitution of 1853, especially under the federal constitution of the United States of Colombia of 1863. But federalism there was accompanied by so much unrest that the unitary form was resumed in 1886 and has not been abandoned since.

Around 1830, however, before the dissolution of the confederations of Central America, Greater Colombia, Bolivia, and Peru, and just before Brazil adopted the 1834 amendment which, while rejecting the word, accepted the institutions of federalism, that form of state prevailed throughout almost all of Latin America. At present only four countries have retained it, namely Argentina, Brazil, Mexico, and Venezuela, while sixteen have adopted the unitary form. It is true nonetheless that the federal state is dominant in Latin America, since it exists in two-thirds of the territory and embraces the same proportion of the people, even excluding Venezuela, where federalism may be only nominal. It should also be added that certain provisions peculiar to federalism have been introduced into unitary states and have somewhat altered their form. Thus a very large number of states have a second legislative chamber, whose role is to provide representation for the provinces instead of the population. Haiti, Cuba, Ecuador, and the Dominican Republic provide for equal senatorial representation for all provinces, while Chile has set up groups of provinces in order to give five senators to each group.

In each of the four federal countries, federalism differs somewhat in its form, and its operation has been influenced by varying historical traditions and social structures as well as by political parties.

PSEUDO-FEDERALISM IN VENEZUELA. Venezuela deserves a place apart. It consists of twenty states, one federal district, and two territories and has proclaimed that the states are self-governing. Although the powers of the federal government are limited and the Senate, as in the United States, gives each of the twenty states two seats in addition to the two seats reserved for the federal district, it does not truly deserve to be included among the federal countries. The reason is that the president enjoys a power incompatible with true federalism—namely, the power to appoint the state governors, in whom executive power is vested, and who are responsible only to him. Many unitary states in Latin America grant greater freedom to their provinces. Despite the terminology adopted by the constitution, Venezuela should be regarded as a relatively centralized unitary state. Next to the prefects, who are the governors responsible to the president, the elected state assemblies are similar (although with broader powers) to the councils of the French departments. Venezuela itself is the product of a dismemberment of the Confederation of Greater Colombia, and federalism was introduced only during a short-lived liberal period in 1864. The fifteen or sixteen subsequent constitutions have retained federalism, but its effects have been lessened because from 1864 to 1958 Venezuela was almost continuously ruled by dictators who cared very little about constitutions.

ARGENTINE FEDERALISM. The Argentine Republic is a federal state consisting of twenty-two provinces, one federal district, and one territory. This is a case of true federalism by aggregation of provinces which, in the early days after independence, succeeded only with great difficulty in uniting with the hated city of Buenos Aires. Although the form of the institutions barely changed after the amendments introduced in 1860 into the constitution of 1853, the operation of those institutions was transformed by the exceptionally rapid and radical changes in the population's ethnic composition, its housing and living conditions. Provincial regionalism has inevitably weakened, since most of the population today consists of first- or second-generation descendants of European immigrants. While some regionalism lingers in provinces whose population has not been renewed by immigration, it is very slight, since almost half the population lives in the capital and its surrounding province. The excessive growth of Buenos Aires and the neighboring region has unbalanced Argentine federalism.

MEXICAN FEDERALISM. Mexico, which at present includes twenty-nine states, two territories, and one federal district, has never abandoned federalism for any length of time. Although the danger of a split into small states was not as serious as in Argentina's early national life, there have been separatist drives. Yucatán in particular was not really tied to the rest of the country. As long as caudillismo endured, the provinces enjoyed a great deal of autonomy. Even under the long rule of Porfirio Díaz (1876–1910), the dictatorial authority of the federal president was carried out through the provincial caudillos whom he had subjugated. At the present time, the face of federalism is very different because of the official party system. Although the party is not a single one, it is so sure of its power that it can impose its leadership upon the governments of the federated states as well as upon the federal government, and upon the various branches of both. The situation is somewhat reminiscent of the USSR, although the party in Mexico is neither monolithic nor totalitarian in outlook. In both countries, but to a lesser extent in Mexico, decentralized institutions are in the service of a centralized party.

BRAZILIAN FEDERALISM. Under normal circumstances the Brazilian federalist regime is the most orderly and most resembles United States federalism. The federation consists of twenty-two states, five territories, and one federal district now situated in Brasília. Legally, however, this is not federalism by aggregation. It was imposed outright after the fall of the Empire in 1891, when the Brazilian nation was already firmly established. Nevertheless, under the veneer of unitarism Brazil has always had an underlying federalist fabric dating back to the early colonial days, when the country was organized into captaincies granted to *donatários*. After independence the monarchy and the monarchists refrained from using the word federalism, generally associated with republicanism, but this did not prevent the monarchy from respecting regional diversities. The Acto Adicional, or amendment of 1834, provided for elected legislative assemblies vested with broad powers, although the emperor retained the prerogative of appointing presidents for the provinces. By imparting a federal form to the Brazilian state, which took the name of the United States of Brazil, the constitution of 1891 only gave its proper name to an existing situation.

The 1891 constitution certainly left too much power to the federated states. Two of these powers were particularly dangerous: that of maintaining local armies and of granting concessions to foreign powers (and even worse of borrowing money from them). Until the 1930 revolution, and even until the coup d'état of Getulio Vargas did away with state armies, the federal government had no assurance that it could impose its will upon the large states. Although the constitution gave the federation more powers than the United States Constitution and although presidential authority was increased, Brazilian federalism of 1891 was more akin to United States federalism before the Civil War, as expressed in the Kentucky and Virginia Resolutions, than to its form in the post-Roosevelt period.

Since Vargas dictatorially imposed centralization with the help of the national armed forces during the nationalistic era, state regionalism has no longer threatened Brazilian unity. Insofar as any such threat exists, it stems, as in the United States on the eve of the Civil War, from sectionalism, by which the overpopulated, needy, and decadent Northeast is ranged against the active, prosperous South. But if regionalism no longer jeopardizes national unity, it remains strong and is the raison d'être of federalism. The political parties are still largely local, and so are political alliances; the president of the republic, notwithstanding his power, cannot assure or prevent the election of a hostile state governor. Unlike Argentina or Mexico, Brazil maintains true federalism more easily because there is a relative balance of power between a few large states, none of which can dominate the federation. In Argentina, the situation is the reverse: Buenos Aires and its surrounding area are as influential as all the other parts of the country put together. In Brazil, the state of São Paulo is effectively counterbalanced by Minas Gerais, which since 1930 has had the help of Rio Grande do Sul. Even before the capital was transferred to Brasília, the city of São Paulo exerted a more powerful economic attraction than Rio de Janeiro and an almost equal intellectual attraction.

Comparison of Latin American and United States Federalism

The federalist regimes of Mexico, Brazil, and Argentina were copied directly from the United States. As in the United States, the principle of aggregation of states is the basis of the distribution of powers between the two categories of government—federal and, depending on the country, state or province. The federal government enjoys only the powers delegated to it, and reserve power is in principle vested in the states. Even Venezuela inscribed this principle in its constitution, where it does not apply. As in the United States Constitution, federalism required a double representation with two legislative houses. One provides popular representation and gives each state a number of representatives proportional to population. The other provides representation for the states and grants each state the same number of senators. There are two senators per state or province in Argentina, Mexico, and Venezuela, and three in Brazil. As in the United States, the federal capitals of Buenos Aires, Brasília, Caracas, and Mexico City are federal districts. Their population, unlike that of Washington, D. C., is represented in the federal assemblies.

The United States system of federal territories has also been adopted by the federal countries of Latin America in order to provide a trusteeship system for those regions not only insufficiently developed to govern themselves but—and this is the main consideration—too sparsely populated and too poor to cover regular state expenses. This system has been used far less extensively and skillfully than in the United States. Only in Argentina has it been effectively applied, preventing regions from becoming states before they have sufficient inhabitants and economic means. The number of provinces has increased slowly and today covers almost the entire expanse of land. In Brazil, however, the system of territories under federal trusteeship was not actually used until much too late, during World War II. At that time President Vargas amputated the Amazon states of over 312,000 square miles of almost uninhabited land in order to add to the Acre territory (wrested from Bolivia by rubber adventurers in 1899) the territories of Guaporé, Rondônia, Rio Branco, and Amapá. Leaving barely explored regions in the care of states themselves too large, poor and underpopulated, such as Pará, Amazonas, and Mato Grosso, undoubtedly delayed their development and fostered the squandering of manpower and land.

Federal institutions in Latin America were directly copied from the United States, but this has not prevented the resulting regimes from acquiring certain individual features present to a more or less marked degree in Brazil, Argentina, and Chile. Some of them result from deliberate changes in order to adapt to the conditions of Latin American political life. Others are a by-product of the different political parties and the presidents' dominant position. Still other differences are only superficial and stem from the difficulty of amending the United States Constitution and the stringent testing of the constitutionality of her laws. In the United States this perforce masks some of the centralization that is changing United States federalism. In Latin America, on the contrary, it is very easy not only to amend but also to change the constitutions altogether, and fairly easy to give them a very broad interpretation. Consequently they can be adapted to a changing reality. The original balance of power between the federation and the states has been shattered in the United States just as in Latin America. What prompts so many analysts to deny that true federalism can exist in Latin America is not the greater hegemony of the federal government but the fact that the hegemony is more obvious.

Distribution of Powers Between the Federation and the States

In principle, in Latin America as well as in the United States, the federal government possesses only the powers delegated to it, but in Latin America they are much broader.

A major difference between the United States and Latin American countries is that the latter, whether federalist or unitary, are civil law countries with a completely or relatively unified national juridical system. Private law as well as penal or business law is codified, and in the few countries where unification is not complete (for example, in Mexico) the federation's member states have no other recourse than to adapt national standards to local needs. In this respect, too, the system is closer to the Soviet system than to the United States. Latin American countries may have state courts in addition to federal courts. Although both categories of jurisdictions may have different competence in *ratione materiae* and *ratione personae*, they apply the same national law. This judicial unity has spared the Latin American federal countries a great deal of the usurpations of power that United States jurists have had to justify in order to permit the federation to pursue one national economic and social policy.

A second difference is that the writers of Latin American constitutions were not limited to providing for the distribution of powers, as were the authors of the Constitution in Philadelphia in an era when the function of government was narrower than it is today. The Latin American writers added to the federal functions of national defense, foreign policy, defense of the freedom of interstate commerce and foreign trade, those of regulation of production, development of public education, and labor legislation. Experience has demonstrated that these tasks must now be federal in scope, since the central government has been entrusted with far more than merely policing the country. Besides, the declarations of rights, inspired by Mexico's socialist constitution and today part of all the constitutions, force the states of the federation to pursue a uniform economic and social policy.

Another difference from the United States Constitution is

that the Latin American federal constitutions usually prescribe
the nature of political and judicial institutions, and the internal
administrative structure of the states. This political uniformity
may seem regrettable in certain respects because it does not
allow for adaptation of political and administrative institutions
to local conditions, developed regions, nor does it permit the
fruitful local political experimentation that took place in the
United States. The uniformity was needed, nonetheless, in order to overcome the dangers of caudillismo. In the United
States, as a matter of fact, the liberty of the states to experiment, in particular in judicial matters and in the procedures
for electing judges, was not always fortunate.

The authors of the Argentine constitution provided for in-
definite enlargement of federal powers when necessary. Thus
Section 16 of Article 67 gives Congress the power "to provide
whatever is conducive to the prosperity of the country, for the
progress and welfare of all the provinces and for the advancement of learning, enacting programs of general and university
instruction, and promoting industry, immigration . . . , the
introduction and establishment of new industries, the importation of foreign capital, etc. . . ."

In Brazil similar opportunities are given the federal government by a form of distribution of powers between the two
categories of government which is closer to the Soviet than to
the United States pattern. For those powers not within the
exclusive purview of the federation, the latter may impose
over-all standards and leave the states—which thus enjoy a
regulatory rather than a legislative power—free to adapt the
standards to local resources and needs. The meticulousness
with which these standards have been laid down in some cases
is obvious from the 120 articles of the Brazilian law of December 20, 1962, which prescribes the *Diretrizes e Bases da
Educação*.

Although federal powers are infinitely broader in Latin
America than in the United States, greater centralization does
not result. A large part of the powers, particularly in economic
matters, which in Latin America have been vested in the
federal government, have in the United States had to be
usurped by the federal government as the role assigned to it by
the authors of the 1789 Constitution has changed. There was

no economic or social need in Latin American countries for the subtle diversions of power that the United States had to resort to in the cases of legislation by indirection, so that the federal government has used its power to regulate interstate transportation in order to prevent the spread of syphilis, or used the power to set up postal agencies to control pornographic mail. The relative centralization authorized by constitution in Latin America had to be introduced through customary law in the United States. This is probably a consequence of the special genius of the Anglo-Saxon culture which enabled the people of the United States to allow their constitution—the most rigid in the world and resting on the strictest judicial control of the constitutionality of laws—to become based on custom to the same extent as the English constitution. In England too, the constitution is never abrogated and seldom amended but also is changing constantly.

It should be added that in Latin America, as in the United States, real centralization stems far less from direct exercise of the powers vested in or usurped by the federal government than from the manner in which it appropriates money. For example, the states cannot discharge their functions without requesting appropriations from the federal government (the equivalent of the United States grants-in-aid), and these are usually granted conditionally. Federally controlled agencies that allot funds and regulate the economy are another form of universal centralization, whether the federal control is direct or indirect.

In conclusion, it is not overstating the case to say that the major difference between United States and Latin American federalism is that the United States federal government uses very effectively the powers gained by encroachment, whereas the powers specifically vested in the Latin American federal governments are often weakened by an inadequate administrative apparatus within a resisting social structure.

Local Administration

Whether the countries are federal or unitary, United States observers are prone to conclude, particularly on the basis of municipal administration, that Latin Americans are averse to local self-government. This conclusion rests primarily on the fact that, in contrast to the United States, Latin American municipalities are never allowed to select the form of their institutions and draw up their own charter. The forms of local government are usually laid down by the federal constitutions or by a uniform legislation provided for by the constitution. Hence, local administration is necessarily very different from that of the United States. It is important, however, to avoid equating centralization and administrative uniformity. Self-government with local freedom hinges on the existence of elected assemblies endowed with sufficiently broad competence, and administrators who are responsible to the assemblies and not to the central government.

In this respect, Latin America as a whole is, at least in principle, far more centralized than the United States, but much less so than France. But neither can one generalize about Latin America on this point.

In the three large federal states, Argentina, Brazil, and Mexico, the administrative structure is relatively simple, since there are no administrative subdivisions between the states and municipalities. It should be added that the municipalities generally embrace huge territories, and these are split up into new municipalities only as the population density increases. They form large rural zones around the town or the village. In Brazil, in 1960, three-quarters of the *municípios* embraced territories varying between 780 and 1950 square miles, while in the states of Amazonas, Pará, and Mato Grosso the município usually exceeds 390,000 square miles.

In Brazil and Mexico the federal constitution guarantees broad autonomy to the municipalities; they are administered by elected assemblies headed by a major or a prefect elected through universal suffrage.

In Argentina the situation is more complex for, while the constitution provides for municipal freedoms, the various provinces of the federation differ in the amount of freedom they give their municipalities. All municipalities have elected councils, but over half the provinces give their presidents the right to appoint the *intendente* or chief of the municipal administration.

Two of the nonfederal countries have an internal organization that provides for local freedoms. In Uruguay the nineteen departments are administered by an elected assembly. Predilection for plural executive power on the national level has resulted in local executive councils chosen by the constituents, instead of mayors. In Cuba before Castro each of the six provinces had an assembly and a governor, both elected by universal suffrage, and the municipalities elected a council and mayor.

Other Latin American countries have an administrative organization closer to the French pattern. Municipalities are administered by an elected council and by a mayor either appointed by the council or elected by universal suffrage. But there are intermediate administrative subdivisions between the states and the municipalities; these departments or provinces are headed by an administrator appointed and removed by the central government. In this group are Chile and five small Central American countries—El Salvador, Costa Rica, Guatemala, Panama, and Honduras. Venezuela should be added despite its semblance of federalism since, although the large subdivisions are called states, the governors are agents of the central power. The states of Venezuela have elected assemblies, however, and each town elects a council that appoints the mayor.

The internal structure of another group of countries is even more centralized than France's since not only are departmental prefects appointed by the president, but even mayors are appointed by either the president or the prefect. Only the assemblies are elected, but they are merely advisory. Bolivia, Colombia, Ecuador, Nicaragua, Peru, the Dominican Republic, and Haiti are in this category. Table 16 shows the administrative structures of a number of Latin American countries. Almost all the countries deny municipal freedoms to the capital city, and some deny them also to a few other large cities.

Thus in their form the institutions preserve those local freedoms that Latin America's own traditions, combined with Anglo-Saxon influence, have led her to regard as basic elements of democracy. The extent to which these freedoms are respected is another matter, however.

One fact is undeniable: the municípios are the center of political life in Latin America. The de facto authority of the

TABLE 16
ADMINISTRATIVE STRUCTURES

Country	States in Federations	Provinces or Departments	Municipalities
Argentina	22 provinces, elected assemblies, elected governors	No departments	Elected councils and (according to the provinces) appointed or elected *intendantes*
Bolivia	Unitary state	9 departments, no assemblies and appointed prefects	Elected councils, appointed mayors
Brazil	22 states, elected assemblies and governors	No departments	Elected councils and mayors
Chile	Unitary state	25 provinces, appointed *intendantes*, elected assemblies	Elected councils and mayors
Colombia	Unitary state	16 departments, appointed governors, elected assemblies	Appointed mayors, elected councils
Costa Rica	Unitary state	7 provinces, appointed governors, no assemblies	Elected councils and mayors
Cuba (1940)	Unitary state	6 provinces, elected governors and assemblies	Elected councils and mayors
Dominican Republic	Unitary state	17 provinces, appointed governors, no assemblies	Elected councils

TABLE 16 (Continued)

Haiti	Unitary state	5 departments, prefects, no elected assemblies	Elected councils
Mexico	29 federated states, elected assemblies and governors	No departments	Elected mayors and councils
Panama	Unitary state	7 provinces, appointed governors, no assemblies	Elected mayors and councils
Paraguay	Unitary state	12 departments, appointed governors, no assemblies	No administrative division outside the department
Peru	Unitary state	23 departments, appointed prefects	No municipal self-government
Uruguay	Unitary state	19 departments, elected legislative councils and executive councils	Elected councils in the cities
Venezuela	20 federated states, appointed governors, elected assemblies	None	Elected councils and mayors

cacique or the colonel rooted itself in the municipalities and still exists in many of them. As long as the cacique does not clash with the government in power, his authority sometimes borders on sovereignty. The existence of such an authority justifies second thoughts about the degree of centralization of Latin American regimes, regardless of their legal aspect. When a cacique actually dominates the local administration and the agents of the central government must obey him if they want to keep their jobs, it hardly matters how strictly they are required to supervise the local administration.

Federal Power of Intervention

Federal constitutions in Latin America give the federation one power that facilitates centralization—that of intervening in the states to protect them against external or internal subversion, and this power can be diverted from its original purpose.

In the United States federal system, the government of the Union has the right if not the duty to use the forces at its disposal to protect the states, primarily against foreign invasion, but also from internal subversion. As expressed in the Constitution of the United States (Article 4, Section 4) the power to intervene is a duty imposed upon the federation: "The United States shall guarantee to every State in this Union a Republican form of government, and shall protect each of them against invasion; and on application of the Legislature, or of the Executive (when the Legislature cannot be convened) against domestic violence." In the United States, except for the Civil War, the federal government had used with the greatest restraint the powers vested in it under this clause. It has not sought to impose upon the states governments of its own choice except during the Reconstruction era that followed the Civil War, and these were carpetbagger governments supported by federal troops. Even the Negro integration crises of the 1950's and '60's have not resulted in any suggestion of takeover by the federal government.

In Latin America, on the other hand, the dangers of caudillismo, the frequent unrest during elections, and the tendency of some heads of state to become dictators have led to frequent use of the power of intervention, often when not requested by the local government. The power of intervention has often been diverted from its purpose and used to further centralization, since in order to restore order it allows the executive to replace local authorities with agents of the central government. Because of frequent interventions and the latent threat of federal interference, local administrations cannot always take advantage of their precariously based freedoms.

Excessive use of the power of intervention varies among the four federal countries. In Venezuela no intervention is needed, since federalism exists only in name and each state governor is a presidential agent. In the three other countries intervention has played a very important role, but Brazil in 1946 took measures to prevent diversion from its original purpose. The measures are effective in normal times, but proved worthless in the coup d'état of 1964.

FEDERAL INTERVENTION IN ARGENTINA. Of the three other countries, it is in the Argentine Republic that the use and abuse of intervention has been most systematic. This is not because Article 5 of the constitution of 1853 (amended in 1860), which regulates interventions, is very different from the article of the United States Constitution which specifies the guarantees of the states. The relevant article of the Argentine constitution reads: "The federal government may intervene in the territory of the Province in order to guarantee the republican form of government, or to repel foreign invasions, and at the request of their constituted authorities, to support or reestablish them, should they have been deposed by sedition or invasion from another Province."

Even if the governments had scruples about construing the constitution too freely, the interpretation of the words "republican form of government" could easily condone abuse of the power of intervention, since the Argentine Supreme Court, deeming intervention to be a political matter, does not regard itself qualified to determine its legality. In the United States, the guarantee of the republican form of government, which has never been invoked, is construed strictly at aiming to prohibit a monarchic regime. It was suggested that this clause be used to prohibit the first experiments in semidirect government through referendum and recall in the western states, by construing republican to mean also representative. But these suggestions were not followed up.

In Argentina, where the threat of caudillismo persisted in the provinces even after 1853, intervention was needed to prevent local dictatorships. A tradition developed whereby the mere claim by a state government that its foes had authoritarian tendencies or seemed to have them was enough to justify intervention.

The interpretation of the words "at the request of their constituted authorities, to support or reestablish them, should they have been deposed" was to permit even far more arbitrary action. The main cause of interventions, which were used under military pressure in 1962 in the face of election results favoring the Peronistas, was the allegation of election fraud: authorities established by fraudulent elections are not the constituted authorities, and hence the federal government is obligated to establish more legitimate ones through new elections. Under these conditions, election results unfavorable to the party that dominates the federal government, or merely unfavorable to the president's friends, may become grounds for intervention. This completely deprives the state of the freedom to pursue the policy of its choice within its constitutional powers. Nothing is easier than for the president to use domestic conflicts—inevitable in a presidential regime which is the regime of the states as well—as a pretext for intervention.

Lastly, it is unfortunate that the Argentine constitution has no provisions regarding the jurisdiction of the various federal authorities with respect to intervention. It simply states that "the federal government may intervene." The respective powers of the president and Congress are not specified. Usage in Argentina, which favored presidential hegemony, established the power of intervention of the President by decree. Congress, in which the provinces and the oppositions are represented, need not be consulted.

Provincial autonomy is more threatened by the power of intervention when the intervention tends to be long-lasting. Intervention is not usually aimed at helping legitimate authorities but, on the contrary, at "rebuilding" a state where the institutions are alleged to be no longer operating legally. The representative of the federation, or *interventor,* who in Latin

America has often been a military man, takes the place of the governor of the state or province. He is endowed with absolute powers, including the discretionary power to comply with or disregard the constitution of the state.

It has been noted [1] that in Argentina 101 federal interventions occurred between 1860 and 1930, 64 of them by presidential decree, although in a substantial number of instances Congress was in session when they were decreed. Out of the 101 interventions of that period, 72 were aimed at organizing elections in order to ensure in each state the victory of the party then in power in the federal government, thus eliminating the opposition in those states. During Irigoyen's first presidency, when the upper-class conservative party suffered its first defeat as Irigoyen brought about the victory of the Radical Civic Union in national elections, the president ordered 20 interventions between 1916 and 1922 in order to impose the rule of his party upon the states. After 1930, during a period of unrest, the pace of the interventions did not slow down. Their use in the 1962 crisis shows that their meaning has not changed. Such use of the institution may have been intended by some of the authors of the constitution. Alberdi, the moving spirit behind the 1853 constitution, had initially proposed to set up a federal intervention power to restore order even when not requested by the local authorities. His proposal was not accepted, but practice made up for this, since out of the 101 interventions before 1930, half had not been requested. Neither were the interventions that President Frondizi had to order in March 1962.

FEDERAL INTERVENTION IN MEXICO. Since the National Revolutionary party (now called the Institutional Revolutionary party) controls all of Mexican political life, it might seem that the power of intervention would seldom need to be used, since the various state governments are usually in the hands of the party over which the president reigns undisputed. Interventions are frequent, nonetheless, because, although the PRI is an official party and dominates all elections, it is not monolithic. Factional or personal struggles are rife within the

[1] Rosendo A. Gomez in *Inter-American Economic Affairs*, December, 1947, pp. 53–73.

party. These struggles, incidentally, have preserved a democratic way of life in Mexico. Suffice it to recall the struggle for influence between the two PRI leaders from 1924 to 1934. Cárdenas, after becoming president, intervened in four states within one year to eliminate the local governments loyal to his foe, Calles. All the elections organized by Cárdenas' representatives were won by his candidates.

Serious guarantees against interventions nevertheless exist in Mexico. The constitutional powers are couched in very broad terms, since the federation must declare that "the constitutional powers of a state have disappeared," but under Article 76 of the constitution the right to decide on intervention rests with the Senate, which must vote for it by a two-thirds majority, and it is the Senate that represents the states. During Congressional recess the power rests with a permanent committee representing Congress. It might be thought therefore that any abuse of intervention is impossible: if the Mexican Senate were as considerate of states rights as is the United States Senate, it would take a major provocation to muster a two-thirds majority of the states.

However, because of the existence of an official party headed by the president, the guarantee is illusory. In practice, the Mexican Senate receives a request for intervention from the Ministry of the Interior and does not dare refuse a request from the head of a party that in fact holds the power of political life and death over the members of the houses. There is no judicial recourse against abuse of the power of intervention, since the Mexican Supreme Court, like that in Argentina, regards decisions to intervene as political acts. Hence it is not within its jurisdiction to judge their constitutionality and it refuses to allow recourse to amparo.

Because of the existence of an official party, resort to intervention is needed much less in Mexico than in Argentina; it is, however, almost as frequent and lends itself to the same excesses, which may be necessary.

FEDERAL INTERVENTION IN BRAZIL. It is certain that the use and abuse of intervention distort the operation of federal institutions in Latin America. On the other hand, without a power of intervention broader and more often used than in the

United States, it is doubtful that federalism would have been able to survive in Latin America without leading to the breakup of the countries involved. The threats to federalism were caciquismo, caudillismo, and communications difficulties, which for so long prevented the populations from being fully integrated into the nation.

The case of Brazil today is probably the most interesting because the power of federal intervention, as revised by the constitution of 1946, does not seem to have provoked abuses in normal circumstances. The federal government has very often been tempted to use it recently, but has resisted the temptation, although it is in Brazil that regionalism has remained the strongest, and most political parties are still regional in character. Under the policy of free elections prevailing in Brazil since the end of the Vargas regime, the party of the president of the republic has been constantly confronted by political foes—often relentless ones—in power in the states. The bitterness of the campaigns against Goulart before he was confirmed as president in 1961, and of the campaigns against Kubitschek in the first years of his presidency, are good examples in point. Still the power of intervention was not used to remove the foes from their positions in the states. In 1962, when the cabinet, angered by the violent attacks of Carlos Lacerda, governor of the state of Guanabara (Rio de Janeiro), asked the president to intervene in that state, he refused.

The grounds for intervention listed in the Brazilian constitution are as numerous as those in the Mexican and Argentine constitutions and might provide as many pretexts for elimination of hostile state governments. The power of intervention is worded in a negative form:

The federal government shall not intervene in the States, except: To maintain the national integrity. To repel foreign invasion. . . . To put an end to civil war. To guarantee the free exercise of any of the state powers. To assure the execution of a judicial order or decision. To reorganize the finances of any State. . . . To assure the observance of. . . . a representative republican form. . . . Municipal autonomy. . . . Prohibition of the reelection (of certain officials) for the period immediately following.

All these clauses had been included in the constitutions of 1891 and 1934 and had given rise to many abuses. Resort to intervention enabled Vargas to get rid of many of those who had resisted him and to institute a dictatorial regime in 1937. He then appointed officers as interventors in many states and through them had governed until 1945 without regard for any constitutional rule. After Vargas' downfall his interventions had a fortunate consequence for the equilibrium of the federal regime. One of his acts, which was not subsequently revoked, was the disbanding of state troops because some of them had become too powerful and hence a threat to national unity. This had been true of the Brigada Militar of the aggressive state of Rio Grande do Sul, which had been able to hold the federal army in check. It was so strong that it had played a crucial role in putting down the São Paulo insurrection in 1932. When Vargas dissolved these local troops the national army became omnipotent, and a local insurrection can no longer succeed.

The government put in power by the military in the Brazil of 1964 did not hesitate to resort to intervention repeatedly. Outwardly the procedure was legal because the government was the master of Congress. But the situation was a revolutionary one, and intervention in the states was not the only illegal act of the revolutionary regime.

The lesson of the Vargas regime was heeded in the period from 1946 to 1964, and there were no abuses of intervention, the main reason being that during that period there was no government of truly authoritarian tendency. Besides, the structure of the Brazilian parties and the persistently local character of some of them, as well as effective control by the special electoral courts, precluded any hope that a president would intervene to cancel election results in a state. He could not, without provoking violence, impose the election of persons of his choice.

Aside from these practical grounds, the provisions contained in the constitution of 1946 have been effective in limiting the power of intervention to its intended aim, that is, the proper operation of the institutions of the states and their defense against external and internal subversion. The president may carry out an intervention when it is requested by the state authorities, the Supreme Court, or the electoral courts. Except when the request is made by the judiciary, the president is required to obtain the authorization of Congress and, in order to do so, to convene Congress if it is not in session. When the intervention aims at reorganizing finances or defending the higher principles of the constitution, Congress alone is empowered to intervene.

It may be truly said that in view of the abuse of the power of intervention as it has always occurred in Mexico and Argentina, and in Brazil under Getulio Vargas, local freedoms are not respected and federalism is only a veneer. The problem then is not the value of Latin American political institutions, but rather the disorderly political life. Federal intervention that suspends the freedoms of the states is only one form—and by no means the worst—of a far more general phenomenon, namely the suspension of constitutional guarantees in case of actual or impending unrest. The situation when the alleged threat of unrest is merely the government's attempt to get rid of constitutional hindrances comes under the same heading.

16. Form of
the Government:
Presidential Dominance

Heeding the fruitful experience of the critical period, the constitution writers of Latin America were aware of two conflicting and equally compelling needs dictated by political and economic conditions in their developing countries. There was on the one hand the need for an executive power stronger than in Europe to prevent the disintegration of their young states, and on the other hand the need to prevent the head of the executive from being tempted to use his dominance as a stepping stone to dictatorship. The existence of caudillismo and the submissiveness of the backward populations to the person of their master made this temptation even stronger.

The ready solution—vesting in the executive power the needed authority while containing its tendency to abuse it—was separation of powers. The French had worked out the principle and the authors of the Latin American constitutions responded to its logic. The presidential regime that had just been devised in the United States to counteract the anarchy of the critical period provided the means. These two sources of inspiration ensured the democratic orthodoxy of the system.

The political organization of the Latin American countries took more definite shape in the middle of the nineteenth century. Its model was the system of separation of powers directly inspired by the United States presidential regime with its principle of interplay of checks and balances to maintain equilibrium between the independent powers. Theoretically, this is the constitutional basis of the Latin American governments.

The authors of the United States Constitution had empirically set up a system of very skillfully balanced powers. They had done so, however, not to apply a given principle of government, but to remedy very definite flaws they had detected in regimes set up during the critical period in the newly sovereign thirteen former colonies. The United States Constitution of 1789 refrains from proclaiming the principle of separation of powers, a term which today is widely acknowledged as not the most fortunate. Possibly because they were Latins who liked to justify their acts by principles, the Latin American constitution framers were on occasion less cautious and in some constitutions specifically invoked the rule of the separation of powers. This, for instance, is the case in Mexico (Article 50 of the constitution of 1853, reiterated in Article 49 of the 1917 constitution):

The supreme power of the Federation is divided for its exercise into the legislative, the executive and the judicial. Two or more of these powers shall never be united in one person or corporation nor shall the legislative power be deposited with one individual except in the case of extraordinary powers being given to the Executive of the Union, in conformity with the provisions of article 29.

The presidential regime is of course nowhere a regime of complete separation of powers, for there always remain some means of collaboration between the executive and the legislative powers. Whenever the means of collaboration provided by the constitution prove insufficient, as they certainly are in the United States, others develop through custom. The essential principle of presidential regimes is that the chief of the executive power, who is also the head of state, is not politically responsible to the houses of congress. The cabinet members who are his agents are appointed and removed by him and do not have to resign if the congress should cast a no-confidence vote. Conversely, the president and his cabinet have no means of direct action upon congress, which cannot be dissolved. The mutual independence of the two powers is ensured by the fact that the president's power, like the power of the members of the legislative assemblies, derives from elections. In some cases, it has been deemed necessary also to ensure the independence of the judicial power by having the judges elected, but usually their independence is assured merely by making them irremovable—a provision that is not always fully respected. In practice the presidential regime in Latin America is sufficiently remote from these principles in their original purity that it is preferable to call it a regime of presidential dominance.

Disequilibrium of the Balance of Powers

Presidential regimes in Latin America and in the United States are very similar in the form of their institutions. Nonetheless, the presidential regime in Latin America is far from operating exactly as in the United States. Most generally the system of checks and balances has not been enough to provide for equilibrium of the powers. The executive and the legislative have not remained separated—which is also the case in the United States. But—and this is peculiar to Latin America—they have remained neither independent nor equal. Indeed, the characteristic feature of the presidential regime in Latin America is that, although the institutions resemble those of the United States, the president usually succeeds in gaining control. Even if we disregard the frequent periods when legality is suspended, his power may be said to verge on hegemony.

Exceptions to presidential hegemony are rare. These are only in Chile and Uruguay, Uruguay, as a way out of this situation, has at times entrusted the executive power to a committee. Congress in Chile is usually quite spirited and tries to use all its constitutional powers. This might result from the long period of parliamentary regime of the French type which lasted from 1891 to 1925 and gave Congress a tradition of aggressiveness that it did not relinquish when the presidential regime was restored. From 1938 to 1946, for instance, the Popular Front presidents Aguirre Cerda and Juan Antonio Ríos were unable to discipline Congresses where the multiplicity of parties made possible only coalition majorities. Until the 1965 elections Congressional hostility prevented President Frei from pursuing his policy.

Presidential hegemony is certainly less well accepted in Brazil than in Spanish America. This may be because in Brazil too, but earlier than in Chile, a parliamentary regime existed for a while under the monarchy, for Dom Pedro was not intolerant of opposition. Another reason may be that federalism in action enables opposition parties to establish solid bases in the states. Brazil's president nevertheless enjoys such power that Ernest Hambloch named his analysis of the country's constitution, in 1935, *His Majesty the President: A Study of Constitutional Brazil.*

In most countries, however, and particularly in Mexico and Argentina, the dominance of the president is such that his power is limited only by his own moderation or the control exerted by the military. Congress is actually unable to initiate laws independently from the president, and almost automatically adopts bills initiated by him without introducing substantial amendments. If the president wishes, broad legislative powers can be delegated to him even when the constitution strictly limits such action. Although almost all countries provide for control of the laws' constitutionality, the judiciary in which this power is vested hesitates to use it against the president and to intervene in issues of a purely political nature. Presidential dominance has become such a permanent characteristic of Latin American regimes that whenever it is absent the regime can no longer operate. Lack of authority on the part of the president does not mean, as in the United States, the increased authority of congress, which assumes leadership in such circumstances, but an inner crisis of the regime that leads to a personal dictatorship or to an authoritarian intervention by the military.

The inherent flaw of the regime of presidential dominance in Latin America is not, as is often alleged, its tendency to give rise to dictatorships. These occur with the same or even greater ease in other regimes. The flaw is rather that this type of regime is apt to conceal dictatorships under the veneer of constitutional forms. They permit the dictator to keep a clear

conscience, since he is not forced openly to violate the constitution. Sometimes the difference between a president who respects the constitution and a dictator who does not lies not so
much in the scope of the powers he enjoys as in the way he
uses them. Only the dictator acts arbitrarily, but both may be
equally authoritarian.

In this type of regime the only guarantee of democracy is
the very short presidential term. The authors of the Latin
American constitutions have not tried to limit the powers of
the president, since broad powers have their advantages, as
much as to set a time limit on his term of office. They have
done this by means of painstaking precautions against any
attempts by the president to perpetuate his stay in power
(*continuismo*) by being reelected or governing through pup-
pets.

Presidential hegemony is so well established and so widespread that many observers firmly believe that the presidential
regime, born in an Anglo-Saxon environment, cannot be use-
fully transplanted into a Latin, especially a Latin American,
setting. They believe that a parliamentary regime transplanted
to Latin America, instead of leading to government by the
legislature as in England, would produce disorder and helplessness. A transplanted United States presidential regime, on
the other hand, would allegedly lead to personal, dictatorial,
and sometimes tyrannical power. If this were so, it could only
be inferred that Latin America is ungovernable and that the
sole choice is between anarchy and dictatorship.

The Latin American regime of presidential dominance is
certainly very different from the United States presidential
regime. This is not necessarily a shortcoming, since Latin
America itself is so different from Anglo-America. The point
to elucidate in order to assess the merits of this particular form
of presidential regime, is not whether it leads to greater concentration of powers in the hands of the president than it
usually does in the United States, but rather whether such
concentration of powers is necessary or not under the prevailing economic, political, and social conditions. Another point is
whether Latin America has been able to achieve this concentration without sacrificing too many political and individual
freedoms.

Presidential Elections

In the past, the influence of the United States Constitution in many instances led to a two-step system of presidential election through indirect suffrage. Until quite recently under the 1940 constitution, Cuba maintained this system, whereby the number of popular votes received by presidential candidates was not counted, and instead each of them was allotted a given number of votes for each province in which he had won the majority. This number was not strictly proportional to the provinces' population. The system of indirect presidential election still exists in Argentina, but the intermediate step of presidential electors does not distort the popular vote on behalf of the thinly populated provinces. Even federal countries such as Brazil and Mexico have given up the somewhat anachronistic system retained in the United States whereby each state designates presidential electors whose number is not exactly proportional to the population figure. It is true that in the United States the indirect nature of the system is no more than theoretical today. The presidential candidates are known before the electors have been selected by the people. The electors who announce their support of one of the candidates are in fact entrusted with a mandate, and they seldom fail to fulfill it. The identical figure of two senators per state which enters into the apportionment of electors to each state continues to distort the representative character of the presidential election as far as popular vote is concerned; this increases the weight of the small states, which are often agricultural and often more conservative than the large industrial states. In this respect the solution adopted in Latin America may therefore appear as more truly democratic than the one retained in the United States. However, it fosters the hegemony of the advanced society and disregard of the backward rural people.

The fact that Latin American federal countries regard the president as being elected only by the population and not by states or provinces might be construed as indicating a lesser attachment of those countries to the reality of federalism. Some political scientists believe that in the United States the representation of states in presidential elections is a remnant of the period when the federal government was the creature of the thirteen former colonies, which had just given up their sovereignty in its favor. In their opinion it has little meaning today since the United States has become a nation, but the system is difficult to abolish because of the existing procedure for amending the Constitution.

Suffrage

The principle accepted today by all Latin American constitutions is election of the president through direct universal suffrage. In recent years most countries have given women the vote. Before 1945 women were eligible to vote in only three countries, Brazil, Uruguay, and Cuba; Peru permitted women to vote only in municipal elections. Since then reform has spread to all the countries, but in some of them the voting age differs according to sex. A remaining major infringement of the principle of universal suffrage, however, is that the most important countries, namely Brazil, Chile, Colombia, and Peru, disenfranchise illiterates, who are extremely numerous. In some countries, the voting age is lower for married men and members of the teaching profession.

A number of Latin American countries have devised fairly effective provisions to ensure fair elections by setting up electoral courts. The system is particularly well organized in Brazil. The superior electoral tribunal consists of two judges selected by the Federal Supreme Tribunal, two by the federal appellate court, one by the appellate court of the federal district, and two appointed by the president. This superior tribunal sets up regional tribunals. The powers of the electoral tribunals are very broad: they set the electoral divisions, register the parties authorized to run candidates (in Brazil the Communist party has not been allowed to do so), and organize and validate the elections.

There is a tendency today to make voting compulsory, as it is in Brazil, Argentina, and eight other countries, but the requirement is largely a sham. Actually a major source of political disorders is the fact that the president's authority is open to question because he is often elected by a very narrow margin. This in turn results from abstentions and the barring of the illiterates from the ballot.

The 1958 elections in Mexico show the difficulty of requiring a politically uneducated population to vote. The official party provides strong leadership for the illiterate masses who enjoy the franchise. On the last registration day, February 15, only 25 percent of the voters had registered. The government extended the registration period and organized a campaign to persuade the shopkeepers in some neighborhoods to grant a 10 percent discount to shoppers upon presentation of a registration card. The number of registrations was still so low that registration time had to be extended again and the pressure increased.

In the other countries where there is no party so well organized as the Mexican PRI, pressure is not so effective. When there are three parties, as there frequently are in Latin America because of splintering and the large role of personalities, the president may be elected by a ridiculously narrow margin. In the 1955 elections in Brazil the number of citizens over 18 was about 25 million but, because of the high percentage of illiterates who were barred, the number of voters was only 15 million, of whom 9 million did not vote. President Kubitschek was elected by 3,077,411 votes—12 percent of the persons over 18—and this in a country where voting is theoretically compulsory. It is thus easier to understand why the opposition finds it difficult to accept defeat. The legitimacy of office founded on universal suffrage is most tenuous when so few constituents have voiced their opinion, especially in countries where, rightly or not, the population believes that electoral fraud is the rule.

In Brazil the military were wise enough to resist the requests of those who wanted them to oppose the installation of Kubitschek and hold new elections. In Peru in 1962, on the contrary, the military took advantage of the situation to seize power. Peru has slightly over 10 million inhabitants and voting is compulsory. Out of the three candidates who ran in 1962, none obtained over 600,000 votes. Furthermore, each of the three candidates obtained roughly the same number of votes—between 480,000 and 557,000. The Peruvian constitution provides that in such a case Congress shall elect the President from among the three candidates since the elections have failed to do so. Public opinion did not count much in the selection of a president for whom only 10 percent of all adults in the country had expressed a preference; furthermore, the deals between the candidates and the members of Congress who had to choose between them showed utter disregard for the opinion of the small fraction of the population that had voted. Thereupon the junta intervened because the leftist candidate, Haya de La Torre, who had a slight margin over his opponent but was detested by the military, decided on the basis of an agreement whose terms were not clear to step aside for General Odría. (Odría was the man who, in order to institute a right-wing dictatorship in 1949, had outlawed Haya de La Torre and forced him to seek asylum in the Colombian embassy.) His withdrawal in 1962 made it all too easy for the military to contend that the elections did not prove anything (whereas they had seldom been freer) and to promise to hold new and better ones. In Chile, with a population exceeding 7 million inhabitants, 4 million of them of voting age, Alessandri had been elected President in 1958 by 386,192 votes.

Presidential Substitute

Under present political conditions, where the existence of a large majority within public opinion is all too rare, presidential elections in themselves always entail the danger of political crisis. This danger is all the greater when the president, whose role is so fully dominant, is unable to fulfill his functions. Several procedures are available in case of presidential resignation or death. Most countries have remained faithful to the United States system of simultaneous election of a vice-president, and as in the United States, the vice-president's only function is to preside over the senate. But events in Brazil have shown the possible drawback of this system. The serious political crisis of 1961-1962 was due to the fact that out of the two main slates in the presidential elections, Jânio Quadros, the presidential candidate of one of them, was the winner but Jango Goulart, the vice-presidential candidate of what was unquestionably the losing slate, was also elected. Therefore, after President Quadros resigned the nation was to be governed by the losing coalition. Such a situation could have been avoided by making it a rule that the President and vice-president must be selected from the same slate.

A few countries have adopted other systems, for instance, the *designado,* which entrusts congress with nominating each year, and usually only for that year, one or several personals who would be called upon to succeed the president. Mexico entrusts Congress with choosing the successor when a crisis occurs. He serves the rest of the presidential term if it is less than four years or organizes elections if the vacancy occurs in the beginning of the six-year presidential term. Table 17 indicates the systems used in the different countries.

Length of Term and Continuismo

Most Latin American constitutions provide for a longer presidential term than does the United States Constitution. Only seven countries, Colombia being the single large one, have adopted the same four-year term as the United States; six countries, including Brazil and Venezuela, have a five-year term; and seven, including Argentina, Mexico, and Chile, provide for six years. The tendency toward longer terms is amply justified by the risk of crisis too often attendant upon presidential elections. On the other hand, length of term is not a factor in greatly increased presidential power as compared to the United States, since this is more than compensated for by the Latin American principle of prohibiting reelection, or at any rate immediate reelection, of a president. In this respect the president's position is definitely less favorable than in the United States, for legally the presidential term may in no case exceed six consecutive years. In the United States, on the other hand, where non-reelection of a President would mean a clear-cut disavowal of his policy, the term tends to be eight years, and Franklin Roosevelt was in office for fourteen years. True enough, this gave rise to the twenty-second Constitutional Amendment, limiting the total term of office to eight years.

The ban on presidential reelection was certainly justified in Latin America, because experience showed that democracy was threatened far more by a long stay in office than by the scope of the president's power. Even outside of coups d'état, this precaution did not always prevent continuismo. Some presidents have taken advantage of the excessive ease with which the constitutions could be amended by congress and have used their authority over congress to have the non-reelection clause

TABLE 17
FORM OF THE PRESIDENCY

Country	Date of Constitution	Duration of Term	Immediately Reeligible?	Provision for Vice-Presidency
Argentina	1957	6 years	No	Yes
Bolivia	1961	4 years	No	Yes
Brazil	1946	5 years	No	Yes
Chile	1925	6 years	No	Members of cabinet
Colombia	1886	4 years	No	A *designado*
Costa Rica	1949	4 years	No	Two vice-presidents
Cuba	1940 constitution theoretically in force; a 1959 organic law gives the Council of Ministers sovereign power to change it			
Dominican Republic	1962	4 years	No	Yes
Ecuador	1946	4 years	No	Yes
El Salvador	1962	5 years	No	Yes
Guatemala	1956	6 years	No	President of Congress
Haiti	1957	6 years	Yes	Yes
Honduras	1957	6 years	No	Yes
Mexico	1917	6 years	In no case	Designation by congress
Nicaragua	1950	6 years	No	Yes
Panama	1946	4 years	No	Two vice-presidents
Paraguay	1940	5 years	Yes	?
Peru	1933	6 years	No	Two vice-presidents
Uruguay	1952	9-member Council, 4 years	No	No
Venezuela	1961	5 years	No	Designated by the cabinet

suspended on their own behalf. The two best-known cases were those of Porfirio Díaz in Mexico, who gave a façade of constitutionality to his 1876–1911 dictatorship, and of Perón, whose constitutional reform of 1949 was aimed in part at authorizing presidential reelection. In order to avert this danger several constitutions specify that the non-reelection clause may not be amended. In Brazil in 1964 Goulart also would have liked to use the pressure of mass demonstrations to push through a constitutional amendment authorizing his reelection.

This means of perpetuating oneself in power verges on illegality and has been used only to establish real dictatorships. There are, however, indirect ways of attaining the same result by outwardly respecting the constitutional forms. They have been used much oftener. The personal prestige of some presidents, the political machines they were able to establish during their stay in power, and their ability to exert pressure during elections enabled them to have successors nominated. These successors regarded themselves as the agents of the man who had arranged for their election, catered to his followers, and, in turn, used their authority to ensure the reelection of their master after the expiration of the statutory interval.

To prevent the president from being tempted to circumvent the immediate non-reelection clause by having a successor nominated to keep his seat warm, Mexico took the ultimate and apparently effective precaution of prohibiting any second term for the president even after an interval. This foiled the attempt by Calles, who had been president from 1924 to 1928, to remain indefinitely and by proxy the master of Mexican politics. Until 1934 Calles managed to have his successors nominated. They were successively Portes Gil, who served for only one year as provisional president; Ortiz Rubio, whom Calles forced to resign in 1932 because he had distributed patronage without consulting him; and Adelardo Rodríguez. But the fourth successor was either less submissive or more skillful. This was Cárdenas, who eliminated Calles completely, pursued his own policy, and reestablished de facto the temporal limit on the presidential term, which by then existed only on paper.

The fear of electoral pressure on behalf of government-backed candidates has also made for a multitude of nonreeligibility clauses against officials—cabinet ministers, military chiefs, sometimes state governors. The chief result of these rather ineffectual provisions is to provoke a flood of resignations in the months preceding presidential elections, thus forcing political maneuvers into the open long before elections.

Presidential continuismo has been one of the worst evils in Latin American political life. Today it persists in its overt form only in the least developed countries. In the countries that include the bulk of the Latin American populations— Brazil, Chile, Mexico, Argentina, and Colombia—the non-reelection rule is one of the most generally respected constitutional rules. Goulart's attempt to have his reelection authorized certainly helped to bring about the Brazilian military coup of 1964. Dictators have established themselves by getting rid of the constitutions, as Perón did in Argentina and Vargas in Brazil, but as soon as the regime of presidential dominance reverts to its constitutional forms, no president may have himself reelected immediately. This is the fruit of efforts to ensure democratic regimes in Latin America, and the major importance of these efforts should not be underestimated.

Mexico is particularly interesting because of the power of the official party. The president, who is its leader during his stay in power, plays a decisive role in choosing his successor. The only important step in the presidential election is the selection of the PRI candidate, who is sure of being elected. As a result, the Mexican president is not really elected but is instead selected by his predecessor with the consent of the heads of the party. Nevertheless, limits are set on any arbitrary presidential behavior, since the president must appease the various factions of a party that is not monolithic. It would be difficult today for the president to impose a candidate vetoed by one of the two main factions that divide the PRI—the leftist *Cardenasista* faction, named after former President Cárdenas, whose popular prestige is still sizable, and the rightist *Alemanista* faction, named after former President Alemán. In the selection of the presidential candidate, instead of using their influence to perpetuate their own policy when they could no longer hold office, the Presidents have often been forced to use it to satisfy opposition factions. Cárdenas, who had steered the Mexican government toward the extreme left, was in 1940 replaced by Ávila Camacho, who was far more moderate. He stopped Cárdenas' agrarian reform policy of collectivist ejidos and instead distributed land in individual plots. Ávila Camacho was replaced in 1946 by Miguel Alemán, whose orientation was frankly rightist. In 1952 Ruíz Cortínez strongly reacted against Alemán's policy and brought the pendulum back toward the center, where it was maintained by his successors López Mateos and Díaz Ordaz. Since the 1940's Mexico has lived under a stable regime of presidential dominance which, although quite authoritarian in spirit, is far from dictatorial, and even further from being totalitarian.

If one accepts the idea that a very strong executive power is indispensable in Latin America because of existing social conditions, it is clear that one of the safeguards to the democratic character of authoritorian regimes is a limitation on the length of the presidential term. A large part of Latin America has been relatively successful in this respect, and hence it would be unfair to state that the presidential regime is ill-suited to Latin America's needs. The United States form of presidential regime did not suit Latin America, and therefore she altered it and adapted it to her own needs. The regime of presidential dominance does not always operate smoothly, but it remains to be proved that there are other, more democratic regimes that could operate better in such difficult circumstances.

The President's Cabinet

As in the United States, the president is assisted by a cabinet whose members are appointed and removed by him. The departments are generally the same as in the United States, but French influence is felt in the widespread institution of a Ministry of the Interior which does not exist under that name in the United States. The existence of such a ministry is easy to justify, since many Latin American countries are unitary states and local administration is controlled by the central government. Such a ministry even in the federal countries is construed as evidence of a trend toward centralization more marked than in the United States. In any case, at least in Mexico, it is certain that the Ministry of the Interior keeps a close watch over the state governments, has been the instigator of many federal interventions in those states, and is an effective tool of the president in promoting the interests of the official party.

In organizing his cabinet a Latin American president has greater freedom than the president of the United States, for his appointments are not subject to senatorial confirmation. The difference, however, is one of form rather than substance, since custom in the United States usually prevents the Senate from questioning the president's choice of cabinet members. Even if such a purely formalistic difference were regarded as favoring a Latin American president, it would be largely outweighed by the requirement of a ministerial countersignature to validate any presidential action. In fact, in most cases this formality scarcely restricts the president's freedom of action, since he may remove the members of his cabinet at will. The need to remove them in order to make his policy prevail over their disapproval is nonetheless a serious decision about which he is apt to have second thoughts. In theory at least, the presidents in Latin America could not have been the authors of the utterance ascribed to Lincoln during a cabinet meeting: "Seven nays, one aye, the aye has it."

Many Latin constitutions contain a provision which might seriously restrict the power of the presidents as compared to that of United States presidents. In the largest part of Latin America—Argentina, Mexico, Venezuela, and before the 1961 parliamentary reform even in Brazil—a parliamentary influence alien to the spirit of the presidential regime had fostered the practice of allowing congress to call cabinet members before it to answer questions. In several countries this practice led to an embryonic parliamentary regime. In Costa Rica and Panama congress may censure the ministers. In Cuba under the 1940 constitution, in Peru under the 1933 constitution, in Bolivia under the 1938 constitution, and in Ecuador under the 1946 constitution a vote of censure requires the cabinet to resign. These countries, with the exception of Cuba, whose constitution has been suspended, do not enjoy the most orderly political life. Such provisions would suffice to ensure the dominance of congress if there were not other means of ensuring presidential dominance. On this point, too, the particular forms of the presidential regime are less favorable to the president than under the United States regime.

Appointive Power

As in the United States, the power to appoint officials is vested in the president. Some authors regard the freedom he enjoys as one of the causes of his dominance as the distribution of public patronage jobs to the politicians loyal to him might increase his influence over congress. It is not quite certain, however, that the situations in the most developed Latin American countries and in the United States differ a great deal in this respect.

The distribution of public offices under the spoils system is a very important element in the relations between the executive and the legislative in any regime having a separation of powers. Even now when the extension of the civil service has greatly curtailed the number of patronage jobs in the United States, the president still has some leeway in their distribution. Some posts can still be assigned upon the suggestion of a senator in whose state they are available, and this is one effective means of executive pressure upon the legislative power. Not so long ago in the United States, for lack of any civil service the spoils system extended to all public offices; and until the second half of the nineteenth century the power, or one might almost say the duty, of the president to distribute jobs to his friends' constituents did not lead to presidential hegemony as it did in Latin America.

Today, as in the United States, most civil servants in Latin America enjoy a status that has greatly restricted presidential arbitrariness. Appointment to high diplomatic posts as a reward to influential voters or wealthy party contributors does not seem as widespread as in the United States. At most, a fairly large number of positions are at the disposal of the presidents despite the tenure of most civil servants. Governmental functions have rapidly developed of late. Hence a very large number of new public posts is created each year, and just because they are new the president has a great deal of freedom in filling them. Franklin D. Roosevelt made very skillful use of that temporary opportunity when the New Deal opened up new public functions by the score.

The growing economic role of the state provides very effective opportunities for pressure almost verging on corruption. The large nationalized industries, the autonomous planning boards for the production of certain industrial or agricultural goods, the credit allocation agencies, and even the social security bureaus provide openings for management posts outside civil service, and since they are very well paid they attract prominent political figures. In addition, many large foreign concerns in Latin America find it advisable in this era of nationalism to hire highly placed figures whose main function is that of protectors. Their presence would not be useful unless they were friends of the government. Governments in all regimes have distributed positions in the semigovernmental sector outside the civil service where salaries are on a par with the private sector. This tool of presidential dominance is particularly effective in Latin America because in most countries this semipublic sector owes its rapid growth to the system of *autarchic* bodies such as the petroleum, steel, and coffee boards. Distribution of these well-paid patronage positions is used to bring the president the backing of the military as well as of the politicians.

Presidential Intervention in the Legislative Process

The major difference between the Latin American and United States presidential regimes is that in Latin America the principle of separation of powers has been modified to allow the president to take part in drafting legislation, and he is even given leadership in the legislative process. Not only have most constitution writers deemed it necessary specifically to empower the president to initiate laws, but under certain conditions they have given him the right to legislate directly, by decree. Although in principle the delegation of legislative power is prohibited, usage has condoned a diversion of the regulatory power that transforms it into legislative power. This might be regarded as one cause of presidential hegemony were it not for the fact that everywhere the new functions of the state have made it necessary to give the head of the government an increasingly large role in framing laws. Initiating legislation and using decree-laws are instruments, not causes, of presidential hegemony.

Initiating of Legislation

Latin American constitutions give the president the right, together with congress, to initiate legislation, Latin America also makes a legal distinction that does not exist in the United States between government bills and private bills from a member of congress or (in some countries) from the supreme court or, in the Mexican federation, from the member states. Government bills are far more likely to be enacted into law than are private bills from congressmen. This legislative power is not an important factor in giving the presidents in Latin America greater dominance than in the United States. It was simply realism on the part of the constitution writers who, coming after their counterparts in the United States, profited by the practical experience north of the border.

The framers of the Philadelphia Constitution defined the president's role in the legislative process in somewhat ambiguous terms. They seemed to give only the power or the obligation to furnish information and recommend measures, as stated in Section 3 of Article II. The tendencies expressed in the Wade-Davis Manifesto of 1864, attempting to restrict the president to a purely executive role, have been repudiated long ago. Presidential messages have become a very effective way, not so much of informing Congress as of putting pressure on it and compelling it, by appealing to public opinion, to enact measures recommended by the president. Actually, by far the largest portion of the legislation in the United States originates with the administration. Times have changed since 1908, when the Senate waxed indignant because a cabinet member was so impudent as to submit to it a fully drafted bill. It is because usage plays such a large role in the application of the United States Constitution that its meaning may be altered while the text remains unchanged. This adjustment to reality prevents the legal recognition that in the United States some bills originate with the president and others with members of Congress, and normally the former are much more likely to become laws.

Despite the United States president's power to intervene in the legislative process, he has not usually achieved the hegemony of Latin American presidents. Not only does Congress quite often refuse to pass bills drafted by the administration and still more often alter them through amendments, but it also very frequently foists upon the president laws intended to orient his policy in the direction it wishes.

The best proof of this independence is the place that the presidential veto has assumed in the United States legislative process. Conflicts between the president and Congress are so commonplace that the president's refusal to approve a bill voted by Congress is a normal stage in the legislative process and provokes no political crisis. From Washington's first presidency to Franklin Roosevelt's second term there were 750 presidential vetoes.

The use of the veto is so much a part of the United States presidential regime that it is sometimes blamed for lending itself to an absurd demagoguery on the part of Congress. The representatives are alleged to try to submit and pass a very large number of measures that they themselves regard as purely demogogic. In this way they can quite safely show their constituents the extent of their good will, since they know all along that the president is there to stop their bills. In such a situation Congress would carefully refrain from using its right to override the presidential veto, which it could do by again voting on the bill and passing it by a two-thirds majority. We may think that the reproach is justified, since out of the 750 presidential vetoes mentioned above, only 49 were overridden. Of these, fifteen occurred during the conflict between Congress and President Andrew Johnson over Reconstruction in the Southern states after the Civil War.

There is no doubt that in Latin America the president is far less often in conflict with congress over bills. The best proof is that he very seldom has had to veto a bill initiated by congress. In most if not all Latin American countries, including Mexico, a government bill may be regarded as voted. The certain success of presidential bills does not mean, however, that the role of congress is nil, for lengthy debates help improve the bills. After all, the major role of the House of Commons in

England's ministerial regime consists of debating government bills that it always adopts in the end.

There is a large difference between Latin America and the United States, but it does not derive from the president's role as laid down by the constitution. The right of initiative in legislation which has been vested in the president in Latin America is not a cause of his dominance. On the contrary, the success of his initiatives is its consequence. Hence the question remains unanswered as to why Latin American legislatures are less free than the United States Congress to use the powers they possess to impose their will. It also remains to be discovered why, when the legislature does use its powers against the president, the move so often ushers in a political crisis jeopardizing the existence of the regime itself.

Partial or Item Veto

There is one difference in veto practice between Latin America and the United States that enables Latin American presidents to influence legislation far more and in a much more flexible manner than in the United States. Whereas constitutional practice in the United States provides only for a total veto, Latin American practice allows partial vetoes. This difference may have far more important effects than is generally thought.

In the United States the veto is a purely negative tool. Barring the rare second passage of the bill with an extraordinary majority, the veto allows the president to dismiss legislation initiated by Congress if he deems it inappropriate. Conversely, the veto is of very little help to the president in obtaining the measures he actually desires. It is said that at most the veto allows for bargaining and enables the president to obtain passage of measures that displease Congress. He achieves this by letting it be known that if he gets what he wants he will not oppose the measures strongly desired by members of Congress, such as those related to patronage for their constituents. On the whole, however, the total veto is of limited effectiveness, for generally it is not by initiating legislation that Congress tries to guide presidential policy. In the United States as elsewhere, despite the separation of powers, the most important laws are those drafted by the administration, and the legislature intervenes by amending the presidential bills to varying degrees. The president then can only choose between accepting a measure which does not fit his needs or rejecting it completely although it was partly what he needed. In this way Congress is usually the winner and presidential dominance is averted.

In Brazil, Mexico, Colombia, and Ecuador, the constitution itself or usage allows the president to veto an item or merely one word in a bill he otherwise approves. This partial veto helps reverse the balance of power in favor of the president, but also lessen the conflicts between the executive and the legislative powers and promotes mutual concessions. While in the United States it is up to Congress to alter through amendment a bill which actually originates with the president, in Latin America it is up to the president to use his partial veto power to amend a bill initiated by congress, or sometimes to restore his own bills to their original form by rejecting amendments.

This Latin American system can be blamed for markedly increasing infringements of the principle of the separation of powers. But since it is acknowledged that infringements are necessary in order to resolve conflicts between the president and congress, it should also be acknowledged that the Latin American forms of veto are more flexible and effective than those of the United States. A whole bill should not have to be rejected because one of its details seems dangerous. The president's power to improve legislation, while at the same time largely satisfying congress, may smooth out many conflicts between the two powers. Partial veto helps eliminate the rider procedure often used in the United States. This is an amendment to a bill which the president would be loath to veto since its substance is essential to his policy. The amendment itself, however, introduces a provision which may not be related to the substance of the bill and which the president would have vetoed if he were free to do so.

Everything depends of course on how a Latin American president uses the very broad steering powers vested in him by the partial veto. He could completely change the trend of proposed legislation and deprive congress of any legislative power. Confronted with such abuse of power congress could always override his veto, and this is particularly easy in countries that do not even require a special majority. In Mexico the rule is the same as in the United States, namely a new vote by the two houses with the special two-thirds majority; in Chile a simple majority is sufficient, in Colombia an absolute majority, and in Ecuador a simple majority at a joint session of the two houses.

It should be noted that very often in Latin America the president possesses hidden means of pressure that deprive the members of congress of the independence needed to override a veto. In the countries where congress is at the complete mercy of the president, he hardly ever needs actually to use the veto to impose his will upon congress. In Mexico, for instance, where Congress is disciplined by the official party, resort to the veto is exceptional.

In Latin America the veto power is most often used in the form of a partial veto, and it seems to help correct errors or vagueness and thus to improve legislation. The item veto is an original Latin American contribution to the presidential regime developed through usage.

Executive Legislation and Suspension of Constitutional Guarantees

It should be noted that in Latin America not only does the president exert a dominant influence on the drafting of legislation by congress, but that a large, perhaps the largest, part of the legislation is drafted directly by the administration, independently of congress. This power results primarily from a very broad construction placed upon ordinance power. In practice the decrees, ordinances, regulations, and instructions may aim not only at enforcing existing legislation but at changing its letter and spirit as well. This inevitable tendency is not peculiar to Latin American governments, but it develops more freely among them because of the supreme courts' reluctance to deal with presidential acts. Since the courts are prone to disqualify themselves on the grounds that these are political acts, there are no effective means of controlling ordinance power.

The Latin American presidents' very broad legislative role

expresses itself mainly through the practice of decree-laws (*decretos con fuerza de Ley*). This is a widespread practice, either because the constitutions provide for it subject to ratification by congress or, more often, because governments resort to constitutional clauses permitting some or all constitutional rules to be suspended in emergencies and enabling congress to empower the president to meet the situation by means of decrees.

All the constitutions provide for such suspension of rules and delegation of the legislative power to the president. All too often, however, the conditions for suspension of constitutional rules are vague. Article 29 of the Mexican constitution of 1917 provides for it in the following words, which have often served as a model:

In case of invasion, of serious disturbance of the public peace, or any other emergency that may place the people in great danger or conflict, only the President of the Mexican Republic, in agreement with the Council of Ministers and with the approval of the Congress of the Union or, and should the latter be in recess, of the permanent commission, may suspend throughout the country or in any part specified, the guarantees that might be an obstacle to a rapid and easy adjustment of the situation. . . . If the suspension is made in time of recess the Congress shall be convoked without delay for the granting of such powers.

The most careful limits to a state of siege seem to have been set by Brazil. Not only must the president immediately convene Congress if it is in recess, but the duration of the state of siege is limited to thirty days and a certain number of specified constitutional guarantees must be maintained. Chile has taken similar precautions but has stated in very broad terms the conditions justifying the state of siege: "When the supreme necessity of the defense of the State, preservation of the constitutional regime, or internal peace may so demand. . . ." Other countries have taken fewer precautions. For instance, Argentina has failed to require the convening of Congress when the president proclaims a state of siege during a recess.

In many countries the suspension of constitutional guarantees is accepted much too easily, and also, in the absence of any control by the courts in essentially political matters, delegations of the legislative power are used simply to speed the passing of legislation outside any emergency. Countless examples could be adduced: it was by decree that the president of Mexico instituted the income tax and that the codes of penal and civil procedure were promulgated; in Honduras a law of 1906 empowered the president to "prepare certain codes of laws"; in Cuba in 1946 during the presidency of Grau San Martín—a short interlude of liberal government by the *Auténtico* party between the two dictatorships of Batista— legislation consisted of three thousand decrees and twenty laws.

The present-day multiplication of economic planning bodies whose powers cannot be accurately defined by the legislator has given the president very broad legislative power.

The administrations' growing share in the drafting of laws is in no way specifically Latin American. It is a general characteristic of the modern state whose functions have multiplied. Latin American presidents are tending to enlarge their regulatory power not only to enforce but also to change the law. All governments tend to do this and are prevented only when sternly controlled by the courts. Legislative power is often delegated to Latin American presidents, and their decrees then have force of law. Elsewhere realistic constitution writers must realize that in emergency situations delegations of legislative power are unavoidable.

In the United States, the Supreme Court strives to enforce the constitutional rule that prohibits such delegation of power. But in order not to paralyze the government, the court then has to differentiate between delegations of power that are inadmissible because they are too broad and would strip Congress of its constitutional role, and delegations of legislative power that are tolerable. The latter are deemed legitimate because they are only partial and define with sufficient precision the policies that Congress wishes the president to carry out. In this case an arbitrary Supreme Court merely substitutes itself for the president and institutes government by the judges.

Bureaucracy and technocracy are not specifically Latin American. What is, or rather what is common to developing countries whose economic and social structures have remained archaic and must be transformed rapidly, is the swift succession of emergencies. These make it difficult or impossible to respect constitutional rules that limit the effectiveness or speed of government action. It is chiefly the frequency of situations calling for arbitrary government action that is at the root of presidential dominance and political instability in Latin America.

17. Subservience of Congress under Regimes of Presidential Dominance

Presidential dominance is accompanied by a relative effacement of congress which should not be overestimated. Despite
the president's prominence on the political scene, some Latin
American congresses have performed a great deal of legislative
work. In the period of remarkable development between 1860
and 1914 which transformed the Argentine Republic, the
Congress of conservative, if often very enlightened, representatives of the oligarchy did some outstanding work. After
the 1912 electoral reform, extreme presidential dominance
and the corresponding effacement of Congress in Argentina
resulted from the democratization of political life when the
Radical Civic Union came to power. Irigoyen, sure of his
popularity, forced Congress to submit by browbeating the
representatives of his party into utter subservience. In Brazil,
where Congress always retained some independence from the
President, it did not confine itself to sterile opposition. Suffice
it to recall Ruy Barbosa's role in strengthening the Brazilian
republic although he never became the president. Congress
declined mainly during Vargas' authoritarian populist regimes.

The very nature of the presidential regime, where the spot-
light is on the president, does not always do justice to congressional achievements. A skillful president usually succeeds in
pushing through his own policy by getting congress to vote the
legislation he needs. He then receives all the credit, although

very often his skill consisted merely in fitting his own desires to the inclinations of a congress whose influence on national policy may be far greater than appears at first sight. No United States president has dominated the scene as much as Franklin Roosevelt, and not merely because his policy was popular but because he was remarkably skillful in managing Congress. Many similar examples could be found. President Kubitschek in Brazil pushed through his main programs, but he certainly considered Congressional opinion. In this respect he differed very much from his successors, Quadros and Goulart, whose clumsiness prevented them from dominating Congress despite their presidential authority and their popularity.

Generally speaking, congresses in Latin America play a much more humble part than do those in the United States. Their role is underplayed while the president's is enhanced because of the frequency of emergency situations where lengthy parliamentary debates are unsuitable.

Caliber of the Parliamentarians

It is useless to cite, as is sometimes done, the low caliber of the parliamentarians. Legislative functions are often said not to attract the most brilliant men in Latin America. Congressmen all too often are alleged to be caciques eager to perpetuate their local authority, or petty politicians anxious to get rich and easy to corrupt, all of them lacking in experience and in national spirit. These are subjective statements; since the upper classes have stopped being the elected representatives anywhere, such statements are being made about all countries. Representative assemblies in Latin America seem to have much the same composition as those everywhere else. The liberal professions, lawyers in particular, are well represented. As elsewhere, serving as a representative tends to become a specific occupation so that congress has its share of professional politicians. Perhaps more than in other parts of the world, there are still members of upper-class families representing a clan rather than a district or a party.

It is probably closer to the truth that in a presidential regime ambitious elites are less attracted than in a parliamentary regime by a career in the legislative assemblies because they are not so powerful. Since the cabinet is small and dominated by the president, and its members are not necessarily former congressmen, the legislators have very few opportunities for advancement to ministerial rank. Furthermore, except for few countries like Chile, the salaries are relatively low and serving in congress is not a good sinecure.

Even in the United States, whose presidential regime is held up as a model, the members of the House of Representatives are said not to be always of the highest caliber. The United States Senate is in a different category: its eminent position and the standing of some of its members may help explain why Congress has been more successful than in Latin America in upholding the prerogatives of the legislative power. Whenever in the United States Congress has either effectively opposed the president's policy, or on the contrary helped him carry it out, most of the credit should go to the Senate. There is a striking difference in prestige and influence between the Senators and the Representatives.

Nowhere in Latin America does the senate seem to enjoy comparable preeminence over the lower house, but the reasons are hard to define. United States Senators, especially today, owe much of their prestige and their influence over the president to their power of treaty ratification. Since foreign policy has become the president's major and most absorbing task, he has gradually involved the Senators in it so as to avoid a mishap such as befell Wilson when the Versailles treaty was rejected. Foreign policy is not so conducive to demagoguery as domestic policy; because of this the Senators have developed a larger sense of responsibility.

The senates in Latin America have the same power of ratifying or rejecting treaties, but foreign policy itself does not have the same vital importance. Furthermore, when the United States was shaping its institutions, the reality of federalism endowed the two Senators from each state as ambassadors with very large powers. The federal government had to be careful not to offend them; this is the source of the special Senatorial authority.

Effects of the Multiplicity of Parties

In addition to the frequent emergencies that force congress to hand its powers over to the president, the nature of the political parties—so different from those in the United States—also contributes to the relative effacement of the assemblies.

In countries living under the regime of a single or official party whose head is the president, there is no need to seek other causes for presidential dominance. In Paraguay, Haiti, and Cuba the question of the relationship between the executive and the legislative is of no interest, since these are not presidential or constitutional regimes, but barely disguised dictatorships. Only in Mexico does a privileged party hold its monopoly under a presidential regime. The overwhelming majority of Congressmen belong to the Institutional Revolutionary party led by the president during his term in office, and no Senator or Deputy can expect to be reelected against the president's will. The relationship between the majority party Deputies and the president is not unlike the relationship of the members of the House of Commons and the prime minister. In Mexico, however, no opposition enjoys real influence or expects some day to accede to power.

The situation is more complex in the rest of Latin America because of the plurality of parties, for instance in Brazil, Chile, Venezuela, and Argentina. A tidy conclusion would be that in a presidential regime the effect of splitting the assemblies into many parties is the opposite of what it is generally believed to be in a parliamentary regime.

It is claimed that under the parliamentary regime the splintering of parties with undisciplined memberships forces the cabinet holding the executive power to rely on coalition majorities. The inevitable propensity of these coalitions to break up provokes frequent cabinet crises or compels the cabinet to exert utmost caution in order to avert them, either of which weakens the executive power. Under a presidential regime, on the contrary, if the assemblies remain divided by the plurality of parties while the executive power, independent of the assemblies, is in the hands of one man, the assemblies' lack of power entails presidential dominance. The party splits and the unruliness of their members increase the president's domination. Many political scientists firmly believe that it is a drawback for assemblies under a presidential regime to have a plurality of parties. In their opinion this regime has the advantage of forcing parties to unite so as not to remain powerless, and so resign themselves to a two-party system. If this is the case, could the difference in the role of congress in Latin America and in the United States stem from the existence of a plurality of parties in the former case and a two-party system in the latter?

This reasoning is far from fully convincing. In the first place, there are a few Latin American countries where only two parties have dominated the political scene. Colombia with the opposing liberals and conservatives, and Uruguay with the opposing blancos and colorados are in that category, and presidential dominance has existed there as well as in the other countries. The belief that the presidential regime tends to favor party unification rests mainly on the observation of the United States political scene, but to a large extent the facts are not correctly interpreted. While it is true that two efficient electoral machines were set up in the United States because they were needed for presidential elections, the fact that there are only two parties is debatable. The lasting vitality of sectionalism in the federal system has, on the contrary, enabled a horde of local parties to survive. These parties have had to come together with their counterparts in other states in order to use one of the electoral machines—Republican or Democratic. It is possible that as national integration is completed and federalism declines, the picture will change and the two electoral machines will end by matching two political parties, but this is certainly not the case now. After elections, the winners who have taken advantage of the services of one of the electoral machines regain their full freedom. The party to which they claim allegiance has no national leader and does not attempt to enforce voting discipline in Congress. As far as the work of Congress outside elections is concerned, the United States has a system of multiple parties, or to be more accurate, of multiple tendencies within two organizations. The organizations allow the tendencies to express themselves freely. It may even be said that in the Senate personalities are far more important than parties. Hence the situation in the United States and in Latin America is not so different as it appears at first sight.

Nonetheless the splits in the United States Congress and the lack of discipline of its members have not weakened this body, unlike the legislatures throughout Latin America.

In the United States the absence of party discipline of Congressmen may promote as well as thwart the president's authority. The president is stronger when the opposition party has the majority in Congress because he can then play up differences and use any temporary majority formed on the basis of current issues, including members of both parties, in order to pursue his policy. Conversely, the president's authority is weakened when his party holds the majority in Congress. This is because he is the leader of only one of the many factions of the majority and the balloting does not necessarily follow party lines. President Kennedy experienced this absence of party discipline. The British parliamentary regime gave rise to two political parties, while the United States federal regime produced a multitude of local parties. The presidential regime did not succeed in convincing party members to unite outside of presidential elections. A multiplicity of local parties also exists in a large portion of Latin America, but presidential elections have not always been enough to prompt the parties to agree, let alone unite in order to run only two candidates. This may be because personality or clan dissensions go deeper, or perhaps because national society is more divided.

Effects of Caciquismo on Party Discipline

One cause of weakened congressional authority in Latin America may be the nature of the ties between the elected representatives and the party to which they claim allegiance, rather than lack of party discipline stemming from the large number of political parties. This does not apply to all parties, but it does to the traditional parties. And practically everywhere in Latin America, these are still a political force essential to any coalition-based majority.

In the United States members of Congress often cross party lines in the course of legislative work. Momentary majorities often arise on a given issue. The Congressmen's freedom does not imply in any way that they are free to disregard their constituents' opinion. Absence of party discipline only results from the fact that adoption of the Republican or Democratic

ticket in order to use one of the two large electoral machines
does not correspond to a set opinion and political platform in
each constituency. In order better to preserve the freedom of
those who run on their tickets, the Republican and Democratic
machines carefully refrain from endorsing too clearcut a platform. Otherwise they might cut themselves off from various
regional party organizations, all claiming allegiance to a single
party although their respective political positions are quite
different. Even if a Senator or a Representative opposes the
president elected on the same ticket, he is not necessarily
disloyal to the local party organization of his state or district or
to his constituents' mandate. In the cities the Democratic party
tends to be reform-minded, and that is the faction a Democratic president belongs to because the majorities come from
the cities. But in the Southern states the Democratic party
resists change, particularly in the rural areas which still dominate the party machines in those states. This is an artificial
domination, and the Supreme Court had to take a stand
against the unfair districting that favored the rural areas. Thus
when a Southern Democrat allied to the most conservative
Republicans endeavors to paralyze the policy of Democratic
Presidents—Kennedy or Johnson—on the national scale, he is
disloyal to the Democratic ticket while remaining entirely
faithful to the conservative tendency of his state. If he should
follow the presidential line, he would be disloyal to his constituents' mandate and chances are he would not be reelected.

The situation is entirely different in Latin America.
Wherever caciquismo or other forms of personalism survive,
the party affiliation of the local political chieftains scarcely
curtails their freedom. The following of the political chief is a
personal one. He does not need party endorsement in order to
be elected. On the contrary, it is he who for any number of
reasons—family tradition, opportunity to play a more important role, better electoral machine—decides to bring his own
clients into a given party, and in a way gives that party his
personal endorsement. It is very difficult to tell what stand a
man elected under such conditions will take, all the more so
because, wherever caciquismo has survived, a vote for the
patrón does not mean that his backward followers have expressed any political opinion.

A Latin American president has powerful means of putting pressure on elected representatives, while the party is completely helpless to impose any discipline on them. The most unexpected alliances may form and dissolve while the parties have no way of knowing on what forces they can actually rely and for how long. This greatly intensifies the means of pressure which, in any regime, belong to the holders of the executive power. Whether they are legitimate or illegitimate, the number of favors the president can hand out does not have to be larger in Latin America than elsewhere. The important thing is that men elected to congress thanks to their personal clientele can obtain favors by being free to choose any profitable political line. Naturally under present conditions in Latin America caciquismo is only a remnant of the past. Modern parties are beginning to discipline their membership. But if caciquismo gives such political freedom to even a small fraction of the congressmen, the president can then play the independents against the organized parties.

This, however, is only a very secondary factor in pushing into the background the assemblies in the Latin American presidential regimes. The essential cause is the imperative need for a strong presidential power in the present stage of rapid transformation of the developing countries.

Structure of the Legislative Power

Whatever causes the differences between the presidential regimes in the United States and in Latin America, it is certainly not the constitutional basis of the legislative power. This power is closely modeled on that of the United States, and whatever changes have occurred have favored the assemblies by introducing the vote of censure—a measure inspired by parliamentary methods. Naturally this does not apply to General Stroessner's dictatorship in Paraguay, where the President's sole duty is to notify the House of his decisions.

As far as the organization of the legislative power is concerned, the general trend in Latin America has been toward adoption of the bicameral legislature, although exceptions are numerous. Costa Rica, Guatemala, Honduras, Panama, El Salvador, and Paraguay have a single house, and Haiti may be placed in the same category since the Senate was eliminated in

1963. It should be noted, though, that Guatemala, which has the largest population of these seven countries, has less than four million inhabitants.

In Argentina, Brazil, Mexico, and to a lesser extent Venezuela, the federal system required two houses in order to provide representation both for population and for the states. The senate represents the states, with an identical number of senators per state regardless of its size. The senate plays or played a somewhat similar role in Bolivia, Ecuador, Haiti, and Cuba (under the 1940 constitution), since these countries are subdivided into departments or provinces with a fixed number of senators for each, which varies from two in Ecuador to twenty-one in Haiti. It is slightly different in Colombia and Chile. In Colombia the number of Senators is proportional to the population, but no province may have less than three Senators or more than nine. In Chile the provinces form groups whose population is roughly the same, and each group selects five Senators. In Ecuador the Senate has been used to provide not only regional representation but also corporate representation. Thus twelve seats are earmarked for the representatives of public education, private education, the armed forces, the trade unions, and various economic interests. The Senate in Nicaragua has a few lifetime members, including the former presidents of the republic. Table 18 indicates the structure of the assemblies.

Today the senates in Latin American countries are elected through direct suffrage under the same conditions as the lower houses. In principle, therefore, they are not intended to provide conservative chambers. Indirectly, though, they are weighted in favor of the rural areas against the large cities. This can weaken the modern reform-minded parties whose backing is generally in the urban population. The distortion also tends to preserve remnants of caciquismo within the traditional parties. It is also conceivable that the mood of the senate is somewhat different from that of the house of representatives because of different minimum age requirements for the two assemblies. Depending on the countries, these range between 21 and 25 for the deputies and between 30 and 35 for the senators.

Of the fourteen countries having a senate, in nine the term of the senators is longer than that of the representatives. This

TABLE 18

FORM OF THE ASSEMBLIES

Country	Upper House, Number of Senators	Duration of Term	Lower House, Number of Deputies	Duration of Term
Argentina	2 senators per province and 2 for the capital	6 years	1 deputy per 100,000 inhabitants	6 years
Bolivia	3 senators per department	6 years	68 deputies	4 years
Brazil	3 senators per state and 3 for the federal capital	8 years	1 deputy per 150,000 inhabitants	4 years
Chile	5 senators per group of provinces	8 years	147 deputies	4 years
Colombia	80 senators	4 years	152 deputies	2 years
Costa Rica	No upper house		57 deputies	4 years
Cuba (1940)	9 senators per province	4 years	1 deputy per 35,000 inhabitants	4 years
Dominican Republic	Under the 1959 organic law all the powers belong to the Council of Ministers			
	1 senator per province and 1 for the capital	5 years	1 deputy per 60,000 inhabitants	5 years
Ecuador	2 senators per province and 12 corporation senators	4 years	1 deputy per 50,000 inhabitants	2 years
El Salvador	No upper house		3 deputies per department	2 years
Guatemala	No upper house		1 deputy per 50,000 inhabitants	4 years
Haiti	21 senators per department; eliminated in 1963	6 years	37 deputies	4 years
Honduras	No upper house		58 deputies	6 years
Mexico	2 senators per state and 2 for the federal capital	6 years	162 deputies	3 years
Nicaragua	16 senators	6 years	42 deputies	6 years
Panama	No upper house		53 deputies	4 years
Paraguay	No upper house; a council of state		1 deputy per 25,000 inhabitants	5 years
Peru	50 senators	6 years	182 deputies	5 years
Uruguay	31 senators	5 years	99 deputies	4 years
Venezuela	2 senators per state and 2 for the federal capital	5 years	233 deputies	5 years

is or was the case in Bolivia, Brazil, Colombia, Chile, Ecuador, Haiti, Mexico, Peru, and Uruguay. The term is twice as long in Brazil, Chile, Colombia, Ecuador, and Mexico; it is only slightly longer in Uruguay, 5 years for the Senate, 4 for the Chamber of Deputies. The longest term is 8 years for the senators in Brazil and in Chile, and the shortest is 4 years in Colombia and Ecuador. For representatives the term varies between 2 and 6 years. The term is the same for both houses in Argentina, Cuba (1940), the Dominican Republic, Nicaragua, and Venezuela. The system of partial renewal of the senate exists only in Argentina, Brazil, Bolivia, and Chile.

The form of election most used today in Latin American countries is proportional representation among the parties, at least for the house of representatives. This is the system in Argentina, Brazil, Chile, Colombia, Ecuador, Uruguay, Nicaragua, and Costa Rica. A frequent drawback of proportional representation systems, which are often very complicated, is that there may be long delays between the election and the proclamation of the results. There is a tendency in Latin America to avoid special elections by using the system of alternates who are elected at the same time as the candidate. A few countries let the party select the successor or entrust congress with the task.

Usually members of the armed forces, frequently the clergy and appointive officials, and sometimes relatives of policy makers, that is, presidents and ministers, are not eligible for legislative seats. Mexico is particularly strict in this respect. Colombia restricts seats in the Senate to men who have proved elsewhere their experience or culture, for instance, former members of the House of Representatives, chiefs of diplomatic missions, Supreme Court justices, members of the Councils of State, university professors, and members of the liberal professions requiring university degrees. As a rule no person discharging functions paid out of public funds may serve in the legislature, but almost everywhere the members of the teaching profession are exempt.

None of this is likely to weaken congress, and on two points the structure of the legislature should even enhance the independence of its members and the effectiveness of their work.

Parliamentary Immunities

Parliamentary immunities are granted very liberally for fear of arbitrary behavior on the part of the executive power. Mexico is an exception, since immunity can be lifted by an absolute majority in the Chamber of Deputies sitting as a grand jury. In most countries immunity may be waived only by a two-thirds majority of the particular chamber of which the person involved is a member. Immunity covers the representatives throughout their term, even during recess. This very broad protection exists in Argentina, Brazil, Bolivia, Venezuela, Costa Rica, Paraguay, Cuba, Haiti, Panama, and Uruguay.

The effects of immunity have not always been fortunate. Immunity was unable to protect the members of congress against arbitrary dictatorships, and in countries where dictatorships are frequent their political foes have been persecuted constantly. On the other hand, parliamentary immunity has served to cover many abuses. One of the most current is protection against libel. Certain newspapers have made libel their trademark and are able to do so with impunity by using the name of a deputy as a front. Lazcano y Mazón [1] quotes statistics used in the debates of the Cuban Constituent Assembly of 1940, according to which over 1,200 common law infractions committed in 39 years by members of Congress had been protected by parliamentary immunity. The infractions included two murders and nine homicides. A favorite method of assemblies to help their members escape prosecution without appearing overly cynical consists in indefinitely postponing any vote to waive the immunity. A few constitutions have tried to correct this situation by setting a short time limit on the vote for lifting the immunity. The abuses have certainly contributed to undermine the prestige of the assemblies.

The relatively small size of the assemblies should make their work easier. To satisfy the military, Latin America has all too often increased the number of generals; on the contrary, in most countries she has limited the number of deputies and

[1] Andrés María Lazcano y Mazon, *Constitución de Cuba,* 3 vols. (Havana, 1941).

senators. Colombia, with the largest senate, has only 80 members. If it is agreed that in order to be effective in their deliberations the assemblies should not be too large, the situation in Latin America seems favorable, since the size of the lower houses ranges from about 50 members in the small countries to about 200 in the largest. Only Brazil, whose population exceeds 60 million inhabitants, has a larger house.

Powers of the Assemblies

The situation in Latin America calls for no special remarks. Agreement of both chambers is necessary for the passage of legislation. Conflicts between them are resolved either (as in Brazil) by a joint meeting of the appropriate committees of each chamber or (as in Venezuela) by a joint meeting of both chambers or (as in Argentina) by a two-thirds majority that allows the assembly originating the bill to override the other assembly.

Parliamentary work in almost all the countries is prepared by specialized permanent committees, as it is in the United States presidential system or the French parliamentary system. Such specialization on the part of the committees often leads to actual tutelage of the executive power by the assemblies. Even in the United States the president has to display great tact in dealing with the major committees, particularly the Senatorial ones; the fate of bills inspired by the executive power is decided in these committees. However, the system has not produced the same effects in Latin America. The investigating committees that exist in Latin America as well as in the United States also play different roles, and in Latin America they cannot appeal to public opinion in order to alter the president's policy.

As in the United States, the assemblies can institute impeachment proceedings for criminal offenses against presidents, ministers, and judges. When the procedure is used against judges, it has often made it all too easy for presidents to get rid of their opponents. This may lead some observers to believe that in countries where the presidents take the greatest liberties with constitutional rules, impeachment might become a tool in the hands of congress to force the president into submission. But even when the president has most flagrantly flouted his obligations, the house of representatives has very seldom used its right to arraign the president before the senate. Abuses of power by the president are much more likely to be penalized by military intervention and revolution than by resort to constitutional procedures.

Congressional Sessions and the Permanent Commission

Some observers have asserted that one cause of presidential dominance is the shortness of parliamentary sessions. It is true that in a few countries regular sessions are very short—two months in Ecuador and Nicaragua, for instance—but these are exceptions. Most of the constitutions provide for a long regular session as a precaution against presidential hegemony—six months in Brazil, nine months in Uruguay. Other countries provide for two annual sessions, and everywhere the sessions may be extended and congress may be called into special session.

In addition a few countries have adopted an institution, called the permanent commission, whose object is to maintain a permanent congressional representation. This is done in Uruguay, El Salvador, Guatemala, Panama, and Mexico. Under the Mexican system, the permanent commission consists of 29 members, of whom 14 are elected by the Senate and 15 by the House of Representatives. This commission may discharge some of the functions of Congress between sessions, for instance, it may agree by a two-thirds vote to suspend constitutional guarantees. Its main role is to call emergency sessions of Congress. In principle, through this delegation of Congress a constant watch is kept over the president. The permanent commission is an old institution in Latin America. It existed as early as 1819 in the second constitution in Venezuela. It is not unlike the Presidium of the Supreme Soviet, but neither in Latin America nor in the USSR has the permanent delegation of the legislative assemblies effectively limited the dominance of the governing power.

Presidential dominance is an obvious fact in Latin America, but it does not stem from the form of the institutions. Its cause should be sought in the nature of the society and the ensuing political problems.

18. Social Causes of Presidential Dominance: The Crisis of Democracy

It is tempting to ascribe the political instability of Latin American countries and the constant drift of the presidential regime toward authoritarianism to the temperament of the populations. This allegedly is due to the fact that Latin populations mixed with Africans and Amerindians differ from Anglo-Saxons. This explanation is of no help, however, not because it is erroneous but because the obvious differences in political behavior are tied to a complex of traits of social rather than ethnic origin—sense of political responsibility, perpetuation of family allegiances, and level of education—which determine the degree of political maturity. Ascribing political behavior to peoples' psychology is tantamount then to ascribing it to lags in social evolution.

Role of Personalization of Power

The reason why the institutions have moved in the direction of personal power may be traced to those same social factors, and also to the propensity of Latin American populations to view power as embodied in a man and their inability to understand it as an abstract concept. Highly developed peoples are supposed to be able to conceive of the government as the rule of law based on majority consent. But illiterate populations, Indians or mestizos, and backward peasants used to the paternalism of an accessible master are bound to regard government as being in the hands of a man whom one can approach because "if he knew what was going on he would stop it and restore justice." This is the "myth of the protective father" that the Latin American president benefits by, just as in the past the hereditary monarchs did.[1] Trust in the equity of the chief necessarily excludes trust in the law. In the presidential regime law is made by congress whose prestige suffers from it, while the president is a chief who can protect the little man.

The amazing parade of individuals and delegations that all day long and sometimes also at night wait in the president's antechamber because they feel they must speak to him is cited as evidence of this Latin American propensity to personalize power. Irigoyen in Argentina was a past master in demagogic exploitation of the little man's faith in the all-powerful president. Although in Perón's time the population was quite advanced, his regime made skillful use of its faith in him. It is true that Perón was no father image. His wife filled the role of personal protector and incarnated power much more than her spouse. In fact, it was Evita Perón's death that shook the regime.

It is quite probable that populations accustomed to paternalism, a segment of whom are still far from integrated into the nation, are more prone to give their allegiance to a man rather than an institution. Personalism, or rather the cult of the personality, has nevertheless not been confined to Latin America or the underdeveloped countries. Even outside the cruel experiences suffered at the hands of Hitler and Mussolini, not to speak of Stalin and many others, power has tended to be personalized even by peoples who believed they were most attached to the rule of law, whenever the regime has allowed them to do so. Royal democracies of the English type have been the most skillful in dealing with the need to personalize power. They have done it by diverting that need toward the person of a sovereign who only holds power symbolically. There is no doubt that the myth of the protective father strikes a chord in Latin America. But then, the United States has not always been immune to it, nor does France seem to be in the 1960's.

[1] William W. Pierson and Federico G. Gil, *Governments of Latin America: The President as the Great Father* (New York, 1957), p. 225.

It is difficult to find a country where personalization of power is more openly accepted and even sought than the haven of political democracy, the United States. Political scientists in the United States, while regarding personalism as the flaw of Latin American presidential regimes, invariably mention that in choosing a presidential candidate in the United States the parties must consider his personal vote-getting abilities. This is far more important than his loyalty to the nominating party or his political platform. When the American people elected Eisenhower they voted for a person rather than for a party or an idea, as shown by the fact that the Democrats wanted him on their ticket as much as the Republicans did.

The major difference between Latin America and the United States with respect to personalization of power is that in the latter, public relations are scientifically organized and geared to that end. All too often Latin American presidents and all those who hold any degree of power waste precious time in proving how accessible they are by interrupting their work at a moment's notice to welcome the worshipers in person. In the United States the same need is fulfilled by periodic if rare hand-shaking or baby-kissing rituals, while television replaces physical presence the rest of the time.

The flaw of the presidential regime might well be its tendency to personalize power. This is why it is legitimately distrusted by those who believe that personalization of power can be avoided, and should be for democracy's sake. On the other hand, if despite its drawbacks the need for personalization of power is so compelling, it is not safe to repress it completely. Since the presidential regime can satisfy the need, it is preferable to the parliamentary regime. It is alleged that in Latin America the need for personalization is especially deep, and if it is completely frustrated by such overly impersonal regimes as the collective executive power in Uruguay, this might promote the advent of dictatorships. The example of the United States throughout its history and that of several Latin American countries show that the presidential regime may allow personalization of power without necessarily evolving toward arbitrary regimes or degenerating into dictatorship.

In Latin America it was especially important to satisfy the need for incarnation of power in the person of the president, since the social structure did not particularly help to enhance his image. On the contrary, incomplete national integration allowed too many family and clan bonds and too many feudal, scattered personal allegiances to linger on. Since the presidential regime embodies national power in one person it may be more effective than any other regime in transferring scattered allegiances to the nation, just as in other times the state has been embodied in the person of the king. The existence of a president makes matters even easier because his election through universal suffrage (even if narrowly based in Latin America) calls for the people's frequent participation in the "coronation" ceremony.

Frequency of Emergencies

The presidential regime in Latin America tends to be distorted and to promote excessive authority for the president, but this does not imply that the regime is ill-suited to Latin America's specific needs or that the people do not know how to use it. The inescapable conclusion, therefore, is that the lack of equilibrium between the president and the assemblies corresponds to specific needs of Latin America and of developing countries in general. The distortion merely shows that the regime is adaptable to different requirements.

Only in theory could one visualize a presidential regime operating under a stable equilibrium between the powers. Actual equilibrium seems impossible, since in order to make the executive and the legislative powers independent from each other, they both are made to rest upon popular suffrage. Although a single electoral body casts the votes, these cannot possibly be identical when only *one* president is elected, together with *a host* of representatives. Besides, as in the United States, most Latin American countries—Brazil, Chile, Colombia, Ecuador, El Salvador, Guatemala, Haiti, Mexico, Panama, and Peru—have different terms for the president and the congressmen. Hence it is inevitable that while the two powers may directly reflect public opinion, they do not reflect exactly the same one.

The United States model of orderly operation of the presidential regime shows that public opinion is always markedly different in senatorial and presidential elections. It also shows the changes in public opinion in off-year elections to the House of Representatives. More than once these off-year elections have brought an opposition majority into the House. Elections to replace a segment of the Senate also change its makeup, although at a slower pace. Hence conflicts between the president and Congress are inevitable.

The parliamentary regime, when it operates properly, is a regime of cooperation between powers, since the cabinet cannot stay in office if it is in serious disagreement with parliament. The presidential regime, on the contrary, is a regime of conflict between powers. Subconsciously observers base their judgment about the operation of the presidential regime in Latin America on the rarity of conflicts. They ascribe the absence of conflicts to the failure of the checks and balances system.

The methods necessary everywhere to resolve these conflicts are bound to break the equilibrium between the powers. The methods may be constitutional, such as the presidential veto, or extra-constitutional, such as the United States Congressional investigating committees aimed at appealing to the people over the president's head, diversion of the treaty ratification power in order to influence foreign or even domestic policy, presidential favors granted to compliant Representatives, or threats of "purges" of unruly ones.

The priceless merit of the United States presidential regime is not that equilibrium between the powers always prevails, but rather that once broken it is generally soon restored. One may speak of equilibrium only over a long period, and the political history of the United States is an alternation of presidential and congressional dominance with occasional spells of dominance by the judiciary.

Thus, from 1829 to 1837 the president so completely dominated federal policy that the period is sometimes called the reign of Jackson. His successor, President Van Buren, found a Congress eager to assert itself. Lincoln's term was one of presidential hegemony, but Congress retaliated by paralyzing Andrew Johnson's unpopular administration and substituting its own policy of Reconstruction in the Southern states. Congressional dominance persisted under Grant's weak and corrupt presidency. Wilson's domination during World War I gave way to the Senate's revolt in 1919. Harding and Coolidge were rather colorless men, but during their presidencies it was the Supreme Court rather than Congress that held the dominant role, so that the United States has had its period of government by judges. Franklin Roosevelt's long hegemony, accompanied by the effacement of a judicial power that had taken too many liberties, gave presidents Truman and Eisenhower Congresses determined to use their prerogatives to the full. Even President Kennedy's popularity was not enough to appease the aggressiveness of the houses.

In Latin America there is no such pendulum motion. Not only are any conflicts almost always resolved in the president's favor, but congress is so submissive that conflicts usually do not arise in the first place. The president, it is true, may be better equipped with both constitutional and hidden means to emerge the winner in any conflict. Still, if congress were determined it could use its irresistible means of pressure, namely the enactment or withholding of legislation and, more specifically, of appropriations. The fact is that congress is far more hesitant than in the United States to use such means and would rather let itself be dominated. The tilting of the scale toward one side is not later compensated by a shift toward the opposite side. Usually presidential hegemony is not halted by congressional rebellion but by palace revolutions or military and popular uprisings.

The regime's rigidity and the relative passivity of congress can be explained without adducing the cult of personality of the president or the congressmen's lack of personality. The periods of presidential dominance in the United States provide clear examples. A president with a strong personality certainly helps bring such periods about, but all of them coincide with times of crisis when rapid, energetic action is imperative. Jackson's preponderance accompanied the crisis of democratization of society that put an end to the domination of the eastern business oligarchies and the southern landed oligarchies and made power accessible to the western farmers. A far more serious crisis, which jeopardized the very existence of the United States, was the abolition of slavery and the Civil War during Lincoln's presidency. Wilson's dominance was tied to the World War I. Roosevelt's was connected with the 1929 depression and prolonged by World War II. In times of unrest the regime has tended as in Latin America to broaden the president's power. In the United States, though, the periods of serious crisis have been few and far between and the regime has had time to regain its balance between crises.

In Latin America the acceleration of history precipitates crises and creates a permanent state of tension. This is because the need to change archaic social structures rapidly creates social problems, compounded by economic problems caused by the need for a rapid rise in the standards of living. These tensions call for frequent resort to emergency powers. The assemblies become accustomed to delegating their powers, and the presidents to wielding them. All this happens, however, because the hegemony really is necessary in view of the political, economic, and social conditions in the developing countries.

Latin America's political instability, the governments' tendency to concentrate power in the hands of the president, the relative abdication of the representative assemblies, even the frequent interruptions of constitutional government by civilian or military dictatorships in no way stem from disaffection of Latin American populations for democratic forms of government. Such unrest, on the contrary, is the inevitable consequence of stubborn efforts of the Latin American populations—or at least of the segment that up to now has influenced political life—to try to maintain democratic forms of government under unfavorable circumstances. Very few developing countries in other parts of the world have worked as hard to preserve democratic governments.

These persistent efforts in pursuit of political democracy and of maximum liberalism in economic planning are the real political hallmark of the largest part of Latin America. Up to now, culturally Latin America has fully belonged to the community of the North Atlantic democracies because their culture was that of Latin America's own ruling class. The culture of the masses, the social structure, and the level of economic development of Latin America, however, did not make it part of that community, and democratic political institutions cannot be expected to operate harmoniously in societies that are not democratic in any respect.

As long as the contradiction has not been resolved, political life of Latin America is bound to be one of constant turmoil. It will be resolved eventually, but the danger is that the easiest way out is to limit the scope of the most progressive institutions instead of rapidly integrating the backward masses. Despite major achievements in Mexico, Chile, Brazil, Colombia, Costa Rica, and even Venezuela, if most of the Latin American population cannot fairly soon gain access to the culture and way of life that up to now have been the privilege of the ruling class, the stubborn efforts made throughout the continent will have been in vain.

Bibliography

BIBLIOGRAPHICAL AIDS

Andrews, David H., *Latin America: A Bibliography of Paperback Books* (Washington, 1964).

Bayitch, Stojan A., *Latin America: A Bibliographical Guide to Economy, History, Law, Politics, and Society* (Miami, 1961). English titles only.

Burr, Robert N., "Recent Developments in Latin American History," *Annals of the American Academy of Political and Social Science* (May 1964), p. 122.

Cline, Howard F., "Latin America," *American Association Guide to Literature* (New York, 1961).

Delgado, Oscar, *Bibliografía latinoamericana sobre reforma agraria y tenencia de la tierra, 1950–1961* (Mexico, 1962).

"Documents Relating to Latin America," *International Social Science Bulletin*, UNESCO, IV, no. 3 (1952), 427–624. Contains an annotated bibliography of official publications and of periodicals.

Geoghegan, Abel I., *Obras de referencia de América latina*, UNESCO (1965).

Humphreys, Robert A., *Latin American History: A Guide to the Literature in English* (London and New York, 1958).

Indice histórico español: bibliografía histórica de España e Hispano-américa (Barcelona, 1953–   ).

Lauerhass, Ludwig, *Communism in Latin America* (Los Angeles, 1962). A bibliography.

Pan American Union, *Education in Latin America: A Partial Bibliography* (Washington, 1958).

————, *Index to Latin American Periodical Literature, 1929–1960,* 8 vols. (Boston, 1962).

Sable, Martin H., *A Guide to Latin American Studies,* 2 vols. (Los Angeles, 1967).

Sánchez Alonso, Benito, *Fuentes de la historia española e hispano--americana,* 3 vols. (Madrid, 1962). The most useful tool for the colonial period.

Wagley, Charles, ed., *Social Science Research on Latin America* (New York, 1965). A very useful collection of bibliographical essays from the various disciplines indicating the status of research in their respective fields.

Zimmerman, Irene, *A Guide to Current Latin American Periodicals: Humanities and Social Sciences* (Gainesville, Fla., 1961).

PERIODICALS

América latina (Rio de Janeiro, 1958–   ).

Anuario de estudios americanos (Seville, 1944–   ).

Bank of London and South America Fortnightly Review (London, 1950–   ).

Ciencias políticas y sociales (Mexico, July 1955–1964).

Cuadernos americanos (Mexico, 1942–   ).

Cuadernos hispano-americanos (Madrid, 1948–   ).

Handbook of Latin American Studies (Gainesville, Fla., 1936–   ).

Hispanic American Report (Stanford, Calif., 1948–1964).

Index to Latin American Periodical Literature, 1929–1960, Pan American Union, 8 vols. (Boston, 1962).

Inter-American Economic Affairs (Washington, June 1947–   ).

Journal of Inter-American Studies (Gainesville, Fla.,1959–   ).

Revista brasileira de estudos políticos (Belo Horizonte, Brazil, 1956–   ).

Revista de estudios políticos (Madrid, 1941–   ). Contains a Latin American section.

Revista inter-americana de ciencias sociales, Organization of American States (Washington, 1950).

Revista mexicana de sociología (Mexico, 1939–   ).

Statistical Abstract of Latin America (Los Angeles, 1955–   ).

El Trimestre Económico (Mexico, 1934–   ).

GENERAL WORKS

Academy of Political Science, *Proceedings* (May 1964). This issue is devoted to "Economic and Political Trends in Latin America."

Accioli Borges, Pompeu, "Graus de Desenvolvimento na América Latina," *Boletim do centro latino americano de pesquisas em ciencias sociaes* (Rio de Janeiro, May, 1958, and August, 1959). A suggested typology.

Adams, R., A. Hohnberg, O. Lewis, R. Patch, S. Gillin, and C. Wagley, *Social Change in Latin America Today* (New York, 1960).

Alexander, Robert J., *Today's Latin America* (New York, 1962).

Allen, Robert Loring, *Soviet Influence in Latin America* (Washington, 1959).

Annals of the American Academy of Political and Social Science (March 1961). This issue is devoted to "Latin American Nationalistic Revolutions."

Arciniegas, Germán, *The Green Continent: A Comprehensive View of Latin America by Its Leading Writers* (New York, 1959).

Bailey, H. M., and A. P. Nasatir, *Latin America: The Development of Its Civilization* (New York, 1960).

Berle, Adolf A., *Latin America: Diplomacy and Reality* (New York, 1962).

Beyhaut, Gustavo, *Süd- und Mittelamerika II. Von der Unabhängigheit bis zur Krise der Gegenwort* (Frankfurt am Main, 1965).

Chang Rodríquez, Eugenio, and Harry Kantor, eds., *La América latina de hoy* (New York, 1961).

Cosío Villegas, Daniel, *American Extremes* (Austin, Tex., 1964). A collection of essays.

————, *Change in Latin America: The Mexican and Cuban Revolutions* (Lincoln, Neb., 1961).

Crawford, William Rex, *A Century of Latin American Thought* (Cambridge, Mass., 1961).

Dávila, Carlos, *We of the Americas* (Chicago and New York, 1949).

Dozer, Donald, *Are We Good Neighbors? Three Decades of Inter-American Relations* (Gainesville, Fla., 1957).

Dreier, John C., *The Organization of American States and the Hemisphere Crisis* (New York, 1962).

Eisenhower, Milton S., *The Wine Is Bitter: The United States and Latin America* (New York, 1963).

Estrada Martínez, Antonio, *Diferencias y semejanzas entre los paises de América latina* (Mexico, 1962).

Fraga Iriborne, Manuel, *Sociedad, política y gobierno en Hispano-américa* (Madrid, 1962).

Galíndez Suárez, Jesús, *Iberoamérica: su evolución política, socio-económica, cultural e internacional* (New York, 1954).

Gerassi, John, *The Great Fear: The Reconquest of Latin America by Latin Americans* (New York, 1963). A series of articles very critical of United States policy.

Gordon, Lincoln, *A New Deal for Latin America* (Boston, 1963).

Gottmann, Jean, *L'Amérique* (Paris, 1960). Geography.

Gourou, Pierre, *The Tropical World* (London, 1961). Geography.

Gozard, Gilles, *Demain, l'Amérique latine* (Paris, 1964).

Hanke, Lewis, *Modern Latin America: Continent in Ferment* (Princeton, 1959). Vol. I, *Mexico and the Caribbean*. Vol. II, *South America*.

Henríquez Ureña, Pedro, *A Concise History of Latin American Culture* (New York, 1965).

Hernández Sánchez-Barba, Mario, *Las tensiones históricos hispano-americanas en el siglo XX* (Madrid, 1961).

Houtart, François, *El cambio social en América latina* (Brussels, 1964). Contains some conclusions of the survey conducted by FERES (International Federation of Catholic Institutes for Social and Socio-Religious Research) consisting of 42 volumes dealing with the period 1962–1965.

James, Preston, *Latin America* (New York, 1950). The standard geography.

Johnson, John J., *Continuity and Change in Latin America* (Stanford, Calif., 1964).

——, *The Military and Society in Latin America* (Stanford, Calif., 1964).

Lambert, Denis, *Les inflations sud-américaines* (Paris, 1959).

Leonard, Olen E., and Charles P. Loomis, eds., *Readings in Latin American Social Organization and Institutions* (East Lansing, Mich., 1953).

Lieuwen, Edwin, *Arms and Politics in Latin America* (New York,

1961). Suggests (on pp. 154–170) a classification on the basis of military interventions.

Madariaga, Salvador de, *Presente y porvenir de Hispanoamérica y otros ensayos* (Buenos Aires, 1959).

Mecham, John L., *Church and State in Latin America* (Chapel Hill, N. C., 1934).

Mende, Tibor, *L'Amérique latine entre en scène* (Paris, 1952). Still one of the best on the subject in French.

Niedergang, Marcel, *Les vingt Amériques latines* (Paris, 1962). The best introduction to the study of Latin America available in French.

Onís, Juan de, ed., *The America of José Martí* (New York, 1953). Important because of the present-day influence of this nineteenth-century Cuban political thinker.

Pan American Union, Department of Economic Affairs, *Economic Survey of Latin America* (Washington, 1961–).

———, Department of Social Affairs, *Estudio social de América latina* (Washington, 1961–).

———, *Tipología socio-económica de los paises latinoamericanos* (Washington, 1964). Contains the findings of Father Vekeman's research project in Santiago, Chile. The most detailed typological study.

Perkins, Dexter, *The United States and Latin America* (Baton Rouge, 1961).

Picón-Salas, Mariano, *A Cultural History of Spanish America* (Berkeley, Calif., 1962).

Pike, Frederick B., *The Conflict Between Church and State in Latin America* (New York, 1963). A collection of essays.

Pike, Frederick B., and William V. D'Antonio, *Religion, Revolution and Reform: New Forces for Change in Latin America* (Notre Dame, 1964).

Porter, Charles O., and Robert J. Alexander, *The Struggle for Democracy in Latin America* (New York, 1961).

Powelson, John P., *Latin America: Today's Economic and Social Revolution* (New York, 1964).

Rouma, Georges, *L'Amérique latine* (Brussels, 1958).

Ruiz García, Enrique, *Iberoamérica entre el bisonte y el toro* (Madrid, 1959).

Sánchez, Luis Alberto, *Existe América latina?* (Mexico, 1945). Caused a great deal of controversy at the time of publication.

Schmieder, Oscar, *Geografía de América latina* (Mexico, 1964).

Schmitt, Karl M., and David D. Burks, *Evolution or Chaos: Dynamics of Latin American Government and Politics* (New York, 1963).

Silvert, Kalman H., *The Conflict Society: Reaction and Revolution in Latin America* (New York, 1966).

Tepaske, John, ed., *Explosive Forces in Latin America* (Columbus, Ohio, 1964).

UNESCO, *Social Aspects of Economic Development in Latin America*, 2 vols. (1963).

Urquidi, Victor L., *The Challenge of Development in Latin America* (New York, 1964).

Whitbeck, Ray H., *et al., The Economic Geography of South America* (New York, 1950).

Zea, Leopoldo, *The Latin American Mind* (Norman, Okla., 1963). An intellectual history.

HISTORICAL BACKGROUND

Amunátegui y Solar, Domingo, *La emancipación de Hispanoamérica* (Santiago, 1936).

Arnoldsson, Sverker, *La leyenda negra, estudios sobre sus origenes* (Goteborg, 1966).

Bannon, John Francis, ed., *Indian Labor in the Spanish Indies: Was There Another Solution?* (Boston, 1966).

Barros Arana, Diego, *Historia general de Chile* (Santiago, 1930).

Basadre, Jorge, *Historia de la república del Perú*, 10 vols. (Lima, 1961–64).

Belaúnde, Victor Andrés, *Bolívar and the Political Thought of the Spanish American Revolution* (Baltimore, 1938).

Bourne, Edward G., *Spain in America* (New York, 1904).

Buarque de Holanda, Sergio, ed., *História geral da civilização brasileira*, 4 vols. (São Paulo, 1962–64).

Calmon, Pedro, *História do Brasil*, 4 vols. (Rio de Janeiro, 1939–47).

Carbia, Rómulo D., *Historia de la leyenda negra hispano-americana* (Madrid, 1944).

Chaunu, Pierre, *L'Amérique et les Amériques* (Paris, 1964).

―――, *Séville et l'Atlantique,* 11 vols. (Paris, 1954–59). Basically a study of economics; contains a complete bibliography.

Cosío Villegas, Daniel, ed., *Historia moderna de México* (Mexico, 1955–65).

Descola, Jean, *La vie quotidienne au Pérou au temps des espagnols (1710–1820)* (Paris, 1962).

Díaz del Castillo, Bernal, *The Conquest of New Spain* (Baltimore, 1963). A classic description of the conquest.

Diffie, Bailey W., *Latin American Civilization: Colonial Period* (Harrisburg, Pa., 1955).

Driver, Harold E., *The Americas on the Eve of Discovery* (Englewood Cliffs, N. J., 1964).

Encina, Francisco Antonio, *Historia de Chile,* 20 vols. (Santiago, 1940–54).

Garcia, Rodolpho, *Ensaio sôbre a história política e administrativa do Brasil, 1500–1810* (Rio de Janeiro, 1956).

García Gallo, Alfonso, *Curso de historia del derecho español,* 2 vols. (Madrid, 1950).

García Samudio, Nicolás, *La independencia de Hispano-américa* (Mexico, 1950).

Gibson, Charles, *The Aztecs Under Spanish Rule: A History of the Indians of the Valley of Mexico, 1519–1810* (Stanford, Calif., 1964).

———, *Spain in America* (New York, Evanston, Ill., and London, 1966). Contains a very useful bibliography.

Hanke, Lewis, *The Spanish Struggle for Justice in the Conquest of America* (Philadelphia, 1959).

Haring, Clarence H., *The Spanish Empire in America* (New York, 1947). The basic work in English.

Humboldt, Alexander von, *Personal Narrative of Travels to the Equinoctial Regions of America During the Years 1799–1804* (London and New York, 1895).

———, *Political Essay on the Kingdom of New Spain,* 4 vols. (New York, 1966). The findings of the well-known scientist, from his visit during the last decades of colonial rule.

Humphreys, Robert A., and John Lynch, *The Origins of the Latin American Revolutions* (New York, 1965).

Juan, Jorge, and Antonio de Ulloa, *Voyage to South America* (New York, 1964). The observations of the authors while on a scientific expedition, first published in 1735.

Kirkpatrick, F. A., *The Spanish Conquistadores* (London, 1963).

Konetzke, Richard, *El imperio español* (Madrid, 1946).

Masur, Gerhard, *Simon Bolívar* (Albuquerque, 1948).

Oliveira Lima, Manuel de, *O Império brasileiro, 1822–1889* (São Paulo, 1927).

——, *O movimento da independência, 1821–1822* (São Paulo, 1922).

Ots Capdequí, José María, *Las instituciones sociales de la América española en el período colonial* (La Plata, Argentina, 1934).

Parry, John, *The Spanish Seaborne Empire* (New York, 1966).

Picón-Salas, Mariano, *A Cultural History of Spanish America* (Berkeley, Calif., 1966).

Prescott, William H., *The Conquest of Mexico* (London, 1843).

Rabasa, Emilio, *La evolución histórica de México* (Mexico, 1956).

Ramos, Roberto, *Bibliografía de la revolución mexicana* (Mexico, 1931–1940). A supplement was published in 1959.

Scelle, Georges, *La traite négrière aux Indes de Castille*, 2 vols. (Paris, 1906).

Simpson, Lesley Byrd, "The Laws of Burgos," *Studies in the Administration of the Indians in New Spain* (Berkeley, Calif., 1934).

Tapié, Victor, *Histoire de l'Amérique latine au xixe siècle* (Paris, 1949).

Varnhagen, Francisco Adolpho de, *História geral de Brasil*, 5 vols. (São Paulo, 1927–1936).

Vianna, Helio, *História do Brasil*, 2 vols. (São Paulo, 1962).

Zavala, Silvio A., *The Colonial Period in the History of the New World* (Mexico, 1962).

SPECIFIC COUNTRIES

ARGENTINA

Alexander, Robert J., *The Perón Era* (New York, 1951).

Blanksten, George I., *Perón's Argentina* (Chicago, 1953).

Ferrer, Aldo, *The Argentine Economy* (Berkeley, Calif., 1967).

Fillol, Tomás Roberto, *Social Factors in Economic Development: The Argentine Case* (Cambridge, Mass., 1961).

Hall, Elvajean, *The Land and People of Argentina* (Philadelphia, 1960).

Levene, Gustavo Gabriel, *La Argentine se hizo así* (Buenos Aires, 1960).

Levene, Ricardo, *A History of Argentina* (New York, 1963).

McGann, Thomas F., *Argentina, the United States, and the Inter-American System, 1880–1914* (Cambridge, Mass., 1957).

Pendle, George, *Argentina* (London and New York, 1963).

Perón, Eva, *My Mission in Life* (New York, 1953).

Rennie, Ysabel Fisk, *The Argentine Republic* (New York, 1945).

Romero, José Luis, *A History of Argentine Political Thought* (Stanford, Calif., 1963).

Scobie, James R., *Argentina, a City and a Nation* (New York, 1964).

Touchard, J., *La République argentine* (Paris, 1961).

Whitaker, Arthur P., *Argentina* (New York, 1965). The best survey available.

BOLIVIA

Alexander, Robert J., *The Bolivian National Revolution* (New Brunswick, N. J., 1958).

Arnade, Charles, *The Emergence of the Republic of Bolivia* (Gainesville, Fla., 1964).

Céspedes, Augusto, *Bolivia* (Washington, 1962).

Leonard, Olen E., *Bolivia: Land, People, and Institutions* (Washington, 1952).

Patch, Richard W., *Bolivia: Decision or Debacle* (New York, 1959).

Zondag, Cornelius, *The Bolivian Economy, 1952–1965* (New York, 1966).

BRAZIL

Bastide, Roger, *Brésil: terre des contrastes* (Paris, 1957).

Bello, José María, *A History of Modern Brazil, 1889–1964* (Stanford, Calif., 1966).

Buarque de Holanda, Sergio, *Raizes do Brasil* (Rio de Janeiro, 1956).

Burns, E. Bradford, ed., *A Documentary History of Brazil* (New York, 1966).

Calogeras, João Pandia, *A History of Brazil* (New York, 1963).

Carneiro Leão, Antonio, *Panorama sociologique du Brésil* (Paris, 1953).

Cruz Costa, João, *History of Ideas in Brazil* (Berkeley, Calif., 1964).

Freyre, Gilberto, *Brazil: An Interpretation* (New York, 1945).

——, *The Masters and the Slaves* (New York, 1964).

——, *New World in the Tropics: The Culture of Modern Brazil* (New York, 1963).

Furtado, Celso, *The Economic Growth of Brazil* (Berkeley, Calif., 1963).

Haring, Clarence H., *Empire in Brazil: A New World Experiment with Monarchy* (Cambridge, Mass., 1958).

Lambert, Jacques, *Le Brésil: Structure social et institutions politiques* (Paris, 1953).

——, *Os dois Brasils* (Rio de Janeiro, 1959).

MacDonald, Norman P., *The Land and People of Brazil* (London, 1959).

Morazé, Charles, *Les trois âges du Brésil* (Paris, 1954).

Morse, Richard M., *From Community to Metropolis: A Biography of São Paulo, Brazil* (Gainesville, Fla., 1958).

Oliveira Vianna, Francisco José de, *Evolução do povo brasileiro* (São Paulo, 1938).

Prado, Caio, Jr., *História economica do Brasil* (São Paulo, 1945).

Ramos, Arthur, *The Negro in Brazil* (Washington, 1939).

Rodríguez, José Honorio, *Aspiraçoes nacionais* (São Paulo, 1963).

Smith, T. Lynn, *Brazil: People and Institutions* (Baton Rouge, La., 1963).

Wagley, Charles, *An Introduction to Brazil* (New York, 1963).

Werneck Sodre, Nelson, *O que se deve ler para conhecer o Brasil* (Rio de Janeiro, 1960). A very useful annotated bibliography.

CHILE

Argüedas, Alcides, *Pueblo enfermo* (Santiago, 1937).

Basadre, Jorge, *Chile, Perú y Bolivia independientes* (Barcelona, 1948).

Butland, Gilbert J., *Chile: An Outline of Its Geography, Economics, and Politics* (London, 1956).

Cohen, Alvin, *Economic Change in Chile, 1929–1959* (Gainesville, Fla., 1960).

Galdames, Luis, *A History of Chile* (New York, 1963).

Gil, Federico, *The Political System of Chile* (New York, 1966).

Halperin, Ernest, *Nationalism and Communism in Chile* (Boston, 1965).

McBride, George M., *Chile, Land and Society* (New York, 1936).

Ostria Gutiérrez, Alberto, *Un pueblo en la cruz* (Santiago, 1956).

Pendle, George, *The Land and People of Chile* (London and New York, 1964).

Siles Salinas, Jorge, *La aventura y el orden* (Santiago, 1956).

Silvert, Kalman H., *Chile, Yesterday and Today* (New York, 1965).

COLOMBIA

Calballero Calderón, Eduardo, *Historia privada de los Colombianos* (Bogotá, 1960).

Hunter, John M., *Emerging Colombia* (Washington, 1962).

Lebret, J. L., *Estudios sobre las condiciones del desarrollo de Colombia*, 2 vols. (Bogotá, 1958).

Martz, John D., *Colombia: A Contemporary Political Survey* (Chapel Hill, N.C., 1962).

Nieto Arteta, Luis E., *Economía y cultura en la historia de Colombia* (Bogotá, 1962).

Ospina Vasquez, Luis, *Industria y protección en Colombia, 1810–1930* (Medellín, Colombia, 1955).

Romoli, Kathleen, *Colombia, Gateway to South America* (New York, 1941).

Whiteford, Andrew H., *Two Cities of Latin America: A Comparative Description of Social Classes* (Beloit, Wis., 1960). A sociological study of Querétaro, Mexico and Popayán, Colombia.

ECUADOR

Blanksten, George T., *Ecuador: Constitutions and Caudillos* (New York, 1963).

Institut d'Etudes Politiques pour l'Amérique Latine (IEPAL), *Equateur* (Montevideo, 1964).

Linke, Lilo, *Ecuador: Country of Contrasts* (London, 1960).

Needler, Martin C., *Anatomy of a Coup d'État: Ecuador, 1963* (Washington, 1964).

Platt, R. R., *Ecuador* (New York, 1960).

Saunder, John V. D., *The Population of Ecuador: A Demographic Analysis* (Gainesville, Fla., 1961).

Watkins, Ralph J., *Expanding Ecuador's Exports: A Commodity-by-Commodity Study with Projections to 1973* (New York, 1966).

MEXICO

Brandenburg, Frank, *The Making of Modern Mexico* (New York, 1964).

Chevalier, François, "Le Mexique contemporain: État des travaux," *Revue française de science politique,* I (1958), 110 ff. Bibliography.

Cline, Howard F., *Mexico: Revolution to Evolution, 1940–1960* (New York, 1963).

————, *The United States and Mexico* (New York, 1963).

Glade, William P., and Charles W. Anderson, *The Political Economy of Mexico* (Madison, Wis., 1963).

Iturriaga, José E., *La estructura social y cultural de México* (Mexico, 1951).

Lewis, Oscar, *The Children of Sánchez: Autobiography of a Mexican Family* (New York, 1961).

————, *Five Families: Mexican Case Studies in the Culture of Poverty* (New York, 1959).

————, *Pedro Martinez: A Mexican Peasant and His Family* (New York, 1964).

Parkes, Henry Bamford, *A History of Mexico* (Boston, 1960).

Ramos, Samuel, *Profile of Man and Culture in Mexico* (Austin, Tex., 1962).

Ross, Stanley R., ed., *Is the Mexican Revolution Dead?* (New York, 1966). A collection of essays.

Simpson, Lesley B., *Many Mexicos,* 4th ed., rev. (Berkeley, Calif., 1966).

Tannenbaum, Frank, *Mexico: The Struggle for Peace and Bread* (New York, 1962).

Vernon, Raymond, *The Dilemma of Mexico's Development* (Cambridge, Mass., 1963).

Whetten, Nathan L., *Rural Mexico* (Chicago, 1958).

Wolf, Eric R., *Sons of the Shaking Earth* (Chicago, 1959). An anthropologist's view of Mexican history and culture.

PARAGUAY

Cardozo, Efraím, *El Paraguay colonial: las raíces de la nacionalidad* (Buenos Aires, 1959).

Kalinski, Charles J., *Independence or Death: The Story of the Paraguayan War* (Gainesville, Fla., 1966).

Pendle, George, *Paraguay, a Riverside Nation* (London and New York, 1956).

PERU

Belaúnde, Victor Andrés, *La realidad nacional* (Lima, 1945).

Ford, Thomas R., *Man and Land in Peru* (Gainesville, Fla., (1962).

Levin, Jonathan, *The Export Economies: Their Pattern of Development in Historical Perspective* (Cambridge, Mass., 1960). An analysis of the guano boom and its effect on the Peruvian economy.

MacLean y Estenós, Roberto, *Sociología del Peru* (Mexico, 1959).

Payne, James, *Labor and Politics in Peru* (New Haven, Conn., 1965).

Stein, William, *Hualcan: Life in the Highlands of Peru* (Ithaca, N. Y., 1961). A very useful general study of contemporary peasant society.

URUGUAY

Lindahl, Goran G., *Uruguay's New Path: A Study in Politics During the First Colegiado, 1917–1933* (Stockholm, 1962).

Pendle, George, *Uruguay, South America's First Welfare State* (London and New York, 1959).

Taylor, Philip B., *Government and Politics of Uruguay* (New Orleans, 1960).

VENEZUELA

Alexander, Robert J., *The Venezuelan Democratic Revolution* (New Brunswick, N. J., 1964).

Brito Figueroa, Federico, *Historia económica y social de Venezuela*, 2 vols. (Caracas, 1965).

Crist, Raymond E., *Venezuela* (New York, 1959). A geographical view.

Institut d'Etudes Politiques pour l'Amérique Latine, *Vénézuela* (Montevideo, 1965).

Lieuwen, Edwin, *Petroleum in Venezuela, a History* (Berkeley, Calif., 1954).

———, *Venezuela* (London, 1961).

Morón, Guillermo, *A History of Venezuela* (New York, 1963).

Picón-Salas, Mariano, *Comprensión de Venezuela* (Caracas, 1955).

Picón-Salas, Mariano, Augusto Mijares, Ramón Diaz Sanchez, Eduardo Arcila Farías, and Juan Liscano, *Venezuela independiente, 1810–1960* (Caracas, 1962). A collection of essays on political, social, economic, and cultural aspects of Venezuela's independence.

Royal Institute of International Affairs, *Venezuela, a Brief Political and Economic Survey* (New York, 1959).

CENTRAL AMERICA

Busey, James L., *Notes on Costa Rican Democracy* (Denver, 1962).

Checchi, Vincent, *Honduras, a Problem in Economic Development* (New York, 1959).

Colvin, Gerard, *The Lands and People of Central America* (New York, 1961).

Follick, Montgomery, *The Twelve Republics* (London, 1952).

Karnes, Thomas L., *The Failure of Union: Central America (1824–1960)* (Chapel Hill, N. C., 1961).

Lloyd, Chester, *Costa Rica and Civilization in the Caribbean* (Madison, 1961).

Martz, John D., *Central America: The Crisis and the Challenge* (Chapel Hill, N. C., 1959).

May, Stacy, *Costa Rica* (New York, 1962).

Monteforte Toledo, Mario, *Guatemala, monografía sociológica* (Mexico, 1965).

Pan American Union, *Honduras* (Washington, 1959).

Parker, Franklin D., *The Central American Republics* (London and New York, 1964). Contains a useful bibliography.

Rodríguez, Mario, *Central America* (Englewood Cliffs, N. J., 1965).

Rosenthal, Mario, *Guatemala, the Story of an Emerging Latin American Democracy* (New York, 1962).

Silvert, Kalman H., *A Study in Government: Guatemala* (New Orleans, 1954).

Stokes, William S., *Honduras, an Area Study in Government* (Madison, Wis., 1950).

Valle Matheu, Jorge del, *Sociología guatemalteca* (Guatemala City, 1950).

Waddell, David A. G., *British Honduras, a Historical and Contemporary Survey* (London and New York, 1961).

Whetten, Nathan L., *Guatemala, the Land and the People* (New Haven, Conn., 1961).

THE CARIBBEAN

Albanell, Norah, *Cuba, Dominican Republic, Haiti, and Puerto Rico* (Gainesville, Fla., 1956). A bibliography.

Draper, Theodore, *Castroism, Theory and Practice* (New York, 1965). The most useful book on the subject.

———, *Castro's Revolution, Myths and Realities* (New York, 1962).

Espaillot, Arturo, *Trujillo: The Last Caesar* (Chicago, 1963).

Fagg, John Edwin, *Cuba, Haiti, and the Dominican Republic* (Englewood Cliffs, N. J., 1965).

Goldenburg, Boris, *The Cuban Revolution and Latin America* (New York, 1965).

Guerra y Sanchez, Ramiro, *Sugar and Society in the Caribbean: An Economic History of Cuban Agriculture* (New Haven, Conn., 1964).

Guilbert, Yves, *El "Infidel" Castro* (Mexico, 1961).

Huberman, Leo, and Paul M. Sweezey, *Cuba: Anatomy of a Revolution* (New York, 1960).

Julien, Claude, *La révolution cubaine* (Paris, 1961).

Kurzman, Dan, *Revolt of the Damned* (New York, 1965). An account of the April 1965 revolt and the United States invasion of the Dominican Republic.

Leyburn, James G., *The Haitian People* (New Haven, Conn., 1966).

MacGaffey, Wyatt, and Clifford H. Barnett, *Cuba, Its People, Its Society, Its Culture* (New Haven, Conn., 1962).

Ortiz, Fernando, *Cuban Counterpoint: Tobacco and Sugar* (New York, 1947).

Phillips, Ruby H., *Cuba: Island of Paradox* (New York, 1959).

Rodman, Selden, *Haiti: The Black Republic* (New York, 1954).

———, *Quisqueya: A History of the Dominican Republic* (Seattle, 1964).

Royal Institute of International Affairs, *Cuba: A Brief Political and Economic Survey* (London, 1958).

Seers, Dudley, *Cuba: The Economic and Social Revolution* (Chapel Hill, N. C., 1964).

Wilgus, A. Curtis, *The Caribbean at Mid-Century* (Gainesville, Fla., 1951).

——, *The Caribbean: Contemporary International Relations* (Gainesville, Fla., 1963).

——, *The Caribbean: Contemporary Trends* (Gainesville, Fla., 1953).

——, *The Caribbean: Education* (Gainesville, Fla., 1960).

——, *The Caribbean: Its Economy* (Gainesville, Fla., 1962).

——, *The Caribbean: Its Natural Resources* (Gainesville, Fla., 1961).

——, *The Caribbean: Its Political Problems* (Gainesville, Fla., 1956).

Wilkerson, Loree, *Fidel Castro's Political Programs from Reformism to "Marxism-Leninism"* (Gainesville, Fla., 1966).

DEMOGRAPHY, ETHNOGRAPHY, AND URBANIZATION

Adams, R. N., et al., *Social Change in Latin America Today* (New York, 1960). Contains population information.

Azevedo, Thales de, *As elites de Côr, um estudo de ascensão social* (São Paulo, 1955).

Bastide, Roger, "The Negro in Latin America," *International Social Science Bulletin,* UNESCO, IV (1952), 435–441.

Bazzanella, W., *Problemas de urbanização na América latina* (Rio de Janeiro, 1960). A bibliography.

Beaujeu-Garnier, Jacqueline, *Geography of Population* (London, 1966).

Bourricaud, François, *Changement à Puno, étude de sociologie andine* (Paris, 1962).

Castro, Baron, *La población hispano-americana a partir de la independencia* (Madrid, 1944).

CELADE (Latin American Center for Demographic Training and Research), "The Demographic Situation in Latin America," *Economic Bulletin for Latin America* (October, 1961).

Comas, Juan, "Latin America," *International Social Science Journal,* UNESCO, II (1961), 292–299.

Costa Pinto, L. A., *O negro no Rio de Janeiro: Relaçoes de raça numa sociedade em mudança* (São Paulo, 1953).

"A Crowding Hemisphere: Population Change in the Americas,"

Annals of the American Academy of Political and Social Science (March 1958).

Dobyns, Henry F., "Estimating Aboriginal American Population: I. An Appraisal of Techniques with a New Hemispheric Estimate," *Current Anthropology* (April 1966).

Dorselaer, Jamie, and Alfonso Gregory, *La urbanización en América latina* (FERES, 1962). Good bibliography.

Harris, Marvin, *Patterns of Race in the Americas* (New York, 1964).

Hauser, Philip Morris, *Urbanization in Latin America* (New York, 1961).

Instituto Inter-americano de Estadística, *La estructura demográfica de las naciones americanas* (Washington, 1959).

Klein, Herbert S., *Slavery in the Americas: A Comparative Study of Cuba and Virginia* (Chicago, 1967).

Merias, George, *Riobamba, Ecuador* (FERES, 1962).

Métraux, Alfred, "The Social and Economic Structure of the Indian Communities of the Andean Region," *International Labour Review* (March 1959), pp. 225–244.

Mörner, Magnus, "The History of Race Relations in Latin America: Some Comments on the State of Research," *Latin American Research Review*, I, no. 3 (1966), 17–44.

Morse, Richard, "Urbanization in Latin America," *Latin American Research Review*, I, no. 1 (1965), 35–74.

Pan American Union, *Materiales para el estudio de la clase media en la América latina*, 6 vols. (Washington, 1950–51). Contains a wealth of material on the social conditions of the nations.

Pierson, Donald, *Negroes in Brazil: A Study of Race Contacts at Bahia* (Chicago, 1942).

Population Bulletin, Washington. April 1961 and October 1962 issues were devoted to Latin America.

"Le Problème des Capitales en Amérique Latine," *Caravelle*, no. 3 (1964). Deals with social, economic, and political aspects of urbanization.

Ramos, Arthur, *As culturas negras no novo mundo* (São Paulo, 1946).

Rens, Jef, "The Andean Programme," *International Labour Review* (December 1961), pp. 423–462.

Ribeiro, Darcy, "The Social Integration of Indigenous Population in Brazil," *International Labour Review* (April 1962), pp. 459–478.

Rosenblat, Angel, *La población indígena y el mestizaje en América,* 2 vols. (Buenos Aires, 1954).

Tannenbaum, Frank, *Slave and Citizen: The Negro in the Americas* (New York, 1946).

United Nations, *Provisional Report on World Population: Prospects as Assessed in 1963* (New York, 1964).

Wagley, Charles, *Race and Class in Rural Brazil* (New York, 1963).

ECONOMICS

Baer, Werner, "The Inflation Controversy in Latin America: A Survey," *Latin American Research Review,* XI, no. 2 (1967), 3–25.

Benham, F. A., and H. A. Holley, *A Short Introduction to the Economy of Latin America* (London and New York, 1961).

Cole, John P., *Latin American Economic and Social Survey* (Washington, 1965).

Furtado, Celso, *The Economic Growth of Brazil* (Berkeley, Calif., 1963).

Gordon, Wendell, *The Political Economy of Latin America* (New York, 1965).

Hirschman, Albert O., *Journeys Toward Progress: Studies in Economic Policy-Making in Latin America* (New York, 1963).

Jones, Tom B., Elizabeth A. Warburton, and Ann Kingsley, eds., *A Bibliography on South American Economic Affairs: Articles in Nineteenth Century Periodicals* (Minneapolis, 1955).

Joslin, David, *A Century of Banking in Latin America, Bank of London and South America Limited, 1862–1962* (New York, 1963).

Lambert, Denis, *Les inflations sud américaines* (Paris, 1959). Extensive bibliography.

Prebisch, Raúl, *Hacía una dinámica del desarrollo latino americano* (Mexico, 1963).

United Nations, Economic Commission for Latin America, *Analyses and Projections of Economic Development* (1953–   ). A series of monographs on individual countries including Argentina, Bolivia, Brazil, Chile, Colombia, Ecuador, El Salvador, Panama, and Peru.

————, *Economic Bulletin for Latin America*. Published twice yearly.

————, *Economic Development of Latin America in the Post-War Period* (New York, 1964).

————, *Economic Survey of Latin America*. Published yearly.

Urquidi, Victor, *Free Trade and Economic Integration in Latin America* (New York, 1964).

Vernon, Raymond, ed., *How Latin America Views the U. S. Investor* (New York, 1966).

Wish, John R., *Economic Development in Latin America: An Annotated Bibliography* (New York, 1966).

AGRICULTURE

Azevedo, Fernando de, *Canaviais e engenhos na vida política do Brasil* (Rio de Janeiro, 1948).

Belaúnde Guinassi, Manuel, *La encomienda en el Perú* (Lima, 1945). Historical background.

Bray, James C., *The Agrarian Problem in Chile* (Santiago, 1961).

Chevalier, François, *Land and Society in Colonial Mexico: The Great Hacienda* (Berkeley, Calif., 1963). The historical process of latifundio formation.

Domínguez, Oscar, *El campesino chileno* (FERES, 1961).

Dumont, René, *Cuba: Intento de crítica constructiva* (Barcelona, 1965).

————, *Lands Alive* (New York, 1965).

Fals Borda, Orlando, *Peasant Society in the Colombian Andes* (Gainesville, Fla., 1955).

Fernández y Fernández, Ramón, *Economía agrícola y reforma agraria* (Mexico, 1962).

Flores, Edmundo, *Tratado de economía agrícola* (Mexico, 1961).

Ford, Thomas R., *Man and Land in Peru* (Gainesville, Fla., 1955).

International Labour Organization, Seventh Conference of the American States Members, "Economic Growth and Social Policy," *International Labour Review* (July 1961).

International Labour Review. Contains notes on agrarian reforms in the following countries: El Salvador (May 1962), p. 511, and (March 1962), p. 294; Chile (April 1963), p. 361; Colombia (June 1962), p. 622; Costa Rica (April 1962), p. 390; Dominican Republic (July 1963), p. 74; Ecuador (December

1964), p. 569; Haiti (December 1962), p. 576; Honduras (June 1963), p. 573; Nicaragua, (January 1964), p. 69; Panama (February 1964), p. 181; Peru (March 1963), p. 258, (September 1963), p. 305, and (October 1964), p. 376.

Matos, Valdemar, *Contribução ao estudo da sesmaria no Brasil* (San Salvador, 1955).

Mendieta y Núñez, Lucio, *El problema agrario de México* (Mexico, 1964).

———, *La reforma agraria de la América latina* (Mexico, 1960).

Métraux, Alfred, "The Social and Economic Structure of the Indian Communities of the Andean Region," *International Labour Review* (March 1959), pp. 225–244.

Monbeig, Pierre, *Pionniers et planteurs de São Paulo* (Paris, 1952). Study of an agricultural area where the latifundio is not predominant.

Ots Capdequí, J. M., *El régimen de la tierra en la América española durante el período colonial* (Santo Domingo, Dominican Republic, 1956). Historical background.

Pan American Union, *La estructura agruperuaria de las naciones americanas* (Washington, 1957).

———, *Plantation Systems in the New World* (Washington, 1959).

———, *Revista inter-americana de ciencias sociales,* no. 2 (1963). This issue was devoted to agrarian problems.

Peña, Moisés T. de la, *El pueblo y su tierra* (Mexico, 1964).

Pérez, Gustavo, *El campesinado colombiano* (Bogotá, 1962).

Picó, Rafael, "Problems of Land Tenure Reform in Latin America," *Journal of Inter-American Studies* (April 1964), p. 144.

Poblete Troncoso, Moisés, *La economía agraria de América latina y el campesino* (Santiago, 1957).

———, "El exodo rural, sus origenes, sus repercuciones," *América latina* (January-June 1962), pp. 41–50. A reliable analysis of the flight from the countryside.

Rodríquez Ochoa, Augustín, *Los systemas de explotación de la tierra en México y sus repercuciones sociales* (Mexico, 1954).

Seminario latino americano sobre problemas de la tenencia y uso de la tierra en América latina, 6 vols. (Mexico, 1954).

Senior, Clarence O., *Land Reform and Democracy* (Gainesville, Fla., 1958). Deals particularly with the communal ejido.

Silva Herzog, Jesús, *El agrarismo mexicano* (Mexico, 1959). A highly critical view.

Simpson, Lesley B., *The Encomienda in New Spain,* 3rd ed. (Berkeley, Calif., 1966). Historical background.

Smith, T. Lynn, *Agrarian Reform in Latin America* (New York, 1965).

Solari, Aldo E., *Estudios sobre la sociedad uruguaya,* 2 vols. (Montevideo, 1964–65).

―――, *Sociología rural nacional* (Montevideo, 1958).

Taylor, Carl, *Rural Life in Argentina* (Baton Rouge, La., 1948).

United Nations, ECLA, "An Agricultural Policy to Expedite the Economic Development of Latin America," *Economic Bulletin for Latin America* (October 1961), pp. 1–12.

―――, *Estudio económico de América latina* (New York, 1959).

―――, *Seminario sobre urbanización en América latina* (Santiago, December 1958).

Wolfe, Marshall, "Rural Settlement Patterns and Social Change in Latin America: Notes for a Strategy of Rural Development," *Latin American Research Review,* I, no. 2 (1966), 5–50.

Zavala, Silvio A., *La encomienda indiana* (Madrid, 1935). Historical background.

Zavala, Silvio A., and Maria Castelo, *Fuentes para la historia del trabajo en Nueva Espana* (Mexico, 1939). Historical background.

EDUCATION AND SOCIAL STRUCTURE

Alarcón Pino, Raúl, *La clase media en Chile* (Santiago, 1947).

Álvarez Andrews, Oscar, "Las clases sociales en Chile," *Revista mexicana de sociología* (May–August 1951), pp. 201–220.

Benjamin, Harold R. W., *Higher Education in the American Republics* (New York, 1965).

Bernal Jiménez, Rafael, "A Sociological Appraisal of Cultural, Political and Economic Problems in Latin America," *International Social Science Bulletin,* UNESCO, IV, no. 3 (1952), 461–470.

Buarque de Holanda, Sergio, *Raízes do Brasil* (Rio de Janeiro, 1956).

Cebollero, Pedro, *Estado actual de la educación secondaria en la América latina* (Washington, 1957).

Corredor, Berta R., and Sergio Torres, *Transformación en el mundo rural latino-americano* (FERES, 1961).

Crevenna, Théo, ed., *Materiales para el estudio de la clase media en la América latina,* 6 vols. (Pan American Union, 1950–51).

Debuyst, Federico, *Las clases sociales en América latina* (FERES, 1962). A broad survey; contains no bibliography.

Díaz, Demetrio, *La educación en Brazil* (FERES, 1961). Díaz is completing a series for FERES which will include Argentina, Chile, Uruguay, Paraguay, Ecuador, Peru, Bolivia, Mexico, Central America, the Caribbean, and (in collaboration with Emilio Pérez) Colombia.

Fernandez, Florestan, *Mudancas sociais no Brasil* (São Paulo, 1960).

Foster, George M., *Tzintzuntzan: Mexican Peasants in a Changing World* (Boston, 1967). Contains important implications for world-wide peasant societies in the twentieth century.

Gannagé, Elias A., *Economie du développement* (Paris, 1962).

Germani, Gino, *Estructura social de la Argentina: Análisis estadístico* (Buenos Aires, 1955). One of the foremost Latin American studies of social structure.

———, *Política y sociedad en una época de transición* (Buenos Aires, 1962).

———, "The Strategy of Fostering Social Mobility," *Social Aspects of Economic Development in Latin America,* UNESCO, I (1963), 211–230.

González Casanova, Pablo, "Sociedad plural y desarrollo: El caso de México," *América latina,* no. 4 (1962), 31.

Havighurst, R., ed., *La sociedad y la educación en América latina* (Buenos Aires, 1963).

Heath, Dwight B., and Richard N. Adams, eds., *Contemporary Cultures and Societies of Latin America* (New York, 1965).

Hirschman, Albert O., "Investment Policies and Dualism in Underdeveloped Countries," *American Economic Review* (September 1957), pp. 550–570.

Hutchinson, Bertram A., *Mobilidade e trabalho* (Rio de Janeiro, 1960).

Iturriaga, Jose E., *La estructura social y cultural de México* (Mexico, 1951).

Johnson, John J., *Political Change in Latin America: The Emergence of the Middle Sector* (Stanford, Calif., 1964).

Konetzke, Richard, *Colección de documentos para la historia de la formación social de Hispanoamérica* (Madrid, 1953).

———, *La esclavitud de los indios como elemento de la estructuración social de Hispanoamérica* (Madrid, 1949).

Lambert, Jacques, "Requirements for Rapid Economic and Social Development," *Social Aspects of Economic Development in Latin America*, UNESCO, 2 vols., I (1963), 50.

Lanning, John T., *Academic Culture in the Spanish Colonies* (New York, 1940).

Lannoy, Juan Luis de, and Gustavo Pérez, *Estructuras demográficas y sociales de Colombia* (FERES, 1961).

Lipset, Seymour Martin, and Aldo Solari, *Elites in Latin America* (New York, 1967).

Mendieta y Núñez, Lucio, *Las clases sociales* (Mexico, 1957).

Myrdal, Gunnar, *Economic Theory and Underdeveloped Regions* (London, 1957).

Navarrete, Ifigenía M. de, *La distribución del ingreso y el desarrollo económico de México* (Mexico, 1960).

Oliveira Vianna, Francisco José de, *Populações meridionaes do Brasil* (São Paulo, 1938). An older classic.

Pan American Union, *El analfabetismo en América según los ultimos censos de población* (Washington, 1958).

Pierson, Donald, *Cruz das Almas: A Brazilian Village* (Washington, 1951).

Rama, Carlos, *Las clases sociales en el Uruguay* (Montevideo, 1960).

Schatz, Sayre P., "A Dual Economy Model of an Underdeveloped Country," *Social Research*, XXIII (1956), 419–432.

"Sociology of Development in Latin America," *International Social Science Journal*, no. 4 (1963), 519–580.

United Nations, ECLA and UNESCO, *Conference on Education and Economic and Social Development in Latin America* (Santiago, 1962).

———, *La situación educativa en la América latina* (New York, 1960).

———, *Social Aspects of Economic Development in Latin America* (New York, 1963). Contains valuable contributions on education by Oscar Vera, Roberto Moreira, and others.

Wagley, Charles, *Amazon Town: A Study of Man in the Tropics* (New York, 1964).

Werneck Sodre, Nelson, *Formação da sociedade brasileira* (Rio de Janeiro, 1944).

Whitaker, Arthur P., ed., *Latin America and the Enlightenment* (Ithaca, N. Y., 1961).

Wolf, Eric, *Peasants* (Englewood Cliffs, N. J., 1966).

CAUDILLISMO AND THE MILITARY

Alba, Víctor, *El militarismo: ensayo sobre un fenómeno político social iberoamericano* (Mexico, 1959).

Alexander, Robert J., "The Army in Politics," in Harold E. Davis, ed., *Government and Politics in Latin America* (New York, 1958).

Bunge, Carlos Octavio, *Nuestro América* (Buenos Aires, 1935). Stresses ethnic factors in caudillismo.

Carro Martínez, Antonio, "El caudillismo americano," *Revista de estudios políticos* (Madrid, May–June 1957), pp. 139–163.

Chapman, Charles E., "The Age of the Caudillos," *Hispanic American Review* (August 1939).

Finer, Samuel E., *The Man on Horseback: The Role of the Military in Politics* (London, 1962).

Fluharty, Vernon Lee, *Dance of the Millions: Military Rule and the Social Revolution in Colombia, 1930–1956* (Pittsburgh, 1957).

García Calderón, Francisco, *Les démocraties latines de l'Amérique* (Paris, 1912). The author sees caudillismo as necessary in view of the conditions.

Germani, Gino, and Kalman Silvert, *Politics, Social Structure, and Military Intervention in Latin America,* I (1961), 62–81.

Gilmore, Robert L., *Caudillism and Militarism in Venezuela* (Athens, Ohio, 1964). Bibliography.

Imaz, José Luis de, "Los que mandan: las fuerzas armadas en Argentina," *América Latina*, IV (1964), 35. Quite good. A book by the author is to be published in Buenos Aires entitled *Los que mandan*.

Janowitz, Morris, *The Military in the Political Development of New Nations* (Chicago, 1964).

Johnson, John J., *The Military and Society in Latin America* (Stanford, Calif., 1964).

Lieuwen, Edwin, *Arms and Politics in Latin America* (New York, 1961).

———, *Generals vs. Presidents, Neomilitarism in Latin America* (New York, 1964).

McAlister, Lyle N., *The "fuero militar" in New Spain, 1764–1800* (Gainesville, Fla., 1957). Background on the military.

Núñez Leal, Victor, *Coronelismo, enxada e voto* (Rio de Janeiro, 1948).

Pierson, William W., and Federico G. Gil, *Governments of Latin America* (New York, 1957). Contains an analysis of caudillismo.

———, "Recent Research and Writings on the Role of the Military in Latin America," *Latin American Research Review*, II, no. 1 (1966), 5–36.

Rabasa, Emilio, *La constitución y la dictatura: estudio sobre la organización política de México* (Mexico, 1950).

Sarmiento, Domingo Faustino, *Life in the Argentine Republic in the Days of the Tyrants* (New York, 1961). First published in 1845; stressed sociological factors.

Vasconcelos, José, *Apuntes para la historia de México desde la conquista hasta la revolucion de 1910* (Mexico, 1943).

Wilgus, A. Curtis, *South American Dictators During the First Century of Independence* (Washington, 1937).

Wyckoff, Theodore, "The Role of the Military in Contemporary Latin American Politics," *Western Political Quarterly* (September 1960), pp. 745–763.

LABOR, POLITICS, AND PARTIES

Alba, Victor, *Historia del comunismo en América latina* (Mexico, 1960).

———, *Historia del movimiento obrero en América latina* (Mexico, 1964).

Alexander, Robert J., *Communism in Latin America* (New Brunswick, N. J., 1960).

———, *Labor Relations in Argentina, Brazil, and Chile* (New York, 1962).

———, "The Latin American Aprista Parties," *Political Science Quarterly* (July 1949), p. 236.

Alexander, Robert J., *Prophets of the Revolution: Profiles of Latin American Leaders* (New York, 1964).

Arcos, Juan, *El sindicalismo en América latina* (FERES, 1963). Contains historical outlines of trade unions in each country.

Arévalo, Juan José, *Anti-Kommunism in Latin America* (New York, 1964).

Arinos de Mello Franco, Afonso, *História e teoria do partido político no direito constitucional brasileiro* (Rio de Janeiro, 1948).

Barbosa de Carvalho, Augusta, *Organização sindical brasileira* (São Paulo, 1952).

Beals, Carleton, "Aprismo: The Rise of Haya de la Torre," *Foreign Affairs* (January 1935).

Blondel, Jean, "Structures politiques et compartement électoral dans l'état de Paraíba, Brésil," *Revue française de science politique* (April 1955), p. 315.

Bourricaud, François, *El sindicalismo en Latinoamérica: los casos de Perú y Brasil* (Barcelona, 1965).

————, "Sur le régime constitutionnel du Pérou," *Revue française de science politique* (March 1955), p. 92.

Castagno, Antonio, *Los partidos políticos argentinos, análisis de los antecedentes del régimen legal* (Buenos Aires, 1959).

Chico Alatorre, Carlos, *Cause y horizontes de la revolución mexicana* (Mexico, 1953).

Christensen, Asher N., *The Evolution of Latin American Government* (New York, 1951). A collection of articles from scholarly reviews.

Clark, Marjorie R., *Organized Labor in Mexico* (Chapel Hill, N. C., 1934).

Cruz-Coke, Ricardo, *Geografía electoral de Chile* (Santiago, 1952).

Edelmann, Alexander, *Latin American Government and Politics* (Homewood, Ill., 1965).

Edwards, Alberto, and Eduardo Frei Montalva, *Historia de los partidos políticos chilenos* (Santiago, 1949).

Fuentes Díaz, Vicente, *Los partidos políticos en México*, 2 vols. (Mexico, 1954–1956).

Harrison, John P., "Learning and Politics in Latin American Universities," *Proceedings of the American Academy of Political Sciences* (May 1964), p. 331.

Haya de La Torre, Víctor Raúl, *Adonde va Indo-América?* (Buenos Aires, 1954).

Kantor, Harry, *The Ideology and Programs of the Peruvian Aprista Movement* (Berkeley, Calif., 1953).

————, "Los partidos populares de América latina," *Journal of Inter-American Studies* (April 1964), p. 221.

Langrod, Michele, "Les forces politiques au Brésil," *Revue française de science politique* (1953), p. 511.

Lombardo Toledano, Vicente, "The Labor Movement," *Annals of the American Academy of Political and Social Sciences* (March 1940), pp. 48–54.

López Aparicio, Alfonso, *El movimiento obrero en México* (Mexico, 1952).

Maier, Joseph, and Richard W. Weatherhead, eds., *Politics of Change in Latin America* (New York, 1964).

Mazo, Gabriel del, *Estudiantes y govierno universitario* (Buenos Aires, 1956).

Melo, Carlos R., *Los partidos políticos argentinos* (Córdoba, 1964).

Mende, Raúl A., *El justicialismo, doctrina y realidad peronista* (Buenos Aires, 1950).

Mendieta y Núñez, Lucio, *Los partidos políticos* (Mexico, 1947).

Needler, Martin C., *Political Systems of Latin America* (Princeton, 1964).

Oliveira Vianna, Francisco José de, *Instituções políticas brasileiras: fondamentos sociais do estado* (Rio de Janeiro, 1955).

Poblete Troncoso, Moisés, *El movimiento obrero latinoamericano* (Mexico, 1946).

————, *The Rise of the Latin American Labor Movement* (New York, 1960).

Potash, Robert, "Argentine Political Parties, 1957–1958," *Journal of Inter-American Studies* (October 1959), pp. 515–524.

Puentes, Milton, *Historia del partido liberal colombiano* (Bogotá, 1961).

Reiser, Pedro, *L'organisation régionale inter-américaine de travailleurs* (Geneva, 1962).

Revista brasileira de estudos políticos (April 1960). A special issue which differentiates the respective ranges of the traditional and the new populist parties.

Rivel Devoto, Juan, *Historia des los partidos políticos en el Uruguay* (Montevideo, 1942).

Rodríquez, Carlos J., *Irigoyen, su revolución política y social* (Buenos Aires, 1943).

Romero Aguirre, Alfonso, *El partido conservador ante la historia* (Bogotá, 1944).

Scott, Robert E., *Mexican Government in Transition* (Urbana, Ill., 1959).

Skidmore, Thomas E., *Politics in Brazil, 1930–1964* (New York, 1967).

Spencer, David, *Student Politics in Latin America* (Philadelphia, 1965).

Távara, Santiago, *Historia de los partidos* (Lima, 1951).

Touraine, Alain, ed., "Ouvriers et syndicats d'Amérique latine," *Sociologie du Travail* (1961). This special issue has articles by François Bourricaud on Peru, Ziz Simao and Alain Touraine on Brazil, and Gino Germani on political consequences.

Viana, Segadas, *O sindicalismo no Brasil* (Rio de Janeiro, 1953).

Walter, Washington W., "Student Politics in Latin America: The Venezuelan Example," *Foreign Affairs* (April 1959).

CONSTITUTIONS, LAW, AND GOVERNMENT

Blanksten, George I., "Bibliography on Latin American Politics and Government," *Inter-American Review of Bibliography* (1954), IV.

Clagett, Helen L., *The Administration of Justice in Latin America* (New York, 1952).

Consejo, Interamericano Económico y Social, *La administración pública en América latina* (Washington, 1955).

Considine, John J., *New Horizons in Latin America* (New York, 1958). On religious freedom.

Eder, Phanor, *A Comparative Survey of Anglo-American and Latin-American Law* (New York, 1950).

——, "Habeas Corpus Disembodied: The Latin American Experience," *Mélanges yntema,* 1960.

——, "Judicial Review in Latin America," *Ohio State Law Journal,* IV (1960), 569–615.

Fitzgibbon, Russell H., *The Constitutions of the Americas* (Chicago, 1948).

Gallardo, Ricardo, *Estudios de derecho constitucional Americano comparado: ensayos sobrela crisis del federalismo* (Madrid, 1961). Extensive bibliography.

Haring, Clarence H., "Federalism in Latin America," Asher N.

Christensen, ed., *Evolution of Latin American Government* (New York, 1951), p. 355.

Hernández Sánchez-Barba, Mario, *Las tensiones históricos hispanoamericanas en el siglo xx* (Madrid, 1961). Deals with the influence of social changes on political life.

Howard, George P., *Religious Liberty in Latin America* (Philadelphia, 1944).

Institute of Hispanic Culture. The institute is currently preparing a collection under the editorship of Manuel Fraga Iribarne. Each volume, devoted to one country, contains a survey of social evolution, an outline of the former constitutions, and the text of the present one.

Miranda, José, *Reformas y tendencias constitucionales recientes de la América latina, 1945–1956* (Mexico, 1957).

Pan American Union, *Human Rights in the American States* (November 1960).

Peaslee, Amos J., *Constitutions of Nations,* 3 vols. (The Hague, 1956). Contains a bibliography on each constitution.

Vivas, Jorge B., *Intervención del gobierno central en los estados miembros de las repúblicas federales* (Buenos Aires, 1957).

ARGENTINA

Alberdi, Juan Bautista, *Del gobierno en Sud América, escritos póstumos,* IV (Buenos Aires, 1895–1901). The organization and attempt at parliamentary rule.

Bielsa, Rafael, *Derecho constitucional argentino* (Buenos Aires, 1954).

Casiello, Juan, *Iglesia y estado en la Argentina* (Buenos Aires, 1948).

García, Rodolfo, *Ensayo sobre la constitución argentina* (Buenos Aires, 1950).

Gómez, Rosendo A., "Intervention in Argentina, 1860–1930," Asher N. Christensen, ed., *Evolution of Latin American Government* (New York, 1951).

Lafont, Julio B., *Historia de la constitución argentina* (Buenos Aires, 1950).

Legón, Faustino, and Samuel W. Medrano, *Las constituciones de la república Argentina de 1811 a 1953* (Madrid, 1953).

Linares, Quintana, *Tratado de la ciencia del derecho constitucional,* 7 vols. (Buenos Aires, 1953–1960).

Pérez Aznar, Ataulfo, *Bases federalistas y comunales de la organización constitucional* (La Plata, 1958).

BOLIVIA

Cleven, Andrew N., *The Political Organization of Bolivia* (Washington, 1940).

Paz Antezerra, Frankin, *Le régime parlementaire en Bolivie* (Paris, 1953).

Trigo, Ciro Félix, ed., *Las constituciones de Bolivia* (Madrid, 1958).

BRAZIL

Arinos de Mello Franco, Alfonso, and Raul Pilla, *Presidencialismo ou parlamentarismo?* (Rio de Janeiro, 1958).

Bibliografia brasileira de dereito constitucional (Rio de Janeiro, 1956).

Calmon, Pedro, *Curso de direito constitucional brasileiro* (Rio de Janeiro, 1951).

Cavalcanti, Themistocles Brandão, *Las constituciones de los Estados Unidos del Brasil* (Madrid, 1958).

Martin, Percy Alvin, "Federalism in Brazil," Asher N. Christensen, ed., *Evolution of Latin American Government* (New York, 1951).

Maximiliano, Carlos, *Comentários à constituição brasileira,* 3 vols. (Rio de Janeiro, 1954).

Oliveira Torres, João Camillo de, *A formação do federalismo no Brasil* (São Paulo, 1961).

Oliveira Vianna, Francisco José de, *Instituções políticas brasileiras,* 2 vols. (Rio de Janeiro, 1955).

Pachego, Claudio, *Tratado das constituciones brasileiras,* 2 vols. (Rio de Janeiro, 1956).

Pontes de Miranda, Francisco, *História e prática do habeas corpus* (Rio de Janeiro, 1955).

CHILE

Amunátegui, Gabriel, *Manual de derecho constitucional* (Santiago, 1950).

Bianchi Rosas, *Breve estudio comparative de las legislaciones del trabajo de Chile y México* (Santiago, 1946).

Donoso, Ricardo, *Desarrollo político y social de Chile desde la Constitución de 1833* (Santiago, 1942).

Edwards, Alberto, *La organización política de Chile* (Santiago, 1955).

COLOMBIA

Dangon, Flores, *Habeas Corpus* (Bogotá, 1960).

Gibson, William M., *The Constitutions of Colombia* (Durham, N. C., 1948).

Pérez, Francisco de Paula, *Derecho constitucional colombiano* (Bogotá, 1954).

ECUADOR

Boya y Boya, Ramiros, *Las constituciones de Ecuador* (Madrid, 1931).

———, *Derecho constitucional ecuatoriano,* 3 vols. (Madrid, 1950).

MEXICO

Deschamps Blanco, Rafael, *El juicio de amparo como medio indirecto de control del sistema federal* (Mexico, 1958).

Echánove Trujillo, Carlos A., "La procédure mexicaine d'amparo," *Revue internationale de droit comparé,* III (1949), 229–248.

León Orantes, Romeo, *El juicio de amparo* (Mexico, 1951).

Mecham, J. Lloyd, "Mexican Federalism," Asher N. Christensen, ed., *Evolution of Latin American Government* (New York, 1951).

Mendieta y Núñez, Lucio, *La administración pública en México* (Mexico, 1943).

Miranda, José, *Las ideas y las instituciones políticas mexicanas* (Mexico, 1952).

Morales, José Ignacio, *Las constituciones de México* (Mexico, 1957).

Ochoa Campos, Moisés, *La reforma municipal: Historia municipal de México* (Mexico, 1955).

Puente Arteaga, Martin, *El municipio en México* (Mexico, 1954).

Rodríguez Treviño, Francisco, *Los derechos de hombre y las garantías sociales* (Mexico, 1948).

Scott, Robert E., *Mexican Government in Transition* (Urbana, Ill., 1964).

Tena Ramírez, Felipe, *Derecho constitucional mexicano* (Mexico, 1964).

PARAGUAY

Sanabria, Salustiano, *Organización política de Paraguay* (Asunción, 1946).

PERU

Alzamora Silva, Lizardo, *Derecho constitucional general y del Perú* (Lima, 1942).

URUGUAY

Gros Espiell, Héctor, and Daniel Hugo Martins, eds., *Constitución uruguaya anotada* (Montevideo, 1958).

Sanguinetti Freire, Alberto, *Legislación social del Uruguay*, 5 vols. (Montevideo, 1952–1959).

VENEZUELA

Aguirre Cerda, Granados, Legislación del trabajo en Venezuela (Caracas, 1947).

Gil Fortoul, José, *Historia constitucional de Venezuela*, 3 vols. (Caracas, 1942).

Ruggeri Parra, Pablo, *Derecho constitucional venezolano* (Merida, Venezuela, 1953).

Sierraalta, Morris, *De los recusos de amparo y habeas corpus en el derecho constitucional venezolano* (Caracas, 1961).

CARIBBEAN AND CENTRAL AMERICA

Álvarez Lejarza, Emilio, *Las constituciones de Nicaragua* (Madrid, 1958).

Gallardo, Ricardo, *Las constituciones de la República Federal de Centro-America* (Madrid, 1958). Very important regarding past attempts at Central American organization.

Gaytia, Victor R., *Las constituciones de Panama* (Madrid, 1954).

Infiestra, Ramón, *Derecho constitucional* (Havana, 1954).

Mariñas Otero, Luis, ed., *Las constituciones de Guatemala* (Madrid, 1958).

Zeladón, Marco Tulio, *Lecciones de derecho constitucional* (San José, Costa Rica, 1945).

Index